A THIRD
BROWSER'S DICTIONARY

Also by John Ciardi in COMMON READER EDITIONS:

A Browser's Dictionary

A Second Browser's Dictionary

A THIRD
BROWSER'S
DICTIONARY

A Compendium of Curious Expressions & Intriguing Facts

JOHN CIARDI

[ORIGINALLY PUBLISHED AS *GOOD WORDS TO YOU*]

THE AKADINE PRESS

A Third Browser's Dictionary

A COMMON READER EDITION published 1998
by The Akadine Press, Inc., by arrangement with HarperCollins Publishers, Inc.

A COMMON READER EDITION and fountain colophon are trademarks
of The Akadine Press, Inc.

ISBN 1-888173-43-2

10 9 8 7 6 5 4 3

To Walter Newman, a man of eager learning
to whom I am indebted for so many insights
and suggestions that rather than thank him
piecemeal in note after note, I do so here
in full title of respect, gratitude, and
affection. Thank you, sir.

SIGNS AND ABBREVIATIONS USED IN THIS DICTIONARY

Signs used in this book

?   In doubt.

*   When placed before a root word, indicates that it cannot be traced beyond the form given.

=   Equals.

<   From.

→   To, yields, yield, leads to, lead to.

'   Indicates a vowel in an unattested form. Thus the stem *forfi-* may be more securely rendered as *f' rf'-* indicating "unspecified vowel."

/   Indicates a consonant shift, as g/h signifies "shift from *g* to *h.*" Similarly, p/f, b/v, d/t, th/t, etc.

'   Indicates the stressed syllable in a word.

Roman numerals indicate centuries. "XVII" should be read "the seventeenth century." To avoid confusion, the first through the fifth centuries and the tenth are written out. All dates are A.D. unless otherwise noted.

General abbreviations

approx.	Approximately.
colloq.	Colloquially. Colloquialism. Colloquial.
dial.	Dialect.
dict.	Dictionary.
dim.	Diminutive.
esp.	Especially.
etymol.	Etymology. Etymological.
exclam.	Exclamation. Exclamatory.

ext.	(Sense) extension (from one meaning of the word to another).
influ.	Influence. Influences. Influenced.
lit.	Literally.
myth.	Mythology.
neg.	Negative.
obs.	Obsolete.
part.	Participle.
perh.	Perhaps.
plu.	Plural.
p.p.	Past participle.
prep.	Preposition.
prob.	Probably.
pron.	Pronounced.
redupl.	Reduplicated from (as *heebie-jeebies*).
ref.	Reference. Refers to.
sing.	Singular.
sthrn.	Southern American regional.
ult.	Ultimately. Ultimate.
usu.	Usually.
wstrn.	Western American regional.

Abbreviations of languages often cited

Am.	American English.
Brit.	British English.
Du.	Dutch.
Eng.	English (since c. XVI).
Fr.	French.
Ger.	German.
Gk.	Greek.
Gmnc.	Common Germanic. Intermediate between Indo-European and the German, Scandinavian, and Dutch languages, as well as Scottish and English.
IE	Indo-European.
It.	Italian.
L.	Latin.
LG	Low German.
MD	Middle Dutch.
ME	Middle English.
MHG	Middle High German.
MLG	Middle Low German.

OD	Old Dutch.
OE	Old English.
OF	Old French.
OHG	Old High German.
OLG	Old Low German.
ON	Old Norse.
Port.	Portuguese.
Sc.	Scottish.
Sp.	Spanish.

Works frequently cited

AHD	*American Heritage Dictionary.*
Bailey	Nathan Bailey, *Universal Etymological English Dictionary* (1721 et seq.).
Brewer	E. Cobham Brewer, *Dictionary of Phrase and Fable.*
Browser's I	John Ciardi, *A Browser's Dictionary.*
Browser's II	John Ciardi, *A Second Browser's Dictionary.*
EDD	*English Dialect Dictionary.*
Grose	Captain Francis Grose, *A Classical Dictionary of the Vulgar Tongue.*
Hyamson	A. M. Hyamson, *A Dictionary of English Phrases.*
Johnson	Samuel Johnson, *Dictionary of the English Language.*
MMM	Mitford M. Mathews, *A Dictionary of Americanisms on Historical Principles.*
NT	*New Testament.*
NWD	*New World Dictionary.*
ODEE	*Oxford Dictionary of English Etymology.* Edited by C. T. Onions (pronounced *On-ee-on*).
OED	*Oxford English Dictionary.*
OT	*Old Testament.*
P. *Catch Phrases*	Eric Partridge, *A Dictionary of Catch Phrases.*
P. *Origins*	Eric Partridge, *Origins, A Short Etymological Dictionary of Modern English.*
P. *Slang*	Eric Partridge, *A Dictionary of Slang and Unconventional English.*
P. *Underworld*	Eric Partridge, *A Dictionary of the Underworld.*
Trench	R. C. Trench, *Dictionary of Obsolete English.*
Weekley	Ernest Weekley, *An Etymological Dictionary of Modern English.*

Wentworth and
    Flexner   Harold Wentworth and Stuart B. Flexner, eds.,
                    Dictionary of American Slang.

I owe a particular and grateful thanks to the original AHD, whose appendix on Indo-European Roots has enormously simplified the hunt. The most recent edition is a step backward.

FOREWORD

Idiom is a seemingly sequential illogic (psycho-logic?) to which native speakers of any particular language become conditioned. It is a language convention and encodement, and we become imprinted with it in something like the way a gosling is inner-directed to follow the first creature it sees. The gosling asks no questions. It does what seems to be its nature. Like it, we follow our language lead even to the point of absurdity.

We say of a lovesick oaf that he is *head over heels* in love, understanding that he is emotionally upside down without knowing which end is up. But is not *head over heels* the proper upright order? In another encodement we might describe a clear-sighted practical businessman as head over heels, meaning that he has his head alertly raised and his feet firmly planted in practicality. In our encodement we say it of the love-smitten when we really mean something like *heels over head.* And it doesn't matter; for having said the opposite of what we mean, we continue to understand what we should have said more logically in the first place.

Or how about *assbackward* for "all turned around"? What is turned around about that? Is not *assbackward* the only right arrangement of any anatomy? Should we not be saying, in logic, *assfrontward?*

Financial advisers, true head-over-heels men with their feet on the ground and their heads alertly raised, speak of *pyramiding* our assets. Does that mean that starting from a broad base we pile our financial future taperingly to an apical vanishing point? (I have had stockbrokers who took pains to arrange things for me in just that way.) Or are we to understand that the pyramid is to be balanced on its apex as we broaden our resources upward and outward? That is an inviting thought, at least on paper, but it puts the figure in such precarious balance that we are left to live under the shadow of an impending crash.

The fact is that we mean neither one nor the other when we speak of pyramiding. The word *pyramid* suggests mass and stability, and in idiomatic use that is what we understand, what we actually say becoming irrelevant. May you stay solvent by whatever legal means are still available. Our idiomatic code is not always as absurd as these examples suggest, but they should be enough to suggest that our language is not an exercise in logic.

Latin *focus* means "hearth." I have seen it anachronistically rendered as "fireplace," but that implies a firepit that is top vented by a flue that passes through a roof or a wall, and that arrangement did not come into use until the development of squeezed, high-rise, tenement housing in medieval walled cities and there caused so many disastrous fires that a legal curfew (in French a *couvre feu*) set an hour at which all fires were to be covered—and so by various extensions to our modern *curfew*. So even to *fudge* for a sort of candy. In the late nineteenth century American college girls "fudged" on their curfew regulations for afterhours gaggles in which they made this candy over a gas flame, so naming it because it was the product of their curfew-fudging. Language, you will note, leads everywhere and mostly away, in this case away from the Roman *focus*.

What the Romans had in place of a fireplace was an open hearth under an opening in the roof. There must have been times in which an adverse wind sent choking smoke through the old *domus,* but without great ill-effect, for the Romans long stayed healthy enough to knock down everyone else.

In flowering idiom the English sense of *focus,* "point at which light rays or sight lines converge," follows from the fact that the Roman family once converged around its *focus.*

Italian also has *focale* and *punto focale* by a like association, but the main derivative in Italian is *fuogo,* fire. Both evolutions can be said to "make sense." But if we understand "sense" to mean "logic," then an equal logic, beginning from what may be called the same premises, has led to widely disparate conclusions.

And therefore it is not logic, but something else.

It is a persuasive something else. The idioms we empower become a power upon us. But idiom is, for example, no way to compile a *Summa theologica.* When our logical Aquinases go to work, they start by fencing out idiom. They invent their own language counters and assemble them into glossaries as they grind on to the definition and placement of everything at large. They create what passes as a new idiom—about as idiomatic as Esperanto. Their followers even learn to speak it, almost as if it were living idiom. But inevitably the living language sneaks up on the monumental system and makes monkeys of the logicians. For man is the language-ape and there are no ape logicians. The language overgrows the systems as jungle overgrows an abandoned temple, and the idioms flash again through the foliage as brilliantly in no sequential order as the dayglow rumps of mandrills at play.

That play speaks us not necessarily as we might prefer to imagine ourselves, but as we are. The language is plotless, and yet it portrays us. It is plotless as the ideal census is plotless: because it leaves nothing out.

There are, of course, gaps. Italian, for example, has no truly idiomatic term for "privacy." In relatively recent legalese, lawyers have translated the essentially British legal concept "right to privacy" as *diritto di reservatezza,* the right to be reserved unto oneself, but in Italian that term is more Aquinian than idiomatic.

Or sometimes the gap is in our knowledge. Despite a long and brilliant scholarship, etymology has found no Indo-European root that means "hair." Unless we have our language from nonmammalian ancestors there must have been such a word. It has simply vanished, and who knows how? The census is never entirely complete, and yet we do have a population.

Within its range there are even evident subgroupings about which we can generalize. *Omen,* for example, began neutrally as "sign from heaven," possibly good, possibly bad. But what does it become in *ominous? Portent* and *portentous* are clearly of this subgroup. *Nemesis* began as the goddess of impartial justice, and, as if to show the language-ape's view of justice, a *nemesis* has become a downfall. Our ancestors may have hoped for heaven, but they have left their language to testify that they feared it.

And so for all decision from on high, whether from God or the State. The carpet of *on the carpet* (French *sur le tapis*) was not a floor covering but the cloth that covered an official desk back when all desks were official. To be *sur le tapis* was to have one's dossier under official review. Aquinian dispassion would insist that the review might be favorable; it could even lead to promotion or to a tax rebate. But as inevitably as idiom speaks us, to be on the carpet means to be in trouble. The idea fills us with a sense of foreboding. And *foreboding,* too, is of this identifiable subgroup, for its original was a mounted messenger galloping in with the *News,* possibly good news. But to the language-ape only no news is good news. He responds to announcement from on high as your great aunt Tillie received telegrams, always with a sense of impending disaster.

In idiom with himself this creature has hoped and has appointed priests and other masters to hope for him, but what he has hoped for most, as this group of words makes clear, is simply to escape notice from on high.

Idiom is more than what is said. It is the creature who speaks it— and necessarily so, else we should all be speaking Aquinian dialects of Computerese.

In some sense the computer does use language (or nonlanguage). As far back as the 1960s—so my dear friend, the late Fletcher Pratt, told me at the time—our government's intelligence gatherers set computers to scan Russian technical papers and to render them in American. Fletcher described some of the computer's problems with idiom in terms I understood at once even in my ignorance, knowing that computers are too orderly to be language sensitive.

Within that orderliness they can scan whole banks of stored instructions, responding as if sensitively. When, for example, they scanned the Russian for the military rank stated as *general-major,* their instruction would order them to render it in American as *major-general.* Instruction: in this case (always a particular) reverse the word order. And the computer, a high-speed moron, dutifully reverses the word order with no sense of what it is doing.

In translating one Russian engineering manual, the computer came up repeatedly with *water goat,* as if it knew what it was writing. Its absurdity became instantly clear when an editor with genetic ties to the language-ape checked the original and found that the computer was trying to express the Russian term for *hydraulic ram.*

Very well—set in one more specific instruction to cover this other case. Perhaps in near infinite time, with every idiomatic variant reduced to an electronic instruction, the computer would be more or less (but never quite) idiomatically naturalized. By that time we language-apes will probably have become extinct, leaving the computers to talk only to themselves, or to whatever successor species their genetic engineering may have created by way of improving on our image.

But even given a googolplectic particularization, the computer would not (and so I shall die believing) pass the examination of any chance survivor of the language species. Nothing but a human being can speak like one.

Fletcher Pratt also told me (what I knew at once to be true) that the computer had trouble with prepositions. Scanning one in Russian, the computer would flash through its bank of instructions and print out a cluster of English prepositions that seemed to qualify electronically. The printout might read, for example, *of, from, for, about, to, toward, alongside, under, over, by, beside.* An editor then had to blue-pencil out all but the one (or, as sometimes in American, two) that passed his human inspection.

Idiom is a force we use to promote what we call understanding. Certainly we could not be ourselves without it. But even as it empowers us, it is also a force upon us. We use it (and are used by it) almost in the way we let our reflexes breathe for us.

In Old French and continuing through Frenchified Middle English and into Shakespeare's time, "nunnation" altered the form of many of our English words. In nunnation initial or terminal *n* may be said to "bounce off" one word and to attach itself, fore or aft, to another.

At the hunt dinners of the feudal system, the horsey lords dined on choice roasts while the hunt attendants at low table chomped down a meat pie made of *nombles,* the chopped organs, tripe, and other guts of the kill. In Middle English this pasty became *a noumbles pie,* then *an omble pie,* and then *umble pie.* Probably because this pasty was a favorite meal of London draymen, some purist decided that *umble* was a Cockney mispronunciation of *humble* and accordingly corrected it incorrectly to *humble pie.*

Similarly, but without the intervening purist, *a napron* became *an apron; an ewt, a newt; a nader, an adder.* Many more words were altered in these patterns, but nunnation was not a fixed rule. *An aunt,* for example, was never *a naunt* (except perhaps in some dialect unknown to me). But did Shakespeare's audiences hear Hamlet saying *married to my nuncle* or *married to mine uncle?*

In our time nunnation is no longer a common force. Yet my younger son, in the American language he spoke at the time of his second birthday, always said *some nother time* and referred to his grandmother as *Ana* for *Nana.*

I must be tentative in this. I have no case to make for intuitive etymology. There may be a scientific explanation beyond the reach of my ignorance. I still wonder if he was not responding to the force of some memory so deep in language itself that it sounds even from the mouths of babes. What, for instance, moves so many American children to say "pasketti" for "spaghetti"? And if that is not an impulse peculiar to the American idiom, why do Italian children not do the same thing (for they do not)?

Consider the Indo-European root *sad-,* replete (heavy with food). It is the base of Latin *satur,* "satiety," and of course of English *sate, sated.* Via Common Germanic it is the base of Old English *saed,* "weary" (heavy with fatigue). In Modern English it has become *sad,* "melancholy" (heavy of heart). "Heavy" has never been the primary sense, nor is it now in standard English (whatever that is). Yet in dialect and in colloquial usages from dialect, *sad,* in all of its historically various forms, has continued to mean heavy. We still say "fate struck him a sad blow." Your great-grandmother (see your local antique shop) used *sad irons,* so called because they are notably heavier than the old *flat irons.* I once heard a Virginia hostess apologize to her guests because her homemade bread had "sad" streaks in it. She meant that the bread had been insufficiently kneaded, as a result of which some strips of the dough lacked enough yeast to make them rise properly. (It was still fine bread.)

This association of "heavy" with "sad" is clearly a folk transmission from generation to generation, and yet its stubborn survival without the sanction of dictionaries and grammatical rule is an evidence of deep language memory.

Our boys at their rough play still establish the pecking order within the boypack by forcing weaker boys to "say uncle" or to "cry uncle" by submitting them to small torments until they yield a title of respect to their tormentors, thereby accepting a subordinate place in the order. The sons of the troglodytes must have played this game at the mouth of the cave. There is no way to trace the formula that far back, but it is attested at least from the early days of the Roman Republic, when boys were made to cry *patrue, me patruissime* (all vocatives), "paternal uncle, my best of paternal uncles!" (Within the patrilineal Roman *gens* the paternal uncle was senior to the *avunculus* or maternal uncle.)

Generation by generation, as the language changed, boys kept the formula, adapting it to the changed forms of their speech but clinging to it in a straight line of descent from dim time to tomorrow in the playgrounds of Sioux City. And although all language (including neologisms once coined) is a transmitted memory that changes constantly, some elements within it seem to be almost mysteriously persistent.

I am, of course, woolgathering. I can no more etymologize sequentially than the alphabetical arrangement of a dictionary can turn into a story line. The etymologist must wander about to find his goodies in whatever order they attract his attention, almost invariably finding more goodies to stop for along the way. It is as if every trail were crossed by so many others that everything leads to a parenthetical something else.

(*Woolgathering,* for example, is certainly worth parenthesizing. On feudal estates the esnes had the right to gather from bushes any tufts of wool snagged from passing sheep. It was an impoverished but precious right, for woolgathering was the one common source of the homespun that clothed the laborers of the estate. The sheep belonged to the lord and to shear one on the sly amounted to poaching, which could be a hanging offense. But although woolgathering was an essential labor, it was not quite a manly one. It was left to children and gaffers who roamed the brush in every direction at once, flitting from tuft to tuft as they happened to catch their attention. And so to the later metaphor for free-association mental rambling. Nor will I resist it as a metaphor for what the etymologist does, for though it may be less than manly work, it remains an essential way of clothing the mixed metaphors we live by. And close parentheses.)

Let me start again with what I will offer as a more-than-parenthetical ramble beginning with *ventriloquist.* The word is readily traceable to Latin *venter*, stomach, and *loqui*, to speak, whence the late Latin form *ventriloquus*, at root, "a belly speaker."

I am already a bit over my head. I do not know positively how a ventriloquist projects his voice. The Romans obviously thought that he did it from his belly (we would say "from the diaphragm"), and that assumption is enough to explain the form of the word, probably accurately.

The modern ventriloquist is an entertainer. The equivalent Greek word, however, is *gastromantis*, from *gaster*, belly, and *mantis*, prophet, oracle, soothsayer. The difference between "to speak" and "to utter divine truth" takes us from what is left of vaudeville to what is left of religion. *Gastromantis* points us back to a shadowy temple priest who stood to one side of the idol and caused it to give forth the voice of the living god!

(And yet another parenthesis. Temple did not always signify "a more or less monumental house of God." The Indo-European base is *tem-*, to cut. The first "temple" was a magic diagram cut [scratched] into the soil by the priest magician. It was a circle, a pentacle, or some other magic figure drawn to an accompaniment of chants, prayers, and spells. Almost certainly the profane were forbidden to cross the line—an act that would have amounted to defiling the altar—and within the line, the inner sanctum, the holy man prophesied usually by "reading" the pluck of a ritually sacrificed animal. It was within his magic enclosure that the holy gut-plucker *contemplated* the will of God and announced it to the people.

Some of these holy places—later to be called *templa* by the Romans —must have acquired a reputation for great sanctity and were probably marked off with stones, which later became walls, which when roofed over were the forerunners—forestanders?—of our modern temples.

The point is that such structures would not have arisen until some time after the first cave-mouth religious rites. The *gastromantis* does not go quite all the way back. Yet there he stands at some time in the late dawn, and since his newly reared temple would be the natural site for the local idol, it would also provide a natural occasion to play down the chicken plucking and to start prophesying from the god's own mouth.

Traces of such religious ventriloquism have been found among the Eskimo and also among peoples of the South Sea islands and of African tribes. Unless we make the unlikely assumption that these peoples developed the trick independently, only great antiquity can explain its distribution among such widely scattered primitives. Or the first *gastromantis* may well have practiced his arts in the open air, before temples were erected.)

In any case he is there to contemplate from the roots of the word: there he stands, there sounds the miracle, and there, beyond all doubt, the awed worshipers hear nothing less than the living voice of the god! There would not yet have been holy books to record the message, but the wise and holy men of the tribe would repeat it to ethnic legend in which it would take form as law to be set down in time as scripture and to remain there to this day as the unalterable truth of the fundamentalist.

Bear in mind that we set out only to track down the origins of a word; and now where are we? Never mind the answer. If there is an answer, the chances are that the question has not been asked deeply enough. I will only say that etymology regularly brings the inquirer to questions of such an order. There can be no doubt that our ancestors heard the living voice of the god. As a member of this species, in idiom with it and with myself, I will only say that I sense something wonderfully and characteristically human in the possibility that our most awed convictions should arise from a vaudeville trick performed in the name of God.

The ventriloquist-priest-gastromancer would, of course, know what he was doing. He must have served a long term as an acolyte, studying his art, performing for the approval of his abbot, suffering punishment when he performed badly. God will not be deceived without practice.

But wait. Would it not be more accurately in the idiom of our species for that trickster-priest, *in the very act of his deception,* to persuade himself despite his long years of practice, perhaps because of them, that *there is no deception,* that the god has entered into the spirit of the trickster and is using the (holy) trick only to speak through it in his living presence? I believe! In idiom with us all, I believe, on the infallible evidence of our idioms, that we are exactly what our languages say we are!

I have been speculating, of course, even wildly perhaps, but from evidence. I am thinking language in a way no extraterrestrial (including the computer) can hear it or, hearing it, recognize it as the idiom of our kind.

In fraud, in holy deception, in the very forms of saying hello and good-bye, idiom speaks the creature that speaks it. It makes no better sense than this creature does. Idiom will not be pared down to formula and certainty. It will change faster than rule can fix it, yet it will remain persistently itself through every change. Peel it back layer by layer and what finally emerges is most like a poem, or the seed of a poem. The essential life of a poem is, above all, in the fact that it *releases* more (more suggestion, insight, possibility, echo, meaning) than can be *said.* If everything is sequential, openly declarable, and therefore paraphraseable, then what has been written is *exactly not* a poem. If the computer can say it, or if one of its temple attendants can say it to the computer (or the computer speak it through him), that is exactly not the language act of this species, and even the commonly carminative rhetoric of our guiding politicians is by comparison human utterance.

The Project

Three to four percent of all the ants
in a given hill die daily, making no
difference to anything except that a month's
a generation. It is the work must go
on and on and on exactly as
it does, it does, it does, it does, it does.

A biologist named Lewis Thomas, who wrote
The Lives of a Cell, said this, not just as fact
(which it merely is) but toward a question: what
is more like this than the endless language act
of twitching generations building tall
the City of Idea from which we fall?

This side of the concluding nova-gasp
ours is the Eternal City, eternal at least
as measured by the ant, the bee, the wasp,
humankind, and every colonial beast
at its mote averages. It makes me dizzy
to think how long how many have been busy

at what they have no way to understand
except as something they can't help but do.
Without it, what could I say when I shake your hand
but grunt maybe, or click, or blubber, or moo?
Or maybe point to the anthill and to this man
who could not have written his book about this plan

no one makes up that makes up all there is?
—Unless you think to spook it to heaven. Ants
don't seem to think to. I myself am a whiz
at doing what I don't know. Then I stop to glance
at what has been done, and I sense in enormous detail
how little we really know of how much we fail.

Key West, Florida

A THIRD
BROWSER'S DICTIONARY

𝒜

Abyssinia   1. Ethiopia. 2. *Coy slang.* I'll be seein' ya. [Am. Common during and after the invasion of Abyssinia by Mussolini, 1935–1936, but the form had some slightly earlier currency. So *Alaska* for "I'll ask her," *Jamaica* for "dja make her?" (i.e., "dja screw her?"). Cf. also *strictly from Hungary* for "strictly from hunger" (i.e., of no account). Such word plays are a bit oafish and have never had a great vogue, but neither do they die out entirely, remaining in limited use by the limited wits of each new generation.]

accidentally on purpose   With malice prepense under cover of inadvertence: *She happened accidentally on purpose to shoot him between the eyes when his back was turned.* [P. *Catch Phrases* cites this form in Brit. slang use by 1880 and into Am. by 1885. Wentworth and Flexner gloss it as "in popular student use c. 1940." I was in the class of 1938 and in graduate school in 1940 and can recall no specifically campus vogue, though it was in some use there as one of many common catchphrases.]

accost   *v.* 1. To approach with intent to speak to. Hence, 2. To solicit. 3. *Commonly specialized sense.* To solicit sexually. [At root, "to come up beside (with intent to speak to)." < L. *ac-*, combining form of *ad*, to; with *costa*, side (COAST). At the end of a voyage a cruise ship might be argued etymologically to *accost* its pier, but the language convention has not sanctioned this sense—and besides all the accosting has been done during the cruise.]

acrobat   A gymnast, a tumbler. [But at root also "a rope walker," < Gk. *batēs*, one who walks, agential form of *batein*, to walk; prefixed *akros*, high (cf. Gk. *akropolis*, the high city). Hence *akrobatēs*, a high walker, a rope walker. Which is sufficiently acrobatic, but *akrobatein* also meant "to walk on tiptoe/on the balls of one's feet"

1

—as gymnasts and tumblers do; thus, whether up on a tightrope, or here on the ground, an acrobat is at root "a high walker."]

acronym   A word formed from the initial letters or first elements of a phrase or title. (So armed services early XX jargon, now generalized, *AWOL* or *awol* for *"a*bsent *witho*ut *l*eave," as distinct from *AWL* or *awl*, *"a*bsent *with l*eave." So also late 1930s *radar* for *"ra*dio *d*etecting *a*nd *r*anging (device)," which see. And so *Nazi* for Ger. *Na*tionalsozi*al*ist. [A late coinage from Gk. roots *akros*, high, extreme, at the extreme limit (ACROPOLIS). In reference to words this sense was specified to "of the beginning." Combined with *nomos*, name. This coinage is Am. and recent. The word does not appear in the first OED (1927), nor until the *1972 Supplement*, the first citation there being from *Notes and Queries* and dated 1943, suggesting an origin during the New Deal (see below).]

HISTORIC. After-the-fact spook etymologists are fond of explaining earlier English word formations as acronyms. *Cop*, they are eager to mis-explain, is from *c*onstable *o*n *p*atrol; *tip*, from *"t*o *i*nsure *p*romptness"; *posh*, from *"p*ort *o*ut, *s*tarboard *h*ome."

For the correct etymologies of these terms see my *Browser's I.* The U.S. Armed Services developed a few bits of early XX acronymic jargon, as AWOL, above, but search as I may I can find no securely attested case of an acronymic word formation in English or American before FDR's New Deal introduced acronymania into Federalese and then into general Am. Even the word for the process was unknown until at least the mid-1930s.

Today many acronyms are coined for catchy effect, and the phrase or the title of the program or organization from which the acronym is supposed to derive is then bumbled about to fit the catchphrase.

The ZIP of the Postal Zip Code is such an ad-agency catchword to suggest the wonders of zippy mail delivery. Only after the acronym was the five-number (now nine) address code officially labeled *Z*one *I*mprovement *P*rogram, as if the zones rather than the deliveries were to be improved.

And consider CARE, as if in Please Care! (Have a heart!) That emotional tug sloganized into the pseudo-acronym, the sponsoring organization had to submit to the clumsy title *C*ooperative (for) *A*merican *R*elief *E*verywhere.

act your age   An admonition: 1. Stop being babyish and silly. 2. Stop pretending to be coyly innocent. *Hence,* Face up to reality in an adult way. [Am. Prob. ca. 1900. P. *Catch Phrases* says this idiom passed into Brit. from Am. ca. 1920.]

adjectival An unspecified unfavorable descriptive. A generic in place of a possibly impolite, obscene, or at least unflattering term: *Yes, he did rather incline to be an adjectival son of a bitch.* [Dating? Far more common in Brit. than in Am. Perhaps of Parliamentary origin, a speaker's arch effort to suggest but avoid uttering a derogation. Cf. the common journalistic "expletive deleted" in reporting the contents of the Nixon tapes. Cf. also Hemingway's use of "obscenity" as a generic in place of the given obscenity, in *For Whom the Bell Tolls.* (Obscenity in the obscenity of your mother's obscenity, you obscenity of an adjectival deleted obscenity.)]

adore 1. To worship: *the adoration of the Magi.* 2. *In loose ext.* (a) To like intensely: *I adore "Rigoletto."* (b) *Further loosened ext.* To like: *I adore prosciutto and fresh figs.* (c) *In utterly debased ext., esp. in the adjectival form.* A conversational mannerism to express enthusiasm for the trivial: *What an adorable new hat!* [One of many terms debased from an originally sacred sense (cf. *charisma, Browser's I* and *epiphany,* below). < L. orare, to pray; prefixed *ad-*, to → *adorare,* to pray to; substantive of p.p. *adoratus,* adored one, the one prayed to, God or a saint. So as a conversational mannerism one hears "they have an adorable house in the woods" (cf. *a divine house*), whereas etymology and literate clerics might reasonably insist that the only truly "adorable house" is a church.]

aegis Also *egis* 1. *At root,* A shield. But 2. Authoritative license, sponsorship, and protection: *Under the aegis of the Medici, Galileo developed the telescope safe from papal interference.* [IE *aig-*, goat. Gk. *aegis,* goatskin; hence goatskin shield.]

HISTORIC. In Gk. mythology the Aegis was the shield given (or variantly, lent) to Athena by Zeus to protect her in the war with the Titans. It was a shield of goatskin (with heavenly powers, of course) stretched on a frame of tough boughs, a shield of the sort still used by primitive tribesmen; and though, in the nature of language, the primitive name could have survived into a much later age, this capitalized *Aegis* must at least suggest that the legend of the war with the Titans dates back to some Stone Age belief. *Aegis* is the only survival in Eng. of this IE root, though a veterinarian who specializes in diseases of goats would be free to label himself an *aigologist* or *aegologist,* a matter of primary concern, I suggest, only to another goat.

A.E.I.O.U.   The five basic vowels. (In many European languages *J*, *W*, and *Y* function as vowels, as *Y* does in English, *W* to a limited extent, and *J* in foreign loanwords.)

These letters are, of course, a natural invitation to a rubric. Emperor Frederick III, archduke of Austria (born 1415, died 1493), amused his imperial nonesuchness by devising the vaunt *Austriae Est Imperare Orbi Universo* or in German *Alles Endreich Ist Oesterreich Unterthan,* Austria's Empire Is Overall Universal. Today *Austria's Empire Is Over Utterly,* but the vowels survive, offering a promise that there may be more to say in future.

affiliate   [At root, "to adopt a child." Our dictionaries commonly parse the root sense as "to adopt a son," from L. *filius,* son, prefixed *ad-,* to, hence, lit. "to be-son (someone)," to adopt. But in the name of unisex principles, L. *filia,* daughter, was as readily available for adoption.] *v.* 1. To attach oneself as a junior associate. Also to become so attached. (Note the surviving metaphor of the common business formula, "affiliated enterprises and the *parent* company.") 2. *Legal.* (a) To return a child to a parent by judicial decree. (b) To determine a disputed paternity or maternity, the court declaring *X* to be the legal child of *Y,* or of *Y* and *Z.* 3. *Archaic.* To take a person as one's child. (Now expressed by *to adopt.*) *Yet, within living memory, whole chorus lines of gold diggers became affiliated with sugar daddies.*

age before beauty   A formula of mock courtesy in yielding precedence to another, as anyone as beautiful as I is obliged to do for anyone as old and creaky as you, if only as evidence of my superior sensibilities. [Origin and dating unknown.]

agenda   (A plural form that now takes a sing. verb.) [L. things to do (or to be done). Plural of *agendum,* neuter present part. of *agere,* to do, to act (upon). And *agendum,* though rare, is standard English for a single item on an agenda. So, one of the rare English words (it may be the only one) that takes a sing. verb with either the plural or the singular form. *Data* is often ignorantly used with a singular verb, as in *this data is not reliable,* but the proper form would be *these data are not reliable.* Or, in the singular, *that is a commonly misread datum.*] A list of matters to be discussed and acted upon at a stated meeting of a social, political, or professional organization. (Technically, the checklist for an airplane taking off is an *agenda,* i.e., things to be done in a stated order, but the word has become specific to the meetings of committees.)

ain't   A natural, inevitable, and irrepressible English contraction, in the first person singular, *ain't I?* for *am I not? I ain't* for *I am not.* [But long beset by starched grammarians, perhaps because so commonly misused for *are we not?* (aren't we?) and *is it not?* (isn't it?). Schooled to avoid this natural form in the right place and feeling that *am I not?* is affectedly formal (it isn't), uncertain abusers of the language resort to such forms as *amn't I?* (perhaps defensible but fortunately rare), *arn't I?* (I are not, thank you), and the ludicrous *aren't I?* with an abusively pronounced *e.* (No, youse arén't not, sweetheart.)

And then, beginning, I believe, in the latter XIX, a whole series of colloq. idioms beginning with *ain't:*]

ain't it the truth! Exclam. How true it is! *ain't love grand!* Often used ironically, as after a lover's quarrel. Then generalized: *"Ain't love grand!" said Norman Abrams, laying down four queens and raking in the pot.* And in this class, among many more: *ain't that a laugh! ain't we got fun! ain't that something!*—all of which may be used straightforwardly or ironically. And also *ain't that the limit!* expressing approval, delight, surprise, dismay (Isn't that about as far as one can go!).

album   [At L. root, "white (tablet)," < *albus,* white. At Eng. root, a book of white (blank) pages. The L. neuter form *album* (ALBUMEN) labeled a tablet (bulletin board) on which public notices were posted. In practice this bulletin-tablet was usually a piece of slate, whereby the original sense "white" was superseded by "blank," i.e., "to be written on." So, when first used in XVII Eng., a white (blank) book for entries and insertions. Since much varied.] 1. A book of blank pages in which to insert collected items. Registers, diaries, logs, and ledgers respond to this definition, but *album* in Eng. has become more or less specific to a collector's book. Primarily: (a) *photograph album.* Often with black pages. (b) *stamp album.* Commonly imprinted with illustrations and designated places for affixing the collected stamps. (c) *autograph album.* Commonly of white or tinted pages on which to collect autographs and penned sentiments. (d) *guest album.* Far more commonly called a *guest book.* An autograph album used as a registry of one's guests. (In all cases the printing, if any, is more or less blanked out by what is affixed or penned.) 2. *Ext.* A trade term for a set of phonograph records in a booklike binder. 3. *Further ext.* A single long-playing record. (It comes in a slip cover and is usually a collection of musical pieces.) 4. *Now antiquarian.* A much-decorated selection of short, high-minded texts for genteel Victorians. A sentimental gift once common. [As if the editors had filled one's autograph album with names, sentiments, and decorations.]

alchemy   The link between the immemorial magic arts and modern science. Humankind's first systematic effort to unlock the secrets of matter by reproducible experiment. Alchemy sought above all else to discover: 1. The elixir of life that would confer immortality; 2. The universal solvent (the alkahest); and 3. The transmutation of base metals to gold. Yet, as astrology underlies modern astronomy, so alchemy underlies modern chemistry. [At root, "the Egyptian art," the root also implying "black magic." Arabic *al kimiya,* the (black) art of transmuting base elements to gold. < Arabic *khem,* black. Whence Gk. *Khēmia,* Egypt (the Black Land).]

alderman   In U.S. an elected official who represents a ward on the municipal council. [Commonly explained as a variant of *elderman,* from *elder,* a senior municipal official, and that derivation is seemingly attested by *church elder.* But in fact the form is from ME in which *alder* meant "most," as in such once-common forms as *alderbest, alderforemost, alderhighest, aldertruest, alderworst.*]

all systems go   1. The space rocket is all in order for launching. 2. *Generalized ext.* All is fine and dandy. (a) Moving ahead in good mechanical working order. (b) Carrying on in good health: *George Burns is counting down to his hundredth birthday with all systems go.* [NASA control-room formula for periodic summary as the countdown proceeds. The form was standard in-group jargon in the late 1950s but was widely disseminated by radio and TV coverage of U.S. space shots beginning early in 1962.]

alp   A high mountain formed in relatively recent geological time and still sharply upthrust. Especially one of the Alps. *the Alps* The central mountain chain of south-central Europe, extending about 800 miles from southeastern France to Albania, the Alps are the dominant geographical feature of Switzerland and of northernmost Italy. [At root, "white" (with the primary, but not exclusive, sense "snow-covered"). Ult. < IE *albho-* white, → L. *albus,* white. (ALBUM, ALBINO.) The Alps, Fr. *les Alpes,* uses the IE root with a b/p, but the unaltered stem *alb-* occurs widely in place-names. So *Albion* as a poetic name for England (the ref. here being not to snow but to the white cliffs of Dover); so *Albania* with ref. to its snow-covered mountains. So, too, the place name *Albany,* but from a personal name, ultimately L. *Albanus,* the white one. *No Albanian albinos are visible in Albany's photo-album of the Alps.*]

Alphonse and Gaston   Comic figures of exaggerated politeness. They have passed into standard catchphrase English bowing to each other and saying "After you, my dear Alphonse. No, after you, my dear Gaston"—and so into a formula of mock courtesy in any context. [P. *Catch Phrases* tells that the formula has passed into Brit. with the names altered to *Claude and Cecil,* noting that in Brit., as of the late 1970s, this catchphrase is far from obsolete. It developed in Brit. use ca. 1940, and Partridge seems to think it is of Canadian origin a few years earlier, adding "current also in U.S." It was current in U.S. ca. 1940 but was in fact just beginning to pass out of use, being by now only in the recall vocabulary of old-timers. But Partridge is wrong about its Canadian origin and about 40 years late.

In 1899 William Randolph Hearst hired Frederick Burr Opper as a comic-strip "artist" for the Hearst *American Journal Examiner.* Two of Opper's comic strips were the long-popular *Happy Hooligan* and *Alphonse and Gaston.* Both survived at least through the 1920s, for I was an avid reader of comic strips then and distinctly remember both of them, at which time they may also have been current in Canada en route to Brit. and to Claude and Cecil.]

aluminum   In Brit. *aluminium.* A metallic element. Symbol Al, atomic number 13. Although it does not occur naturally and is somewhat difficult to extract, aluminum is the commonest metal in the earth's crust. It is silvery, ductile, and relatively light though strong. For these reasons, and because it is relatively resistant to corrosion, it has found many uses, especially as the outer skin of modern airplanes. [< L. *alumen,* alum. The name coined by English chemist Sir Humphrey Davy, who first isolated the metal in 1809 from a naturally occurring potash alum. Davy first called it *alumina,* and this name survives to label various naturally occurring oxides of aluminum, e.g., corundum and emory.]

HISTORIC. The following note is from the financial section of the *New York Times,* July 28, 1983: "In the 1830's when aluminum sold for $545 a pound, Napoleon III used it to serve royalty at state dinners, relegating lesser guests on gold and silver. [sic] Later in the century [after a new production process was developed], the price plummeted to 57 cents a pound . . . a level that made aluminum better suited to soda cans than [to?] dinner service." [Note to the

Times: 1. Did Napoleon III buy his aluminum with U.S. dollars? 2. Aluminum soda cans did not begin to litter public places until XX.]

Amazon[1]   *Gk. myth.* A race of warrior women, fierce cavalry, and especially adept with bow, spear, and war axe. They captured men for mating purposes but exiled them to the limits of the Amazonian kingdom (said to be near the Caspian Sea) after the first, fine, careless rapture. If a male child was born, it was sent to live with its exiled father; if a girl child, it was reared to the true battle axe. The Amazons fought at Troy for the Trojans, and Achilles is said to have killed the Amazonian queen after a fierce battle. As legend often had it, the Amazons cut off a breast for greater ease in using the bow. [The name of these warrior women is ultimately < IE *magh-*, to fight, to be powerful. Modified to *maz-* → Old Iranian *ho-maz-on,* the warrior (*ho* being the masculine definite article), whence perhaps into Greek with *ha,* feminine definite article as *ha-maz-on,* the (feminine) warrior.

The same IE stem, modified in Gmnc., probably with the *g* silenced as in later Eng. *might,* suffixed *-t-,* and compounded with *hildis* or *hildaz,* battle, is the base of the feminine name *Matilda,* (she who is) mighty in battle. *When she is done waltzing, Matilda turns out to be an Amazon.*

Amazon[2]   The river that flows eastward, mostly through Brazil, rising in the Andes. It is the second longest river on earth, its calculated length of 4,000 miles making it slightly shorter than the Nile (4,145) but longer than the Yangtze (3,400); but had the North American continent been settled from the west and the Missouri discovered before the Mississippi, whereby what is now the upper Mississippi might have been regarded as a tributary joining the main flow at what is now St. Louis, the total headwaters-to-Gulf-of-Mexico flow of the Missouri so conceived would be just short of 4,000 miles. [So called because an explorer of this dark, long water reported that his party had been attacked by female warriors, whereby he dubbed it the River of the Amazons. Had he been drunk it might have been called the Vinoveritas. Had he been suffering from sex-deprivation, as he probably was, it might have been called the Lacanucchi. Nature, having no language for a rebuttal, is forced to bear the names placed upon it by the beast that talks, remaining perhaps serene in the assumption that all names wear off.]

amerce   *Law.* (Standard but rare.) 1. To fine. To mulct. To impose a monetary penalty or to seize property at the discretion of the court, along with or in lieu of other penalties. [Most sources gloss such a legal imposition as "arbitrary," basing their gloss largely on Norman French *à merci*, at the mercy (of the court), and the courts from XI to XIV did tend to be arbitrary in upholding Norman claims against Saxon defendants; but if this chapter of legal history is proximate justification for the assertion of arbitrary process, the ultimate (and surviving) root sense is "legal (i.e., precedented/judicial) action in imposing a penalty in money and goods"—and this is the sense of L. *ad merces* "(judgment directed) against wages, goods, property (rather than against the person of the defendant)." In a similar judgment some recent obscenity trials against books have brought charges *in rem*, against the thing (itself), in which the book is confiscated if found guilty of obscenity, but the author, publisher, bookseller, et al., are not otherwise punished.

The form of the word is ult. < Italic *merc-*, commercial goods, wares. → L. *merx* (stem *merc-*), same sense. (MERCHANT.) Variantly L. *merces,* wages. (MERCENARY.) And so Fr. *merci,* Eng. *mercy,* lit. "gift of good (things)." And also Mercury (L. *Mercurius*), because he, the most rapid comer and goer, was (among other things) the god of sea commerce. It. *merce* is still in common use for "wares, things for sale." The combination of these senses cannot fail to suggest a probable origin of the term in the Common Mediterranean of sea traders.]

Ananias   Three men of this name are mentioned in Acts, the first and best known having become a scriptural figure of the Liar. He was one of the Jews who was early converted to belief in Christ. Commanded, along with his fellow converts, to sell their houses and land and to bring the money to Peter for distribution "unto every man according as he had need" (Acts 4:35), Ananias, with the approval of his wife, held back part of the money he had received, and fell dead when Peter rebuked him, saying, "thou hast not lied unto men, but unto God" (Acts 5:4). And in Acts 5:5: "And Ananias hearing these words fell down, and gave up the ghost." Note that Ananias went more than halfway: he did accept the faith, and he did sell his land and bring part of the money received to Peter, holding back a pittance, just in case. But there is power in words: once Peter accused him of lying to God, he became the symbol of the liar.

Ananias Club 1. A group organized to compete in telling tall tales. 2. The collective liars of this world, i.e., the human race. [Informal Liars' Clubs were part of the Colonial scene from the moment the first locals sat around a cracker barrel in the first general store, and probably earlier. The name *Ananias Club* was first used in 1896 (MMM). The name was later popularized by Theodore Roosevelt, who denounced all of his political opponents as charter members.]

anatomy 1. The study of the bodily parts of organisms. 2. *Obs.* A skeleton. 3. *Slang.* The body. *park the anatomy, baby = put [your] body down [here], sex object.* 4. Any detailed close examination: *anatomy of a murder.* [Gk. *ana,* up; *tomē,* an act of cutting, substantive form of p.p. of *temnein,* to cut. Cf. *atom* (same base, *tom-,* with neg. prefix *a-;* at root, "not cuttable/irreducible"—because the particle called an atom was anciently held to be the irreducible basic unit of all matter). Cf., also, obs. *atomie,* a being, especially a tiny sprite. The obs. sense "skeleton" is clearly implicit in the root sense "cut up," i.e., "what is left when all else has been cut up/away."]

HISTORIC. Times change and old words take on new senses. The Greeks, largely deterred by a religious awe of dead bodies, did not dissect them for study. Arabs did so about 300 B.C. under the Ptolemies, but surgery, except for amputations and Caesarian sections, and bloodletting (if that may be called surgery) was not practiced except by barbers, physicians scorning such "butcher's work." Human dissection did not occur in Europe until the Renaissance, a few crude autopsies being undertaken in XIV for legal reasons. In XV such artists as da Vinci, Dürer, and Michelangelo did some dissection for their anatomical studies. In XVI Vasalius published the first extensive anatomical work based on scientific dissection, but the dissection of cadavers remained under a religious and legal cloud in England until well into XIX.

anile Old womanish. [L. *ănīlis,* adj., like an old woman; < *ănŭs,* old woman. The noun is feminine with a masculine ending, a survival from the fact the IE *an-* signified a grandparent or elder ancestor *of either sex.* The form is curiously rare in English. I have known even speakers and writers who normally use the language with great precision to use *senile* without sex distinction; and so, commonly, our standard dictionaries. The admirable (in its first edition) AHD not only defines *senile* as "pertaining to old age" (noting no sex distinction), but in tracing the word to L. defines *senex* as "old" though its sense is specifically "old man." Be it noted, however, that Statius anticipated this blurring of the sex distinction by using *senex* for old woman. Dante later sneaked Statius into heaven on questionable grounds, but he might have argued that since there are no sexes there, all was well.]

answer [The root sense survives clearly in the idiom *to answer to the charge,* to defend oneself against a more or less legal accusation. The second element is ult. < IE *swer-, swor-,* to speak solemnly under witness of the gods, as in ritual or under oath. The first element is OE *and,* akin to L. *anti,* against. The OE compound *andswerian* might as readily have developed the understood sense "to denounce," but signified instead "to speak in one's own defense, to rebut a charge."

But now: *n.* 1. A reply to a question: *"If the question is how,"* said the tortoise, *"the answer is 'slowly.'"* 2. The solution to a problem or a mathematical process. 3. An action in response to: *His answer was a punch in the nose.* 4. *In the root sense,* A legal defense.

v. 1. To respond to a question or a charge. 2. To be sufficient for a purpose: *Any lifeboat will answer the need of a drowning man.* 3. To conform to stipulations: *he answers the description.* 4. To respond to a signal or control: *this sloop answers the helm well.* 5. To be made to pay for or atone: *You will answer for this insult.*

answerable 1. Responsible for. Capable of being held to account. 2. Capable of being resolved, explained: *Life is the unanswerable question.*

answer back To sass. To reply disrespectfully. To respond argumentatively when one has a duty to obey.

antipodes (pron. with four syllables, in earlier Eng. with three.) The opposite side of the earth's sphere. *antipodal* 1. Of "down under." 2. *Ext.* Diametrically opposed in any way. *The Antipodes* A group of small uninhabited islands about 24 miles southeast of New Zealand. So called because they are exactly antipodal to Greenwich, England, on the meridian from which Greenwich mean time is calculated. [These are more or less fanciful terms from an early metaphysical geography still groping with the new concept of a spherical planet but still conceiving it as if it were flat. Like noses pressed against plate glass at the same point but from opposite sides, the feet of persons "down under" were said to oppose those of a person on this side. < Gk. *anti,* opposite; *pous,* foot, *podes,* feet.]

HISTORIC. From the old metaphysical geography, see rare but surviving *antiscian (an-tish'-'n)* A person, *X,* on the same meridian as *Y* but on the other side of the equator. *X* and *Y* were therefore said to throw their shadows in opposite directions. And if one allows for the sun's annual course north and south of the equator, the theory is as defensible as it is irrelevant. In any case, the word derives < *anti-;* with Gk. *skia,* shadow. Cf. *squirrel;* and in *Browser's I, cynosure.*)

Also **ascian** *(ash-y'-'n),* lit., a "no-shadow"; < *skia;* with neg. prefix *a-.* One who lives on the equator. So called because twice a year, when the sun is directly overhead, he is said to cast no shadow.

apes in hell: to lead apes in hell　　The semiproverbial punishment of women who die as old maids. [Obs. The origin of this saying, common in XVI, remains a scholar's mystery. In full, as if proverbial, "Old maids must/shall lead apes in hell." Seems to imply, as a sentiment of that male-dominant society, that women who do not win the society of men on earth will be reduced to the company of apes in hell.

Shakespeare refers to this saying in *The Taming of the Shrew,* II.1.34 (ca. 1605); but the first attestation is from Lyly, *Euphues* (1579): "But certes I will either lead a virgins life in earth (though I lead apes in hel) or els follow thee." My guess is that the reference is to a lost XV folktale, for had it been in common use in Chaucer's time (1340?–1400) it would seem nearly impossible for him to have written the Wife of Bath's tale without putting an ape-in-hell reference into her mouth, she being the least likely infernal-ape-tender of our literature.

Defenders of women's rights (of whom I am timidly and warily one, though only timid and wary of the movement's rhetoric, not of its cause) will not be pleased by the idea of this long-obsolete saying, but it is there, and it is too nearly Russian or Big Brotherish to revise history in order to advance present cause.]

apothecary　　1. A pharmacist, druggist. *(In Brit.,* called *chemist.)* 2. His place of business. [Gk. *apotithenai,* to store away. In late L. in the agential form *apothēcārius,* storekeeper, shopkeeper ("one who stores things away") → OF *apotecaire,* whence *apotecarie.* I have been unable to fix the point at which the general-merchandise storekeeper became specifically a dealer first in alchemical and then in chemical-medical materials.]

arithmetic　　The basic branch of mathematics that deals with addition, subtraction, multiplication, and division. [At root, "the art of counting," < Gk. *hē arithmātikē technē,* the technique of counting, < *arithmein,* to count, < *arithmos,* number. And see *mathematics.*]

aroint   Begone. [Of unknown origin, but used by Shakespeare, once in *King Lear* and most notably in *Macbeth,* I.1 (the witches' scene): "Aroynt thee, Witch, the rompe-fed Ronyon cries."]

HISTORIC. A few English writers have picked up this unknown word from Shakespeare. It can hardly be said to be a working Americanism, but every high-school graduate who stayed awake in English class has met it once, if only long enough to be puzzled by it.

There is no record of its use before Shakespeare, but Charles MacKay, *Lost Beauties of the English Language* (London, 1874), offers an ingenious bit of spook etymology on *aroint.* He reports that in Scottish highland superstition a twig from the rowan tree, or mountain ash, was a charm for repelling witches. (Cf. the power of wolfbane to repel Dracula's invasion of the Late Late Movies.) MacKay therefore suggests that "aroint thee witch" is a misprint for "a rowan-tree, witch."

Why seek the unidentifiable truth when spook ingenuity can be so engaging?

arrow of Alcestes   One of the great heroic folk metaphors. An arrow fired with such speed that it catches fire by friction with the air.

MYTHO-HISTORIC. When Aeneas and his followers reached Sicily (where some of them remained when he went on to Italy), his father, Anchises, died. *Aeneid* V recounts the funeral ritual and the memorial games. Toward the end of the games Alcestes, a local king-hero, fired his arrow with such force that it caught fire in the sky and passed from view like a departing comet. The flight of the flaming arrow became a sign of the passage of the great soul of Anchises, and though all the prizes had already been awarded, Aeneas loaded Alcestes with memorial gifts.

I rank this metaphor with the Arthurian figure of Arthur's defeat of the wicked Mordred. Arthur struck his evil nephew such a blow with his lance that when he withdrew it, a shaft of light passed clear through Mordred's falling body, making a circle of light inside Mordred's shadow as he fell to the ground.

The Alcestes figure is immortally in place in the *Aeneid,* and Dante has assured the Arthurean figure a second immortal place in his *Commedia.* Yet although these two inventions rank as supreme narrative metaphors of folk legend, neither is sufficiently well known.

art   1. *In vague common usage.* Painting, sculpture, architecture, poetry, music, dance, drama, belles lettres. (Note that artist once meant "scholar." So Shakespeare, *Troilus and Cressida* III. 3, "the artist and the unread," i.e., illiterate.) 2. The skill, knack, knowledge of a process: *The art of cabinet making begins with a feel for the grain of wood.* [In the Middle Ages the arts of man (we would now say artisanship or craft) were all the skills by which he won a living from nature. Dante's usurers, for example, are punished for *violence against art* because they do not practice these skills as God commanded, earning their bread in the sweat of their brows, but rather sit idly, letting their money work for them unnaturally.]

artist 1. A practitioner of art, sense 1. 2. A stage performer. Also circus, television, movie, music: *AFTRA, the American Federation of Television and Radio Artists.* 3. *In common usage.* An especially skilled, or smoothly persuasive, person: *bullshit artist, con artist.*

arty Pretentiously mannered. **artful** Resourcefully deceiving. **artificial** False. Unnatural. Ersatz. **articulate** 1. To join together: *The delicate articulations of the parts of the skull.* 2. To give oral shape to [to join words together in good order]. **artifice** A deceiving pretense. **artisan** A skilled craftsman. [The common denominator of all these variously extended senses is in the IE root *ar-*, to join together, suffixed *-t-* → L. *artus,* joint (ARTHRITIS), also tight; hence, "to join together closely."]

PSEUDO-HISTORIC. The story is variously told that when Sir Christopher Wren completed St. Paul's Cathedral, Queen Anne inspected it and told him it was "artificial, aweful, and amusing," at which Sir Christopher glowed with approval from on high. The story was almost certainly invented by a later etymologist (all such are unreliable), but if it lies, it does so toward a truth. In XVIII *artificial* meant "characterized by high art," *aweful* meant (as it should indeed still mean) "inspiring awe," and *amusing* meant "entrancing, having the power to seize upon the soul as the Muses do."

artesian well   A deep-bored well. (In the past the name implied a well from which water flowed to the surface by internal pressure, but today, especially in areas where increased drilling has lowered the water table, artesian water must often be pumped.) [After *Artois,* a province of France anciently called *Artesian.* There, near the town of Lilliers, a bored well sunk in 1126 struck an aquifer between two layers of impervious rock and the internal pressure caused an abundant surface flow.

HISTORIC. I do not know the depth of this XII *puit Artesian.* It must have been relatively shallow. The *Encyclopedia Britannica* leaves the matter in doubt, noting cryptically, "The renowned flowing well . . . started in A.D. 1126 at Lilliers . . . *may* [italics mine] have been bored." Other sources date the major flow as beginning in mid-XVIII, and whatever happened in the intervening 600 years, the later well was auger-bored. The *Encyclopedia Britannica* adds that the ancient Chinese, using bamboo as piping, drilled wells to depths of 5,000 feet on the edge of the Gobi Desert, a labor of decades accomplished with a primitive pile driver, the crushed rock being then extracted by an auger. Thirst drives deep.

asbestos A white or light gray mineral of magnesium silicate. As indicated by the folk name *earthflax* it is found in, or can be readily separated into, long fibers easily carded, spun, and woven. [The name is, at root, a misnomer meaning "unquenchable [stuff]." The form is < Gk. *sbennunai,* to quench; with *a-*, negative prefix. The adjectival form, from the p.p. stem, *asbestos,* unquenchable. L. borrowed the accusative, *asbeston.* Because of the whiteness of the stuff, the form was sometimes altered to *albeston* < L. *albus,* white. Both *abeston* and *albeston* occur in OF, whence XIV Eng. *albestone,* as "white stone." But *abiston* and *asbeston* are also attested with the sense "mysterious unquenchable stone," a sense that must have been an alchemist's mystery, for no one seems to have known the meaning of "unquenchable." In XVII *asbestos* labeled a fireproof fabric woven of threads spun from asbestos fibers.

The odd misnomer is traceable to the Greeks, who seem to have confused asbestos with quicklime. Both are white, and both have mysterious properties. I can think of nothing else they have in common, but this much was enough for the Greek (mis)connection. Quicklime is calcium oxide, made by baking limestone at 500° to 600° C. When water is poured into dry quicklime, it seethes, smokes, heats up, and starts to swell. It is also corrosive. Given enough water, it swells to about twice its dry volume; but the Greeks seemed to think there were no limits to this reaction, i.e., that the stuff was unquenchable. Confused on that point, they doubled confusion by calling asbestos "the unquenchable."]

HISTORIC. Asbestos has had wide recent industrial and home uses until the discovery that continued inhalation of asbestos fibers leads to fatal lung diseases. Early asbestos came from Cyprus. The ancients made fireproof "perpetual" lampwicks of asbestos fibers, and such wicks were known to have been used in Rome in the temple of Vesta. Pliny the Elder notes that in very early Rome the noble dead were cremated in asbestos shrouds. Wilfred Funk, *Word Origins and Their Romantic Stories* (New York 1950), in a reference I am unable to confirm, writes, "The Greeks and Romans made napkins of asbestos. . . . when they were dirty, the users simply threw them into the fire and pulled them out again with their pearly whiteness restored." Perhaps; though I suspect that the few who could afford asbestos napery had slaves enough to handle the laundry.

astronomy   The scientific observation and analysis of heavenly bodies and of their motions, emissions, and evolutionary changes. [Gk. *astron,* star; *nomos,* name, law, orderly selection and arrangement.] Ult. < IE *nem-,* to assign place to. Gk. *astronomos,* astronomer, which is in one root sense "star-placer." The Greeks may have had in mind the placement of stars within the established constellations, as if joining the star dots by imaginary lines to produce such legendary figures as Orion, the Pleiades, etc. Almost all early cultures have played this game of connect-the-dots, producing many configurations. *astrology* A system of divination based on the assumption that the positions of the stars and planets in relation to the zodiac influence and predict human events. [Gk. ASTRON; with *logos,* word, study of, law.]

HISTORIC. Almost identical at root and now antithetical in their senses, these two words did not begin to become distinct until the Renaissance, and did not completely divide until the establishment of early modern scientific method in XVIII–XIX. *Chemist* similarly separated from *alchemist* and *physics* from *metaphysics* at about this time, though Shakespeare, *Sonnet XIV,* clearly had in mind two incompatible senses for *astronomy:*

> Not from the stars do I my judgments pluck,
> And yet methinks I have astronomy,
> But not to tell of good or evil luck,
> Of plagues, of dearths, of seasons' quality.

Wyclif in his ME rendering of Leviticus 19:31 uses *astronomer* for what we would call *astrologer,* but does so with firm religious disapproval: "Bowe ye not to astronomyers, neither axe ye onything of fals dyvynours." The same passage is rendered as follows in the King James version: "Regard not them that have familiar spirits, neither seek after wizards, to be defiled by them."

Either text will do for the horoscope page of your daily newspaper.

atonement   [Earlier, and into XVII, *at-one-ment,* the act of becoming one with (implicitly, after some divisive offense). Bailey defines the word as "Reconcilement, appeasing of anger. But Wyclif's ME Bible renders it as "make an onement" and "set at onement." As a religious term, one seeks to atone for sin by offering God prayers, penance, and good works. Thus the root sense, *reunion,* has yielded to:] Satisfaction rendered for an offense.

attire 1. Clothing. In earlier usage, more or less elaborate formal dress (as one would not readily say "attired in rags and tatters"). But as many terms blur in the pretentiousness of advertising, also applied to any clothing, as, e.g., *casual attire* for lounging clothes. 2. *Heraldry.* The antlers of a deer. [And this heraldic sense is the key to earlier usage when the word was specific to headdress, implicitly to such headdress as tiaras, crowns, miters, and other formal and ornate head emblems of status. So OF *atours,* at root, of the tower, of the top, of the crown of the head. Of obscure Mediterranean origin. But the sense "headdress" is explicit in Leviticus 16:4, "And with the linen miter shall he be attired." It was this root sense that permitted Milton to speak of time as "attired [i.e., crowned] with stars" (where our unwary understanding today would be "clothed with stars").

Earlier *to tire,* to adorn. And earlier, the noun *attire* specified headdress, headband, tiara, crown, hat or helmet of office.

Tire (Brit. *tyre*) is the "dressing" of a wheel rim, earlier an iron band, now commonly of rubber or inflated rubber. The root sense "upper/of the head" has been here superseded by outer (as viewed from the hub), perhaps as all directions from the center of the earth are up and away.]

attorney Now, specifically, a lawyer. But the common *attorney at law,* a surviving archaic formula, was not originally a redundancy, for up to ca. 1800 *attorney* signified any man authorized to act for another in any matter (cf. the standard legal phrase *power of attorney,* which is not specific to lawyers but empowers any authorized person to execute legal and financial papers in the name of the person granting, or surrendering, the power). Trench supplies an apt instance of earlier usage from *A Short Catechism* (1553): "Our everlasting and only High Bishop; our only attorney, only mediator, only peace maker between God and man." [At root, "one who takes the place [turn] of another." IE *ter-,* to turn → L. *tornare,* to turn (TORNADO). With *a(d)-* prefix → OF *atorner,* lit., to turn to, but operatively, to assign. So with a variant but coherent sense the old-style Eng. legalism *to attorn,* to acknowledge a new owner as one's landlord, i.e., to turn to him, to assign to him the rights once vested in the former landlord.]

aubergine   1. The eggplant (which see). 2. *Color.* The color of the purple-brown variety of eggplant, especially as a fabric color. [The plant is of eastern and southern Asia and has been cultivated there since earliest times. I can find no information on whether the leading varieties there were the white or the purple eggplant. The Sanskrit name, of unknown origin, was *vatin-ganah* → Persian *bādin-gān* → Arabic *albādindjān* → XVII Sp. (Catalan) *alberginia,* whence Fr. *aubergine.* OED renders Fr. *aubergine* as a dim. form of *auberge, alberge,* a kind of peach, and also notes it as being akin to Sp. *alberchigo, alverchiga,* apricot. I know of no way in which an eggplant resembles a peach or an apricot, unless it be in the fact that the first varieties cultivated in Europe were much smaller than those now common. The XVIII Eng. folkname *eggplant* (Ger. *Eierpflanze*) clearly suggests that the first variety cultivated in England was white and probably small (perhaps the size of a peach or large apricot). But note that the color *aubergine* is always with ref. to the deep purplish-brown varieties.

It is quite possible that the various names labeled different varieties at different times, as often happens with the names of plants. *Rosemary* is etymologically from L. *ros marina,* sea dew, but no one is sure what specific plant was so labeled. *Primrose* is etymologically from *prima rosa* with *rosa* as a generic for "flower," hence, "first flower [of spring]." The name, however, has been applied to different flowers at different times, and what we now call the primrose is clearly not the first flower of spring.]

au pair   [Fr. at par, but with the sense "in an equal trade." *Par,* in English, has come to mean "at a stated value." At root, however, it is L. *par,* equal, even. So in It. *paro sparo,* even [and] odd. And see *umpire,* at root, "the unequal one," i.e., the third or odd man between the presumably even and equal contestants, as in a duel.] 1. *At root,* A bartering of goods or services, as when the milkman and the baker trade milk and bread. *But most commonly now,* 2. An arrangement whereby British families began, in the years before WWII, to exchange children with Continental families for a mutually "broadening" residence. [Some U.S. families have made similar arrangements, but the more common practice here centers on the:] *au pair girl* A foreign girl with good references taken into a U.S. home for an agreed time, usu. with some stipend and with travel paid, in return for child tending and some housekeeping.

$\mathcal{B}$

babushka   See *kerchief.* A piece of cloth, usually a square, worn over the head and tied under the chin. It is almost invariably folded diagonally and put on as a triangle. A common item of the European peasant woman's dress even today. [< Russian *babushka,* grandmother, by association, because old peasant women almost invariably wear such head coverings. Girls also wear them, but the grandmothers have preempted the label.]

back to back   *Baseball, since ca. 1900* (and long generalized). Sequentially. One after the other. *back-to-back home runs* = two in a row: *Remember when Reggie Jackson hit three back-to-back homers in one World Series Game?* [I do, as a matter of fact, but after the third, what was his position in relation to the other two, and after the second, what was his position relative to the first and third? I hope the question will show the absurdity of this Am. idiom. Not that it matters, for we tolerate many such absurdities. Common *time clock* is certainly an idiotic redundancy. (What else is any clock for?) See also *assbackward* for "all turned around." So, too, *head over heels* for "all upside down." The systematic illogic we call idiom has a large tolerance for absurdity.]

back to square one   Back to the beginning again (after having made an initial progress). [From board games in which a player places a counter on a starting square and advances it through consecutive numbered or labeled squares according to rolls of the dice. A common penalty for landing on a particular square is to be sent back to start all over again. The game concept goes back at least to mid-XIX and probably earlier, but the idiomatic specification is relatively recent. P. *Catch Phrases* puts it out of reach of human understanding by saying that it was popularized by BBC commentators on Brit. football. Certainly standard in Am. by the end of WWII. And cf. *back to the drawing board,* which developed a bit

earlier, originally with reference to a failed trial run of a complicated mechanical system. Implies: "We have worked hard but we
seem to have overlooked something and must start all over again."]

badger game   The extortionist's scheme in which a woman lures a
man to her room for promised sex which is interrupted (usually
after being secretly photographed) by her irate "husband." The
man is then made to pay blackmail to avoid publicity or a beating,
the photographs remaining for future blackmail (badgering) after
his wallet has been emptied and his identity established. The ideal
victim is a "respectable" conventioneer in the big city for a whim
away from whom. [Am. late XIX. The term is usually explained as
a form of "badgering," with a reference to the once-common British practice of baiting animals. Queen Elizabeth, for example, is
known to have attended a bear baiting in which nine hounds were
killed before the shackled bear was finished off. In England bulls
about to be slaughtered were once required by law to be baited by
bulldogs at a post commonly placed in front of the house of the lord
mayor. Ponies, sometimes with monkeys tied to their backs, were
also baited as a public sport. The word "garden" in the name of an
English pub originally meant that the place had a baiting arena as
part of its entertainment. In badger baiting, the badger was placed
in a pit that had a lairlike hole in the center for the badger to back
into, though only partway, and the betting was on how many dogs
it would kill with its formidable claws and teeth before the pack
killed it.

This original badgering was a bloody game and Am. *badgering*
has come to mean something like "insistent teasing," rather than
a bloody assault. The criminal's badger game could be for blood;
various forms of animal baiting persisted into XIX U.S., and this
origin of the term cannot be disregarded. But there is an even
stronger case to be made for the derivation from Romany *bajour,*
a wad of money as a swindler's take. Gypsy women were prized for
their ability as *bajour women,* usually as fortune tellers who extracted large sums from the gullible on pretext that the money was
cursed, and had to be purified in a small bag with magic charms,
the bag then being switched (the Gypsy switch) for another that
contained a wad of newspaper.

In tribal tradition Gypsy women were rigidly chaste. They were
not, however, above luring a man into their fortune-telling stall and
leading him behind the drapes with a promise of sex, which was
then interrupted by a raging and knife-wielding husband who
picked the victim clean as the price of not cutting his throat.

Several accounts, most recently a *New Yorker* series on the Gypsy in America, describe this *bajour* game as a common Gypsy swindle. Nor is the Gypsy flimflam unknown to native rogues. Gypsies first appeared in Britain toward the end of XV and entered into various wary alliances with native rogues, at least to the extent that Brit. thieves' cant by late XVI had incorporated many Gypsy terms, some of the most common (with their Romany meaning) being: *shiv* (knife), *pal* (brother), *masher* (smooth-talking swindler), *cosh* (stout stick, a cooking spit), *Posh* (see *Browser's I*), and indirectly *rum go* (a Rom, i.e., Gypsy, hence "queer" thing; this term, of course being a Brit. ref. to Gypsies rather than from Romany).]

baffle To foil. To thwart. To stump, esp. by setting a problem beyond one's powers of solution: *Moriarty baffled even Holmes.* **baffling** 1. Puzzling. Difficult to solve. 2. Beyond solution. **bafflegab** *Am. only.* 1. Loud double-talk [makes no sense]. 2. A deceitful spiel [pretends to make sense but doesn't]. **baffleplate** A plate or grid for controlling the flow of liquids under pressure, esp. to prevent roiling and eddying; or such a plate for controlling and deflecting burning gases within a system; and in electronics, a device for controlling electromagnetic flow. [The uncertain root sense is "to block and rechannel," prob. (??) < OF *bafouer*, to cheat, to hoodwink (to divert and misdirect to one's advantage).

But earlier, to disgrace publicly. This is Shakespeare's sense in *Twelfth Night* V.i: "Alas poor fool how they have baffled thee." And see Spenser, *Faerie Queen* V.3, for a description of the public debasement of a false knight, reading him, so to speak, out of the corps:

> First he his beard did shave and foully shent.
> Then from him rent his shield, and it reversed
> And blotted out his arms with falsehood blent,
> And himself *baffled,* and his arms unhersed,
> And broke his sword in twain, and all his armor spersed.

Baffled here may be taken for "stripped of all insignias of honor."]

bagatelle [Commonly referred to OF *bague,* a bundle; the OF dim. form *bagatel* then explained as a little bundle of nothing much. But the root is It. *bagatella* modified < It. and L. *bacca,* berry. The root sense is, therefore, "a little berry," i.e., a (bright and shiny) nothing much.] 1. A trifling thing. 2. *Jewelry.* A gem-studded bauble: *My girl thinks diamond bagatelles are the berries.* 3. A short piece of light music or light verse. ["A nothing much."] 4. A game played with billiard balls and a cue on a long narrow table with nine holes (!) at one end. [So I have read in various nonexplaining dictionaries. The game is unknown to me. To the best of my knowledge, no bagatelle table is to be found in the U.S. and no poolroom proprietor known to me has ever heard of or seen one. (Long and narrow with nine holes at one end! That's not a pool table but an apple sorter!)]

baldachin [It. *baldacchino*, at root, "[ornate] brocade of Baghdad [used as a canopy]." < *Baldacco*, the It. name for Baghdad.] 1. An ornate canopy above an altar, usually of richly gold-brocaded silk. Also a similar canopy above a throne or carried above a monarch, a high church official, or an icon when borne in procession (as similar canopies where placed above the thrones of oriental monarchs, or carried above them when they were borne in procession). 2. *Architectural ext.* A stone altar canopy, usually ornately carved.

ball and chain 1. A large iron ball attached by a chain to an ankle fetter to restrain prisoners, as a punishment or to inhibit escape. Used in the U.S. on southern chain gangs (of roadworkers) up to about WWII. 2. A wife. Sometimes an insistently altar-bound girlfriend. [Am. whimsical. Common since 1890s. P. *Slang* says it was anglicized ca. 1920 by way of Canada. But note that Partridge, by fixed habit, and usu. without supporting evidence, seems to think that all Americanisms that have been anglicized made it to Brit. by a Canadian way-station, as if there were no direct lines of communication between the U.S. and the U.K.]

ball bearing 1. A spherical metal weight-bearing mechanical device commonly contained in series in a ring that permits free rotation of a shaft, distributing the weight and reducing friction. 2. Such an assembly of mechanical bearings. ["Ball-shaped device that bears weight." The name seems inevitable through habituation. But note It. *cuscino à sfera*, literally, spherical cushion. And if that label rings strange, it is yet identical with ours, a ball being a sphere, and a weight-bearing, weight-distributing member being, in engineer's terms, a cushion.]

ball park *n.* [Since XIX Am.] A baseball playing field, especially one equipped with at least bleachers for spectators. Now such a field with more or less of the elaborate facilities of commercialized fran-

chise sports. **ball-park** (adj.) Labels a general estimate within broad
limits. *a ball-park figure* A figure somewhere inside a general
range. Also *in the ball park* More or less in the neighborhood of:
and *out of the ball park* Beyond negotiable limits. [Corporate and
federal robotic English of the latter 1950s. The image is of a fly ball
landing somewhere within the broad expanse of the baseball playing field (i.e., not over the fence and out of reach), hence within a
negotiable area. I believe but cannot demonstrate that ball park
succeeded *parameters* in pandemic robotic usage in the years just
after WWII.]

balmy *Slang.* (This is the Am. alteration of Brit. *barmy,* but since the
l in one and the *r* in the other are commonly suppressed, the
pronunciation is essentially the same.) *adj.* Crazy (or at least notably eccentric). Out of one's mind. In slang equivalence, "not all
there." [Since XVI. First applied to a mad roving beggar, a Tom o'
Bedlam, a St. Bartholomew's man, *Bartholomew* corrupted to
Barmy, St. Barmy in the same sort of slurring that altered *Bethlehem* to *Bedlam.*]

HISTORIC. With Henry VIII's break from Rome and the suppression of the monasteries, many church properties were seized
and converted to other than clerical use. The Hospice of St. Mary
of Bethlehem was converted to an insane asylum soon known as
Bedlam, and though the name suggests horror, it was the institution of an intended mercy for the mad and only the second such
asylum to be established in Europe (the first was in Grenada, Spain,
founded ca. 1450).

The wards at Bedlam were separately named after saints, St.
Bartholomew's ward being for the nonviolent. These nonviolent
inmates were often released to wander and live as they could by
begging (Tom o' Bedlam) and were commonly known as *Barmy's*
and, soon, *barmies.*

Another ward for nonviolent mental cases was named after
Abraham, whence released patients were alternatively called
Abraham men or *Abram men.* They sometimes wandered loosely
fettered, the chains being as much for identity as for restraint. It
was the crudest sort of care for the mentally ill, but such was the
poverty of XVI London that the condition of these Barmies and
Abrams was good enough to tempt the poorest of beggars to chain
themselves and wander as released Bedlamites, whence, in obsolete thieves' cant, *to Abraham, to Abram,* to play Tom o' Bedlam.
Halitosis is better than no breath at all.

bananas Crazy. [Am. slang since 1890s. For no better reason than the fact that bananas curve. Hence, they are not straight. So when one stops thinking straight, he is said to be bananas—as anyone soon will be if he tries to make strict logic of the process of slang-word formation. And to complicate things further:] *to go bananas* To fly into a frenzy. To rage. To go violently crazy.

bandit [IE *bhā-*, to speak, suffixed *-n-* → *bhan-*, *ban-*. (It must be assumed that the suffix occurred early for with standard bh/f it appears in L. *infans,* infant, at root, "being that does not—yet—speak"; and also in Gmnc., *ban-*, whence OE *bannan,* to summon by legal decree, to proclaim (BAN, BANISH, BANNS).

In old It. *bandire,* to muster, to call together into a band (joining a band, either of soldiers or of brigands, involved the ritual speaking of solemn oaths). So *banditto,* a member of such a band (lit., "a ganged-up man"). Bandit may perhaps be explained as "one banned by the solemn pronunciation of a decree," and that sense cannot be disputed, but "the act of speaking a solemn oath of loyalty to the band" is the primary root sense. In Mafia patois a *made man* or a *sworn man* is one who has joined with such an oath.] 1. A member of an outlaw gang. 2. *Common ext.* An armed stick-up man. [Though he operate alone, he uses violence or the threat of violence in the manner of bandit gangs.] 3. *Further common ext.* A merchant or professional man whose prices or fees are exorbitant.

one-armed bandit A slot machine. [Whimsical Am. slang, ca. 1900 or a bit later. Because, though it has only one arm (the lever), it empties the victim's pockets as thoroughly as does any bandit; and because it, so to speak, reaches out to detain its victim as he is passing by.]

bandit Special use, WWII. An enemy fighter plane. [Primarily RAF, though sometimes borrowed by the Eighth Air Force, which was based in England. The common USAF term, however, was *bogie,* < *bogieman* (because he will get you if he can).]

barbecue 1. *Am.* A cookout or picnic featuring meat cooked on a spit (or now, on a grill). 2. The meat so prepared originally by spitting a whole steer, hog, or other animal. 3. *In loose association.* An outdoor grill. Also *to barbecue,* to prepare meat in one of these ways or in a recent variant thereof. [< Taino (Carib), the original word is unknown but evident in derived Sp. *barbacoa,* a framework of sticks for smoking meat or drying fish. *Buccaneer,* pirate, < Fr. *boucanier,* < native Brazilian *boucan,* such a framework for grilling or drying meat and fish, is a related word, for Caribbean pirates prepared their sea rations on such frameworks. The sometime offered derivation from Fr. *barbe à cou,* beard to tail, with ref. to spitting a whole animal, is ingenious but without substance.]

barbershop quartet　A male quartet specializing in a cappella ornate harmonies of usually sentimental songs. [But though commonly linked in the popular mind with the Gay Nineties—because such groups commonly appear in Gay Nineties costumes and specialize in songs of that era—the name did not come into being until 1925 (MMM).]

HISTORIC. The name harks back to the old barbershop when men commonly went there daily to be shaved. Regular customers had their names ornamented and fired on individual shaving mugs that were stored for them on a rack of open shelves in most barber shops. Except in very small towns in which men still gather to watch haircuts (after they have sat around watching the grass grow), most of us have forgotten to what extent the old barbershop was a social center. I have no doubt that local singing groups were part of that regular attendance, their styles modeled on the then wildly popular minstrel shows or on gospel singers and vaudeville turns, and also on the popular Gay Nineties institution of the singing waiter. But though these antecedents are clear, the term *barbershop quartet* developed only later. By now *Barbershop Quartets* (an official name) have formed a national alliance with regional and national sing-offs for prizes.

barghest, barguest　*Brit. folk-spookery.* A howling night thing commonly in the form of a wild dog. The sight or sound of it is a sign of approaching misfortune (cf. the dire significance of having a black cat cross one's path). [The second element is certainly a folk variant of ghost, Ger. *Geist.* The first element may be from Brit. dialect *bargh,* ridge; akin to Ger. *Berg,* mountain; ult. < IE *bhergh-,* high. If so taken, the root sense is "ridge howler" or "ridge hound." But the first element may as reasonably be derived from *bark;* ult. from IE *bha-,* to speak, to make sound, to sound off; and the root sense would then be "barking ghost" or "howling goblin." The superstition suggests the Irish *banshees,* weird sisters whose wailing foreshadows a death in the house.

The word is hardly an Americanism. I cannot help but note, however, the number of howling spooks who have gathered as guests around my wet bar, as an infallible omen that all bottles will be empty next morning and the house in ruin. I begin to sense that dark forces are afoot and that the *barguests* (I choose that as the Am. form) are massing for a last descent upon us. Several of my last Chinese fortune cookies have also contained dark hints. Toward a more cheerful commerce, however, and to keep omen untainted by money, I have asked the publisher not to compute the cost of setting this entry in the price of the book. It is here offered at no cost as a public-service announcement.]

Barnburner   A New York State (Equal Rights) Reform Democrat of the 1840s. [Said to be so zealous for reform that he would burn down the barn to get rid of the rats. Now archaic but not entirely dead: were any president to call his opponents barnburners, the label would surely come into daily use again.]

baron   1. With various later designations, a minor feudal war chief holding his title of nobility directly from the liege lord or sovereign. In general, the lowest rank of nobility, though in 1611 England established the degree of *baronet,* a subbaron. [< medieval L. * *baro* (stem *barōn*-), man, warrior, knight, minor war chief.] 2. A powerful financier: *the robber barons of the XIX railroads.* [Because in the feudal system barons commonly ruled outlying territories and often murdered, enslaved, or at least robbed all strangers who wandered into their holdings without a heavy armed guard.] 3. A double sirloin roast, or a saddle of lamb or mutton. [A whimsical play on "noble cut of meat." Akin to the play on *sirloin* or Fr., *surloigne,* lit., "above the loin (cut)." Despite that sufficiently clear Fr. etymon, endless variant stories have been told of drunken or simply merry princes who drew their swords and dubbed this noble cut of meat, saying, "Arise. I dub thee Sir Loin." *Baron,* for the double sirloin and the saddle of lamb or mutton, is almost certainly a similar whimsy, and equally unattestable. (But why name it after the lowest title of nobility? Why did the original jokester not create it a "duke of beef, or of lamb, or of mutton?" It does take something close to a king to afford it nowadays.)]

Bartlett pear   Also *bartlett pear* and *bartlett* A popular early pear first imported from England in the 1820s. [After Enoch Bartlett of Dorchester, Mass., who developed, distributed, and popularized this fruit in the U.S.]

bassinet   An infant's crib raised on four legs to about waist height, often with a curved hood over one end, originally, and still often, of basket weave, but now also of various synthetic materials. (Funk and Wagnalls, *Britannica World Language Dictionary,* gives the additional senses: 1. Small basket for infant's clothing. 2. A kind of perambulator. Maybe in Brit. My notebook shows that when I asked forty-one American mothers, none recognized the term in these senses. You may ask the forty-second yourself.) [Fr. *bassinet,* small basin < OF *bacinet,* dim. form of *bacin,* basin. < medieval L. *bacchinus,* dim. form of low L. *bacca,* a vessel for carrying liquid. L. *bacca* also means "berry," and may be, though uncertainly, akin to Bacchus, with ref. to the bowl from which he drank wine, the grape being his "berry."

Fr. *basinet,* earlier *bascinet* and *basnet,* also derives < OF *bacinet,* small basin, but labeled a light, basin-shaped medieval helmet, first worn in England by soldiers of Edward I (reigned 1272–1307) in his conquest of Wales. (It was at this time that his Basque mercenaries brought *Jingo,* the Basque word for God, and *by Jingo!* into English: see *Browser's I.*)

It takes many odd pieces of drunken and bloody time to put one infant to sleep.]

Bastille   1. The infamous fortress prison of Paris into which royal prisoners were thrown, often to be forgotten. It was captured July 14, 1789 in the first great victory of the French Revolution, and July 14 is still celebrated in France as a holiday that closely corresponds to our Fourth of July. 2. *As a journalistic flourish, usually lowercase,* Any clink, cooler, hoosegow, pokey, jug, or similar public rest home. [ME *bastille,* a jail < OF *bastide,* prob. based on a p.p. form of *bastir,* to build. Cf. ME *basten,* to build, of obscure Gmnc. origin but akin to *bastion.* In medieval France *bastide,* later *bastille,* signified a strong point (easily used as a prison) outside the city walls but at no great distance from them. Its purpose in siege warfare was to provide a base for sorties against the rear of the besieging enemy. The Bastille was originally so situated outside of Paris, and then enclosed by the new walls of the expanded city.

HISTORIC. In medieval Italy *borghetti,* little "cities," regularly developed a short distance beyond the city walls on roads leading to the main gates of the city. These, however, were simply points convenient to fields, flocks, and vineyards, and were unfortified or only lightly so, the inhabitants fleeing to the city with their flocks in times of danger.

As the cities expanded, their enlarged walls took in these *borghetti* as distinct quarters of the new city, with customs and an individual flavor developed over centuries of living apart. Many lexicographers have assumed that *ghetto* derives from *(bor)ghetto,* but wrongly so. For the complicated but correct etymology of *ghetto* (given, as I believe, for the first time in English) see *Browser's I.*]

bat 1. The only flying mammal. It resembles a mouse, but has long needlelike teeth with extended canines; usually insectivorous, but some bats are bloodsuckers, and there are fruit bats. 2. An especially ugly old woman. Commonly *an old bat.* (I once observed closely a bat trapped between a lower window and a lowered upper one, and will testify that it is a notably hideous creature.) [Ult. < IE *bhlag-*, to strike (with understood reference to beating wings). Via Gmnc. with g/k → ON *ledhrblaka*, bat (lit. "leather flapper," with "leather wings" understood. Into ME under Danelaw altered to *bakka.* Both *backe* and *bat* were in use in XVI, but the earlier common name was *rearmouse* < OE *hreremus* (in which *hrere* is of unknown origin and meaning; with *mus,* mouse; but prob. akin to Gmnc. *fledermaus,* flutter mouse).]

    bats in the belfry A metaphor for "crazy." [*Belfry* taken as "head"; bats as strange unpredictable shapes (notions) flitting through it.]

    blind as a bat Utterly blind. [Folk metaphor based on the incorrect assumption that bats, since they thread their way through lightless caves and shun daylight, are blind. They do have echolocation sensors, but also sharp eyes with especially good night vision.]

    But *bat* as a cudgel is < L. *batuere,* to strike, to beat. And *bat* as a wad of cotton or wool *(cotton batting)* derives from the fact that the fibers used to be beaten to clean them.

bathos [Gk. *bathos,* depth, deep; BATHOSPHERE.] 1. A ludicrous lapse from the sublime to the ridiculous by a writer incapable of sublimity in the first place. 2. Cloying sentimentality (a reach for false depths of feeling). *adj.* **bathetic** [*Batho-* as a scientific combining form has ample precedent, as above, and also in *batholith,* deep-lying rock, esp. a magmatic intrusion far below the surface. As a noun, coined by Alexander Pope in mid-XVIII in his *Dunciad,* a satiric "epic" of literary lackwits; a variant of *pathos,* feeling. Pope intended his variant to label the ridiculous opposite of true *pathos* conceived as the zenith of which bathos is the nadir.]

battle [L. **battuere,* to beat (assault and) BATTERY.] *Now* 1. An engagement of armed forces. 2. *Ext.* Any intense dispute: *the battle of the sexes.* [But earlier, not the conflict but the forces arrayed for it, this earlier sense surviving in *battle line*, a formation for attack or defense. Old It. *battaglia*, a military troop; with augmentative suffix *-one* → *battaglione*, a large war force, usually five companies. BATTALION. The transition to the modern sense occurred in XVI, Shakespeare using the word in both the old and the modern senses. In *Henry V* IV he means "battle array" in "Each battle [body of troops] sees the other's umbered face;" but cf. *The Taming of the Shrew* II, "Have I not in pitched battle heard . . . ?"]

battle ax(e) 1. Up to XVI a common weapon for close-order hacking, often combined with a spike or hook or both. 2. Often as *old battle axe* A shrewishly or hard-nosed adversary female. [P. *Slang* stresses "old woman," dating the term from 1910 or 1920 U.S. and Canada (and also Australia, New Zealand, and oddly South Africa), but in Am. often labels one's wife or "ball and chain" or "the war department" in which "old" expresses familiarity (the breeding ground of contempt) rather than aged.]

battle cry A shout (earlier *slogan*) by soldiers worked up to blood lust. (It seems to be a military fact that men die more eagerly as they bellow louder.)

battle royal 1. *Chivalric*, A fight to the death. 2. *But now, variously:* (a) A free-for-all. A donnybrook. (b) A domestic discussion in which the crockery flies. [Most of my dictionaries, starched into old habit, give the sense "a battle on a large scale." But would any American in touch with his own idiom and history speak of Gettysburg, El Alamein, or Anzio as a battle royal?]

bazooka 1. *WWII.* A recoilless rocket launcher resembling a long, flared pipe, usually fired from an infantryman's shoulder with an assistant usually acting as the loader. Used primarily as an antitank weapon at close range. [Because of its fancied resemblance to:] 2. A raucous, trombone-like instrument homemade of gas pipes and a metal funnel. [Invented and popularized by Bob Burns, popular Arkansas hillbilly comedian of the 1920s and 1930s. As part of his stage signature, Burns regularly interrupted his comic routine to blurt into his noisemaker. He seems, too, to have invented the name, prob. as a variant of *kazoo* (metathesized to *zooka* and prefixed *ba-*). The word was borrowed by infantry men because of some perceived resemblance in these two ungainly instruments. (And because the bazooka was supposed to "blow away" the tank?)]

beauty sleep This fixed idiom is now applied to any period of regular repose conducive to one's health and therefore, especially with reference to a woman, to one's beauty. But note that up to early

XX and the general adoption of the light bulb, this idiom was specific to *sleep before midnight.* There is no fixed principle that sleep after midnight is less healthy than earlier sleep, but a woman who stayed up regularly till the small hours was thought to be dissipating, and also exposing herself to "unhealthy" night airs. In the age of candles and oil lamps only the conspicuously wealthy "burned midnight oil." The normal hour of bedtime was soon after dusk. So the old proverb stressed both the health advantages and the money saved on candles and oil lamps (and throwing in wisdom as an extra inducement): "Early to bed and early to rise / Will make you healthy, and wealthy, and wise."

because it's there The now-standard reply of mountain climbers when asked, "Why would you want to climb that mountain?" And as a basic fact of the sport, no mountain can be climbed until it is there. Now generalized into a catchphrase that can be used in many contexts. [There seems to be no way to attribute it to any particular mountain. It is a sentiment that would come naturally to any addicted mountain climber when pestered by a flatland reporter. But since WWII and a number of publicized and televised assaults on Everest and other notable peaks, the phrase has become a standard of the sport, escaping also into general usage. *Asked why she had to go and lose it at the Astor, the Dean of Women replied, "Because it's there!" Now everyone knows that's where it is—or used to be before it was torn down.*]

Beefeater 1. *Brit.* A yeoman of the guard. A member of the red-uniformed elite corps best known to Americans as guardians of the Tower of London. 2. *Am.* Also *Beefeater's* A much-promoted brand of gin that uses an image of such a guard as its trademark logo. [There is no explanation for this name. Although these yeomen of the guard existed much earlier, this name was applied to them only in XVIII (according to ODEE). Some sources derive the name from Fr. *buffetier,* a short leather jacket, but these guards are not known to have used such jackets as part of their uniform. *Buffetier* could mean an attendant at a sideboard (buffet), but the yeoman's functions did not commonly include such service. If these guards later adopted beef as a main diet (by name association) it could not have been their traditional mess, for beef and the choice cuts of venison were reserved for the lords, servants and hunt attendants making do with meat pies of organs, tripe, and chopped intestines. (See *humble pie, Browser's I.*) Nor is there any record of a feudal grant to establish a beef diet for these honor guards.

There is a possible precedent in the fact that English, in avoiding the word *peasant* for what were in effect feudal sharecroppers, called them *bacon eaters*. Yeoman, a freeholder, was a class one step up from these peasants, as beef was held to be a step up from pork, and they may have been designated beefeaters accordingly, though the dating is late for such an association. With all possible sources of their name in doubt, the Beefeaters must stand to it under a row of question marks rampant.]

beer [At root, "the drink." Ult. < IE *poi-*, variant *pi-*, to drink. There was prob. some redupl. form, perhaps *pi-po-*, and this with a simple p/b, perhaps intermediately *pi-bo-*, *bi-bo-* → L. *bibere*, to drink (IMBIBE, BIBULOUS). Vulgar L. *biber*, beverage, thing to drink; and this was borrowed into VI Ger., modified to *bier* by German monastic brewers for a drink they then began to brew with hops, thus distinguishing it from the much older ale, which was brewed from malt without hops. OE *bēor*. The ME forms *ber, bere, beere* existed but were so rare that they are not found in Chaucer (nor in *Piers Plowman*). Ale remained the basic British drink. Brewing with hops was probably not reintroduced from Germany into Britain until XV, and not common until late XVI or early XVII.] 1. A drink brewed from hops and malt fermented at a relatively low temperature, and generally with a much lower alcoholic content by volume than that of wine. 2. *Ext. by analogy*. Various, usually carbonated, soft drinks flavored with roots, bark, or both. (Am. *ginger ale* roughly corresponds to Brit. *ginger beer*, but *ginger beer* may also be found here, and the drink so labeled is sharper and tarter—more gingery—than ginger ale. *Root beer* is about the same on either side of the Atlantic—though self-styled experts will argue this point.)

    beery 1. Like beer: *Most of his sentiments have a fine beery flavor*. 2. In one's cups and maudlin.

    beer baron A wealthy brewer. [A number of great British fortunes were built on breweries; cf. A. E. Housman, "Epilogue":

        Oh many a peer of England brews
        Livelier liquor than the Muse.]

    beer belly Am. 1. A pot belly developed by generous consumption of the caloric brew. 2. A beer sot. Also *beer barrel Am.* A beer sot. (He pours the stuff in as if he were the barrel.)

    beer jerk A bartender. [Am. Now rare, and prob. obs. By analogy to the once-common *soda jerk*, common from late XIX to about 1940 for the counter man behind a soda fountain.]

    beer joint Generic for a small neighborhood drinking place that usually sells other drinks but primarily tap beer. [*Joint* came into slang originally with the sense "place where things meet": *What I didn't learn at my mother's knee, I picked up at other low joints.*]

beer and skittles Primarily Brit. slang. The easy life (in pure Am., *the life of Reilly*). [*Beer,* for plenty to drink; *skittles,* a once-popular pub game; known but not common in U.S.]

to cry in one's beer 1. To become maudlin drunk. 2. To weep and mourn while enjoying the good things. (It is obviously far better to giggle into one's champagne.)

used beer Urine. [The stuff does work its way through steady beer drinkers in a hurry. But any number of U.S. beer joints have found a point of high humor in labeling their restrooms "Used Beer Department."]

bee(s) in the bonnet Like bats in the belfry, an idiom signifying mental aberration. [Earlier *to have bees in the head* or *in the brain* (which will certainly do as an image of a confused mental buzz) and so given by John Heywood in his 1546 compilation of English proverbs, the first such work to be published in English.

The image may be related to the old folk belief that the *earwig* (see *Browser's II*) bored through the human ear and into the brain.

Robert Herrick never exactly said *bees in the bonnet,* but he was the first to suggest that phrasing in "Mad Maud's Song," 1648:

> Ah! woe is me, woe, woe is me.
> Alack and well-a-day!
> For pity, sir, find out that bee
> Which bore my love away!
> —I'll seek him in your bonnet brave,
> I'll seek him in your eyes.

Hardly a highwater mark of English poetry, but idiom is where one finds it.]

bee's knees: it's the bee's knees It is swell, the best there is, peaches and cream, supermelogorgeous, the cat's pajamas, the cat's meow. [All of these formulas were fad fast-talk catchphrases of the Am. 1920s, all now archaic but recalled, often in foolish nostalgia, by doddering obsolescents. Some defy all efforts to fix an origin. All seemed to do as smart rhetorical flourishes in an age when it seemed apt to refrain from calling someone a liar and to label him instead as "a fabricator of terminological inexactitudes." *Bee's knees,* however, must derive from "business" ("It will really give you the business"—it will be a memorable experience.) Business, perhaps, as pronounced by an Italian immigrant—*beesa-neesa*. It might suggest the concurrently popular *none of your beeswax* for "none of your business," but if there is a connection, no one has found it.]

Befana, la Befana   In Italy and parts of southern Germany, the Christmas fairy. She is commonly depicted as an ancient witch, but she is benign. She corresponds to our Santa Claus except that she brings her gifts on Twelfth Night or Epiphany (Jan. 6). She is said to put ashes in the stockings of bad children, but this is a parental slander of *la Befana:* come Christmas, no one can be so fiendish as to give brats only what they truly deserve. [It., a folk corruption of the feminine given name Epifania, Epiphany, the day on which *la Befana* performs her eternal penance by paying homage to the generic child (as she once failed to do for the Christ child when she ignored the Magi.)]

HISTORIC. Americans who are in Rome in the winter know the *Befana* as a haggard but kindly old witch among the symbolic Christmas figures. In the traditional pre-Christmas fair in Piazza Navona all sorts of crèche figures and Befana figurines are on festive sale, but the Befana never appears in or near the crèche scene. She is displayed only at a lonely distance from it.

The legend has it that the Magi passed her house on their way to adore the Christ child, but that she was too busy to stop her work or even to look up to pay them homage, saying she would wait to see them when they were on their way back. They returned home by another route, however, and she was left to wait forever to see the glory she had slighted. It does not pay to slight the offered splendor: buy many copies of this book well in advance for truly glorious Christmas giving.

beleaguer   To besiege. [The immediate source is Du. *belegeren,* < *be-,* around (akin to "by"); *leger,* camp. Into Eng. in late XVI (a spate of Dutch words entered English at that time). The essential sense, "to camp around," implies "to combine forces around (in threatening position)." And "combined force(s)" is root-implicit in *league,* < L. *ligare,* to bind together. In Am. slang, "to league up against."]

NOTE. It is not root-consonant to say "Judith beleaguered me." Judith is my wife and has unusual talents, as for example she can surround me in a single look. Even she, however, is incapable of beleaguering me without the aid of the rest of the family—which she has on call.

Not to be confused with *league,* an archaic measure of distance equal to three miles, < L. *leuga,* of obscure Celtic origin. So *seven league boots* = no less than 21 miles to a step (now theoretically almost possible if one walks—very slowly—to a forward lavatory on an SST). So *Half a league, half a league, half a league onward,* as Tennyson rendered the charge of the Light Brigade. Could he have meant a four-and-a-half-mile charge at full gallop? Call it poetic license. In any case, the Russians, as horse lovers, shortened the course for most, and finally for all.

bell [The form is a pure survival of IE *bhel-,* to roar (BELLOW, BAWL), the original sense surviving in Gmnc., but into OE *belle* with a sense shift to "bell," the root sense surviving in *bellow.*] 1. A more-or-less resonant cup (usually metal, and always metal in the time of OE) with a clapper. 2. *Ext. by analogy.* A bell-shaped flower: *bluebells.* 3. *Nautical.* A time signal: *eight bells.* 4. Any rung signal: *death bell, passing bell, church bell, alarm bell.*

sound as a bell *Of things,* In excellent working order. Of persons, *Vibrantly healthy.* [Like liberty, of course, bells crack, but this metaphor predates the national corruption of concept.]

that rings a bell That wakens a responsive chord in memory. [But always said with the implication that though it gives off a familiar signal, the hearer cannot quite identify what is being signaled.]

with bells on Festively prepared. [Like a carriage horse with gay bells on its harness.]

to bell the cat To act with great daring. [From the ancient folktale, retold in *Piers Plowman,* in which the wise old mouse proposed that if someone hung a bell on the sleeping cat, it would no longer be able to sneak up silently on unsuspecting mice. All present agreed on the value of such an early-warning system, but none dared undertake the installation.]

bell, book, and candle 1. The basic formula of the ritual of excommunication from the Roman Catholic church, and so from the hope of eternal grace. 2. *Ext.* Utterly. With total and eternal denunciation: *Granddaddy drove Aunt Clara out of the house by bell, book, and candle.*

HISTORIC. Until as late as ca. 1950 in America (at which time a few Roman Catholic priests were disciplined for clinging to the original doctrine, among them a Father Feeney who served as a sort of chaplain to Harvard students) it was firm doctrine that salvation was available only through the Roman Catholic church.

The papal coat of arms still has two keys in its crest, one to open the gates of heaven and one to lock them, and these keys were given in trust by Christ to the pope as His vicar on earth, to him and to no other. Excommunication was the dread public ritual of exclusion from eternal hope.

Bells were rung as a public announcement that a soul was to be ritually cursed. The curse was then read from a *book*, concluding, "Be they removed from the book of Life [here the book is closed], and as this *candle* is cast from the sight of men [here the lighted candle is extinguished by being dashed to the ground], so be their souls cast from the sight of God into the deepest pit of hell. Amen." The church bells (as distinct from the small hand bell used at the altar) were then clanged discordantly, and in their jangle the damned soul passed from grace forever.

bender A bout of drinking: *He went off on a three-day bender and hasn't straightened out since.* [Common Am. slang. Cf. *to bend an elbow,* to have a drink. Hence *Elbow Room,* the name of a chain of Midwest drinking places; *room* signifying both *common room, meeting place,* and *space,* as in *room to swing a cat.* But in Brit. slang from XVIII to ca. 1875, a hard drinker (one given to sustained elbow bending). So in the less-than-immortal poetry of Allen Ramsey:

> Now lend your lungs, ye *benders* fine
> Wha ken the benefit of wine.]

berm The paved or graveled shoulder of a road. Alternatively, a narrow, grassy road shoulder. [So in Am. since ca. 1850, originally with ref. to barge canals. MMM cites as an 1854 definition cited in *Notes and Queries,* "The bank of a canal opposite to the towing path," a usage closest to the root sense. AHD (2d—and inferior—edition) gives other senses (that have about faded from Am.): 1. A narrow ledge or shelf, as along a slope; 2. A ledge between the parapet and moat of a fortification. AHD derives the term < Fr. *berme* (with senses 1 and 2 above) and MD *berm;* but both are < Ger. *Berme,* path along a dike.]

big store, the The fully developed U.S. confidence game, as opposed to the petty swindle. [*Big store* was the con man's term for such installations as fake banks, betting parlors, Western Union offices, and other seemingly authentic business establishments set up and manned by teams of confidence men to mislead their victims.]

HISTORIC. From late XIX up to the stock-market crash of 1929 big-store confidence men relied on local specialists who could set up at need elaborate business establishments, a fake bank for example, fully equipped with tellers, bank officers, and customers who seemed to be transacting business with real money. A victim ("the mark") could be taken into such a "store" and be assured by the president of the bank (a hired swindler) that the proposed scheme was a sure-fire one-in-a-million golden opportunity.

Local specialists set up such banks (or other offices) in what had once been an actual bank building, leasing the fake premises at need to a confidence man who had a victim to fleece. Such elaborate false establishments must necessarily have been known to the police who had, therefore, to be paid off. The cities corrupt enough to offer such large facilities were organized along two main routes, one from Denver to Kansas City to Miami, sometimes with stops in New Orleans; the other from Chicago to Miami, sometimes with stops in Kansas City and New Orleans. The most successful of the big-store swindlers regularly traveled these routes in seasonal migrations, and they played for big stakes. Yellow Kid Weill, a Chicago-based big-store confidence man claimed in his autobiography to have swindled at least $5 million from 1900 to the beginning of WWI.

bill 1. An assertedly accurate, sometimes itemized, semilegible statement of charges. 2. A posted notice of offerings: *theatrical bill, bill of fare.* 3. A piece of paper money: *phony as a nine-dollar bill.* 4. A legal document presented to a court stating detailed charges: *bill of particulars.* 5. A printed public announcement of an event, as a store sale; also a wanted poster: *handbill.* 6. A proposal presented to a legislature for enactment. 7. *Slang,* A hundred dollars: *Tom Swales dropped three bills in the second race.* [At root, "an official document," originally one marked with wax and a seal. (So *papal bull.* In many European countries receipts are not entirely authorized unless they are written on paper marked with a tax stamp bought at a state store. In It., *carta bollata,* stamped [official] paper.) < L. *bulla,* 1. A ball, a bubble ("rounded, swollen thing"); 2. A magical charm (a small pouch stuffed with magical substances usually worn around the neck. Also, be it noted, apt to root sense, "rounded, swollen thing," which is the sense of IE root *beu-, bheu-,* whence also BULL (at root, "animal that swells up—BELLOWS—with ref. to sexual tumescence). And some bills are still a lot of bull.]

A number of common idiomatic uses, mostly self-evident, in-

clude: *billboard* 1. A generally large, commonly lighted, flat vertical surface for displaying posters. 2. *Specialized TV use,* The endless list of titles, credits, cast, and production staff that precedes a
program, using up air time in the name of entertainment. *billfold*
A wallet. *billhead* A statement of charges on which the name of the
charging firm is printed, with its address, logo, and instructions for
payment.

   bill of attainder Brit. law, obs. A decree declaring, without
trial, that a person is guilty of treason or some other high crime for
which he is to be put to death with loss of all privileges and honors.
[His honor (in chivalry more than life itself) is declared, old style,
to be atteint (tainted).]

   bill of exchange A letter from a principal to an agent directing
the agent to give a specified sum to the designated person. *bill of
fare* A menu. *bill of health* A medical certification of physical
condition. Originally issued to a ship's captain as part of his port
clearance, certifying that the ship was free of contagious disease.
a clean bill of health Generalized. An approval. *bill of lading* An
itemized inventory of goods as part of a cargo or shipment. Also the
total inventory of goods aboard a carrier. *Bill of Rights* 1. The first
ten amendments to the Constitution of the United States. 2. A
declaration by the English Parliament, enacted 1689, limiting the
power of the crown over English subjects. *bill of sale* A signed
document certifying transfer of private property other than real
estate, which is deeded). [All idioms listed in this paragraph have
the common senses, 1. More or less authorized; 2. Itemization or
clearance.]

billion   [< Fr. *bi-,* two, twice; with (m)illion; < It. *milione,* the
majorative/augmentative form of *mille,* 1,000. A confused word-
formation all the way: the Italian etymon means "a big thousand,"
and the French augmentation to *billion* is, at root, 2 million. The
confusion is further confused by the fact that Europeans count by
a system far different from that used in U.S.; see below.] In Am.
1,000,000,000; one followed by nine zeroes; a thousand million.

   WARNING. Take accurate count of your traveler's checks when
traveling in Europe, where they will be called *cheques,* and where
this number is called a *milliard,* a billion there being what we call
a trillion. (Note also that *milliard* is at root *milli-,* 1,000, or thousands; with the pejorative suffix *-ard* as in *bastard, dotard, stinkard.*
Hence, at root, "a bad thousand.") With such variances in ways of
keeping count, free spenders will need a guide to foreign price lists:

Table of Conversion for U.S. Travelers Abroad: A Guide to Tipping

British and Continental	U.S.	Number of zeroes following the one
million	million	6
milliard	billion	9
billion	trillion	12
thousand billion	quadrillion	15
trillion	quintillion	18
thousand trillion	sextillion	21
quadrillion	septillion	24
thousand quadrillion	octillion	27
quintillion	nonillion	30
thousand quintillion	decillion	33

The European system continues to *decillion* (1 with 60 zeroes) and *centillion* (1 with 600 zeroes), but not even Ronald Reagan tips that high. Note that an American who leaves a tip of what he calls a decillion dollars will be short of the European scale by $1,000,-000,000,000,000,000,000,000,000 (one thousand quadrillion), the dead beat.

bingo *n.* An elaborated form of lotto, a game played with cards of numbered squares to be matched by numbered counters shaken from a box, the first player to match a vertical or horizontal line of numbers being the winner. Gambling bingo, originally licensed as a fund-raising activity of churches and social groups (Play Bingo for God!), has developed many variants and is commonly played with two or more cards at a time. (Bingo addicts buy as many cards as they can manage and pray for winners, pray, in fact, rather harder than they do in church.) [The game intermediate between simple Lotto and Bingo was Beano, so called because players once marked their winning squares with beans (now with various counters). The cards' gridwork was marked B-E-A-N-O across the top (later B-I-N-G-O). The game master calling his numbers says, for example, "Under the B—13. Under O—4." And so on. A player who completed a vertical or horizontal line cried, "Beano!" (now "Bingo!"). The game master thereupon cried in formal litany, "Beano! Do not remove your beans: the player may be wrong!" And so, though with variants, in Bingo. Whence:] 1. *Exclam.* A player's cry of triumph. 2. *Ext.* Any cry of triumph: —*Preacher. I now pronounce you man and wife.* —*Judith. Bingo!*

bird: a little bird told me   A fixed formula for saying, "I know and never mind how I found out." [But though used casually, and sometimes lightly, that formula has deep roots, and even biblical precedent: Ecclesiastes 10:20, "Curse not the king, no, not in thy thought . . . for a bird of the air shall carry thy voice, and that which hath wings shall tell the matter."

In the proverbs of many languages rumor and calumny are said to take wing. So in a XIX survival in the "Latest Decalogue" by Arthur Hugh Clough:

> Thou shalt not slander. Let the lie
> Have time on its own wings to fly.

Our species has many languages but a limited stock of natural metaphors. "Wings of rumor" (and so the "little bird") is one of these ancient, almost universal metaphors.

And note that the flight of birds (they fly, so to speak, close to God) was once studied religiously for omens (news from God). However joshingly we use this formula it is still haunted by a memory of deeply religious belief.]

bivouac   A field encampment. Troops bivouac for the night while on the march. They do so in the open, without prepared defense positions, depending for safety on the watches they post. [And so the root sense, "double watch" (because fewer guards would be necessary in a prepared position). Fr. < XII Swiss-German *bei-wacht*, < *bei*, two, twice; *wacht*, watch. In Ger. *Beiwache, Bei-wacht*, a bivouac.]

black flag   A plain black flag as the traditional ensign of besieging forces to indicate that no quarter would be given the defenders. This ensign may have originated in the Middle Ages, but the custom of utterly destroying walled cities and all their defenders is immemorial. The Romans not only killed all the people of Carthage but tore down the city and salted the surrounding fields. The hordes of Genghis Khan used terror as a strategy to encourage the surrender of besieged cities. After the city had been taken and the troops had been turned loose to slaughter all hands, a few were always allowed to escape to spread the word of what happened to those who resisted.

In a late variant (Feb.–March, 1836), Mexican forces under General Santa Anna besieged the Alamo for 11 days, during which relays of musicians played a traditional death song to inform the defenders that none would be spared. Davy Crockett and Colonel

James Bowie died there, probably humming the air that had been dinned into their heads during those 11 days and nights.

Today in the tradition of determined eradication *Black Flag* survives as the registered trade name of an insecticide widely advertised with the motto, "It kills bugs dead."

blackguard   (pronounced *blag'-'rd;* more common in Brit. than in Am.) 1. A term of aristocratic contempt for those who perform the most menial, dirtiest (and most essential) tasks. Thorstein Veblen's "Theory of the Leisure Class" analyzes these caste assumptions. 2. A low, dirty person of no social position. Hence assumed, more or less accurately, to be immoral, dishonest, and cowardly.

HISTORIC. Noble families regularly traveled from one castle to another (in old style, they "made a progress"), trailed by supply wagons and servants. Rather than stock several castles with expensive cooking gear, drinking vessels, table service, bedding, and other household linens, they tended to take the stuff with them. The most menial servants traveled in the last wagons with the pots and pans (as if "guarding" the sooty gear that "blackened" them; and once in residence, these servants worked closest to soot, grease, and manure.

And the most commonly offered explanation derives the term from them, which is probably apt, but not securely attested. The term was certainly applied to pot wallopers and scullery drudges of the officers' mess wagons who brought up the rear of marching columns, and who were generally the first to run if attacked. John Webster, English dramatist whose short life straddled 1600, caught all of the tone of the word in *The White Devil:* "A lousy slave, that within this twenty years rode with the *black guard* in the Duke's carriage (read "retinue" for "carriage"), 'mongst spits and dripping pans!"

Black Maria   A black van, originally horse drawn, for rounding up drunk and disorderly persons and for conveying criminals from raided premises. It was a large boxlike van with wooden benches along either side, a barred rear door, and a step or two below the door for climbing into the van. [Police term since early XIX Am. *Black* because of the traditional color. *Maria* perhaps after Maria Lee, a black woman of Boston ca. 1825. She is variously and vaguely reported to have assisted police in rounding up disorderly persons, hoodlums, and thieves. Through the mist of unspecified reports she seems to emerge as some sort of police informant, quick tempered and powerful of body.

P. *Slang* notes that the form had passed into Brit. use by ca. 1870. I am just old enough to have a hazy memory of the last horse-drawn Black Marias on the streets of Boston a bit after 1920. They were then replaced by wagonlike trucks resembling horse-drawn carriages, but these have since been superseded by various wire-screened buses.

In a separate evolution *Black Maria* was transferred in WWI to an American field piece that belched a great cloud of black smoke. But that name was not certainly a transfer from the police roundup van. The Germans, curiously, had a similar term, *Schwarze Maria,* for our heavy, smoky explosive shells.]

Blighty *Brit.* England. [In the language of British servicemen overseas. Not used by Americans but well known to them from various nostalgic service songs and from Brit. war movies.] *back to Blighty* Back to England (from service overseas). [A XIX Anglo-Indian gift of the British Empire. All sources point to Arabic *waliya,* he rules, *wilāyat,* realm; whence Urdu *walayate,* foreign and Hindi *wilāyati, vilāyati, bilāyati,* foreign, and since the ubiquitous imperial Britishers were the most prominent foreigners, the associated sense England (where the blighters came from). Brit. servicemen, having the term explained to them as meaning England/Great Britain, corrupted *bilāyati* to *b'l-aye-ti,* whence *Blighty,* becoming nostalgic about it because they were far from home and needed to get drunk and mournful when they weren't killing or on parade.]

Bluegrass State The proudly self-proclaimed nickname of Kentucky. *blue grass (Poa pratensis),* a lush grass usually said to be indigenous to the Eurasian plains and naturalized to the limestone-rich soil and climate of Kentucky. Various Kentucky historians, however, including Dr. Eslie Asbury, surgeon, raconteur, and well-known breeder of race horses, insist that the bluegrass was there when the first white settlers reached Kentucky. (I know Dr. Asbury to be a learned and an accurate man, but I do not have the facts.)

I have driven across Kentucky many times, even on the Bluegrass Highway, without seeing any but green grass. A number of natives have assured me that I have seen only cropped pastures, and that the blueness of the bluegrass becomes visible only when the grass is allowed to go to seed, the seed covering having a distinctly blue cast. Maybe. Others have added that the blueness of bluegrass is visible only when the sun is low and a soft wind tosses the heads of the grass. Maybe.

Kentuckians tend to agree on nothing entirely, but I choose to agree with Dr. Asbury, who attributes the blueness (in season) to the small blue flowers this grass bears. Even in season, they are not commonly visible because the grass is usually cropped.

blue law(s)   The legal enactment and enforcement of church rulings on matters of religious observance and morals. [The term is commonly explained by the asserted fact that such laws were published on blue paper or were bound in blue covers. But paper was a scarce and expensive import in the early colonies. I have been able to find no scholar who has seen a volume of such laws published on blue paper, or bound in covers that have remained certifiably blue over the centuries. Nor would the Puritan fathers distinguish, as we do, between church and state.

I have been further defeated in trying to find a secure first dating for this Am. idiom. It may not have developed until late XIX. By that time *blue nose* (which see) had become a common term for *Puritan,* and the "blueness" of these laws may more reasonably be attributed to frostbitten souls than to nonexistent blue paper.]

HISTORIC. The New England colonies were essentially theocracies that believed the Day of Doom was fast approaching and that Satan was waging a last desperate campaign for Christian souls. (He already had the devilish Indians.) The Salem witchcraft trials, begun in 1692, were the most notable outbreak of this religio-legal hysteria, but earlier in XVII Connecticut had hanged Quakers as heretical presences, and Massachusetts had legally ordered that two drunken and dissolute men undergo an improvement of their characters by being sold into slavery.

Blue laws and their derivatives have continued, though with lessening legal force, to prescribe religious and moral behavior. It remains possible in some states for a married couple to break the law by their sexual behavior in the privacy of their beds. Into the 1970s books have been legally banned for offending what justices have called "community standards" (in effect, Cotton Mather's blue-nose standards).

Today it is still commonly illegal to operate a drinking place or a package store within a certain distance of a church, or to sell liquor anywhere during the hours of Sunday morning church services. Until sometime after WWII it was illegal for many stores to open on Sunday, and all athletic contests were forbidden.

The blue laws, however, ran afoul of the religious frenzy of sports fans and of the episcopal power of TV. Sunday professional sports are now an established ritual of holy big money, and not all the ghostly fury of the blue-nose founding fathers shall prevail against the dividend-bearing separation of church and state.

blue nose 1. A New England colonial name for a Nova Scotian. [Whimsical; because down-easters, mostly fishermen in cold waters, were said to have their noses frostbitten blue.] 2. *Later, esp. in the Am. of XIX immigrants and their children.* A rigorously puritanical person of Spartan habits. (Generally implies moral snooping into the habits of others and, certainly, disapproval of them.)

B'nai B'rith A confraternity of Jewish men established in New York City in 1843, now functioning throughout the U.S. and to some extent in Canada. [Transliterated Hebrew, "sons of the covenant." Sometimes rendered "children of the covenant," but with no offense to Women's Rights activists, I must note that B'nai B'rith is for males only, and that male children are properly called sons.]

B.O. *An ad agency bugaboo.* 1. Body odor. [One of the functions of advertising is to create social anxieties in order to sell products that will relieve them. Soap advertising, especially for Lifebuoy deodorant soap, began to sensitize the public to social terror of emitting a strong sweaty or otherwise offensive odor. I have not tracked down the exact beginning of the B.O. campaign, perhaps as early as the 1920s, but the term was squarely in the American consciousness by the beginning of WWII.] 2. A term waiting for an apt extension, toward which I offer: *Don Rickels is Hollywood's most publicized case of psychic B.O. His every line is an exhalation of sulfur dioxide.*

bodice *Dressmaking.* 1. The part of a woman's dress above the waist. 2. A vestlike, laced, tight, outer garment worn over a blouse. 3. *Obs.* A corset. [In XVI and in slightly earlier Sc. sense 3 was a *pair of bodies. Bodice* is, in fact, simply a slightly altered form of *bodies.*
Cf. *midriff,* the only surviving form of obs. *riff,* body. Ult. < IE *krep-,* body; with k/h and p/f in Gmnc. → OE *hriff,* body. But note that an altered form of this same IE root, *korp-,* is the base of L. *corpus,* body.]

bohunk Also *hunky* 1. An ethnic slur term for an immigrant from central Europe. 2. *Generalized ext.* A disparaging label for any immigrant not specifically identified as a limey, spic, dago, kraut, polack, frog, etc. [Since early XX, esp. in the coal mines, steel mills, and Chicago stockyards. Most native American workers had only a foggy notion of the peoples of central Europe. The name is almost certainly a slurring-with-alteration of *Bo(hemian)* and *Hung(arian)* but with the sense also slurred to imply "all dem furriners from queer places."]

boloney   1. The Am. corruption of *sausage of Bologna*. 2. *boloney!* Slang. Exclamation of contemptuous dismissal, dissent, rejection. Worthless stuff! [In its pure native form *Bologna, bologna,* a large sausage native to Bologna, Italy, is reputedly edible, and even thought by some (mostly the manufacturers) to qualify as a delicacy. Perhaps so. At its best it is not filet mignon. In most American imitations it is a ground-up mess of heavily seasoned inferior ground meat and chopped guts, the cheapest of cold cuts (except perhaps for souse or head cheese), fit only for sandwiches in the lunch pails of the cheapest day laborers. The connection between *chopped meat/ground guts* and *bosh, tripe, worthless stuff* is obvious.]

   that's a lot of (a bunch of) boloney That's worthless stuff. *no matter how you slice it, it's (still) boloney* Fancy it up anyway you like, I still won't swallow it. *to be full of boloney* To be worthless/ full of worthless stuff. [A slightly minced form of *to be full of shit.*]

   boloney bulls, boloneys Chicago stockyards (and diffused) since mid XIX. Bulls and old steers too tough for choice cuts, fit only for stew meat and for grinding into sausage meat. *Boloneys* fetch the lowest prices at livestock auctions. [MMM cites as a livestock quotation in the Chicago *Tribune,* June 14, 1947: "Cattle Prime Steers, $28.00–$30.00. Bulls, bologna, common-choice, $15.50–$18.00.]

booze   In Am. a generic term for hard liquor. Also specific to Am. *booze hound* An alcoholic. And in both Brit. and Am. many related variants as: *boozy* Inebriated. *to booze it up* To drink heavily. [ME *bous,* ale, beer, wine. (There was no hard liquor of any consequence.) *bouse,* to drink heavily. < MD *būsen* (now Du. *buisen*), to drink to excess.]

   HISTORIC. Often wrongly attributed to an early XIX American distiller named Booz. For the 1840 presidential campaign in which General William Henry Harrison (Old Tippecanoe) trounced the incumbent Martin Van Buren (see *O.K.* in *Browser's I*), the Booz distillery put out a whiskey bottle, now a collector's item, pressed in the form of a log cabin and prominently marked BOOZ. The bottle was supposed to commemorate Harrison's humble birth in a log cabin. He was in fact the son of a substantial Virginia plantation owner, but Americans like their presidential legends aside from fact, and good whiskey can make almost anything true enough for political purposes. The word *booze,* however, was in English usage for centuries before this Booz was distilled from his family genes.

bother *n.* 1. A minor source of annoyance: *Don't go to the bother of dying of trivial causes.* 2. An irksome person. *v.* 1. To annoy, to pester, to interfere with: *He doesn't bother me.* 2. To go to a deal of trouble for: *Don't bother to wait up for me, warden.* 3. *Exclam.: Bother! Oh, bother!* Expresses mild annoyance. (Primarily Brit. but in limited Am. use.) [Origin guessed at but in doubt. Jonathan Swift used the form *bodder* in early XVIII, and guessing from the fact that he was born in Ireland, NWD, 2d ed., speculates, "prob. Anglo-Irish for POTHER." AHD, 1st ed., suggests, "perhaps from Irish *buaidhrim,* I vex." ODEE notes, "first recorded from the writings of Irishmen (T. Sheridan, Swift, Sterne), and doubtless of Anglo–Ir. origin, but no plausible Ir. source can be adduced." I take the ODEE to be definitive in this, and offer these three citations as a clarification of the lexicographers' use of "prob." and "perh.," which mean, "guess follows." It does, however, seem reasonable to guess that in this case the wind is from Ireland.]

    botheration Bother. [A rhetorical dialect flourish modeled, I guess, on *tarnal/tarnation* < *eternal/tarnal: Dairy farming, said Uncle Hiram, is a tarnal fuss-doodle and botheration.*

Bowie knife A heavy hunting, fighting, and throwing knife with a hilt, crosspiece, and strong single-edge steel blade about fifteen inches long that broadens out from the hilt and then rounds back to a point. [Such a knife was popularized by Jim Bowie, frontiersman who died at the Alamo, 1836. But though intimately associated with Jim Bowie, the surviving evidence indicates that it was designed by Rezin P. Bowie, Jim's brother. Also called whimsically an *Arkansas toothpick.*]

box A container, commonly of wood (though also of many other materials), commonly with a lid. [See *pyx,* < Gk. *puxis,* a small, lidded container for medications, money, and other small, valuable objects. They were traditionally made of fine-grained boxwood, an evergreen shrub or tree *(Buxus sempervirens),* and L. *pyxus* firmly specified a boxwood chest; but though botanical names are pertinacious, the same name has been applied to different plants over the centuries. It is not certain, therefore, which plant the Greeks and Romans intended by *puxis, pyxus, buxus.*

In one now-archaic usage, *Christmas box* in XVI–XVII labeled not a lidded box but a ceramic container slotted for coins, a sort of piggy bank posted in churches to be shattered and the coins distributed as Christmas alms.]

in a box Variantly *boxed in* Confined. In trouble. Closed off from free action.

jurors' box A variously railed-off or closed-off section of a courtroom for seating a jury. [The same extension of the sense "container" functions in such forms as *box seat* and *coachman's box.*]

to sell against the box Wall St. To sell short a number of shares one continues to hold long. Primarily a way of locking in a profit until one's holding qualifies for capital gains rather than short-term gains tax rates. One pays additional commissions in setting up and clearing the box, but makes a larger after-taxes profit.

to box a number In various legal and illegal numbers games to bet that a particular three or four numbers will come out not necessarily in order. A boxed play pays off at lower odds but offers more chances of winning something. Variantly, one may box a number by playing all its permutations to win, but that play involves many separate bets.

to box the compass ["Box" with a slightly extended sense of "to enclose completely."] 1. To recite the points of the compass in proper order, beginning, "North, nor' nor'east by north three quarters north, . . . half north, . . . a quarter north," etc. naming the 64 points, old style. Today headings are given in degrees, East being 90°, South being 180°, West being 270°, and North being 360°. 2. *Rare.* To turn a vessel in a full circle.

boxcar [Am. XIX.] A roofed and sided (not slatted) railroad car, usu. with central sliding doors on both sides. *boxcars At dice.* The roll of two sixes. It is craps, and if made on the opening roll, it loses. [Am. XIX. From preceding. By whimsical association of the twelve dots in two solid rows to a railroad boxcar (or to two boxcars hooked up together).]

box Street slang. The cunt as a (not so) sealed container.

jack-in-the-box 1. *In Am.* A child's toy consisting usually of a clown's head and arms mounted on a spring inside a usually colorfully decorated box, and set to pop up and spread its arms when the lid catch is released. [OED attests this sense in English by 1702 but in a context that suggests it was by then long familiar.] 2. A busily inane person who keeps popping up, as for example in the U.S.

Senate. [These are the two senses that function in modern Am. In Brit. that word has had many now archaic senses, as: card sharper, small swindler (XVI) and also as a derisive label for communion wafers in the pyx. From XVII, and still surviving, jack-in-the-box has labeled a kind of firework. In XVII, now obs., a peddler who stood inside a portable stall. And since XVIII various valves and mechanical devices have been so called in Brit. shop talk.

But *to box,* to strike sharply, is of unknown origin first occurring in ME with cognates in MHG. *boxer* A pugilist. [From preceding. One who strikes sharp blows. This sense first evolved in XVIII. And *to box, boxer,* and *boxing* have spread to most European languages. In Italian, for example, prize fights are commonly put on at *il boxing club,* the English words being given an Italian pronunciation.]

Boxer A XIX Chinese nationalist whose aim was to drive foreigners out of heavily partitioned China. The secret nationalist society practiced the martial arts and was called in Chinese *i ho chuan* (or *chuen*), righteous harmonious fists (as in the mystique of the martial arts) and rendered in English the Boxers. In 1900 in what has been called the Boxer Rebellion or the Boxer Uprising, the righteous fists occupied Peking, but were bloodily defeated by a combined international force of British, German, French, American, Russian, and Japanese.

braggadocio   *n.* 1. A swaggering braggart who turns out to be a coward. 2. Pompous, empty self-assertion. [Coined by Edmund Spenser, *Faerie Queene,* as the name of his allegorical figure of a coward; < bragg(art), plus an Italianate ending. After Braggadocio has loudly puffed his valor, his exploits, his glorious shield, and other spoils of war, including the lovely lady he rescued and who now dotes on him, various outraged champions enter, give him the lie, take back the articles he has stolen, claim the lady, and drive him away with jeers and sneers. Spenser's form is a curious one. *Bragadocchio* would have been a more persuasive Italian form, or *Bragadoccio.* The surviving form *braggadocio* conforms to no known orthography.]

HISTORIC. It was in Spenser's time that young English gentlemen began, as a matter of fixed tradition, to make the Grand Tour of the Continent with a long stay in Italy, where they developed an exaggerated taste for Italian styles, manners, and customs. Returning to England, many such displayed themselves as swaggering fops with affected manners and elaborate tales of personal conquests. Writers found them to be an irresistible target of ridicule, dubbing them "macaronis." Spenser's not quite likely italianization of the allegorical name was undoubtedly suggested by his disadmiration for these macaronis.

brainstorm 1. Intense mental activity producing a bright new idea. [In this sense the term is cited by MMM in 1948, the only earlier ref., dated 1894, being a loose medical label for "sudden and severe phenomena due to some cerebral disturbance." But in the aftermath of FDR's *brain trust* (which see), brainstorming acquired the new significance:] 2. An intense analytical assault upon a problem by a panel of specialists who presumably bring a sum total of expertise and analytic and creative intellect to the solution of a problem. Such brainstorming en masse is the basis of the *think tank* (which see) in which the "best" minds available work together on a common problem or series of problems. At one level, this is the process of the advanced research laboratory; at another, of the cram session in, say, an advertising agency, in which all the "experts" conjoin to work up the most effective drivel for selling New and Improved Drek. Inevitably now the computer is involved in the discussion at all levels.

brain trust Any group of experts, especially scientific and academic theorists and analysts, assembled to analyze, discuss, and attempt to find solutions to complex new problems. *Trust*, as if the assembled panel of experts constituted a monopoly of available *brain* (intellect). From the New Deal of FDR. On taking office, President Roosevelt instituted far-reaching changes in national economic policy, depending heavily on advice from a group of academic economic theorists. Such later projects as the TVA and Los Alamos required formidable arrays of scientists, planners, and theorists. In time even big industry followed this *think tank* (which see) method of attacking problems, and developed *brainstorming*. See also *brainstorm*.

bribe A covert payment, either in money or in other valuable considerations, to win the favor of a person in a position of power and trust. Hence, a subornation of office. [A word of shifting senses. Based on OF *brimber, *briber,* to beg, → ME *briben* with the sense change to "to steal." And thence to the present sense.]

HISTORIC. The King James version of the Bible, published 1611, renders Matthew 23:25: "Woe unto you, scribes and Pharisees, hypocrites! for ye make clean the outside of the cup and of the platter, and within they are full of *extortion and excess.*" The same text was rendered in the Geneva Bible, published 51 years earlier: *"bribery and excess,"* a usage of *bribery* that may be taken to be intermediate between earlier "pilferage" and the modern sense.

bridge¹   1. A span or series of spans supporting a passageway across a declivity or water. [Root sense, "eyebrow." IE *bhru-,* eyebrow, via Gmnc. → OE *bru,* eyebrow, the form surviving in *brow.* Suffixed in Gmnc., prob. form being *brü-g'-* → OE *brycg,* bridge, with a root sense "arched thing"; and though modern arched bridges commonly have wide spans, early English bridges were supported by numerous narrow stone arches, as many as 12 or 18 being used to cross a relatively narrow river, much in the manner of Roman aqueduct construction. < ME *brigge.* Obscurely, however, OE *brycg* may also be akin to Gmnc. roots intending log road, a construction of (unarched) beams. The sense "brow," however, is clearly dominant. With many extensions, among them:] 2. A denture spanning the gap between natural teeth. 3. *Music.* (a) A usu. wooden upright that raises the strings of an instrument above the sounding board. (b) A musical passage connecting two themes or movements. 4. The upper bony ridge of the nose. 5. The piece connecting the two lenses of spectacles and resting on this nose ridge. 6. A raised, forward, transverse platform from which a ship is directed. 7. *Billiards.* An upright form attached at right angles to a long handle, and with three to five rounded indentions to hold the cue stick when the player cannot reach to hold it by hand.

   bridgehead 1. Either end of a bridge. 2. *Military.* A position established on the enemy's side of a bridge, and around it, to protect the advance of one's own units.

   Bridge of Sighs 1. Venice. A small, enclosed, slightly arched bridge across a narrow canal between the Doge's Palace and the Venetian prison. [Those condemned by the doge's court crossed it on their way to prison, with reason enough to sigh. If returned to favor, they might smile on the way back, but few returned, and those who were finally set free were let out the prison gate, seldom returning by way of the doge's court. Hence, a one-way passage to sorrow. It still exists.] 2. *By analogy.* In New York City such an upper-level passageway that once connected the criminal court building and the Tombs Prison. [With the difference that many sighed while crossing this bridge, but it was commonly used for both going and coming during a trial.]

   to burn one's bridges (behind one) In various senses to pledge oneself to forge on and do or die, having left oneself no line of retreat. (The equivalent of *burning one's boats.*)

we'll cross that bridge when we come to it To move ahead, attending to present problems and deferring future problems until they arise. *Since Chappaquiddick, Ted Kennedy will never again be free to say in public, "we'll cross that bridge when we come to it."*

water under the bridge Said of anything gone by: *Why rake up all that water we passed under the bridge when there are still rivers to cross, unless we have burned them behind us.*

rope bridge A down-curving, swaying passage across a gap between two elevations. In simplest form a hawser drawn across a gap between two rock faces, and equipped on either side with lesser lines to serve as handholds, but commonly with two or more hawsers bearing a transverse boardwalk. The rope bridge of Thornton Wilder's *The Bridge at San Luis Rey* was such a boardwalk span.

on the bridge At the command post of a ship. (But *to abridge* is < L. *abbreviare,* to shorten, to abbreviate, by way of OF *abregier,* whence ME *abregen.* The XV form *to abridge* was certainly influ. by *bridge.*)

bridge² The card game in its various forms. [Earlier whist, and called in XVIII *biritch,* one of the few English forms of Slavic origin, the name being a ref. to the bidding, < Russian *birich,* official caller, one who reads proclamations, a herald and crier. ODEE says the game was "Said to be played in Constantinople and the Near East in the 1870s" and speculates on a Levantine or Russian origin.]

brigand An armed robber. A bandit. Commonly, though not necessarily, one of a group. [At root, a fighter; whence, a plunderer, robber, looter. Ult. from Old It. *briga,* fight, strife, conflict, perhaps of obscure Celtic origin (the Celts left a number of ancient traces in northern Italy). → old It. *brigata,* a company of soldiers (BRIGADE); *brigante,* a footsoldier; and also *brigantina* (BRIGANTINE), earlier specifically designating a Mediterranean pirate ship (not necessarily, as in Eng., a sailing vessel with both fore-and-aft and square sails). In XIV Eng., a light infantry irregular; but by XV, a bandit (perhaps because such militia, disbanded but still armed, robbed and looted on the way home, though note that armed robbery was already implicit in XIV It. *brigantino* for pirate ship).]

broad arrow *Great Britain.* The figure of an arrow with broad barbs and a very short shaft with no notch, used to mark various sorts of crown property. It is probably best known to Americans in British historic films involving prisoners, their prison uniforms being stenciled with the broad arrow. [Obviously not an Americanism. This entry is mainly in reply to written inquiries from listeners to my National Public Radio word commentary. The origin of this symbol is unknown but it had become sufficiently established by 1698 to cause William III to forbid its use on private property.]

brochure   A pamphlet. Now in the most general understanding one containing a commercial offering and prospectus, but any folded-over page describing an offering or a project passes as a brochure. [But commonly a pamphlet, often illustrated, of at least six or eight pages. At root, "booklet/pamphlet with stitched pages." < Fr. *brocher,* to sew.]

broker   A dealer who buys, sells, or negotiates for another on commission, but unless qualified in Am., one who deals in securities, a stockbroker. But in ME *love brokier, brocour,* a pimp. Intermediately, those who negotiated marriages and dowries have been called *marriage brokers.* [But at root, "a dealer in wine," i.e., "one who broaches wine barrels." < ME *brocour,* broacher, < OF *brochier,* to broach, to tap a barrel. Later *broker,* a wine salesman.]

brook   To endure, tolerate, put up with. [Usu. followed by "no," as in *to brook no interference.* But earlier without the negative. So Spenser, *Faerie Queene* III.4.43–44:

> But fairely well she thrived and well did brook
> Her noble deeds, ne her right cause for aught forsook.

In which *brook* has the sense of cognate Ger. *brauchen,* to use, to make use of.
    Ult. < IE *bhrug-,* harvest, fruitage. With standard bh/f → L. *frugis,* of fruit (nominative *frux*). FRUGAL. Variantly, L. *fructus,* enjoyment (of the fruits of). USUFRUCT. Verb form *frui,* to enjoy (the fruits of). FRUITION.
    This IE stem with g/k → Gmnc. *bruk-* → OE *brucan,* to enjoy. (As in the pleasure of eating the fruits of one's harvest.) Cf. earlier *to stomach, to have stomach for,* and now more commonly *to have no stomach for,* and *she just can't stomach him.*
    Diamond Lil would brook no denial, nor did she ever meet a man she couldn't stomach.]

Brooklyn   The first foreign country one comes to east of lower Manhattan. It used to threaten invasion at regular intervals before the Dodgers moved west, since which time it has been unable to extricate itself from its own image. [Commonly parsed as Du. *Broucke-len,* broken land, a ref. to its jagged coastline. And plausibly so, but in earlier Eng., with Du. cognates, *lin, linn, lynn,* signified a body of water, a pool or small lake sufficient to be the headwaters of a river or brook, and though this rendering is less plausible, it cannot be ignored.]

brut   *Champagne.* A designation for champagne aged and marketed with no added sugar. [Surviving OF *brut,* rough, plain < L. *brutus,* heavy, basic, unaltered.]

HISTORIC. In normal process champagne is bottled and aged for three months, the bottles being progressively tipped until they are upside down. The bottles are then left for a further three to nine months until the impurities have settled to the bottom of the cork. The cork is then pulled, the impurities shot off, and the bottles recorked, the lesser vintages for shipping, the choicer vintages for further aging. Before recorking, a small amount of syrup mixed with old champagne may be added. If the amount of additive is minimal the champagne is designated *sec,* dry; if a little more, *demi sec,* half dry; and if yet more, *doux,* sweet. *Brut* designates that no syrup whatever has been added.

American champagnes, for reasons beyond reason, are some times further designated *extra dry,* which can only mean a champagne a touch drier than *sec* but sweeter than *brut.*

buccaneer   1. A pirate of the Spanish Main. 2. *Ext.* Any swashbuckling, rapacious person. [< Carib-pidgin *boucan,* strips of meat smoked or sun-dried on a rack (jerky) as a sea provision, whence Fr. *boucanier* 1. One who prepares such meat. 2. One who eats it; hence a pirate who uses it as a sea provision.

Some have suggested a derivation from Simon Boccanera or Boccanegra, immortalized in Verdi's opera of that name. Boccanegra was a Venetian ship's captain who turned against Venice to become a pirate. But though *Boccanera* (Blackmouth) and *buccaneer* conform nicely, *buccaneer* did not come into use until XVI, more than a century after Boccanera's death, and he was little known until immortalized by Verdi in late XIX. *Boucan → boucanier → buccaneer,* on the other hand, is an attested sequence and immediately proximate in time and place to the bloody piracy of the Spanish Main.]

Bucephalus   [The Latinized form of Gk. *Boukephalos,* bull-headed, < *bous,* bull; *kephalos,* adj. form of *kephalē,* head. MEGALOCE-

PHALIC.] The mythicized warhorse of Alexander the Great.

HISTORIC. Alexander did, of course, have a chief warhorse and it was boyishly named Bullheaded, but legends accrete to power, and in this one the real horse is said to have been a wild stallion singled out by an oracle as a hero test, for only the man who broke and rode him could win to the crown of Macedonia, after which the rest of the world was only an easy lope away.

buffalo *v.* Also *to be buffaloed; he has me buffaloed, I've got him buffaloed,* etc. To confuse, bewilder, render incapable of effective action. The person buffaloed senses that he is in trouble or danger but has been manipulated into a situation in which he is unable to take any effective action but can only fidget and await the worst. [*Western frontier.* From the brief era of the massive buffalo hunts that began in the late 1860s and ended ca. 1870 when the herds that had once stretched from horizon to horizon had been virtually wiped out.

In common understanding *to be buffaloed* is taken to mean something like "unable to go on because one's way is blocked by a buffalo or a herd of buffaloes." The true situation is far more complicated, and it is in fact the *buffalo* that is *buffaloed.*]

HISTORIC. The years of the massive buffalo hunt included some incidental slaughter by adventuring sportsmen, but the virtual extinction of the Great Plains herds was the work of professional hunters who collected only the once-prized hides, leaving the carcasses to rot. (Curiously, the great Eastern demand for these hides fell to nothing at just the time the buffalo became rare.)

Professional hunters did not ride the herds down, shooting at the gallop. They approached a "stand" of buffalo cautiously for fear of "spooking" it, set up a fixed firing position, and fired into the herd for hours at a stretch, often killing hundreds of buffalo in a day. To keep the herd from stampeding, these professionals aimed for a clean kill of the dominant bulls, knowing the herd took its direction instinctively from these leaders. If the bull was dropped more or less cleanly in its tracks, the harem would sniff uneasily at the carcass, finding no motive for action in it, though the smell of blood made the cows nervous. The continued firing and the succession of deaths would leave the harems milling anxiously without triggering the flight response. And so on until a bad shot wounded a beast without dropping it. That injured beast, goaded by pain, would writhe in panic, its action finally moving the already spooked herd to stampede out of range.

Thus it was not the hunter but the herd that was said *to be buffaloed* for as long as the hunter (or hunters) could keep it in its uneasy "stand," indecisively awaiting its own end.

To buffalo and *to be buffaloed* passed into general Am. idiom about 1880, remaining in somewhat confused usage because few who used these idioms understood the sense in which the plains hunters had first coined it.

For a superb fictional account of this hunting method see part 2, chapter 4 of John Williams's *Butcher's Crossing,* a book long overdue for reissue in paperback.

bugaboo   1. *Root sense.* A thing or being that inspires terror. 2. *Now more often,* The same but taken to be imaginary and obsessive: *At ninety-two she no longer makes a bugaboo of every wrinkle but only of the points at which two or more wrinkles cross.* [The precedents for this form seem to be Welsh *bwga* (in which *w* = *u*), ghost, hobgoblin (BOGEY MAN); and Cornish *buccaboo,* the devil. See also ODEE: "The OF demon-name *Bugibus* may be of Celtic origin." In XVI, and still surviving, the common form was *bugbear. Bugaboo* is first attested in XVII.]

bullpen   *Baseball.* The enclosure, just off the playing field, in which relief pitchers wait and in which, on signal from the manager, they warm up by throwing practice pitches. (Some parks lack such an enclosure, the pitchers warming up at need on a strip outside the foul line while someone stands by to warn them of foul balls that might otherwise bean them. They are yet said to be in the bullpen.) [Am. late XIX. As with many baseball terms, there are more legends about the derivation than there are derivations. Joe Garagiola (no etymologist he), *Baseball Is a Funny Game,* says that in 1909 the Bull Durham Tobacco Company placed posters of its trademark bull around the fences, offering 50 dollars to any batter who hit a bull. Garagiola traces the term to one such bull poster behind the relief pitchers' enclosure.

But Garagiola is at least thirty years late. The Cincinnati *Enquirer,* May 7, 1877, reported that general admission to a ball game there was 50 cents, but that standing space in an enclosure beyond the outfield was available for 10 cents or three for a quarter. These customers, the reporter asserts, were herded like bulls in a pen.

The *Enquirer* reporter does not exactly call these enclosures *bullpens,* to be sure. And neither of these sources is definitive. Bullpen is a simple, natural metaphor suggested by large, bull-like athletes moving about in an enclosure (pen), and the name implicit in the *Enquirer's* report had become fixed baseball idiom by sometime in the 1880s. I cannot find it in use before then.]

burnsides   And now, oddly, *sideburns.* A form of beard cultivated down the side of the cheeks, often merging loopingly with a full handlebar moustache, but with shaved lower lip and jaws. [After Union General Ambrose Burnside, ineffective and twice-relieved commander of the Army of the Potomac in the Civil War. He affected this style of facial hair in a style rather more distinguished than his military performance.

Burnside was a politically well-established functionary who passed as a figure of power in his time, and who passed out of it unnoticed. The curiously inverted *sideburns,* I will speculate, makes some sort of spectrally idiomatic sense as hair that "burns" (smokes) along the "sides" of the face, and that spectral logic has turned out to be more persuasive upon the language than the faded memory of the man—perhaps in the same way that the Dwy Thrwy continues to thread through New York State in memory of What'sisname.]

bush   [IE *bheu-,* to grow, *busk-,* a bush ("thing that grows"). Which, with common k/h, is recognizably Eng. *bush.*] 1. A low-growing shrub. (A loose category, for some bushes grow as high as many common trees. The distinction, if it can be made, is in the fact that most trees tend to have a main single trunk, whereas most bushes come out of the ground with many branches.) 2. A small clump of vegetation. 3. *With "the,"* The land on which such vegetation grows, as distinct from a forest. Hence, back country: *out in the bush, back in the bush.* 3. *Slang.* Pubic hair.

bush league Baseball. A minor league. [Made up of teams in the "back country" as distinct from the big city franchises of the major leagues. And fancifully because these minor-league teams are said to play where bushes grow in the outfield.] *bushie n.* A minor-league player. Hence *adj.* Inferior, amateurish, unseasoned.

bushed Slang. Weary. Exhausted. [As if from trekking through the bush.]

bushwhacker 1. *In colonial and early XIX Am.* A settler. [One who clears bushes (and fells trees) to create tillage. Hence a back-country farmer. (This sense has passed into Australian to label a dweller in the back country.)] 2. *In Civil War.* A backwoods guerilla. 3. *In post-Civil War western, and diffused.* One who strikes ("whacks") from ambush. And corresponding verb senses.

bushy 1. Shaggy, bushy browed. 2. Densely covered with bushes. [Note (now rare) *bosky*, covered with trees. *Bosky*, as noted, is from the same stem before k/h, whereby the two words are from a single source but with differentiated senses, as in *bushy bosk*, a wooded area with heavy undergrowth.

beat about the bush To avoid direct encounter. [Said originally of a cowardly hound that does not pursue game when it takes cover, but circles around the thicket in which the game is hiding.]

beat the bushes (for) To solicit support for a political candidate or cause. To round up votes. [From the work of dogs and beaters who thrash through the bushes to flush game for the hunters.]

bushel   *v.* To mend or alter clothing. *bushel store* The shop of a tailor whose primary work is mending, alteration, and pressing rather than the making of clothing. [Both terms are now rare but were once common. One of my uncles operated a *bushel store* in East Boston until about WWII and I never heard his shop called anything else. His section of East Boston, earlier Irish, was a Little Italy, and I know that *bushel store* was in standard use by Italian immigrants, though the word is from Gmnc. *bozan*, to tap repeatedly. (So, by ext., "to make repeated strokes with a needle.") Ult. < IE *bhau*, to strike. BASH, BASTE. (Not akin to *bushel*, a dry measure, which is from obscure Gmnc. sources.)]

by and by, by-and-by   Eventually. In the remote, and even the remotest, future. So, in one version of the old Wobbly song, "There'll be pie in the sky by and by," meaning in the afterlife. So also the hymn, "In the sweet by-and-by." [And so in English since ca. 1800, but this is a complete sense reversal, the earlier sense being, "at once, immediately, right now." So in the 1611 King James version of the Bible, in which Mark 6:25–27 leaves no doubt that Salome wanted things to come to a head *right now:* "And she came in *straightway with haste* unto the king, and asked, saying, I will that thou give me *by and by* in a charger the head of John the Baptist. . . . And *immediately* the king sent an executioner." (Italics mine.)

I am unable to account for this reversal of meaning, especially since the root sense "right here, right now" survives in such common idioms as *standing by* and *hard by*. Nor is there any evidence to indicate that the sense of the idiom was influenced by "bye-bye," with the suggestion of going away (off into time).]

$\mathcal{C}$

cake *n.* 1. A variously shaped confection of flour, sweeteners, flavorings, and often fruits and nuts, commonly iced more or less ornamentally. 2. Any rounded wad: *a cake of soap. v.* To form into a wad. Also, to become encrusted: *caked-on dirt.* [Gmnc. **kak-*, clump, wad, disk. Into Eng. as *cake* < ON *kaka* with root senses, the transmission being under IX–X Danelaw. By XIII, loaf; by XV, a honey-sweetened confection (cane sugar was not commonly available in Europe until late XVII), probably a fruit cake; by XVI, in Scotland, oaten bread baked in flat disks (this the forerunner of modern *pancake, wheatcake*). But though the primary sense is now "sweetened baked confection," the Gmnc. root sense has never ceased to function.]

take the cake Take the prize. Esp. in the indignant exclam., *Well, doesn't that take the cake!* which implies that the prize is for some brazen or outlandish or at least surprising action. (XIX Am. < *cakewalk,* below.)

cakewalk A fancy strutting contest developed among American Negroes. [I was told by Sidney Bechet that such strutting was a common Sunday-afternoon amusement on the XVIII plantation in the common meeting place called Congo Square. Because they feared an uprising and because they had heard of African drum-talk, the whites forbade drums. The slaves, therefore, improvised musical instruments, blew into jugs, hummed and sang, and beat time with their feet in fancy steps or by beating on their bodies or clapping hands. Sidney would have been repeating old folk talk, but other sources confirm his account. By mid-XIX strutting contests had developed with prizes for the fanciest stepper, and by late XIX the standard prize was an ornate cake. Cake walking, not necessarily for a cake, also became a specialty of high-stepping, hip-swiveling marshals of black marching groups; and such strutting was carried over into the dance routines of later black stage dancers, inevitably to be imitated by white performers who often wore blackface makeup (and in Minstrel Shows, always).

MMM, writing in 1950, adds: "Now a walk in which those participating pay for the privilege of walking to music on a numbered floor, each one hoping that when the music stops he will be on a lucky number and thus receive a cake as a prize." I have no further information on this festivity but believe MMM's "walking" was in fact "strutting."

piece of cake [WWII RAF slang.] 1. Said of something as easy and pleasant as eating a piece of cake, as, for instance, a successful bombing mission that takes few or no losses. —And then, with the British stiff-upper-lip sense-reversal:] 2. A disastrously bloody engagement.

caked Covered with thick adhesive dirt, as mud or dust, but not, for example, with oil. To be caked the covering substance must be thick, as if layer on layer, and more or less crumbly.

canister   1. A container for dry foods, especially tea. Commonly of thin metal with a tight-fitting lid. 2. *Artillery*. An antipersonnel shell consisting of a thin metal casing packed with small shot and designed to explode in air, thereby advancing civilization by ripping flesh in all directions, which is just what those buggers on the other side deserve, and the more so when you think they are about to attack. Also **canister shot**. 3. *By association with preceding.* The filter of a gas mask, the filtering and neutralizing material being packed in a replaceable cylinder. [The primary association with tea packed in sealed metal cans may suggest to American-speaking readers (tin) CAN with the modified agential suffix -*ister* (here, "thing that does for canning"); but in Brit. one says *tin*, which would yield "tinster" or "tinister," and in any case the term predates the packing of tea in metal containers.

The enduring sense (it being the material that has changed) is "container." < Gk. *kaneon, kanastron*, rush basket, especially a pannier, < Gk. *kanna*, rush, reed (of uncertain Semitic origin).]

cant   1. A specialized group jargon. *thieves' cant*. 2. Hypocritical and deceiving talk: *the pious cant of mendicant friars*. 3. *Rare*. The singsong whining supplications and formulas of professional beggars. (Note that the function of cant is to deceive and persuade. The slightly different function of thieves' cant is to communicate within the hearing of a potential victim without letting him know what deception is afoot. Perhaps the densest cant in modern Am. usage is that used by carnival people. Two carnie swifties can stand in front of you and itemize their plans for fleecing you without speaking a word you are likely to understand.) [Sense 3, common in XVI, came first and is certainly akin to *chant* < Fr. *chanter,* to sing, < L. *cantare.* And note that in long-standing slang an informer who speaks to the police is said to "sing," and is called (more recently in Am.) a "canary" ("bird" that "sings"). Scottish and Erse *canty,* talkative, may be partly from this source (here used by Robert Burns):

> The clashan yill (ale) had made me *canty.*
> I was na' foo (not drunk) but just had plenty.

But here Gaelic *cainnt,* speech, and *cainnteach,* talkative, cannot be ignored in what is probably a convergent evolution.]

canter   *Horsemanship.* A moderate gallop. A brisk but smooth and easy pace a good horse can maintain for a considerable distance. [< *Canterbury.* In XVII *Canterbury gallop, Canterbury trot.* And in XVIII also *to canterbury* (now obs.). Because this was said to be the pace at which mounted pilgrims rode to Canterbury to pay homage to St. Thomas à Becket, martyred in the cathedral there in 1170.

It is impossible, however, to believe that this gait was invented by the pilgrims. They were chance-encounter groups that could not have had enough time together to school their horses to a unison. Rather, the canter came to be associated with them as the easy, miles-consuming pace at which they rode in bands over the sometimes dangerous highways.]

Canuck   A shifting term for a Canadian; once pejorative, now commonly accepted by Canadians as a fond nickname. (Cf. *jayhawker,* once the opprobrious designation of a bloody Kansan guerilla, now proudly asserted by Kansans as their nickname.) [Perhaps from the Scottish-Canadian surname *Connaught* (the *g* is pronounced). In Quebec French *a conaught, conugt, canuck* became a designation for a British Canadian. This derivation is not securely attested, but *Canuck* did first function as a French Canadian's contemptuous term for a Britisher. (Cf. Mexican *gringo.*)

In an odd reversal, *Canuck* became a more-or-less pejorative upper New England name for the large French Canadian population there (a silent minority until their labor unions politicized them, whereupon they discovered they outnumbered the Yankees and became a new political force).]

HISTORIC. Over the centuries, of course, many New England French Canadians became anglicized. In an early version of his poem "The Witch of Coos," Robert Frost wrote that he looked at the mailbox and the name read Tophil Lajway, an obviously anglicized form (though Frost does not say so) of Théophile La Joie.

canvas 1. A strong, coarse cloth woven originally of flax or hemp, later with cotton added. It was used for sails, tents, carriage shades, heavy outer clothing, tarpaulins, and other heavy service. 2. Sailcloth. A sail. 3. *When woven fine and stretched and sized (but since Helen Frankenthaler, used unsized by some artists):* (a) The ground for an oil painting. (b) An oil painting. 4. The floor of a boxing ring. (Because it is canvas-covered over thin padding. In wrestling the floor of the ring—when there is one—is the mat.) [At root, "hempen cloth." < Gk. *kannabis,* hemp, marijuana. L. *cannabis.* With b/v and slightly altered → ME *canevas.*]

under canvas In a tent. *to crowd on canvas Nautical.* To spread more sail, to spread all possible sail (for speed, as in flight or hot pursuit, or for racing). *on the canvas Boxing.* Knocked down.

canvasback 1. A North American duck with a reddish brown head and neck and a pale back said to be the color of undyed, coarse, hempen canvas. 2. *Am. boxing, jocular slang.* A boxer who tends to take things lying down. [Exuberant whimsical XIX. Because he has been knocked down so often that his back is turning to canvas by long, intimate association.]

canvass *v.* 1. *In Am.* To conduct a careful survey of an area, especially of opinion within that area, consulting (ideally) everyone there: *a house-to-house canvass of voting opinion.* (Now largely replaced by the poll, a carefully selected small sampling presumed to reflect total opinion—as it regularly does—except when it is wrong.) 2. *Primarily Brit.* To conduct such a survey in search of votes for a given candidate. 3. *Brit. only.* To examine in painstaking detail. [< *canvas.* The various extended senses derive from the fact that coarse canvas was once used for sifting; hence, fine search.

In XVI colloq. *to canvass* was to toss someone in a piece of canvas (cf. *toss in a blanket*) in hazing or roistering or derision, but there seems to have been no survival of this sense.] *The campus canvass on cannabis use went to pot.*

card shark 1. In gambler's parlance, a "mechanic," i.e., one who manipulates the deck dishonestly. 2. An especially skilled but honest player. [The shark as a rapacious predator is an obvious symbol for a violent grabber, and so *loan shark,* a usurious extortionist who enforces his demands by violence. But *shark,* in both Brit. and Am. XIX slang, also signified a pickpocket, a sly rather than a violent snatcher. And in this sense *shark* seems to have interacted with XVIII Brit. *sharp* or *sharper* (esp. in *card sharper*), a sly but not violent cheat. By now *card shark* and *card sharp* work in Am. as distinctions without a difference.]

carriage [IE *kers-,* to run. And that root sense, via L., has developed in five main ways. 1. *Course.* The route run. 2. *Courier.* A runner. 3. The way one runs, carries oneself. 4. Car. L. *carrus,* cart, chariot. 5. *Obs.* Cargo, luggage, haulage (things carried in a car). The senses now functioning in Eng. are:] 1. A vehicle. 2. One's personal bearing.

HISTORIC. The earlier sense, approximately *luggage* (stuff to be lugged) is clear in Acts 21:15, King James version (1611): "And after those days we took up our carriages [i.e., the things we were carrying with us] and went up to Jerusalem." Perhaps the nearest surviving cognates of this sense are *bundles* or *impedimenta.* If these are sent by a conveyance, they are haulage, trucking, a cargo, or a shipment. But one may yet ask the genie of the English language why a cargo goes by ship whereas a shipment goes by car.

cataclysm 1. In common semiliterate usage any far-ranging violent upheaval of nature or of warfare: *the volcanic cataclysm that destroyed Pompeii; the cataclysmic attacks of the German blitzkrieg.* 2. *But at root,* A flood: *Noah rode out the cataclysm.* [< Gk. *kata,* down, but functioning also as an intensive prefix; with *klusmai,* I inundate (said the Father of Waters). From *kluzein,* to wash, to wash over, to wash away. Ult., with sense unchanged, < IE *kleu-.* CLOACA. (As St. Peter says to Dante in *Paradiso* XVII, denouncing the corrupt Pope Boniface VIII, "fatt'ha del cimitereo mio cloaca" —he has made a sewer of his sepulcher (the Vatican, Rome in general.) In Dante's mind, that corruption would qualify as cataclysmic impiety.]

catastrophe 1. A disastrous turn of fortune: *the catastrophe of the Titanic/of the recent American presidency.* 2. *In hyperbolic colloq.* Anything less than ideal: *Judith's dinner party was a catastrophe: everyone came.* 3. *In literary criticism.* The event in a drama or a novel, especially in a tragic one, that precipitates the final resolution of the story. [And this last is closest to the root sense, which is "down turn." < Gk. *kata,* down; *strephein,* to turn. TROPHY.

STROPHE. TROPE. HELIOTROPE. *After a redundant number of victories the Red Baron's career took a catastrophic downturn into a nosedive.*]

catechism 1. The primer of religious faith, originally of the Roman Catholic church, detailing the basic tenets of the faith in question-and-answer form for young readers and for the oral instruction of the preliterate and illiterate. (The answers, though simplified, are held to be inalterable truths, though maturer believers will search the questions and answers more deeply. In the *Paradiso,* as a final examination before mounting to the peak of heaven, Dante responds to a catechism test by the souls of the great saints. His answers are a bit beyond the primer but close to its intent. In part, of course, Dante is suggesting that one must become as a little child in order to enter heaven. Yet he would certainly declare that the great truths of the faith do not change from what the child is taught.) [< Gk. *ēkhein,* to sound repeatedly. ECHO. With prefix *kat(a),* down → *katēkhein,* lit., to echo down, effective sense, to instruct orally by rote repetition.]

    to catechize 1. To teach (religious dogma) by rote question and answer. Hence 2. To question one insistently and searchingly in order to arrive at the truth. And also 3. To search and examine carefully a proposition or series of propositions. [Sense 3 developed in XVI, the sense shift being from "echoing dogmatic fundamentals by rote" to "close analysis." The common link is obviously the pertinacity of the questioning, but the catechism calls not for analytical examination but rote recitation.]

catgut A tough, thin cord made from the dried intestines of animals, primarily those of sheep. In the age before plastics catgut was in common use for stringing tennis rackets and stringed instruments, and also for surgical sutures. [The common suggestion is that *catgut* was substituted for *sheepgut* because stringed instruments seem to caterwaul when played by beginners. Other sources are more cautious, glossing the term, as the AHD does, "The reason for the naming is unknown." Yet the OED lists *kit* as an obsolete term for a small fiddle, whence, though not attested, *kitgut* would follow naturally, and thence *catgut,* almost as an etymological Q.E.D.]

catty *adj.* Mean and spiteful. [All sources gloss this common form as "like a cat," conceiving the cat to have its back up, its claws out, and its hiss working. There seems to be no way of contesting this assumption, and yet I am drawn to It. *cattivo* as a source, or at least as an influence. Since XVI in England it has been a tradition for young gentlemen (and later, to some extent, ladies) to make a grand tour of the Continent with a long stay in Italy. Young fops who returned from Italy with elaborate wardrobes and more elaborate imitations of Italian mannerisms were called in XVI *macaronis,* in XVII *fantastics,* and in XVIII *enthusiasts.* Their lisping affectations were liberally sprinkled with mispronounced Italian words and phrases.

Italian *cattivo* now means "naughty" when applied to a child. It would best be rendered in English by old-style *caitiff,* the most despicable of persons. At root it is "captive," and by historical association "cowardly slave." To be captured in battle was to become a slave, and generally a despised one, for any true warrior (the noble Roman) would die in battle or commit suicide sooner than be captured and enslaved. At root, therefore, *cattivo* meant not only "base slave" but "despised coward." Who could expect anything but petty malice from such a one?

I can only suggest, in no defiance of the reference to cats, that there was an open line of transmission for *cattivo,* that in the common British slurring of foreign words and phrases, it could readily have become *catti(vo),* and that the sense of *cattivo* is closer to the sense of *catty* than it is to most feline fluffs. To which I must add that search as I may—and I have searched—I cannot find any attestation of *cattivo* in this sense in earlier English. In *Amadeus* the emperor accuses the spiteful Salieri of being "a little *cattivo,*" and could that usage be shown to be historically accurate, I would claim it as an attestation, but the emperor is of course speaking in a contemporary play. For these reasons, I can only offer *cattivo* as an unattested possibility, but not as pure cat yowl.]

caviar   Also, but primarily Brit., *caviare.* 1. Variously preserved roe of the sturgeon. (Whence *beluga caviar* < Russ. *byeluga,* sturgeon; lit., "big white fish," < *byelii,* white.) 2. *In commercial misusage,* The similarly treated black small roe of various other fishes: *lumpfish caviar.* 3. A symbol of luxury and of cultivated taste. (Because those who have not cultivated a taste for this very expensive delicacy often reject it as being too salty—as it sometimes is, for which reason many gourmets insist on fresh caviar. See Shakespeare, *Hamlet* II.ii.457, "'twas caviare to the general," in which "general" is not a military rank but "the generality of uncultivated persons, the masses, the ignorant masses." And note that Shakespeare, prob. in the interest of meter, uses the modern two-and-a-half-syllable form, whereas the common XVI form *caviarie* was three-and-a-half. [And prob. via Fr. from It. *caviaro* < Turk. *khav-yar*, roe (lit. "egg bearing").

One of the few English words of Turkish origin. Caviar itself is of Russian origin and is called in Russ. *ikrá,* but it was introduced to Western Europe by Turkish sea traders.

Many new products have been named after the traders who introduced them. So *Venetian blind* because these slatted window shades were introduced into Europe by the Venetians, though they are called in It. *persiani,* after Persia, the nation of origin.

And see *turkey (Browser's I)* which, though indigenous to the Americas, is named after the country of Turkey (because the first settlers took the turkey to be a guinea fowl (from the Guinea coast of Africa), which was in turn called turkey fowl in England because it was introduced there by Turkish traders.]

cemetery   A graveyard. [An early Christian euphemism, and in some-ways an awkward one. < Gk. *koimētēron,* sleeping quarters, but specifically, slave quarters. L. had *dormire,* to sleep, but did not evolve *dormitorium* (DORMITORY) for sleeping room, using *cubiculum* (CUBICLE) for this purpose. It did however adopt the altered Gk. form *coemētērium* for "the hall in which soldiers of a garrison slept," what we call a barracks or barracks room. Early Christian writers then adopted the Latinized Greek form for "resting place/ sleeping place of the dead," applying it first to the catacombs, and later to any consecrated burial ground. Whence It. *cimitero,* Fr. *cimetière.* This early euphemism of *sleeping* for *dead* ignored the early sense, slave quarters, for the true soul was not enslaved but set free by death. It may have picked up from the Latin association, "resting place of the militia of Christ." We are queasy about death. If any preacher presumes to stand above my corpse (whenever) and say I am not dead but only asleep, I instruct my friends to explain to the man that I am damned well as dead as I am ever going to be, and gone (to quote, of course, myself) into "the dormitory tombs where old boys sleep." (And see, in note to *cataclysm,* the citation of ghostly St. Peter's *cimitereo mio* as early XIV Italian for "my sepulcher.")]

censure   *n.* A strongly expressed adverse judgment. (In the U.S. Congress a vote of censure is one step short of an action to impeach.) And corresponding verb. [IE *kens-*, to pronounce solemnly. → L. *cēnsēre,* to assess, to judge. So *censor,* A Roman magistrate (one who pronounces solemnly in the name of the law). But cf. English *censor,* an official who acts to suppress expression on (his) moral grounds. (He may examine and approve, but when, having been given legal authority to suppress, has any man not exercised his authority, at least to some extent?)]

HISTORIC. This is one of a class of words that were, at root, neutral, but that have acquired a dire sense. So *bode,* originally news (good or bad), became foreboding (bad). *Omen* and *portent,* originally signs from heaven (good or bad), became *ominous* and *portentous* (bad). So *on the carpet,* at neutral root, under judicial or official review, came to mean *in trouble.*

These are conclusions from deep in the folk mind, for though the masses of mankind have appointed (or had appointed unto them) priests to hope and pray for them, and though they have tried as best they could to accept their temporal rulers, they have asked above all to pass unnoticed by heaven or the state, long experience having led them to equate any notice from on high with trouble. Ask anyone about to be audited by the I.R.S. Technically, he might even get some money back, but who expects good to come of an audit?

cerement   More commonly in plu. *cerements* In common burial practice before the repulsive usages of modern embalming, the waxed sheet(s) in which the dead were wrapped for burial. (Commonly in the plu. because the wrapping took more than one sheet.) [< L. *cera,* wax, because once the dead were wrapped more or less like mummies the sheets were impregnated with a preservative of liquid wax or beeswax or with a mixture of the two.]

HISTORIC. This earlier practice was akin to Egyptian mummification, the Egyptian dead also being swathed, anointed, and waxed in this way. Legend long had it that the Egyptians had developed secret powerful preservatives. The fact is that Egyptian mummies were primarily preserved by the desiccatingly arid climate. Museum keepers in non-Egyptian climes have been hard put to it to preserve even thoroughly desiccated mummies. There is in the cemetery of Middlebury, Vermont the grave of a young Egyptian prince bought once for the museum of the town of Middlebury. Stored away in a Vermont attic when the museum was closed the mummy began to rot, and the good Vermonters decided to give it a "decent Christian burial."

One of the most famous pictures from English literature is the etching (I believe it is an etching) of John Donne, Dean of St. Paul's Cathedral, who on the Sunday before his death rose from his bed and delivered his own funeral sermon dressed in his winding sheet and elaborate topknot. At the time of the sermon the winding sheet(s) were not yet waxed and thereby made into cerements, but they almost certainly were "cered" a few days later for the burial.

chameleon 1. One of various small lizards with the ability to blend into its background by changing its color. 2. *Obvious ext.* A highly changeable person. (Though when applied to a person the label implies deceit rather than protective anonymity.) [But this protective talent does not figure in the creature's name, which is, at root, "ground lion," < Gk. *khamai,* on the ground; with *leon,* lion. The association with lion, I will speculate, is by association with the brightly colored gill-like membranes these creatures sometimes project from the back of their heads, conceived in fantasy to be something like a lion's mane, and also with the profile of the snout.]

chaps Cowboy gear. Seatless trousers of tough steerhide or of unsheared sheepskin used to protect the legs of a horseman from thorns. [Earlier *chaparejos, chaparehos,* < Mexican Sp. *chapareros,* < Sp. *chaparro,* thicket, grove, but in Mexico and the Southwest *chaparral,* with particular reference to thorny desert shrubbery, as of the stunted evergreen oak; with Sp. *aparejo,* equipment; hence, "(leg) gear worn against the thorns of the chaparral." Because cumbersome is better than bloody.]

charge [IE *kers-,* to run (CONCUR, COURIER, COURSE, CURSIVE) → L. *currere,* to run (p.p. *cursus*). Also *carrus,* (a) A wain (two-wheeled wagon). (b) Chariot. Late L. *carricare,* to load a cart (CARGO). → OF *chargier,* ME *chargen.* The two basic senses are: 1. from *carrus,* wagon, To load. A load. 2. From *carrus,* chariot, To run forward in an assault. Such an assault. *The charge of the Light Brigade.*] *v.* 1. To place a burden upon. (*I charge you to obey* is old style, but survives in *to charge a jury,* what the judge does when he explains to it its functions and responsibilities.) 2. In various senses, to lay a burden upon. 3. To set a price ("the burden of payment"). 4. *Electricity.* (a) To replenish a storage battery. (b) To energize a circuit. 5. To assault as in a military thrust. 6. To load, as a weapon. 7. *Heraldry.* To emblazon with armorial devices. (And corresponding noun senses.)

    to charge (be charged) with Legal. To accuse (be accused) of an offense. ["To place the burden (onus) upon."]

    charge account An arrangement for buying on credit. [The burden of payment is, so to speak, placed upon the account.] *charge it* Said of items or services so bought: enter the cost on the charge account. ("Load it up.")

get a charge out of Am. slang. To derive a pleasing sensation or thrill from. [Dating uncertain, but technological, fixed to early XX when electrical wiring became common, the essential metaphor being of the sensation received from an electrical contact. But the idiom always implies a pleasantly thrilling, slight tingle, as in the maudliness of popular song lyrics, *I get a charge out of you,* a sentiment never sung to an electric chair.]

take charge To assume direction, command. ["To assume the burden of responsibility." In Brit. ca. 1890 (OED Supplement) this idiom had the sense "to go out of control, usually with disastrous results, but primarily with ref. to a naval gun or artillery piece that blows up when misfired or loaded with an excessive explosive charge." In any case this sense has never functioned in Am.]

Chicago bankroll A large roll of paper money consisting of one or two large bills wrapped around a core of ones, used as flash money, primarily by confidence men. [Circa 1900. Because from late XIX until the stock market crash of 1929, Chicago was one major center of the *big store* confidence game. See *big store.*]

chicken [ME *chicken* < OE *cicen* (both *c*s pronounced as *k*s). Perhaps, as some assert, < IE *ku-*, hollow, rounded, whence, female (CUP, CUNT). But the form is at least as likely echoic, deriving from *kik* or *kuk* in kuk-kuk-kuk-kuk, rendered in English as *cluck-cluck,* though I have always questioned the pronunciation of the *l* in chicken-speak.] 1. Any of the common domestic fowl: *chicken coop.* 2. *Specifically.* A young female bird, about seven months and not yet a fully grown, established layer. (Hens, i.e., established layers, are too tough for pan frying and are generally stewed or stuffed and roasted—though note that on coming from the oven they are billed as *roast chicken,* never as *roast hen.* All menus are the work of professional liars.) And note *she's no chicken* She's not as young and tender as she used to be. She has seen better days. [Jonathan Swift is probably the first to have used this idiom in writing, in *Stella's Birthday,* 1720.] *adj.* Cowardly. [Chickens run in squawking terror from intruders.] *to chicken out, to chicken, to turn chicken* To be/become cowardly. [Some attribute this idiom to cockfighting, asserting that a cock is said to turn chicken when it turns and runs. I am hardly an academy on cockfighting. I suppose someone may have used this idiom in connection with fighting cocks, but the only one I have been able to find is *to show the white feather.* (See *white, Browser's I.*) *chicken-hearted* 1. Faint-hearted. [First recorded in English in Bunyan's *Pilgrim's Progress,* 1684.]

chimera 1. With a capital *C* (in old style *Chimaera*) a monster from the dark side of the Greek mythical imagination; a fire-breathing she-goat with a lion's head and a serpent for a tail. A devourer of human flesh, she was the daughter of the vaguely monstrous Typhon, whose mother Gaea (GEOLOGY) was an ancient goddess associated with the deep earth from which the Titans sprang. In family tradition, she was said to be half woman and half dragon. True to family tradition, Typhon (whose monstrosity was more asserted than specified) begot, in addition to the Chimera, such creatures as Cerberus, the Hydra, and the Sphinx. This tightly knit family group seems to be most of what the Greeks had in place of horror movies, until Zeus, perhaps to purify local entertainment, caused Typhon to burst into flame and buried him at the base of Mt. Etna (old style, Aetna), the Sicilian volcano in which he still smolders and periodically erupts. Hence, 2. (lowercase) A ridiculous, imaginary invention. *Also* 3. *Biology.* An organism made up of tissues from genetically distinct parents. Some such may occur naturally but they are more commonly the product of grafting.

chimerical Unreal, fantastic, absurd, impossible though asserted to be real. (The root sense "hideous man-eating monster" has receded, to be replaced by "wildly improbable.") [The etymology: 1. IE *ghiem-*, winter. With gh/h → L. *hiemalis*, of winter. HIEMAL. 2. With gh/kh → Gk. *khimaira*, at root, a yearling, i.e., "animal one winter old," but by the Gk. language convention, specifically "yearling (adult) she-goat." Hence, the functioning sense "she-goat." (I can find nothing to explain the sexual specification.) 3. The mythological monster, as above, probably conceived as being lusty as a goat while simultaneously as sneaky as a serpent and as voracious as a lion.]

chimney 1. A flue for the passage of smoke, gases, and (alas) escaping heat. 2. Any more or less similar device as (a) The glass sleeve around the flame of a kerosene lamp, (b) A vertical or nearly vertical, long, narrow fissure in a rock face, (c) A vertical vein of ore, or (d) A volcanic vent. *up the chimney* Gone and lost forever. And commonly *he smokes like a chimney* Said of one who chain-smokes. [The ultimate etymology is obscure. Gk. *kaminos*, oven, furnace, the earliest secure base, may be from a suffixed variant of IE *keu-*, to burn, whence Gk. *kaein*, to burn (whence, from the p.p. stem, CAUSTIC). But the homonymous IE stem *keu*, swelling, hole, arched opening, suffixed *-w-*, and with w/v is certainly the stem of L. *cavus*, cave, and a large oven is a sort of cave.

Late L. *camīnatā* echoes the Gk. but is prob. from *camera cam-*

īnāta, room with a hearth (it is sometimes rendered "room with a fireplace," but Roman houses had nothing corresponding to the modern fireplace, but rather a firepit or brazier placed under a hole in the roof. In any case, one walked in there and stood by the hearth for the warmth, whence the association with "walk-in place," whence:) OF *chiminee,* ME *chimnee,* a flue. But also L. and It. *caminare,* to walk, and Fr. *chemin,* a road ("place for walking"). And so the compounding of the sense from "furnace, oven" to "passageway" to "passageway for smoke."]

HISTORICAL. As noted, chimneys were a late (medieval) development in great palaces and in the huddle of walled cities. A number of disastrous fires ravaged such medieval cities, leading to the imposition of legal *curfews* (see *Browser's I,* originally OF *couvrefeu, curfeu,* cover (put out) the fire (at a stated hour).

The Roman equivalent of the fireplace was L. *focus,* a hearth or firepit under a hole in the roof. English *focus,* point at which sight lines converge, follows because the L. *focus* was the point at which the family converged. And so, too, It. *punto focale,* focal point, but the primary It. derivation is *fuoco,* fire (See *Browser's I*).

There is also *to fornicate,* from L. *fornicatio,* arched brickwork, as in the cellars of great buildings, and also in the construction of ovens, whence L. *fornax,* oven, It. *forno,* Eng. *furnace.* The poor of Rome had hovels in the ruins of old cellar works and there, too, the cheapest whores had their cribs. In his youth, our common father Publius Vulgus descended into these fornications for his whim away from home, and there early Christian writers denounced him for fornication, naming the sin after the place of the sinning.

chip off the old block A child said to resemble its father. [A longstanding absurd figure for a child–father relationship. In XVII the form was *chip of the same block* (and note that in that male-dominant society it was the father, not the mother, who was taken to be the original block). Either a wood chip or a stone chip. One would certainly hope for a better-formed offspring; the chip, whether of stone or wood, is a worthless fragment. And what can it grow into? We are accustomed to the idiom, however, and without examining it closely, we simply take it to mean that the child is of the same material as the father. I have known any number of disastrous father–son teams to take great, mutual, stupid pleasure at being so likened.]

chiropractic   Medical treatment by manual adjustment of the joints and vertebrae. (In original practice chiropractors prescribed no medication but, a dollar being a dollar, most now sell "special" (i.e., expensive) vitamins to their patients. [Term coined ca. 1880 by Rev. Samuel H. Weed of Bloomington, Illinois while undergoing treatment by this then new method. Weed coined the term < Gk. *cheir,* hand; *praktika,* method, or *praktikos,* efficient. At root, therefore, "hand method," "manipulative practice."]

chop suey   [Chinese *tsa-sui,* odds and ends.] A specialty of American Chinese restaurants but unknown to China (unless the name be applied there to a clean-up-the-kitchen hash). Here, a fried mixture long on bean sprouts and miscellaneous chopped vegetables, often with diced meat or small shrimps. Though a mongrel dish, it can be delicious. (And see *chow mein.*)
   chop suey joint A Chinese–American restaurant, especially a low-priced hole in the wall. [A synecdoche in which the most commonly known dish serves to label the whole—often elaborate—menu.]

chowder   A thick soup, often almost a stew, of fish or shellfish simmered with vegetables, especially diced potatoes, and bits of crisped bacon. In the U.S. clam chowder is especially popular (if you can find the clams in it) and almost as good as mussel chowder. The two standard variants are *New England clam chowder,* prepared with milk, and *Manhattan clam chowder,* cooked in a thin, variously flavored tomato broth. [At root, "hot pot," i.e., the contents of such a pot. Ult. < IE *kel-,* warm, heat → L. *caldus, calidus,* hot; whence Late L. *caldāria,* caldron, → OF *chaudiere;* ME *chaudier, chowdier, chowder.*]
   chowderhead A dimwit. [Am. Dating unknown. One whose brains have been chopped up and stewed. Cf. *clabberhead, churnhead, puddinghead, meathead, mushhead,* and many more derogatives implying chopped up or pulped brains.]

Chowder and Marching Society (Club)   An arch name for a social gathering. Often in more-or-less elaborated form, as, *The Aloysius X. McGillicuddy Chowder and Marching Society.* [XIX ethnic groups commonly marched to parks or to the city limits for a Sunday picnic and beer bust with a "festive" chowder as the main fare. They often marched to their picnics to music and bearing banners. I have searched for and not found any group that called itself specifically a "chowder and marching society/club," but city politicians often organized such outings in which constituents "marched" for McGillicuddy, ate his "chowder," and drank his beer (for which the city would pay later). It is probably by association with these politically sponsored outings that the name came into being in whimsical usage to label any quaintly busy social group that seeks to be insistently festive.]

chow mein [< Mandarin Chinese *ch'ao' mein,* fried noodles.] Like *chop suey* (which see), an ersatz specialty of Chinese–American restaurants with little standing in Chinese cuisine. In effect a hash of vegetables and finely chopped meat or shrimp named after the fried noodles over which it is served. (But though it lacks culinary breeding it can still be delicious.)

Christmas tree A small evergreen set up in the house, sometimes with a rootball, more usually hewn and set in a holder, to be decorated and draped with lights as part of the family Christmas festival. Also a full-grown tree, usually a spruce set up with the aid of heavy machinery in a public outdoor place, the annual giant Christmas tree of Rockefeller Center, for example. The Christmas tree custom is now so firmly established that the raising and distribution of these family fire hazards has become a considerable commerce, good bushy trees selling for $2.00 to $3.00 per foot, with the price rising annually.

HISTORIC. Originally a custom of the Teutonic Yule *(Jul),* the dead of winter festival, absorbed ca. VII–VIII into the Christian nativity festival. The Teutons were anciently forest people and Druidic tree worshipers. (*Druid* is at root IE *dru-,* tree; *wid-* to see; → *dru-wid-,* one who sees [knows about the spirits of] trees.) The Teutonic Yule log and *Tannenbaum* are simple survivals from Druidism. In Europe the custom of the Christmas tree is largely restricted to the Nordic countries.

Though now a fixed part of the Christmas observance in the U.S. (and Canada), the Christmas tree had no part in Colonial observance, but was popularized here by German settlers beginning ca. 1840. MMM cites Harriet Martineau, *Retrospect of Western Travel,* II (1838): "I was present at the introduction into the new country of the spectacle of the German Christmas-tree."

Donald Hall, editor of *The Oxford Book of Children's Verse,* in a note to the curious poetry of German-born Eliza Lee Follen (1787–1860) dates the introduction of the Christmas tree to America as early as 1825 and places it in Cambridge, Mass. He writes: "Eliza Lee Follen was married to Charles Follen, Harvard's first instructor in German, and it is asserted [?] that their house introduced the Christmas tree to the United States."

I do not know the source of the questioned assertion, but Hall's specifications seem reasonable, and all Martineau is really saying is that her 1838 tree was *her* introduction to the custom.

chug-a-lug   A carouse in which beer drinkers try to down the largest possible pitcher of beer without stopping while fellow carousers chant, "Here's to ———, he's true blue. He's a rounder through and through. So drink chug-a-lug, chug-a-lug, chug-a-lug," the refrain continuing for as long as the rounder keeps drinking. Also verb, *to chug-a-lug* To swill beer competitively. [Echoic. A variant of the *glug-glug* sound of drinking. The trick in chug-a-lugging, I am told, though I have never been tempted to try it, is to open one's throat and to pour the beer down without gluttal gulping. A popular game among collegians on a beer bust, it was raised to a new power by Dylan Thomas, who completed his protracted alcoholic suicide by chug-a-lugging a bottle of scotch at the White Horse Tavern in Greenwich Village, the doctors reporting that he died of "an alcoholic insult to the brain."]

churl   A contemptible, base fellow. *Rare in Am. but survives in the adj. churlish* Vulgar, mean, contemptible. [An aristocratic sneer word. Once in good standing, it is < Gmnc. **karlaz,* man (CARL, CHARLES), whence OE *ceorl* (read the *c* as a *k*), man, freeman, not an esne or a serf; hence, implied a minor free landowner, later a "yeoman," a free man of the lowest class; whence ME *churl,* free man, husband, man. But as the label of the lowest figure in the scale of free men, the word by XIII already implied "bumpkin, lout, mannerless yokel," and by XVI, prob. because of the frugality of the small farmer, the sense "miser, surly person" was added. The word has ever since been a term of contempt, and a fair clue to the major English landholder's view of the small farmer whose fields milord felt free to trample when riding to hounds.]

ciao   (Pronounced *chau.*) Informal for either hello or good-bye. An interchangeable "hi" and "so long." [It. but internationalized by tourism and Italian movies, and now common in Am. metropolitan use, though probably not in Hoxie, Arkansas (unless Miller Williams has introduced it there). The form, via various north Italian dialects, is from *schiavo,* slave, by way of *(s)chia(v)o,* with the *k* sound of the *ch* softened. The present (much altered) sense is by association with the floridities of epistolary courtesies. In English, for example, a common letter sign-off was long "y^r humble and obedient servant, etc." In more florid Italian it would not seem too much to sign off with, "your obsequious and devoted slave." Thence, by association, to the sense *good-bye,* and then also *hello,* though more nearly *so long* and *hi* (with the implicit sense "fondly").]

civilization   1. The way *we* do things according to principles above and beyond most of *them.* (Cf. the Iranian view of the U.S.A., and vice versa.) 2. *Colloq.* The big city as opposed to the boondocks: *They went to New Jersey for a week and couldn't wait to get back to Times Square and civilization.* [< L. *civis,* a citizen conceived as one who is ritual in discharging the religious and legal responsibilities of being a free Roman. Note that inflexible Cato of Utica, never noted for what we now call *civility,* was a model of the true *civis.*]

HISTORIC. Trench offers a curiously contradictory note on *civilization* (he is making the point that *civility,* once, as above, a matter of ritual observance, had come to mean no more than surface—and often dissembling—politeness): "The gradual departure of all deeper significance from *civility* has obliged the creation of another word, *civilization,* which only came up toward the conclusion of the last [XVIII] century. Johnson does not know it in his *Dictionary* except as a technical legal term, to express the turning of a criminal process into a civil one; and according to Boswell, altogether disallowed it in the sense which it has now acquired." [So he did know the word existed, but rejected it. Fair enough: I feel the same way about Ronald Reagan. But note that Bailey does not give *civilization,* and for *to civilize* offers only, "To make courteous and tractable; to polish Manners."]

cliché   A trite expression. A stereotype. [Originally a printer's term based on Ger. *Klitsch,* a lump of clay, with reference to metal casting in a clay matrix, specifically printing plates so cast; whence Fr. *clicher,* to stereotype, to cast a printing plate in this way. Stereotype printing was invented in 1725, but the term *clicher* (and thence, *cliché*) was probably not in general use before ca. 1785, for the opposition of handset printers blocked the use of matrix-cast metal printing plates for about 60 years. The first stereotype or cliché plates in common use were cast in a matrix of papier-mâché, but by 1800 plaster of Paris was more common. Then in XIX what had been a printers' method acquired the associated sense "set words in set order," with a further later extension to "trite, preset, and unalterable" (with reference not only to phrasing but to emotional responses, stage situations, and anything pat and predictable): *Parenthood is the cliché that follows rash improvisation.*]

cliffhanger 1. *Early movies.* An adventure serial in which each episode leaves the viewer in suspense. [Am. Since slightly before WWI, and in common use by 1920, because early Nickelodeons (cinema houses that charged a nickel for admission) traditionally ran adventure serials, the most popular of which being probably *The Perils of Pauline.* In these serials the fair damsel in episode after episode flees from uncounted dangers, each episode ending with what seems to be her final destruction. Chased by the fiendish villain, for example, she falls off a cliff to certain death, and the screen darkens to flash the message "Continued Next Week." In the next episode, it turns out the heroine has grabbed a bush growing a foot down the side of the cliff. Hardly panting, she pulls herself to safety, is once more pursued by danger, and falls into new disaster only to be "Continued Next Week." And so:] 2. Any narration or performance the episodes of which climax in false danger. 3. Any suspenseful action or narration: *Since World War II the Cabinet's discussions of the national budget have been a series of cliffhangers, always continued to new disasters.*

clip joint 1. A low establishment that cheats customers by charging inflated prices. [*Clip,* to shear, to cut off from, to cheat. Akin to Brit. *clip,* a sharp blow; but also with precedent in *to clip coinage,* to debase coinage, esp. gold coins, by shaving off some of the metal content. *Joint,* Am. XIX, public meeting place, low meeting place: *What I didn't learn at my mother's knee, I learned at other low joints.*] 2. *Am. whimsical.* A barber shop. [Place (joint) for getting one's hair clipped.]

clue Something that points to the solution of a problem, riddle, mystery. (Up to XV, and with some survival in Brit., *clew,* but in Am. this form means a ball of thread or of yarn.) [And "ball of thread" is, in fact, the root sense. The evolved sense, "indication of a solution," is by association with Greek myth, for which see note.

The form is < IE *gel-, gl'-,* to make into a ball or wad. With g/k in Gmnc. → OE *cliewan,* 1. Ball of thread or yarn. 2. To make into such a ball. (CLOD, CLUB, CLUMP.) ME *clewe* meant both our *clew* and *clue.*]

MYTHO-HISTORIC. As a vengeance for the murder of his son by the Athenians, King Minos of Crete extracted every nine years a

tribute of seven maidens and seven youths to be fed to the Minotaur, the unnatural son of Queen Pasiphaë, sired by a white bull
from the sea. This monster was kept in an underground labyrinth
so intricate that none who entered could find the way out. It lived
on an atypical ruminant's diet of human flesh, though fourteen
Greek teenagers every nine years was something less than a pro-
tein-glut. Perhaps Minos eked out its diet with a ration of Cretans
who had fallen out of his favor.

The hero Theseus, Duke of Athens, volunteered to sail to Crete
with the next Greek ration in order to kill the Minotaur. Ariadne,
princess of Crete and half-sister of the monster, fell in love with
Theseus at sight and gave him a clew of thread to unwind behind
him as he searched the labyrinth. (He might have thought of that
himself, but heroes are seldom notably bright, and then the story
would have lacked a female lead.)

Having found and killed the Minotaur, Theseus found his way
out of the cavern by following the thread he had unwound from
Ariadne's clew. To show his gratitude, he took her with him when
he sailed for Greece. To show the dangers of fooling around with
Greek heroes, he abandoned her on Naxos. But to show that love
conquers all, Ariadne married the god Dionysus and bore him,
among other children, a son named Oenopion, who is said to have
invented wine making. Ariadne was later immortalized into the
company of the gods and smiled in heaven long after Theseus had
thrown his last bull. Love conquers all.

(But in view of this history, can there be, strictly speaking, such
a thing as *a false clue?* Or can a clue only be broken, covered, or
moved?)

clumsy   1. Fumblingly awkward. 2. Not responsive to good handling:
a clumsy scow. 3. Lacking social graces: *He made a clumsy bow.*
4. Lacking finesse, persuasion, plausibility: *a clumsy excuse.* [Of
obscure Gmnc. origin. Perhaps akin to *clump* (rude cluster), but
clumpsy is unattested and does not square with the first ME form
clumsen, which came into English under IX–X Danelaw with the
sense "numb with cold." The modern sense is a natural evolution
from *benumbed with cold* to *awkward.* The association with cold
has disappeared from the word (but might yet be revived in such
a poetic figure as "clumsy icebergs growling in the fjord"). If the
connection between *frozen numb* and *awkward* is not apparent,
try the etymological exercise of performing brain surgery in a walk-
in freezer.]

cobble¹ Equally *cobblestone* A rounded stone roughly the size and shape of a loaf of supermarket bread, once in common use for paving streets. [Mid-XIX Am. < from *cob coal,* also called *cobble,* a chunk of soft coal. In being hauled about, chunks of soft coal would have their edges chipped away and rounded off, as anthracite would not. Several dictionaries define *cobble* as a "naturally rounded" stone, but this specification would apply only questionably to cob coal and not at all to cobblestones for paving. (See below.)]

HISTORIC. The streets of many U.S. cities are still often paved with cobblestones, though these stones are now usu. covered with asphalt tar. (See *macadam.*) These stone "loaves" provided a durable surface resistant to steel-rimmed wagon wheels and horses' hooves, though sometimes slippery. But these stones were not naturally rounded.

My mother as an Italian immigrant girl of about 14 in the late 1890s had her first American job carrying slings of cobblestones to the men who were paving or repaving Haymarket Square in Boston. Her 10-hour stints were spent in carrying four cobblestones at a time to the paving crews from a pile where another crew chipped and rounded the stones to roughly the same size and shape. Those *hand-rounded* stones are still there under the asphalt surface that I have never walked except memorially.

cobble² *v.* To repair shoes. [*Cobbler,* one who repairs shoes, is now distinct from *shoemaker,* though the distinction was once blurred, perh. because of the obscure origin of ME *cobelere* (of untraced OF origin), which meant both.]

cobbler n. 1. A sort of British sangria made of wine and sweetened citrus juices, often with the addition of a liqueur. [Origin uncertain. Perh. by some arbitrary and lost association with the cobbler's trade. Cf. *boilermaker,* neat whiskey with a beer chaser, as if specific to the drinking habits of the boilermaker's trade.] 2. A deep-dish fruit pie with a thick upper crust. [Origin unknown. Could the name be by association with the uppers of a boot tacked to a last and waiting for a sole to be attached? Doubtful.]

sherry cobbler A still-common bar order consisting of a few ounces of sweet sherry made even more disgusting by adding sugared fizz-water. [First mentioned by Washington Irving in 1807. See *cocktail, Browser's I.*]

cobble³ *v. Slang.* In early adolescent U.S. boy-packs, to cobble is the gang act of seizing a boy and ripping his fly open (or pulling down his pants) to examine his genitals, the stated object being "to see what he's got." It is often concluded by spitting on his genitals if they are not hairy and well developed. (The true purpose, of course, is to establish a gang pecking order, though the ritual must vary from gang to gang. Boys come to full puberty at varying ages, some not developing mature genitals till late in their teens. Early developers, of course, boast over much of their manhood and scorn any boy with a prepubescent "fishing worm.") [I have not seen this verb discussed in any dictionary, though it was standard slang in Boston in the 1920s and 1930s, probably with precedents in XIX, for though I cannot trace this verb's specific evolution to the sense given, there are several bits of XIX and early XX Brit. slang in which *cobblers,* for reasons I cannot establish, have to do with male genitals in one way or another, especially with testicles; and in late XIX Brit. rhyming slang *cobbler's awls* meant "balls" (testicles).]

coffin corner   Any of the four corners of the American football grid-iron within a few yards of the goal line. [Because a punter tried to angle his kick to go out of bounds as near the goal line as possible, the ball then being dead at that point. If it is downed much inside the five-yard line, the receiving team must line up with its backfield in the end zone, a position in which a broken play might lose not only yards but points.

If the kicking team can down the ball or tackle the receiver close to the goal line in the center of the field, the effect is essentially the same; but punters aim for the corners, *coffin corner* is an effective alliteration, and jocks, in the first place, do not much care what one calls it so long as the opposing team can be put in the hole preliminary to burial.]

cogito ergo sum   [L. I think, therefore I am.] The first premise of the philosophy of René Descartes, French philosopher and mathematician (1596–1650). Perhaps the best known of philosophical assertions; certainly one of the most widely accepted assertions of flawed reasoning.

HISTORIC. For more than a century after the death of Descartes, the literate accepted this assertion as if it were an axiom. Many still do, though it has often been refuted, perhaps most notably by Immanuel Kant (1724–1804), as a quibble in which the word "I" is used in two different senses, which are equated pointlessly. In simplest terms, the "I" of "I think" is a unit of experience; the "I" of "I am," a substantial entity. In effect, Descartes asserted:

$$I_1 = I_2$$

In a disguised circular argument, Descartes asserted in his premise the conclusion he was setting out to prove.

I fantasize, therefore I am a fantasy. You disagree, therefore you are disagreeable.

cognate *adj.* 1. Related by blood. Having a common ancestor. 2. *Etymology.* Label for words derived from the same root: *"Kind" and "native" are ultimately cognate.* 3. *Loose extension.* Alike in some way: *Peaches Browning was intimately cognate with Daddy's money.* [L. *co(m)*-, with, together; *gnatus,* variant of *natus,* p.p. of *nasci,* to be born.]

NOTE. Latin *cognatus* labeled any blood relationship on either the paternal or maternal side. English *agnate,* standard but rare, is < L. *agnatus,* related on the paternal side. Maternal relationship was signified by *enātus* (< *e(x)* with *natus,* born from, issued from) and is the root of rare English *enate,* substantially obscured by *innate,* inborn.

Many Latin words that made clear sex distinctions have produced blurred derivatives in English and especially in American. Our word *uncle* is from L. *avunculus,* which is specifically a maternal uncle. A paternal uncle took precedence in the Roman *gens* (clan) and was specifically a *patruus,* a relationship for which English has no one-word label, but must say "paternal uncle" or "uncle on the father's side" (which both involve the root contradiction, "paternal maternal uncle"). And see *anile* and *senile.*

colophon 1. In earliest bookmaking, a publisher's note at the end of the book to explain the type, paper, and press used. In early XVI such information began to appear on the title page, whence the word now means: 2. The publisher's name, logo, and company data as they appear on the title page or elsewhere in the front matter. But still 3. *Especially in folios of art prints and in limited editions,* A note on the last page giving details of the paper, type font, press, and often the number of copies printed, along with the handwritten number of the particular copy. [Ult. < IE *kel*-, hill, place of prominence. (COLUMN.) Gk. *colophon* meant, among other things, the final stroke in forming a letter of the alphabet, a serif. There is no linear connection with Colophon, one of the twelve Ionian cities of Asia Minor, which may have been so named because of its hills, a survival of the IE root sense.]

comfort *n.* 1. Ease. 2. Solace. *v.* To solace, ease, satisfy, relieve, console. [But at root, "to strengthen (one's sense of well-being)." < L.

fortis, strong; prefixed *cum*, with. And so Shakespeare, *As You Like It* II. vi, "For my sake be comfortable [i.e., strengthen yourself]; hold death awhile at arm's end." *Comfortare* does not appear in classical L., but late L. *confortare* is well attested, whence OF *conforter*, ME *conforten*, all with the sense "to strengthen."]
  comforter 1. One who gives comfort to another. 2. A quilt. *comfort station* A public place for relieving oneself. (Hardly a source of strength, it does soothe and relieve at need.) *comfortable* At ease, soothing, in good being. *in comfortable circumstances* Less than filthy rich but securely beyond want. *comfy Informal intimate.* Comfortable. Snug.

comma [At root, "thing cut off." Gk. *komma*, L. *comma*, a cut, a cut-off part of a sentence. < Gk. *kaplein*, to cut. Ult. < IE *(s)kep-*, *k'p-*, to cut off, to hack. The grammatical extended sense "mark of a subsection of a sentence" was established in Greek.] The punctuation mark (,) used to mark minor divisions in a sentence or elements in a series: *Proust is the unchallenged master of commatose prose; not even Faulkner is a rated challenger.*

concubine [IE *kup-*, to bend over. → L. *cubare*, to lie down; *concubare*, to lie down with, to sleep with. INCUBUS. SUCCUBUS.] 1. *Old style.* A woman who regularly shares the bed and quarters of a man to whom she is not married. A mistress. In the neologism created by the 1980 census forms, a *posslq* (person of opposite sex sharing living quarters). 2. *In many polygamous societies (perhaps in all),* An additional wife not equal in status to wife number one. Variantly, a woman attached to a harem lord's sexstock, sometimes as a slave, sometimes by a marriage ritual, sometimes by a ritual somewhat less than marriage.
  HISTORIC. Nothing in the word roots specifies that a concubine be female. Traditionally, the word has been largely limited to females, but not always. One of the charges Henry VIII caused to be fabricated against Anne Boleyn was that she procured "divers of the king's daily and familiar servants to be her adulterers and concubines." Henry had female servants, to be sure, but no least rumor of lesbianism has ever attached to Anne. Nor would girlish gaiety classify as "adultery."

conjure 1. *Now primarily,* To work magic, as in a stage performance. So the agential form *conjuror* A stage illusionist. 2. *But earlier,* To summon a spirit by one of the formulas and incantations of magic, usually of black magic for an evil purpose, though exorcists, practicing what has to be called white magic, may summon evil spirits only to expel them. Usu., in this sense, *to conjure up* (up, that is, from the various lower depths in which evil spirits are said to dwell. Angels are not conjured, but prayer that seeks their mediation would have to call them *down*). 3. *But in English into XVII,* To conspire with. To join with other in swearing to follow a course of (evil) action. [So Milton, *Paradise Lost* II, describes Satan as he who "conjured against the Highest," which implies a swearing together for evil purposes. (But also *I conjure you to keep this vow,* which has the effective sense, "I call upon you by all that is sacred," which picks up the root sense of solemnity—already implicit in *vow*— without the later implicit summoning of spirits.) Ult. < IE *yewes-, iewes-, iewo-,* law (which would include religious as well as civil ritual, hence implying a recitation of solemn formulas) → L. *jus,* law; *jūrare,* to swear (as one still swears at law by religious writings, though civil libertarians may now choose to affirm without religious implication); prefixed form *conjurare,* to swear with, together, by.]

   to conjure up When used without the earlier spook-associations, to summon to someone's, or to one's own, imagination: *Her nudity did not quite conjure up the days of my youth, alas.*

   a name to conjure with 1. In black magic, the true secret name of a spirit or fiend. It was an ancient belief, with some voodoo survival, that to know such a name gave the magician a power over that spirit, who, when properly summoned, was forced to respond. (Any error in the conjuration, of course, left the would-be magician at the power of the spirit or fiend.) 2. *Usually ironically.* The name of an authoritative or pseudo-authoritative person, cited as a power or claimed as a sponsor: *Hugh Hefner—now there's a name to conjure with in fluffdom.*

conn   *v.* To steer a ship. *n.* 1. The post of the helmsman. 2. The act of steering a course. [The double *n* form, now a naval standard, is a variant of earlier *con,* from still earlier *cond, cund,* < ME *conduen,* OF *conduire,* to guide, to conduct, < L. *condūcēre,* < *dūcēre,* to lead, to guide; with prefix *con,* with, here functioning primarily as an intensive.]

   to take the conn 1. To assume command responsibility for a ship's course. 2. To take the helm (as the helmsman does under the orders of the bridge commander).

   conning tower 1. The pilot house of a warship. But in general usage, 2. The elevated structure atop the pressure hull of a submarine.

consensus   General agreement. [Via Fr. < L. *consentire,* to share an opinion, to go along with. Ult. < IE *sent-,* course taken, to go in a chosen direction, to head for. (In Gmnc. this root becomes *sin(n)-,* journey; whence, as a distant cousin, the witchcraft term *widdershins,* backward journey, course taken against the natural way. See *Browser's I.*)]

NOTE. But what exactly is a general agreement? At root, *general agreement* would imply that an opinion put to a vote would be approved by a majority. Yet a five-to-four vote in favor does not quite constitute a consensus, the term implying a more general or even overwhelming meeting of minds: *The consensus of the American people has approved Spiro Agnew's journey to obscurity.*

General consensus is common but redundant. *Unanimous consensus* might be defended by arguing that it implies total rather than merely substantial agreement, yet *unanimous feeling* or *unanimous sentiment* is certainly clearer.

coolie   [In XVII in India a Brit. term for a native unskilled laborer. Prob. (but ?) < Hindi *kuli,* laborer, < Koli, Kuli, the name of an aboriginal hill-tribe whose people were widely used as bearers and for heavy labor. By early XIX British colonial overseers were using the term to signify laborers brought from India and China to be overworked in other countries. But in Am. XIX, beginning on the West Coast, specific to:] 1. A Chinese laborer. 2. *Loose ext.* Any Chinese in the U.S.A.: *The western half of the transcontinental railroad was built with coolie labor.*

HISTORIC. In Hawaii many Japanese worked as laborers in XIX. Many of them did coolie labor, but if they were ever called coolies there, I can find no record of that label. Nor can I find any clear record that Japanese laborers ever mixed on work crews with the Chinese. The white overseers, in their innate contempt, would have lumped Japanese and Chinese together as "slant-eyed heathens," but the two groups tend not to mix.

coon   1. Short form of raccoon. [Itself a corruption of the Amerind name for this creature, the Algonquinian form (unexplained) having been rendered in English syllabification as something like *arath kone.*] A primarily carnivorous and nocturnal North American mammal with a rich fur, marvelously manipulative hands, masklike facial markings, and bushy cross-striped tail. It is said to wash its food before eating and is therefore called in Italian *il cane lavatore,* the dog that washes; but that label is probably a reference to its fish-eating along streams. Usually it does not wash its food if the food is already clean. 2. A vanishing bigot's name for a Negro. [Perhaps because raccoons forage at night, raiding chicken coops, kitchen gardens, and stored food supplies; whence the bigot's contemptuous dismissal of blacks as sly nocturnal varmints too shiftless to work for a living.]

coonskin The pelt of a raccoon, seldom depilated and usually with the tail still attached. *coonskin hat* A round flat cap of coonskin with the tail dangling down the back of the wearer's neck. Such hats were the common headwear of XVII–XIX woodsmen.

to nail the coonskin to the barn door In general, to get any job over and done with, as in getting rid of a night-raiding varmint and acquiring a trophy. [In treating a hide, woodsmen stretched it on a flat surface for salting and scraping, and the barn door not only provided such a surface but offered a place to display the trophy. Raccoons were hunted for food, for their pelts, and because they have a taste for the farmer's chickens, crops, and stored food. Persistent survivalists, they now commonly prowl suburban garbage cans, tipping them over and strewing a mess by the back door.

Perhaps the last most notably inept use of this country phrase was by President Lyndon B. Johnson as the desired resolution of the disastrous nonwar in Vietnam.]

cootie   *Slang.* A body louse. Esp. *Pediculis humanus capitus,* literally "human head louse," whence sometimes it is called "head louse," perhaps to distinguish it from body louse; but if so the label is merely confusing, since the species remains the same. [The unabridged NWD published by Delair, 1981, glosses: "Army slang, prob. < WWI." It does not mention which army. If the AEF, then the Yanks picked it up from the Tommies among other rich biota of life in the trenches, but the British army, in turn, picked it up from XIX Brit. navy slang, which derives from Malay *kutu,* louse.

But why is the term universally classified as slang? Many other terms have come into English from the Far East as gifts of the British Empire—a few among them being *bungalow, pajamas, verandah, sacred cow, nabob*—and none of these is called slang. I ask the question and am unable to answer it, but it should be asked. Could it be slang because of its "low" transmission via the forecastle?)]

HISTORIC. For many years, in the time that many American houses had an attached barn or carriage house or at least a livestock pen, all of which provided fine breeding places for them, cooties were a national presence only partly suppressed by regular coal-oil shampoos.

I knew Boston's North End slum in the 1920s, and though there were no barns or carriage houses there, substitute scurrying life forms offered cooties a preferred habitat there. Not only were cooties and coal-oil shampoos common, but boys in summer commonly had their heads shaved, a style commonly dubbed in patois a *scotch-a-melone scotch-a* being from It. *scocciare* with now-primary sense to bore, to annoy, but at root, to grate, to rasp, to scratch (see *hopscotch, Browser's I*). A *scotch-a-melone* is at root, "a scraped melon"; and a common boy's nickname in reference to this tonsorial style was "Haircut."

I had offered this iota of forgotten history in memory of cooties past with some idea that modern sanitation had removed this presence from us. Then in the Miami *Herald,* Dec. 3, 1984, I came upon a feature that declared head lice to be "a national epidemic" and claimed that almost all Florida children are cootie infested. Life goes on.

cordon bleu [Fr., blue ribbon.] 1. In Am. a term reserved for high cuisine and the pretensions of various restaurants. Common also in trade names to connote excellent food or wine. 2. Originally, Fr. *un cordon bleu* signified a chevalier of the Order of the Holy Ghost, which under the Bourbon kings (1589–1793 and 1814–1830) was the highest order of chivalry. [Because the decoration of this order was worn suspended from a blue ribbon. The association with high cuisine stems from the fact that a famous group of these post hoc flowers of French chivalry met regularly for dinners of such distinction that *cordon bleu* came to signify the heights of French cuisine, a *cordon-bleu chef* being one qualified to prepare dinners for these great flowers of lost chivalry.]

HISTORIC. The highest British Order (of the Bath) was also, and is, worn on a blue ribbon, but perhaps as one notable distinction between the British and the French, *blue ribbon* has never become established as a term of high cuisine. In trademarks, it tends to label beer *(Pabst Blue Ribbon)* rather than truffles; and in horse shows, dog shows, and state fairs, it signifies the first prize.

corposant Another name for *St. Elmo's fire* (which see). [This Eng. form dates from XVII < Port. *corpo santo,* holy body, body of the saint, the Port. sailor's name for this luminescence he believed to be the visible body of the seaman's saint-protector.]

costive [Ult. < IE *steip-,* to stick together, to squeeze, to compress; → L. *stipare,* prefixed *con,* with, → *constipare,* to squeeze together (the bowels); p.p. *constipatus* → OF *costivé*, ME *costif.*] 1. Constipated. Also, Causing constipation: *The costive content of TV commercials.* 2. *Exts. by association*, (a) Sluggish. (b) Niggardly (giving out nothing).

coxswain (pron. *kăk's'n*) 1. *Naval.* A rating, originally in charge of a small boat. (a) As steersman and director of rowers. (b) As steersman of a small powerboat. Also an unrated person performing these functions. 2. *In crew (rowing competition).* The one in the stern facing forward. He counts the cadence and tends the tiller. Traditionally a small person directing powerful hulks, he is the one heaved off the pier and into the water in celebration of victory. [< *cock(boat), cockle;* with *swain*, at root, "son," in extended usage, "junior person in charge of a specific minor task."] Cf. *boatswain* (pron. *bō's'n*).

crack A remark: *No more of your cracks, please.* [Long naturalized to American colloq., perhaps since colonial times, but native to Sc. with the sense "sayings, turns of speech, native idioms." Sir Walter Scott praised his friend John Jamieson, author of the first comprehensive Scottish dictionary, as "full of auld Scottish cracks." This Sc. use is a curious evolution via Gmnc., < IE *ger-*, to give off sound, to say; but at root echoic of the hoarse grating cry of such birds as herons and crows. With g/k and in the zero-grade form IE *ger-* → *kr-*, whence CROW, CRANE. So OE *craccian*, to give off sound, to utter, to grate, to croak (CROAK).]

NOTE. 1. Not to be confused with wisecrack < wisecracker < *wiseacre*, which is at root MD *wijseggher* and OHG *wissago*, soothsayer (at root Gmnc. *wiss*, wise, with *sager*, sayer. And so OE *witsega*, soothsayer, prophet. (Though *crack* has certainly influenced the modification of *wiseacre* to *wisecracker*.)

2. I have never found a satisfactory explanation of the fixed Am. idiom *Georgia cracker*, but cannot resist the thought that this sense of *crack* in combination with *wiseacre/wisecracker* is probably relevant.

crass Gross, vulgar, offensive. [Akin to *grease* (which see). < L. * *crassus*, which had the root sense "animal fat" but also the extended senses, "viscous, repulsive, dense, stupid."]

crisscross *n.* A pattern of crossing lines. *v.* 1. To mark with such a pattern, as in *X*ing out a typed passage. 2. To move in such a pattern, as drill teams and marching bands often do. But used primarily as an *adj.* Crossing several times or more: *crisscross overhead ramps.* (The formal resemblance to a reduplication gives the term a frequentative force, as if a crossing were a single intersection of lines; and a crisscrossing, a pattern of intersections.) [But at root a noun only, a *Christ's cross.* From hornbooks, first common in XVIII in the elementary instruction to children of the emerging mercantile class in Britain. A hornbook, it may be well to explain, was a wooden paddle covered with a thin sheet of transparent horn on which children could copy (and easily wipe away) instructional models placed under the sheet. The first and commonest model, often imprinted in a line across the top of the sheet of horn, was an alphabet that concluded with an ampersand and began with a cross, the Cross of Christ, as a pious designation that the young student was receiving Christian instruction. There is no doubt of this origin but no certain explanation of the way this model line of type, *the Christ's cross line,* acquired the present sense of *crisscross* —perhaps because children often crisscrossed their copy before wiping it off the horn.]

crocodile tears   A hypocritical show of grief. [Medieval bestiaries rarely left out the crocodile and the assertion that it wept, as if sorrowfully, while eating its victims. Various pious explanations of this purportedly genuine grief were offered. Crocodiles do, of course, tend to eat in shallow water and might readily splash about while gorging, causing water to stream down their faces. Or the force of mastication might cause their eyes to water. I have never dined with a crocodile and cannot attest, but on whatever basis of fact or fancy, crocodile tears have long been a standard image in English idiom. They are mentioned as early as 1356 in Sir John Maundeville's *Voyage.*]

crying: for crying out loud!   Exclamation of vexation. [A minced oath. A late-XIX Am. altered form of *for Christ's sake!* or *Chrissake!* As if the speaker had started so say *"for Christ . . ."* when he thought better of speaking the oath and shifted to the meaningless *". . . ing out loud!" Gee! Geez!* and *Gee whiz!* are similarly bitten off and altered forms of *Jesus.*]

cummerbund   Now commonly a waistband cut to resemble the bottom of a man's vest, sometimes with pockets, worn over the tops of the trousers in men's formal wear, commonly fastened in the back. Earlier an ornamental pleated sash knotted at one side with the tasseled ends hanging loose, used as ornamental wear by gentlemen of India and adopted and adapted for formal wear by the British in XIX. [But at root, "loin cloth." Hindi < Persian *kamarband* < *kamar*, loins, with *band*, band, sash, cloth, swaddling band; though by the time it became known to British colonials this originally humble garment had become ornate and formal. The vowel alterations are part of the Englishman's easy disregard of ignorant foreigners and their queer languages. Cf. *Rotten Row* in Hyde Park, originally *Rue du Roi*, designating the king's bridle path—but what do those Frenchies, even the royal ones, know about proper English place-names?]

$\mathcal{D}$

daiquiri　A popular mixed drink, originally of rum, lime juice, and sugar, served over cracked ice; now with many variants such as the strawberry daiquiri, which is more nearly a dessert of artificially flavored strawberry slush than a cocktail. [After Daiquiri in Cuba, where the U.S. Navy is said to have been introduced to the original concoction, importing it to the Army and Navy Club in Washington, where it became, and remains, a favorite.]

HISTORIC. Time-Life's "Cookbooks of the World" (1970) credits the Washington Army and Navy Club with introducing the daiquiri to the U.S. after the Spanish-American War of 1898, naming the original discoverer as Admiral Lucius W. Johnson, saying that he and his men "landed on the [desperately hot] beach at Daiquiri [and] a man invited them all for a drink," which they named the daiquiri.

[Question: Where on a desperately hot day in Cuba in 1898 did "the man" get shaved ice? Yes, there was a sea trade in pond ice stored in sawdust, and ice so stored was taken in fast packets to India, surviving two equatorial crossings. It is possible that a wealthy Cuban might have a cellarhole of prewar ice. But ???]

Time-Life erred in ascribing the discovery to Admiral Johnson. My friend Lieutenant Commander Arnold S. Lott, as a naval historian who passed all his courses in Arithmetic I, noted that Admiral Johnson died in 1968 at age 85. He would have been 15 in 1898 and notably junior to his own rank. Navy records do not show who was in command at Daiquiri, and there is still that doubt about the ice; but have a daiquiri and all will be well.

daisy-cutter　A term that keeps turning up in English and that will almost certainly turn up again, though now in seeming abeyance. 1. *Among British horsemen since XVIII.* A horse that does not raise its feet high [said therefore to cut the heads off daisies]. 2. *Cricket.* A ball bowled along the sward. 3. *WWI.* The GI name for a Japanese anti-personnel bomb not much larger than a grenade. These were dropped from planes with contact fuses and with lengths of bamboo fixed in their noses, causing them to go off in air and "to cut daisies" in all directions.

HISTORIC. A crude but deadly weapon. Compare the heavy bombing at Dunkirk with more sophisticated and heavy bombs that buried themselves in sand that muffled their deadly explosions. Had the German bombs been rigged in the Japanese manner to go off about six feet in air, the British might well have had nothing left to evacuate from Dunkirk.

Dan to Beersheba   All over the place. *to wander from Dan to Beersheba* is to go everywhere. [The idiom would be understood wherever the Bible is closely read. It was especially common in colonial America and through XIX and survives in the Bible Belt. As set forth in Judges 20:2, Dan is the northernmost limit of the Holy Land; Beersheba, the southernmost; hence who goes from one to the other has covered it all. Except for exception noted, the idiom is now rare in Am. *I've looked from Dan to Beersheba, and I still can't find that there Vatican.*]

derive   [L. *derivare*, to draw water from a river, as for irrigation, < *de*, from, with *rivus*, watercourse, stream.
RIVER. (Specifically, water flowing between banks. And so cognate *ripa*, bank of a river. Cf. English *arrive*, at root, L. *ad ripam*, to the riverbank, and by ext. to the shore. RIPARIAN. To arrive is, at root, to come to shore, to the bank—and can one, therefore, *arrive at mid-ocean* without some violence to the root sense of honorable browsers?)] By various sense exts. (with the root sense systematically ignored) to draw almost anything from a source not entirely one's own. [So a *derivative literary style* (a pejorative label) is one drawn from that of another writer. Or one may *derive* his income from his grandmother's will—which in a sense makes the source his, though not of his making. In the root sense one may say the XIX inland pirates *derived* substantial booty from the Ohio River (see *Salt River, Browser's I*); but no native speaker of Am. has thought to say that Huck Finn *derived* many a catfish from the Mississippi.]

despot   In all senses and by the same association with absolute power, now (though not at root) identical with *tyrant*, which see. [Ult. < IE *dem-*, house (DOMICILE. And with d/t, via Gmnc. TIMBER, at root, "material from which a house is built"); with IE *pot'-*, master (POTENTATE. And also L. *potis,* power). At root, therefore, "master of a household," or in the common redundant form "lord and master [of a house]." In various cognate forms in Near Eastern languages, king, ruler. Also applies to Greek Orthodox bishops and metropolitans.]

desultory *adj.* (Accent on first syllable) [< L. *salire,* to leap (SOMERSAULT); prefixed *de-,* down, lit. to leap down, but effective sense, to leap about. From participial stem *sult-,* L. *desultor,* leaper.

In Roman circuses one performer rode upright on two horses leaping from one to the other at full gallop. He was commonly booked as *Desultor.* But in English the term is primarily associated with mental rather than physical leaping. Today *desultory* is the sort of homework our children do while watching TV.] Incoherent. Mentally disjunct. (In slang, *grasshoppering,* leaping from one idea or topic to another in no predictable sequence.)

deuce[1] In various exclamations, the devil. *What the deuce! The deuce with it!* (Obs. *A deuce on it!*) *What the deuce are you doing?* [This particular devil is, at root, from Ger. *Daus,* hobgoblin. (And note *to play the deuce with,* to play hob with.) Certainly influenced in part by the roll of two (deuce, craps) at dice, but the etymological trace is clearly to LG *was der daus!* what the deuce. No link can be established between this form and L. *deus,* God.]

deuce[2] *Tennis.* The score, forty all. [From Fr., in which the game is said to be *à deux,* because to win, a player must score two successive points. (If his opponent scores a point, the player must score three in a row, one to bring the opponent back to deuce, then two in a row to win.)]

diadem Unless specified as a piece of ornate jeweled headdress, a crown as the symbol of royal power. [Gk. *diadema,* crown, from *v. diadein,* < from *dein,* to bind, prefixed *dia-,* through, but here with the sense "around." *diadēdenai,* I bind around. The original reference was to the ornate turbans worn by the Persians, to which Persian kings bound an ornately embroidered blue-and-white band as a symbol of majesty. I do not know by what encrustations of pompous symbolism such bands became the mark of royal authority, but the Greeks carried over to metal crowns this word that originally signified a cloth band.]

dice: no dice   1. *Crap shooting.* A roll of the dice that does not count. [If a die, or both dice, go off the table, or land cocked on money or chips, or do not bounce off the backboard, or fall out of the shooter's hand before he is prepared to roll, or in some cases, subject to local rules, if a player or the shooter calls "no dice" before the roll is completed, the roll does not count for or against any bet, and the dice are to be rolled again. 2. *In generalized use,* Nothing doing. [But generally with the implication "you lose," which is not implicit in the gambler's sense. One who asks a loan or another favor and who is told, "No dice," is in effect rejected coldly.

This sense, more negative than the neutral gambler's original, may be influenced by the horse player's *no price,* said of a horse not worth betting on at any odds, a sure loser; and so in generalized usage, a person said to be no price is beyond hope. So, *when Lefty finds out about you, you'll be no price* = you'll be as good as dead to all hope (and dead in fact soon thereafter).

The term is Am. and prob. back to the beginnings of crap shooting here, but I have found it recorded nowhere until Lester Berrey and Melvin Van Den Bark noted it in their *American Thesaurus of Slang* (New York, 1942).]

diesel   *In early XX Diesel engine* An internal combustion engine that does away with sparkplugs by compressing air to incandescence for igniting a spray of heavy oil. Diesels were used originally in heavy equipment, trucks, locomotives, and ships, but have recently been refined for use in pleasure vehicles. [Eponymous. After the German inventor, Rudolf Diesel (1858–1913). *Diesel engine* was once the language equivalent of *Ford car,* but Ford has been prominent enough to keep his name capitalized, whereas Diesel has been lowercased into the language.]

diesel fumes The noxious exhaust of diesel engines as in the exhalations from the rear of New York City buses, esp. on sultry days. But generalized, as in *diesel-mouth,* for one with bad breath. *Hell, I think, must be diesel.*

NOTE. For the confused distinction between *engine* and *motor,* see *motor.*

digs, diggings   Brit. One's lodgings. [Familiar to readers of Brit. novels, but though now a Brit. usage, and obs. in Am., the term originated in Wisconsin ca. 1840 when miners of galena ore holed up in their diggings for the winter. (Australian opal miners of today live in elaborate underground digs to escape the heat of the barren "outback." In one TV documentary I saw, even the local school is in such digs.)

P. *Slang* says the term was anglicized in late 1850s. Hence, it has had well over a century to become naturalized there.]

Diogenes   A Greek cynic philosopher, ca. 412–323 B.C. Studiedly indifferent to worldly pomps and possessions, he sought to find a trace of honesty in the world, and his remarks on its rarity gave birth to the legend that he went about at night with a lantern in search of an honest man. He is not known to have found one, except himself, but he had clearly set the rules so that only he could win.

MYTHO-HISTORIC. The shades of the Greek underworld begin as pale as death and then dim out until they cannot be identified, an obvious parallel to what happens to bodies in the grave. Yet Orpheus, descending into the shadows, would have no trouble identifying the shade of Diogenes. Adam was said by Christian legend to be the most identifiable man in the world because he had no belly button, was short one rib, and was perfect in beauty, having been directly created by God. So the shade of Diogenes must be short in stature because he was forever holding up his lantern to shine it in men's faces; it must have been one heavily muscled arm from the labor of holding aloft that lamp equipped with a powerful, hence heavy, reflector; and it must bear the scars of the many blows he suffered when he crept up on strangers in the dark and startled them by flashing that light in their eyes. It had to be night work, of course, for all men seem to pass as honest during the day.

diploma   [Gk. *diploos,* double (lit., "twofold") → *diploma. At root,* 1. Thing folded double. *But effectively,* 2. An official document.

There is some historic uncertainty here. Many, probably most, ancient Greek documents were in the form of scrolls. As above, however, the etymological evidence is that some documents (none of which has survived) were on doubled-over papyrus or parchment. It seems likely that ancient Greek contracts were drawn up in duplicate, folded over, and then divided, one copy going to each of the contracting parties.

If so, the later practice of indentures may have stemmed from the Greek practice. An indenture was, originally, a contract drawn up in duplicate on a large sheet of paper which was then divided by irregular serrations, the authenticity of the copies being established when the serrations were refitted together. The now archaic form *charter party* was such a serrated contract, < Fr. *carte parti,* divided paper. Legal-size paper called *fool'scap* (from Italian *foglio capo,* large sheet; and later identified with the fool'scap watermark, which was in fact suggested by *foglio capo*), was such a large sheet to be divided by serrations. Legal refinements accrued inevitably, but the Gk. *diploma* may have been ancestral to these forms.] *n.* A document, esp. one certifying that a particular person has satisfactorily completed a course of study.

    diplomat An official certified by official documents of his country.

    diplomate A physician certified as a specialist by a board of examiners.

    diplomatic immunity 1. Immunity from legal process extended to documented representatives of a foreign county while in another country on diplomatic assignment. Persons so exempted can only be declared persona non grata and sent home for whatever legal action their governments may think fit. 2. The right of Arab consular clerks to double-park on Fifth Avenue and to protest formally when local residents slash their tires.

diptych   A pair of hinged wooden panels painted or carved (or both), most commonly depicting religious figures, though art is capable of endless variations, the essence being that when the hinged panels are opened at an angle, they are free-standing. (The hinged double portrait of wife and children sometimes found standing on an executive's desk is technically as much a diptych as paired icons would be.) [At root, "twofold." < Gk. *ptukhē,* a fold; prefixed *di(s),* two. The association of such panels with pious portrayals is Christian. The Greek *diptukha* was a hinged pair of waxed tablets on which a merchant could scratch accounts, and so made that the waxed surfaces did not touch when it was folded shut.]

    HISTORIC. The idea of such paired, hinged tablets might quite likely have been adapted for religious purposes as temple decorations or for a home shrine, but if so, no firmly identifiable examples have survived from ancient Greece. The earliest known examples are Christian icons, and such icons were most commonly *triptychs* (see *triptych*) in a pious evocation of the Trinity. A quadruple panel —a *tetraptych*—would, of course, be possible but awkward, and would be less apt to religious symbolism than the triple panel.

discombobulate   *Slang.* To discomfit. To confuse. To disconcert. To throw into consternation. To flabber one's ghasts. [Primarily sthrn. regional, prob. since late XIX but since widely disseminated. My army instructors in WWII were overwhelmingly southerners and *discombobulate,* along with such flourishes as *absogoddamntively* and *possifuckinglutely* flowed from them constantly in a late flowering akin to the exuberant rhetoric of the Jacksonian Era. But the precedent is more likely Brit. XIX slang *bamblusterate,* same sense, prob. elaborated from earlier *bamboozle.*]

disinterest   Active and principled impartiality in judgment, arbitration, or other dealings. The essence of disinterest is impartiality, freedom from self-seeking or bias. [L. *interesse,* at root, to be between; effective sense, to be involved in; with neg. prefix.]

NOTE. The confusion of *disinterested* and *uninterested* is a common and especially offensive Am. illiteracy. *Disinterest* tends to imply an active involvement carefully guarded from personal bias. To be *uninterested* is to be indifferent and unconcerned. Part of the reason for this common error is that there is no firm etymological explanation for the distinction. It is a useful and vital distinction imposed not by the word roots but by the language convention.

On a recent TV soap opera a wife was made to say, "I cannot have a baby because my husband is *disinterested* in me." It is true that most babies are the result of a strong personal bias, but she meant that her husband was uninterested in her. He may in fact have had an active interest in making sure she did not spread her level of diction to another generation.

doggone!   Variantly *doggone it! Exclam.* 1. Of minor vexation: *Doggone it, this coffee is cold!* 2. Or of intense approval: *Doggone, we had a good time!* Also as an adj.: *We had a doggone good time!* [Am. early XIX. In a stereotyped oversimplification most, if not all, dictionaries explain the form as a minced oath for *God damn!* Thus, on the order of *What the Sam Hill!* for *What the damn hell!* And cf. *crying out loud!*

And *doggone* might follow as a way of evading *goddamn,* as *goddamn* could be substituted in either of the examples given above. But this common explanation, though plausible, does not sufficiently weigh the early forms, which are cited in OED as "dog on't" (1826) and "Take that, dog-on-you!" (1872). These forms seem to suggest earlier *a pox on you!* The root sense is probably not *goddamn it!* but "[sic] a dog on it!"—a sufficiently summary form of rejection if the dog is well fanged; or, perhaps, variantly, "may a dog shit on it!" which will also do as a cursory appraisal.]

dogma   An infallibly stated, not-to-be-questioned, inalterable (at least in theory) tenet of a particular faith. [Ult. < IE *dek-, dok-,* to take, to accept. DOCTRINE. → Gk. *dokein,* to appear to be, to seem, to be apparent. And *dogma,* 1. An opinion (as if "what is apparent to me"). 2. A decree (as if "that which is true because I say so").

The IE root functions only in words concerning opinions and beliefs; not "to take physically" or "to accept a material object," but to accept mentally. Related words are *doctor* (learned teacher), *decent* (taken to be intellectually or morally proper), *docile* (mentally acceptant) and *decorous* (seemly).]

dog-tired Utterly exhausted. [Prob. not akin to dog/canine, but (though unattested) < Norse (Swedish *dag,* very. Prob. into English dial. and colloq. under IX–X Danelaw. Note Shakespeare, *I Henry IV* III.iii, "dog cheap," very cheap.]

DOM The rubric form of the motto of the Benedictine order. [As if *D. O. M.* for *Deo optimo maximo,* God the best and greatest, but I have never seen the letters separated by periods. Hardly a standard Am. form but prominently set forth on the labels of bottles of authentic *Benedictine liqueur* and *Benedictine and Brandy* (B & B), and whatever the state of the kingDOM, these remain reasonably common articles of commerce and advertising.]

Doppler effect [After Austrian physicist Christian Johann Doppler (1803–1853).] An apparent change in the frequency of sound waves caused by the relative motion of the sound source and the hearer. As the hearer speeds toward the source of the sound, the sound waves (which travel at 1,200 feet per second) reach him at a higher frequency (and, therefore, pitch); as he speeds away, the process is reversed.

The phenomenon is now well known to all motorists. If a truck sounds its horn while approaching at 60 mph a motorist who approaches at the same speed, the sound waves still travel at 1,200 ft/sec, but are intercepted at 1,200 ft/sec plus 120 mph, an approximate increase in frequency of 176 ft/sec, rising to a climactic wave, and fading at about 1,124 ft/sec. (My physics and mathematics are crude in this, but the experience is now common. It could not have been to Doppler. Having died in 1853, he may have had some approximation of this auditory effect on a fast-moving train, but the more likely fact is that he theorized what we have all since experienced.)

dormouse 1. The mouselike creature that fell asleep at the Mad Hatter's Tea Party in Lewis Carroll's *Alice in Wonderland.* [Most readers assume this creature to be a sort of mouse somehow associated with doors, as if originally "(in)door mouse," which is to say, "not a field mouse"; and all the Alice illustrations I have seen encourage this assumption. The creature is not a mouse, and it fell asleep at the tea party, I suggest, because Lewis Carroll knew that its Fr. name is *dormeuse,* sleepy one.] 2. A small European squirrel of the family *Gliridae.* Like the common squirrel, it inhabits trees, but more often bushes. Unlike the squirrel, it is nocturnal. It also has an unusually long period of hibernation, and this, together with the fact that it is sometimes found asleep during the day, led to the Fr. label *la dormeuse,* corrupted in Eng. to *dormouse.* [When *les dormeuses* have fattened up for their long hibernation, they are esteemed by the French as a gourmet delicacy. Americans, commonly squeamish about unusual foods and associating these creatures with mice, may shudder at the thought of eating them, but colonial and XIX Americans used squirrels as a pot-shot staple. The *Williamsburg Art of Cookery,* based on a Virginia cookbook of 1742, gives three recipes for Brunswick Stew. Two of them specify squirrel as an ingredient if available, suggesting chicken as a substitute.]

downstairs *Am. boxing.* The belly, esp. as a target for a boxer's punching. [Since ca. 1885. Belly flab is the first sign that a fighter is not in top condition. *To hammer him downstairs,* therefore, is to weaken him and set him up for a knockout blow to the jaw, though the head has never been called *upstairs* in boxing slang.]

duds Clothing. [Of unknown origin. Common in ME and in Scottish. Once, and now again, applies to clothing of any kind. So the early ballad line, "Let a' his duddies fa'." So Burns, "Tam o' Shanter," in which the witches, for freedom of motion, cast off "their duddies to the work." But in XVII *dudman,* a scarecrow (made of old rags). And "used clothing, rags" was then the primary sense. Daniel Defoe (ca. 1660–1731) mentioned that at the Sturbridge Fair near Cambridge, the booth that dealt in secondhand clothing was called the *Duddery.* XVIII Brit. *dud,* a rag.

Dud for a sham, a counterfeit, an incompetent person, a failure is similarly of unknown origin, perhaps by association with the intermediate sense "rag, discarded thing," except that these senses began to emerge ca. 1900. The sense "unexploded artillery shell" is not attested in OED until 1915. Etymology has been a dud on this one.]

duff The ass. One's rear end. *Get fresh with him and he'll knock you on your duff.* [Origin obscure. Standard Am. slang since early XX. P. *Slang* notes *duff* as an adjective in late XIX Brit. slang, with the sense, no good, inferior. He does not explain the derivation but cites it as originally Glaswegian. Perhaps into Am. with a sense shift to "inferior end (of an inferior person?)." There is no evident connection with doff, as in, "to doff one's hat."]

dumbbell¹ An exercise device consisting of weights secured to either end of a short, usu. metal, bar. [The weights were once commonly spherical, or off-spherical; and earlier crudely bell-shaped. They now usu. consist of discs that can be fastened to a metal bar to increase the weight. The intermediate bell-form suggests dumb (mute, nonringing) bells, but by association with a vanished device.]

HISTORIC. *Dumbbells* precedes any form of this exercise device as we know it. It was noted that church bellringers developed great upper-torso strength in years of ringing the changes. Gentlemen of XVII–XVIII (including Joseph Addison, who has written about his rig) exercised on a device resembling a bellringer's ropes, attached through a pulley to various weights. This device simulated the work of bellringing, though the imaginary "bells" were "dumb." The later, and simpler, barbell device, had crudely bell-shaped weights by association with this earlier and rather cumbersome rig.

dumbbell² A stupid person. [A late Am. development. OE *dumb* had the senses, 1. Mute. 2. Stupid. But the second sense faded from Brit. usage. It survived in German *dumm,* whence *Dummkopf,* blockhead, and was brought to America by German immigrants. Dumb in this second sense was almost certainly in colonial usage, at least in Pennsylvania. In any case it is attested in James Fenimore Cooper by 1823. *Dumbbell,* however, is not attested before 1914, and is generally attributed to T. A. (Tad) Dorgan, popular comic-strip cartoonist. Several sources have advanced the suggestion that the term was originally specific to women, beginning as *dumb belle,* and *Dumb Dora,* a popular comic strip that first appeared in 1914, may give some credence to this suggestion. In any case, *dumb belle* remains unattested. The functional sense is "head that does not work (like a bell that does not ring)."]

dumps: in the dumps Sad. Dispirited. Lost in mental gloom. [*Dumps* here a transfer word, resembling, but not (at least immediately) akin to Swedish *dumpa,* to throw down; whence *city dump,* place where refuse is thrown (down). This *dump* is < OD *domp,* mist, fog (DAMP); hence, at root, *in the dumps* means "befogged in gloom." Except that some, as Witherington, may fight on. So the "Ballad of Chevy Chase":

> I weep indeed for Witherington
> He was in doleful dumps.
> For when his legs were smitten off
> He fought upon his stumps.]

dupe   *n.* An easily deceived fool. v. To mislead and take advantage of the gullible. [At root, "of (like) the hoopoe." Cf. current slang "bird brain" for "fool"; and "it's for the birds," for "it is ridiculous/ worthless." The hoopoe is a common European bird with a twitchy crest, bizarre markings, and mannerisms that have made it a symbol of clownish stupidity (though it has at least passed the test by evolution, and it is not certain that those who think of it as stupid will do so). OF *huppe,* hoopoe is regularly glossed as "origin unknown," but only by those who have not heard its cry, which sounds much like *hoo-hoop!* Hence Fr. *duppe,* and still-surviving Brit. dialect *dupe,* the hoopoe; < the curious OF form *de huppe,* in which *de* seems to function as an article (akin to Gmnc. *der*). ODEE cites a XV Eng. text in which *duppe* is cited as a low or cant term for a fool. *To dupe* < Fr. *duper,* to deceive, has been in Eng. use since XVIII, but this sense is an extension by loose association: nothing in the behavior of the hoopoe shows it to be easily deceived, or not at least by man.]

dusie   A oner. A splendid thing. *it's a dusie* It is an eye-popping wonder. But ironically *that guy is a real dusie* implies that he is a stinker, or sometimes that he is loony. [After the Duesenburg automobile of which the Model A, first offered for sale in 1921, was the first straight-eight and the first with four-wheel hydraulic brakes. Superbly engineered to racing specifications, it was the fastest road car of its time of J and supercharged SJ models, first sold in 1929. Duesenburgs went out of production just before WWII and only about 500 of the J and SJ models were made. Except for a few late models, Duesenburg made only the power plant and chassis, the 1930 price being about 9,000 depression dollars. Buyers had their own customized bodies made. Show people seem to have been especially drawn to these showboats on wheels. Greta Garbo flashed about in a Model A. Gary Cooper and Clark Gable had

1930s customized models. Mae West had at least two, and some say three, elaborately customized.

About 250 survive. In a 1970 auction, one fetched over $300,-000. Today, one in good condition would be expected to fetch at least $1 million. It's a dusie!]

ℰ

Edison As *Bell* is now a standard name for the various telephone systems of the U.S.A., after Alexander Graham Bell, who was not clearly the first to invent the telephone but the first to patent it; so *Edison* is now a standard name for an electric power company, after Thomas Alva Edison, who in 1880 first illuminated his laboratory in Menlo Park, N.J. with an incandescent light bulb.

Illuminating gas had been in use in large U.S. cities since early XIX (see *locofoco* in *Browser's I*) and remained in common use into the 1930s, the raw flame of the gas jet commonly diffused through a fine ceramic mesh called a mantle. Naturally enough there were superstitious rumors about the possible ill-effects of the newfangled light bulb. To allay them, the XIX Edison Co. distributed signs to be posted, primarily in hotel rooms. I cannot duplicate the ornate fonts of the old hand presses but those signs, with various printer's embellishments, read:

This Room Is Equipped With

EDISON ELECTRIC LIGHT

**Do not attempt to light with
match. Simply turn key
on wall by the door.**

━━━ ＜ ∙ ＜ ＞ ∙∙∙∙ ＜ ＞ ∙ ＞ ━━━

**The use of electricity for lighting
is in no way harmful to health
nor does it affect the soundness
of sleep**

eerie *adj.* Ghostly, weird. In the aura of evil spirits. [OE *earg,* ME *eri,* evil, maleficent. But the word fell out of common English usage, passing into Scottish, from which it reentered English in

XVIII with an aura of spooky things that go bump in the night.

Ult. from the widely dispersed IE root *er-*, to move, to set in motion; hence to be animate, to exist. ARE. Variant stem *or-* → L. *orire*, to arise, to be born ("to move into life"). ORIGIN. ORIENT, ABORT. With guttural suffix → Gk. *orkheisthai*, I dance. ORCHESTRA. Variantly, with *g* suffix → Gk. *ergon*, work ("exertion of motion"). ERG. Similarly suffixed and with vowel variation in Gmnc. → OE *earg*, as above; also to Ger. *arg*, bad, evil, mischievous, guileful; whence also Ger. *arglos*, naïve, ingenuous.

It seems to be in German or in late Gmnc. that the root sense "motion" became associated with evil ("there's dirty work afoot"), and so to "fast, snatching demons," as in *Schnellegeist*, an evil snatcher ("fast-moving spook").]

HISTORIC. Harry Truman as president once used, in a press conference, the eerie dialect word *snollygoster*. It sent all reporters scurrying for dictionaries, and one traced it as far as one Am. dialect dictionary that defined it as "a shylock." A shylock will do as a furtive, fast snatcher; but the word was transmitted to Am. dialect from *Schnellegeist* by way of Pennsylvania Dutch, in which some variant form served as the word for bogeyman, ghost that snatches. Harry Truman came by it natively enough, for when the Missouri territory was opened, it was settled about equally by Pennsylvania Dutch (not necessarily Amish) and by southerners.

effete   Nonproductive, sterile, decadent; with associated senses overrefined, incapable of bringing forth good ideas or work: *Modern painting is what happened when effete painters stopped looking at girls and persuaded themselves that they had a better idea.* (Which is only partly true, but who has a whole truth?) [Root sense, "exhausted by childbirth/no longer capable of conceiving or bearing a child." In the root sense only a woman can be effete; but her male companion has had his equivalent in the passé F.O.B. for "fucked-out buck." < L. *effetus* 1. Having borne a child (fetus). 2. Exhausted by childbearing and no longer capable of conceiving or bearing one. < *efferre*, to bear (as if from *ex-*, out of; with *ferre*, ult. < IE *dhe-*, to suck, to give suck; with standard shift of the voiced stop *dh* to *f* in Latin, as shown by Grimm's Law → Latin stem *fe-* → *ferre*, *fetus*, *femina*. *Sooner or later parenthood becomes the accumulated inefficacy of the effete.*]

egg, good egg, bad (rotten) egg   A person; a good person; a bad (rotten) person. [An egg is an obvious image of entity. Yet its slang use egg in your beer / 101

for *chap* came late. P. *Slang* notes *bad egg,* one who disappoints expectation, in Brit. slang from mid-XIX, followed ca. 1900 by *good egg,* and in late 1918 by *old egg,* old chap.

Rotten egg, as in the child's playful taunt, "last one in is a rotten egg," is undoubtedly earlier (though I cannot date it) but does not mean so much an individual as a stink/stinker. The taunt (and invitation) would have been as effective had it read, "last one in is a flat tire."

When in *Macbeth* the murderers come after Macduff but kill his young son instead, they say, "What, you egg! Young fry of treachery!" But this Shakespearean usage is not a precedent, for *egg* here means "roe" (unhatched thing), especially as followed (in the slightly mixed metaphor) by "fry." Nor did this Shakespearean figure pass into English usage.]

egghead   Also, but less commonly, *eggdome* An intellectual. [*Highbrow,* lit., a person with a receding hairline, which has long signified a person of intellectual and arty tastes. An *egghead* is a highbrow whose hair has receded all the way to his nape, but remains distinct from Am. slang *skinhead,* which means simply "bald," with no intellectual implication. The original *egghead* was prob. Adlai Stevenson, who was bald, intellectual, and an unconvincing presidential candidate, first in 1952; but the term came to be applied to the intellectuals who supported his candidacy, and then retroactively to FDR's *brain trust* (which see). Among the anthropoid, lowbrow furheads of Main Street, it became a term of contempt and of distrust for anyone who could quote a book or speak in anything other than the established clichés.]

egg in your beer   In the mocking Am. phrase, *whaddaya want—egg in your beer?* reprimanding a person who asks for a luxury beyond reason, or at least proportion. Variantly, *You want egg in your beer, go check into the Ritz,* implying, "Don't look for luxurious pampering among us plain folks." [A well-established Am. idiom ignored, to the best of my knowledge, by all sources. Dating unknown, but perhaps of XIX origin. I am not a beer drinker, but none of many I have questioned have ever heard of breaking an egg into beer. Lacking firm information (eagerly solicited) I can only speculate that this is a transfer idiom from "egg with your beer." (But I cannot find that form anywhere.) Many beer joints keep jars of variously pickled eggs on the counter for sale to those who wish to munch as they swig. "Egg with your beer" might refer to a moocher who gets someone to buy him a glass of beer and then asks, additionally, for an egg; hence, one not satisfied with a little, but who wants it all. Plausible, but ???]

egg on To urge. To incite. [Sometimes but wrongly explained as a corruption of "to edge on," but this is a straight-line evolution from IE *ak-*, sharp (ACUTE, ACRID), with k/g in Gmnc. → ON *eggia*, to spur, goad, incite (EAGER). OE *eggian* has the ON senses. The ME form was *eggen.* "They that egge a consente to the sinne bin partners of the sinne" (Chaucer, The Parson's Tale). Chaucer also used eggement for "incitement." *The last time I went on stage I was incited to the exit, both egged off and tomatoed off. I knew I shouldn't have tried to play Salome.*]

eggplant The plant and fruit, most commonly of the deep, purplish-brown, squash-shaped variety. There is, however, a white variety, generally more rounded and often smaller. First OED citation is dated 1767. It is a folkname, and clearly a ref. to the smaller white variety, which was probably the first to be introduced into English gardens. Folknames are generally accurate, and this one simply would make no sense with ref. to the various purple varieties, also called *aubergine* (which see) and, earlier, *Guinea squash.* The young white fruit, however, does resemble an egg. Cf. Ger. *Eierpflanze,* lit. "eggs plant" or "plant of eggs." But It. *melanzana* clearly refers to the purple variety, < Gk. *melanos,* black; with *zana,* basket, hence with root sense "black basket."

SOCIO-HISTORIC. Vineland, N.J., boosts itself as the Eggplant Capital of the World; a booster's hyperbole. It does, however, grow and ship about half of the commercial eggplants of the eastern U.S.A. In boosters' ritual, it has an annual Eggplant Festival with an Eggplant Queen (always in an aubergine gown), and a feast consisting of many different eggplant dishes topped off with eggplant cake and washed down, alas, with eggplant wine.

eggshell Aside from its literal signification, a worthless thing once cracked and the egg removed. (Though in the rituals of high cuisine eggshells, ever plentiful in restaurants, are essential in purifying and repurifying consommé. So to all things their seasons and stations.) [Shakespeare, *Hamlet* IV.iv:

> Exposing what is mortal and unsure
> To all that fortune, death, and danger dare,
> Even for an egg-shell.

So Hamlet, soliloquizing on the passage of Fortinbras and his army.

Note that he might have said, "Even for a trifle/a mere trifle/a worthless trifle." Every standard word-form would have been forceless. Shakespeare therefore brushed *words* aside in order to insert a *thing* (image), whereupon, in the natural course of language, the thing became idiom.]

eggbeater 1. The kitchen device. Distinct from a whisk in having a crank and gears to rotate wires that do the work of the whisk. Later an electric device. 2. An early, now faded, name for a helicopter, but the kindred names *chopper* and *whirlybird* survive.

eighta from Decatah (county seat of Wise) *Crap shooting.* The traditional cry of a shooter who seeks to roll an eight in order to make his point. [Am. Dating uncertain but prob. mid-XIX. This cry is probable in two parts. The first suggests the rhyming slang characteristic of black English. Cf. the traditional cry by a roller seeking a four: *Little Joe from Kokimo. Eighta from Decatah* was by itself enough to provide a rhyming chant and was probably in use before someone—probably from Texas—added the tag about the county seat, for according to my search of U.S. counties, only Wise County, Texas has as its county seat Decatur.

Crap shooters in the U.S. have always tended to call on their Lady Luck with about the same enthusiasm of a stadium crowd cheering for its team. There has always been a certain flash about "talking to the dice," often with the sort of exuberant whimsy that has marked sthrn. country rhetoric. Perhaps the most ornate of these cries, the standard one for summoning a nine, is *Nina!* commonly elaborated to *Nina with the golden boobies!* commonly further elaborated to *Nina with the golden boobies, come home to love you big-titted slut!*]

Elmo: St. Elmo's fire A luminous glow observed by sailors at the tips of masts and at yardarms, during or before electrical storms. It has also been observed at the tips of steeples and trees, and recently about the wingtips of airplanes. Never entirely explained, the phenomenon is prob. a luminous discharge of static electricity.

HISTORIC. St. Elmo is the English name of St. Peter Gonzalez (ca. 1190–1246), a Spanish Dominican who spent most of his life working with seafarers of the Spanish coast. He was canonized as the patron of seamen. His feast day is April 14.

For reasons I am unable to explain he was once commonly confused with Erasmus, an auxiliary saint martyred under Diocletian (Feast Day, June 2). I can find no record that Erasmus had anything to do with the sea, but *Elmo* is a corruption of *Erasmus* by some such sequence as *Erasmo* → *Ermo* → *Elmo*.

This luminosity is associated with electrical storms, and piously superstitious sailors took it to be the visible body and radiance of their patron saint descended to protect them, whence the Port. name for this phenomenon *corpo santo,* lit. body of the saint, or saintly body, the Port. name passing into XVII Eng. as *corposant.*

The phenomenon, of course, and various legends about it preceded Christianity. Roman sailors took this luminosity as a sign that Castor and Pollux had descended to protect them, as they once defended the Romans and even fought with them in their victory over the Latians in the battle of Lake Regillus, ca. 496 B.C.

emancipation   [At root, "the act of unhanding." < L, *manus,* hand; prefixed *e(x)-,* away from. But L. *manus* was powerfully operative with the sense "controlling hand of authority." MANAGEMENT, MANDATE, MANIFEST, MANUMIT; all still retain in Eng. a part of the original sense of the authority of the master's hand. In early Roman law, ritual required the master to lay his hand on a newly acquired slave to symbolize possession and absolute authority. Later this ritual was neglected when gangs of slaves were acquired to work country estates, but it continued in the case of house slaves and personal attendants. And the freeing ceremony of emancipation or manumission, the removal of the master's controlling hand, being a personal recognition, continued in force.] 1. The act of freeing a slave: *The Emancipation Proclamation.* 2. *Ext.* Applied to some, but not all, forms of release from imposed authority: *the emancipated woman.* (But note that among other emancipated persons, prisoners are released, servicemen are discharged, and hostages are set free or ransomed.)

emery   An abrasive polishing agent made of impure ground corundum. [Gk. **smuris,* emery, powdered corundum. The initial *s* may have been retained in the vulgar L. name for this powder (prob., though unattested, *smericulum,* and again in OF *esmeril,* which underwent a common alteration to *emeri,* whence ME *emery.* Thus, through minor alteration, the same word since the beginning.]

     emery bag, emery ball, emery strawberry A pincushion filled with emery powder. In common use through XIX and into XX for keeping pins and needles clean. They were, in effect, polished by every insertion into the powder. [The first two names are self-evident. The third, because the industrious housewife and her needle cannot be kept from decorating, whence the bag or ball was sewn to look like a fruit. I would not be surprised to find an emery apple, but given red flannel in common supply, a large strawberry was inevitable.]

HISTORIC. Before the development of stainless steel, needles and pins were commonly plagued by rust, making them brittle, hard to pass through heavy material, and likely to stain fabrics they were passed through. Fine needles and pins, moreover, were scarce and expensive before they began to be mass produced in late XIX. Through most of XIX even nails were usually hand forged, and mass-produced wood screws were not commonly available until the 1890s. The prudent housewife-seamstress preserved her needles and pins by using her emery bag not only for safe keeping, but as a scourer, polisher, and to some extent as a desiccant.

eminence grise   A revered senior figure. A senior statesman, a good gray poet, an esteemed artist or social figure at the still-functioning end of a notable career. (But also used for one retired from and above the battle.) [A loan phrase from the Fr. for "gray eminence" with "gray" as a ref. to hoary-headed old age.]

HISTORIC. First applied to Father Joseph (Père Joseph) François Leclerc du Tremblay (1577–1638), a French soldier who turned priest and again soldier and diplomat, serving as the intimate counselor of Richelieu. He died at age 71 just as he was about to be created a cardinal. The austerity of his personal life, together with his enormous influence on French and European affairs, created about him an aura that led to the common appelation, *l'éminence grise.*

engine   1. *Now.* A mechanical device for converting energy into motion. 2. *Earlier.* Any ingenious device. [In XIII such devices as battering rams, catapults, and siege towers were called engines. A tank may yet be called "an engine of war." The human brain has been called an engine. Root sense, "ingenious device." Ult. < IE *gen(e)-*, to give birth (GENERATE). See stem *gen-* in *Browser's I.* Whence L. *ingenium,* genius, inborn talent, skill.]

USAGE. Since early XIX *engine* has more or less connoted "self-mover," prob. by association with locomotive engine, and *motor* has connoted "device fixed in place." I have also seen the suggested distinction that an engine carries its power source with it, and that a *motor* has its power supplied from outside. Yet the distinctions blur. A three-engine plane was once commonly called a *tri-motor* and the Ford Motor Company manufactures engines. Yet the language convention dictates electric *motor*, never *engine*. And so steam *engine*, internal combustion *engine*, diesel *engine*, never *motor*.

English   Also *english* Spin imparted to a ball to control its motion, as in billiards. [Shortened from earlier *body English*, involuntary body motions whereby a player (as a bowler, for example) seeks to "speak" to the ball to direct it to the exact target. Cf. *body language*.

Dating and point of origin uncertain. P. *Slang* (Supplement) assigns *english* a Canadian origin ca. 1918 and seems to imply that *body English* is also Canadian. This work, however, tends almost systematically to assign a Canadian origin to Americanisms that have passed into Brit. use, as if they could not make it across the Atlantic without a Canadian visa. Webster's NWD, without citation or comment, stars *body English* as an Americanism. I can only guess that both terms were in Am. use before 1900.]

English horn   Also but less commonly *cor anglais*. This instrument is not a horn but a double-reed woodwind akin to the oboe but pitched a fifth lower, slightly larger, and ending in a bulblike bell. The reed is placed in a metal crook at the top of the instrument and at an angle to it. [Developed in Vienna ca. 1760, it was called *cor* because early specimens were curved (like the horn of a bull?), this type remaining common until ca. 1900. It is now largely replaced by a straight form first exhibited in Paris in 1839.

Some find the name mysterious, for if it is not a horn, neither has it any specific connection with England. The *Encyclopedia Britannica* goes as far as to suggest that it may be named after the "Anglo-Hanoverian bugle horn," but the suggestion seems random, especially since no instrument was ever given that name. In the absence of firm evidence, I can only suggest that it must first have been called *cors anglé*, angled horn, with reference to the placement of the mouthpiece at an angle to the body of the instrument. If so, English emerged in the name because *Anglais* is a homonym of *angle*. This derivation is speculative but speaks louder on its own merits than any nonexistent bugle.]

epicure   1. *As now commonly understood*, A Feinschmecker. One with elegant taste in food and drink. 2. *Earlier*, One devoted to the pursuit of every sort of physical pleasure and gratification. A hedonist (in the root sense of Gk. *hēdonē*, pleasure). But the sense includes gourmet, gourmand, libertine, aesthete. (Note that *epicu-*

rean functions as an adj. but also as a noun, and when capitalized, in the root sense:) **Epicurean** A follower of the Greek philosopher Epicurus (died 270 B.C.), who taught that the gods take no interest in the doings of mankind, that there is no immortality of the soul, and that the one good of mortal existence is to seek pleasure and gratification while avoiding pain.

HISTORIC. Such a doctrine brought the medieval followers of Epicurus into head-on conflict with Catholic doctrine. In his *Inferno,* Dante dooms the Epicureans to the top circle of the middle hell, where they are punished for the sin of violence against God, the sin contained in their heresy. Because they insisted that there is no life after death, they are made to lie in eternal tombs which, as a further reminder, are full of raging fires. With Dante's use of this label as a point of reference, we may see how much the sense of the word has softened since early XIV.

epiphany   [Gk. *epi-,* near, about (but here primarily as an intensive prefix); with *phainein,* to show; hence, a manifestation, a revelation.] 1. *Theology.* A manifestation of divinity. A revelation. 2. *Capitalized.* The Christian festival of the Twelfth Night (January 6), celebrating the revelation to the Magi of Christ's divine nature. 3. *Literary criticism.* A term for something like "the moment of revelation" in a piece of writing. [Like *charisma* (which see) for what books on salesmanship used to call "personal dynamism," *epiphany* is an overreach word that was soon picked up by intellectual apes and enshrined as a Big Word on Campus (BWOC). In its name English majors spontaneously gave up mere reading in an obsessive hunt for *epiphanies* so profound that not even the author was aware of them.]

e pur si muove   [It. "And still it moves."] A formula for recanting a recantation.

HISTORIC. Under the aegis of the powerful Medici, Galileo Galilei (1564–1642) came from exile to Florence and developed the first telescope, demonstrating thereby (against church teaching) that the earth moved around the sun. Upon the death of his powerful patron he was forced to recant. Even this decree was in deference to the still-powerful Medici, for a standard punishment for heresy was the stake.

Galileo, in no mood to be barbecued, made a ritual public recantation of his findings and was spared. He is reputed to have muttered after the recantation, "e pur si muove," but he was no fool, and of course he did not, for had he done so he would have burned.

He certainly kept his mental reservations, but it must have been his admirers—probably his later admirers—who phrased his sentiments for him as if he himself had spoken them.

escrow   1. A legal agreement reserving a grant of money or property in the custody of a third party until the grantee has waited a specified time or has satisfied other conditions specified by the grantor. 2. *As a mortgage condition,* Sums stipulated to be set aside for taxes, insurance, and specially specified maintenance, and paid by the mortgagee in addition to the scheduled payments on principal and interest. [At root, "piece of paper cut from a larger piece." Effective root sense, "legal document." The form of the word is ult. < IE *sker-*, to cut; zero-grade form *skr'-* (SCRATCH, SCRAPE, SCREW, SCORE). The sense is from legal history.]
    HISTORIC. Before modern methods of making copies by carbon or by reproduction, documents were written at least twice in what was called "fair copies," on an extra-large (legal-size) piece of *fool'-scap* (so called < Italian *foglio capo,* large sheet, master sheet; later watermarked with a jester's belled cap as a matter of word association). These copies were then cut apart with an irregular serrated edge *(indenture),* the validity of the separated documents being established when the "teeth" of the *indenture* (the word now means "legal document") matched. The root sense of *escrow* is a variant reference to this method of copying and verifying legal documents.

Eskimo Pie   The registered trade name of a chocolate-covered ice-cream bar on a stick. Now fixed in the vocabulary of every child, and thence to decrepitude. [Am. Introduced in 1921. One of the early commercial uses of electrical refrigeration. Popsicle (obviously based on *popup* and *icicle*) followed to market (and into standard Am.) about 1928, along with various frozen puddings. The most recent of this genre may be the chocolate-covered ice-cream ball sold from supermarket freezers for storage in the now-common home freezer.]
    HISTORIC. Manufactured ice began to be common in the early 1920s, frozen foods following soon thereafter, made newly possible by refrigeration coils. From the early 1920s until WWII the iceman's horse-drawn wagon commonly delivered "made ice," basically in 100-pound blocks that showed a definite crystalline structure resembling that of refrigerator ice-cubes. The earlier pond ice (the ponds were not always polluted) tended to fewer crystalline striations and to fewer air bubbles.

The young probably need to be told that pond ice in proper storage and well covered with sawdust would keep from winter to winter-again. Nor was a surface coating of sawdust a problem, for it would disappear with the first melt. Ice, if clean to begin with, is self-cleaning as it melts.

Today's frozen foods require a temperature below that of natural ice.

every man has his price Some settle for less, some hold out for more, but everyone can be bought. [A cynically accurate generalization, now semiproverbial, and in fact a sort of folk-evolution; but this one is late, and is a folk corruption of the XVIII original, "all those men have their price" (which could be argued to imply that other men, not of that group, might be incorruptible). With or without that implication, the original was said by Robert Walpole, first earl of Oxford (1676–1754), prime minister of England 1721–1742. In his ever-stormy political career Walpole seemed to specialize in making enemies, all of whom he believed to be venal, probably with sufficient reason. In any case he was saying, "all my enemies are crooks," a specification far removed from that of the surviving altered generalization.

For a similar much-altered sense see *Philadelphia lawyer (Browser's I)*. As W. H. Auden wrote, "The words of the dead man / Are modified in the guts of the living."]

execrate To damn. To denounce. To declare one's hatred of. [Up to XVIII to pronounce a formal malediction upon. Since then the formal malediction has lost most of the terror that caused, say, Rigoletto to recoil, saying, "Quel vecchio mi ha maledotto!" spoken in deep fear for his immortal soul and its future. In XIX and XX the sense has become more nearly, "harsh denunciation" (but without magico-religious consequences to the soul of the person so denounced).

But earlier execration tended to be formal and spiritually powerful (see *bell, book, and candle* for the ultimate execration). < L. *execrāri*, to pronounce a religiously powerful curse upon, < *sacrāre*, to make sacred, to consecrate, < *sacer*, sacred (SACERDOTAL); with prefix *ex-*, here meaning "opposite of." Ult. < IE *sak-*, sacred, to sanctify. SACROSANCT, CORPOSANT, SAINT, CONSECRATE.]

experience meeting *Archaic.* A religious service in which members of the congregation rise and testify to the validity and depth of their religious experiences. [In Am. common use by mid-XIX, though the act of giving open-meeting testimony to religious experience had precedent in British dissident sects of XVIII and even XVII. Such testifying survives in the meetings of various fundamentalist revivalist groups. And something of the sort goes on, though at the altar of psychology, in group therapy, and in what are now called "encounter groups." Today also called "consciousness-raising sessions."]

eye-opener   1. Any revelation that shows things as they truly are, i.e., "opens one's eyes" to reality: *It was an eye-opener to find Millicent in bed with the rest of my barbershop quartet, and in close harmony.* 2. A prebreakfast drink of hard liquor, especially when one is hung over. [Sense 1 was in Am. use through all of XIX with British precedents. Cf. the timeless expression *nine days (days') wonder,* based on the observation that cats and puppies open their eyes after nine days and begin to see the world as it really is. Sense 2, though with a sense shift, has been in use about as long.]

$\mathcal{F}$

face: put on her face   To apply cosmetics. [P. *Slang* gives this form as Brit., ca. 1931. Perhaps. I believe it was in Am. use a bit earlier than that, but memory plays tricks, and I can find no attestation. In any case the form has long been common in Am. The cosmetic kit is a standard article of ladies' luggage, and it is now common for an American woman to refer to her kit as "my face."]

faculty   1. Inherent capability (in plu., one's total inherent capabilities): *to strain one's faculties.* 2. The instructional body of a school, as distinct from the administrative, public-relations, and fund-raising staffs: *Old deans never die; they simply lose their faculties.* [< L. *facilis,* facile; *facultas,* enabling (facilitating) power. *Anyone can learn from a sage: learn to learn from a fool and the whole world is your faculty.*]

fame   Widespread favorable recognition: *Churchill was a famous statesman; Hitler, an infamous one.* (Sometimes confused with *reputation,* but there is a distinction to be preserved. Charles A. Lindbergh, for example, was famous the instant he completed his transatlantic flight, and before he had acquired any general reputation.) [At root, "what is said (about)." < L. *fama,* talk, < *fari* to talk, to speak. Akin to Gk. *phanai,* to talk. Both are ult. < IE *bha-,* to speak. The voiced stop *bh-,* as demonstrated by Grimm, alters to *f* (prob. in Italic) on passing into Latin, whence, with a verb suffix, → L. *fari.* The same stem underwent a bh/ph (prob. in Hellenic), and with an *-m-* suffix became Gk. *phēmē,* a saying, a thing said.

Is the IE root *bha-* ult. echoic of the "ba-ba-ba" of infant prattle? I know of no way to answer the question with any certainty, but it must be asked. And note Gk. *barbaros,* stranger, enemy (BARBARIAN), but at root "one of those (contemptible people) whose speech sounds like nothing but ba-ba-ba."]

family 1. A parent-and-offspring group; mother, father, and the children. But readily extended to include as many as four generations, and extended again to include the whole kinship group of nephews, nieces, and cousins. 2. Any related group: *family of man, of languages, of ideas.* 3. In the Mafia, a crime group under a single head *(capo).* This family is often a kinship group, but nonkin are usually taken into it on certain strict conditions. [< L. *familia,* a household, including the servants. < **famulus,* servant.]

all in the family In private and privileged standing. Not a public matter.

family jewels Whimsical. The penis, especially Daddy's. [See *schmuck.*]

family name A surname. [Rare in English until ca. 1200, and then restricted to landed persons of rank. In Wales surnames did not come into common use until late XIX. In *Browser's I,* see *surname, nickname.*]

family tree 1. A genealogical record starting with any two progenitors as roots and the descendants as branches. 2. A diagram of this trace. 3. Anyone's historical line of descent, if he or she has one.

in the family way Pregnant.

familial Of the family.

familiar adj. 1. Root sense, "of the family." [But this root sense has been largely usurped by *familial.* Hence the more recent, and primary senses:] 2. Usual, habituated, intimate: *"Young man," she said, "you are becoming too familiar." n.* A witch's or warlock's attendant spirit, often in animal form. Also commonly *familiar spirit.* And archaically, *a familiar* A servant. [This is, of course, the root sense.]

family hold back Also often *f.h.b.* A common admonition by a middle-class matron who is having guests for dinner and is not sure there will be enough of the "special dish" she has prepared. The family is to eat only lightly of that dish lest there be none left if a guest asks for seconds. (I say "middle-class matron" because the wealthy would not need to scrimp in trying to make an impression, because the farm wife would heap her table as a matter of course, and because the poor cannot afford to pretend.) [I had always assumed this to be an Am. formula, but P. *Catch Phrases* glosses it as Brit., since mid-XIX, giving the primary Brit. forms as *family, hands off!* and *family, hold off.* I have always heard the Am. variant as an equally stressed "family-hold-back," whereas P. treats the Brit. variant as *"family—hold off!"* P. says this form was common up to WWII. If it is passing in Brit. it seems to remain current in Am.]

fantod, fantad   And commonly, *the fantods* The condition of being unstrung, ill at ease; of having the heebie-jeebies: *Ted Gorey divides his time between his cats and his fantods.* [OED calls it an "unmeaning formation suggested by FANTASTIC." The earliest citation is 1867 nautical, "a name given to the fidgets of officers." In 1883, W. C. Russell, in *Sailors' Language,* defines it variantly as, "A fiddling officer who is always bothering over something small." But Mark Twain, *Huckleberry Finn* (1884), "they always gave me the fan-tads" (made me eerily uneasy). (Twain, in his river-pilot days, seems to have picked up a number of nautical terms, prob. from sailors in New Orleans—see *galleywest, Browser's I.*) His hyphenation here suggests that he understood the term as, perhaps, "the fantasy tadpoles, or toads." In any case this bit of language whimsy comes down without an etymological trace.

　　The fantods are enough to give one the *mulligrubs,* mental, psychic depression. This form is cited by OED as "a grotesque arbitrary formation," prob. < *mouldy* or *mealy grubs.* And between the fantods and mulligrubs, see *megrim.*]

Fata Morgana   An ancient bit of folk spookery, the legend common to most of Europe in various forms. [It. "the fairy Morgana," which may be rendered "the pale witch." Prob. < Arabic *mārgān,* coral (conceived as "pale stone").

　　(Prob. akin to Gk. *margarita,* pearl. And the stem *margarit-* functions in most Romance languages, and in German, for "daisy" (pale flower, pearl flower). The tequila drink called in Spanish *margarita* is named after the daisy, because the wet glasses are dipped in salt, acquiring a white rim.

　　In Italian folk legend Fata Morgana labels a mirage commonly observed off the Calabrian coast. It causes objects to appear inverted and was believed to be caused by witchcraft.

　　The legendary witch of such doings turned up in England as *Morgan le Fay,* Morgana the Witch, the nebulous sister of King Arthur. Arthur, of course, had magic powers of his own, his legend deriving from the Dawn Age figure of the absolute tribal chief who was king, father, witch doctor, rainmaker, and demigod. In later legend, however, most of Arthur's magic powers were subsumed by Merlin, in whose shadow pale Morgan/Morgana grew ever dimmer. *Fata* should be rendered as Fay or Witch, not as Fate.]

fawn[1] *v.* Usu. *fawn upon* 1. To show obsequious but sincere pleasure, as dogs sometimes do. 2. To show obsequious pleasure but self-seekingly. [Of obscure Gmnc. origin. OE *faegnian,* to show pleasure, to take pleasure in. With the *g* silenced, as commonly happened in going from OE to ME → *fain,* as in archaic, "I fain would," i.e., I would gladly.]

fawn[2] *n.* 1. A young deer. 2. The tawny color of a young deer. [Ult. < IE *dhei-,* to suck (as does an infant). As demonstrated by Grimm's Law the voiced stop *dh-* regularly changes to *f* in passing into Latin, whence the new root *fei-,* which, suffixed *-to-,* became Latin *fetus,* an offspring ("newborn sucking thing"), whence Eng. *fetus,* with sense alteration to "embryo" ("a soon-will-be-sucking thing"). I do not understand how L. *fetus* became OF *feon, foun,* which came to mean "a young animal," but ME took over *foun,* with later alteration to *fawn,* and narrowed the sense further to "a young deer."]

featherbed *n.* ["Bed" here for "mattress."] 1. A tick stuffed with feathers, and ideally with pure down. *Hence,* 2. A symbol of luxury.

HISTORIC. The fairy-tale princess so delicate that she was bruised by a pea placed under twenty mattresses must have been used to beds of purest goose-down. But it was scarce. The ideal down is found only on the breast and on some of the body parts under the wings of the goose. The number of geese that had to be plucked to stuff one mattress with such down presumed a diet available only to kings and great lords. Mistresses of lesser estate dreamed that by saving goose-down all their lives and passing it on to their children they might endow the family with a true down featherbed, if only in a number of generations. In necessary practice, however, small feathers were mixed with the down. But even small feathers have incipient barbs whose points can work through the fabric of the ticking—and imagine how such protruding points might scratch the fairy-tale princess. Beds were rated by their down content, the very best being free of feathers. Good featherbeds were family treasures passed on from generation to generation. The "second-best bed" mentioned in Shakespeare's reputed will was such a mattress of less than pure down.

Any reasonably good featherbed represented luxury at a time that most people slept on hay or straw. As late as XIX straw remained the main mattress filling, replaced then by finely shaved wood curlings. See *excelsior* in *Browser's I.* Padded inner-spring mattresses are a technology that was not available even in crude form much before 1900.

featherbedding   *Union work rules.* The practice of protecting jobs by insisting that wages be paid to workers who have nothing to do. Also in the verb form *to featherbed* To insist by union contract that workers with nothing to do be retained on the payroll as idle presences. [From *featherbed,* especially in sense 2, to be luxuriously idle.]

HISTORIC. In U.S. unionism featherbedding was originally associated with the firemen on railroad locomotives. When in the 1920s U.S. railroads converted variously to diesel or to electric locomotives, the fireman was no longer needed for passing coal. He continued to ride in the locomotive, however, because the union protected his job, arguing in part that he was an apprentice engineer and could not otherwise learn the trade. Since that time featherbedding has become especially common in the theater, insuring pay for musicians who do not play and for stage hands who have no work to do, or who have only token tasks. The earliest use of the term, however, was Brit. P. *Slang* dates it from early XX as "the practice of making things very easy for an elderly or indisposed member of a gang of *e.g.* dockers."

Fell, Doctor Fell   Any senior person one dislikes, especially a pedant. [After John Fell (1625–1686), dean of Christchurch, Oxford. He expelled Tom Brown and achieved a doggerel immortality in Brown's jingle, known to all literate persons:

> I do not like thee, Doctor Fell,
> The reason why I cannot tell;
> But this alone I know full well—
> I do not like thee Doctor Fell.

If Tom Brown's Latin was no better than his prosody, Dr. Fell probably acted reasonably in "rusticating" him, but this bit of doggerel has survived, probably because everyone has at some time had a teacher who would do for Dr. Fell.]

felon   *n.* 1. *Now, at law.* Person guilty of a crime more serious than a misdemeanor. 2. *Earlier.* A villain. A depraved person. At root, a term of revulsion. There is some evidence that the root *fel-, fell-* once expressed the revulsion some men feel for homosexual *fellatio,* the associated sense having once possibly been what taboo slang calls "cocksucker," this sense being not attested but strongly suggested by the various senses this root has developed in various languages. OED touches upon this speculation but recoils from the discussion as an unmentionable.

The discussion is further confused by the fact that two IE roots seem to have merged here. 1. *dhei-*, to suck (primarily, what an infant does); with the regular shift dh/f and suffixed *-l-* → L. *fellare*, to suck. (The same root, suffixed *-m-*, → 1. *femina*, woman ("she who gives suck.") 2. *ghel-*, brightness, to shine (YELLOW). With another regular shift of gh/f → L. *fel*, bile, venom, odious stuff. (So It. *veleno*, poison. Akin to Danish *fael*, foul. And note that in Eng. *felon* also means "whitlow," a bright, discolored, pus-filled inflammation near a fingernail. This association, let me suggest, is not too far from that of a swollen penis about to discharge (puslike) semen.)

These merged(?) roots have functioned in various languages with the senses: deadly, foul, unnatural, merciless, pus, to suck. It is this distribution of senses that leads to the conjecture about early association with the idea "disgustingly perverted, 'unnatural' sex." Some of the associated senses in English are in the following terms.

fellatio The act of taking the penis into the mouth for stimulation/discharge. [New L. < L. *fellatus* < *fellare*, to suck.]

fell Deadly. Merciless. Godlessly unrestrained. Perverse. See Danish *fael*, above. [Like *felon* the word earlier connoted utter villainy/perversion, and has come to mean "legally culpable." Shakespeare illustrates both senses. In *Titus Andromachus* V.iii., "For these fell faults our brothers were beheaded." (Sense: "legal guilt.") And in *Midsummer Night's Dream* V.i., "That no compunctions, visitings of nature / Shake my fell purpose" ("determined evil beyond all restraint of God or man").]

felo da se Also *felo de se* Plu. *felones (feles) da se. In church and legal L.* Suicide (viewed as a mortal sin, depravity, foul violation of God's order of things).

HISTORIC. Dante places the suicides in hell. Denied even human semblance (since they threw theirs away) they grow inside stunted bushes fed upon by loathsome Harpies. Only when the Harpies tear them can they speak or lament—as they bleed.

Yet (see notes to *catty-caitiff-cattivo*), in Roman convention, suicide was the only honorable course for a soldier about to be captured and enslaved ("to die like a Roman"). Cato of Utica killed himself in this high Roman tradition, and Dante, who condones nothing in the similar suicide of Pier delle Vigne, gives Cato an honored post as the guardian of the shores of purgatory, with the promise of further honors to come on Judgment Day.

And still traditional church practice has denied to suicides holy rites and burial in holy ground, for their souls were believed to be damned to hell.

felony murder Law. Murder committed in the course of a felony. [Equivalent, strictly speaking, to a charge of first degree murder brought against *all the criminal accomplices.* If it is possible to believe a lawyer, one informed me that when three hoods held up a liquor store and the proprietor shot and killed one of them, the other two were charged with felony murder of the well-deceased on the grounds that their felony was the direct cause of his social improvement by means of gunshot wounds.]

fettle   *In metallurgy. v.* To line a form or hearth with sand or loose ore before pouring molten metal. *n.* The lining material so used. [This special technical sense, implying "to make fit for use," is the only common survival except for the frozen word formula *in fine fettle.* Earlier *fettle* signified to make fit or to be prepared in any context: so *ill fettled meal,* ill-prepared meal; and *well fettled arms,* weapons in good battle order. Ult. < IE *ped-,* container, contained. With p/f and d/t in Gmnc. → OE *faet,* tun, *fetel,* girdle. (Akin to Ger. *Fessel,* chain, band; ON *fetill,* strap, bandage. All these early senses imply "thing that contains"; the associated sense has become "contained and therefore ready." So:) ME *fetten,* to give shape to, to make ready. Now, as noted, obs. except in:] *in fine fettle* In excellent bodily or spiritual condition. [Said of a living thing, as of a person or of a race horse ready to run. Implies health, alertness, good spirits. For things, i.e., mechanisms, one might say *in fine kilter* except that idiom never developed such a positive construction, though the negative *out of kilter,* not working, is common. (For *kilter,* see *Browser's I.*)]

fiddle-dee-dee   Stuff and nonsense. An idea or remark dismissed as inane trivia. [A language element still in common use. Boswell reports its use by Johnson in XVIII, but it was almost certainly earlier, with precedent in XVI *fiddle-faddle,* same sense (as if "no more than a dee-dee played by a fiddler.")]

field corn   Corn raised as food for livestock, as distinct from *sweet corn* or, sometimes, *eating corn* or *garden corn* grown for human consumption, though field corn, if picked young and tender, can be eaten boiled or roasted. [Am. prob. XIX (post-colonial) for it was in XIX that the table varieties of sweet corn were developed, colonial corn being for both the farmer and the farm animals. In a sense this is an absurd name long sanctioned by the idiomatic convention. Cf. *head over heels* (the proper order of things) for upside down; *ass-backward* (ditto) for in reversed order, and also well-established *time clock* (what else is a clock for?) for *punch clock*. One might reasonably ask, "Where else would you raise corn if not in a field —in the house?" A partial answer is supplied by *garden corn,* i.e., corn not raised in a (large) field. Were language a matter of logic, *fodder corn* might be asserted as the only defensible name; but damn the absurdity, full idiom ahead, for *field corn* seems to be firmly fixed in the American language, and since neither the farmer nor his livestock seems to object to this phrasing, the logician is left clientless.]

fifth column   Any organization that aims to infiltrate a government or other organization and to overthrow it from within. In U.S. political rhetoric the term came to be applied to crypto-Communists, then to any American Communist, and then to any political opponent whose views one sought to stigmatize as treasonous. [But the original fifth columnists were Spanish Franco-Fascists. In 1936, during the Spanish War between largely leftist loyalists and fascist insurgents led by Generalissimo Francisco Franco with the support of Hitler, Mussolini, and a large force of Muslims, General Emilio Mola, leading the attack on Madrid, was reported as saying that he had four columns attacking from outside the city, and a fifth column working within it to assist him by sabotage and guerrilla warfare. Whether the phrase was his or coined by a journalist, it became almost instantly fixed as a term of political rhetoric.]

find 'em, fool 'em, fuck 'em, and forget 'em   The first of the standing orders in the "Macho Manual of Arms" by Bombastus Braggadocio. [I was first drilled to these orders in WWII and received them as essential GI pith, but P. *Catch Phrases* lists *find, fool, fuck—and forget* in Brit. naval use since ca. 1890.]

Flatbush   "Out there," from Manhattan. [Du. *t'vlacke bos,* lit., the flat woods (bosk), in effect, "the treed plain." *Bosky* has some survival in literary usage for "woodsy," and we are accustomed to *bosc pear,* though few associate the name with "woods pear," and *bosk* for woods is standard but beyond the colloquial vocabulary. The rareness of these senses in common usage, combined with the fact Dutch *bos* meant nothing to English-speaking settlers (and *vlacke,* less), offers a good example of what happens to the pronunciation of strange or unknown word elements, though I suppose the Du.

name might as readily have been corrupted to Fatbuzz or Flatboss, or Flatbooze, or Blackbooze—except that who would want to live there?—except that who wants to in any case?]

flibbertigibbet   *In Am.,* A prattling, inane, gossipy person, but primarily an impertinent overtalkative or smarty child who affects airs. [In earlier Brit., and surviving, a gossipy woman who pays attention to everything but her own business. An exuberant formation. The earliest form cited by OED (1549) is flibbergib, soon followed by Mrs. Flibber de Jibb, a form that suggests a flapping jibsail (her tongue), but early altered as if under the influence of *gibbet,* though perh. as the result of some lost reduplicative form, such as *flibb-ity jibb-ity.*

   Medieval writers often gave grotesquely comic (gargoyle) names to fiends. In this tradition, Dante named some of his friends *Graffiacane* (Dog Scratcher), *Malacoda* (Bad Tail), and *Barbariccia* (Curlybeard). Langland in *Piers Plowman* gave us *Ragamuffyn* (see *ragamuffin*). And Harsnet's *Popish Impostures* mentions the fiend *Flibberdigibbet* along with *Hoberdidance* and others. But those who have cited *flibbertigibbet* as "originally a fiend's name" have ignored the fact that *Popish Impostures* was published in 1603, more than half a century after the first attested use with the very different sense given above. Harsnet was following the medieval tradition in fiends' names, but he borrowed this one from existing English sources.]

foible   A minor personal weakness, habit, trait, inclination. [OF *foible,* variant of *faible,* weak. But Fr. *foible,* in fencing, became a noun designating the weaker, more pliable half of a sword blade from its midpoint to its point, the half from midpoint to hilt being called the *forte* (which see).]

foment   To incite, to instigate an action, esp. a disturbance. Most commonly in *to foment a riot.* It would not do, for instance, to say, *Pope John Paul is forever fomenting peace.* [At root, "to treat with heat (as in bringing a boil to a head)," to apply a poultice or hot compress.

   The form of the word is ult. < IE *dh'gwh-,* to burn. The voiced stop *dh* regularly changes to *f* in Latin (Grimm's Law), and the *(g)w(h)* to *v,* whence altered skeletal stem *fv-* → *fovere,* to apply heat (FEVER), p.p. *fomentus,* treated with heat, substantive *fomentum,* poultice.]

forte [< L. *fortis*, strong. (So *fort*, a strongpoint.) So *pianoforte*, lit., "(instrument that plays) soft (and) strong." Ult. < IE *bhergh-*, high. (See *bhergh-*, *Browser's I*.) The sense evolution over the millennia has been from *high* to *high place* (a militarily defensible position for a nomad's encampment) to *settlement defended by high walls* (Pitts*burgh*), to *strong*. With a standard shift of the voiced stop *bh* to *f* in Latin → abbreviated skeletal (vowel swallowed) root *f'r-*, with suffix *-t-* → L. *fortis*, strong.

But the special sense of *forte* (pron. *fort*) in Fr. and Eng. is from fencing, as below.] 1. One's strong point, that at which one excels. *Bea Snyder's forte is a weakness for Bob.* 2. *At root, in fencing.* The relatively inflexible part of a sword blade, especially of a rapier, between the middle and the hilt. [The weaker, more pliable, other half is the *foible*. A fencer who receives his opponent's *foible* on his *forte* is in a desirable position to parry and counterthrust. *Bob is Bea's foible* (see *foible*).]

founder *v.* 1. *Of a ship.* To fill with water and go to the bottom. 2. *Of a draft horse.* (a) To bloat and sicken. (b) To collapse due to overwork. (Horses are stupid enough to allow themselves to be worked, literally, to death.) (c) *Loose ext.* To go lame. [The nautical sense, though it has become primary as draft horses began to disappear, is only since XVI. ODEE cites XIII use with the sense, "to smash," which I find no way to explain. By XIV to founder signified (of a horse) "to stumble and fall," and also "to go lame." These senses can be found in Chaucer, *afounder,* and form and sense responds consonantly to OF *afondre,* to go down, < L. *fundus,* bottom.]

free *adj.* (also *v.*) At liberty. Not captive, enslaved, or subject to the will of another. With endless extensions, as in: *duty-free,* not subject to impost; *vermin-free,* rid of; *free-form,* not subject to formal academic rules; *the room is free,* not occupied; *free ride,* at no cost; *to make free,* to disregard conventional rules. The common sense is "unhindered, not beset by, not subject to imposed control." [At root, "to love," or "like a loved one (as opposed to an enslaved person)." Ult. < IE *pri-,* to love; with p/f → Gmnc. *fri-,* to love, loved one. In Teutonic mythology *Frigg,* wife of Odin, corresponds to Aphrodite-Venus. She is the mother goddess of love. *Freya,* her daughter, is also at root "she who loves" and is undoubtedly the manifestation of Aphrodite-Venus in youth. Our *Friday* (OE *frigedaeg*) is probably named for both. OE *frēo,* free. But note also *frēond,* friend, with root sense "cherished freeman."

As war seems to have been a principal occupation of the Teutons, and as captives became slaves, great households were divided into the loved and cherished free members, and those who were simply owned and to be commanded and worked. A master might, of course, become infatuated by a slave and free her (or him). And so a slant etymological origin on *free love.* Be friendly, children.]

free lunch   1. A more-or-less elaborate buffet from which saloon patrons might help themselves to a snack or sandwich with their drinks. (Survives in the common custom of serving hot hors d'oeuvres to drinking patrons during happy hour(s).) 2. *Ext.* Something for nothing: *There ain't no free lunch.* = (in any context) They may call it free but you end up paying for anything you get. Also *he thinks life is a free lunch.* Implies that he will find out it isn't. [From Am. social history. After the wary watchfulness of saloon keepers in making sure patrons did not eat out of proportion to what they spent at the bar; and especially in keeping "bums" from walking in to freeload without buying a drink.]

freeze   [The IE root *preus-* had the double sense 1. To freeze. 2. To burn (as with the sting of cold?) Into L. *prurire,* to yearn for ("burn for, burn with desire for"). PRURIENT. But also, shedding the terminal *s* of the stem and with a standard L. suffix → *pruina,* rime, hoarfrost; thus both root senses function in Latin. But same root with p/f in Gmnc. (prob. form *fruisan,* to freeze) → OE *frēosan,* to freeze; ME *fresen,* p.p. *frosen.* The second root sense "to burn" has never functioned in English, as in Latin.] *v.* 1. *Primary sense.* To change from a liquid to a crystalline solid because of cold. *Hence,* (a) To become stiff with cold: *the laundry froze on the line.* (b) To become clogged by cold: *Drain the pipes or they will freeze.* 2. To die or suffer bodily damage by exposure to low temperatures. And so, hyperbolically, for "to be cold to a lesser degree": *I freeze when I go to their apartment.* 3. To chill, as in preserving food: *We freeze most of our strawberry crop. n.* 1. A period of cold weather: *there will be a freeze tonight.* 2. A cessation, an imposed halt, the act of fixing a condition in status quo: *a wage freeze.* [This slightly extended sense (from verb sense 3, above) has become endemic in journalese and federalese. If storers and distributors of frozen beef began to thaw it at an excessive rate, I should not be surprised to hear that some federal agency had declared a *thaw freeze.*]

And note the imperative *Freeze!* The standard command to anyone held in one's gunsights, signifying: "Don't move a muscle (or I will shoot!") And also:

freeze out 1. To force out, to ignore, to boycott. [Prob. by association with "giving one the *cold shoulder* (see *Browser's II*), this one frozen. 2. *Business and gambling.* To force out of a venture by raising the stakes. [At root, "to make inoperative."]

freeze in one's tracks To become instantly motionless. [See *freeze!* above. Here, as if caught or about to be caught in an act of stealth. A brass band, for example, may halt, but it does so too openly to freeze in its tracks.]

freeze onto Slang. To hold on as firmly as ice to a mast or line.

till hell freezes over Never. [Long-standing colloq. based on the assumption that hell is a sort of volcanic cellar and cannot freeze. Dante's Inferno has a core of ice, but it could hardly be imagined to freeze *over.*]

freeze-dry To preserve certain dry foods by rapid freezing in a high vacuum. [Freeze-dried coffee is perhaps the commonest example (after dehydrating the brew) but bear in mind that substantial parts of the universe are naturally in a freeze-dried condition. So, *the freeze-dried universe.*]

Friday: man Friday   and also, as a **XX** variant, especially for a private secretary, *girl Friday* An utterly faithful (and at origin, at least) cringingly servile servant-factotum. [From *The Life and Strange Surprising Adventures of Robinson Crusoe* (1719), by Daniel Defoe. Crusoe was cast away on an uninhabited island of the Caribbean. There (on a Friday) he discovered a native of those parts who had put to sea pursued by bloodthirsty enemies. Crusoe saved the wretch, naming him after the day on which he found him, and Friday became his totally devoted servitor.]

HISTORIC. Defoe's book was a romanticized version of the adventures of Alexander Selkirk, who spent the years from 1704 to 1709 on the then-uninhabited Juan Fernandez Island off the coast of Chile. Selkirk was not a castaway but a seaman in bitter dispute with his captain. When the ship stopped at Juan Fernandez for water, Selkirk insisted on being left behind. At the last minute he regretted his decision and asked to be taken aboard but the captain had had enough of him and sailed away, having left some basic provisions. In early XVIII that coast was not exactly heavily traveled, but what ships came there did tend to stop at Juan Fernandez for water. The captain had reason to believe that another ship would stop there in five or six years, and if it turned out to be ten or twelve, so much the better—at least he was rid of Selkirk and his constant carping. Such is the stuff of Romance.

frig [< L. *fricare*, to rub; *frico* or *frigo*, I rub. Prob., though unattested, first in Brit. university slang. Common in Am. slang since XIX.] An all-purpose substitute for *to fuck*, perhaps a minced form. [So: *frig it, frig you, all I got was frigged, to hell with the whole frigging mess.*]

HISTORIC. If it now passes as a minced form of *fuck*, it did not always do so. When ca. 1950 Norman Mailer wrote *The Naked and the Dead* about WWII GIs, he had to record the fact that "fucking" had been dulled in GI use to an all-purpose intensive and appeared almost automatically before nouns. The publishing mores of that time did not allow him to say "fucking rifle/Army/butter/officers," twelve times a page. He ended up substituting "ruttin' " for this part of the litany. I am told that *frigging* was considered as a more immediate substitute but that the publisher thought it was too strong. Times change.

Fritz 1. A common German nickname for Friedrich. [Friedrich II, king of Prussia from 1740 to 1786, was fondly called in his old age *der alte Fritz*, the old Fritz.] 2. Also a common German male given name in its own right. 3. In U.S., a common nickname for any male with a German surname. 4. In WWI, a Brit. and U.S. generic for a German soldier. [P. *Slang* cites it in Brit. use from 1914 but less common than Jerry, < Ger(man)y, from 1917 to 1918. Fritz and *Kraut*, however, were in common use by the AEF from 1917 to 1918. *Kraut* was a derogative generic < *sauerkraut;* akin to Fr. *Boche* < *caboche*, pate, thick skull, thick head, < OF *cabace*, (bump)head.]

fritz: on the fritz Out of order. 1. Commonly said of a machine in need of, or beyond, repair. 2. But also said of one's health: *He has been on the fritz since his operation.* Also as a verb, To put out of order, to ruin, to destroy: *"That fritzed it,"* as the man said when his toupee fell into the blender. [Am. slang. Now rare except in old-timer use. All citations in Wentworth and Flexner are from 1928 to 1943. Not akin to preceding *Fritz*. There is in fact no recorded evidence of origin or derivation. This may be an idiom properly glossed "u & u," origin unknown and by now unknowable.

But to borrow a choice locution from Partridge, I will "trepidate" that it is akin to "all petered out," in which *peter* is from L. *petere*, to fart (at root, "like a long tapering fart—it trails off to nothing"). This idiom was once common in ref. to a mineral vein that had played out, i.e., gone back to rock (L. *petra*).

In the 1930s I worked as a ditch digger and a jackhammer

operator under various Italian straw bosses whose common way of signaling that a machine was down or that the work had reached a dead end was to gesture thumbs down (sometimes with both hands) while blowing a lip-fart, *pf'tt,* commonly with a trilled *r*— *pfrrrit!* "She'sa all *pfrritt!*" I came to think of this as some sort of regional south Italian gesture-with-sound-effects, but in Michigan in 1941 I worked for a Swedish landscaper who kept abusing heavy machinery (borrowed from the Ford Motor Company) and who signaled frequent equipment failure in the same way. Trepidation is not assertion, but if this once common sound-effect gesture is not the source of the idiom, then the etymological case is on the *pfrrrit,* and the verdict must be "u & u."

William Morris and Mary Morris, *Dictionary of Word and Phrase Origins* (New York 1962–), suggest a derivation from the once-popular comic strip *The Katzenjammer Kids* drawn originally (for Hearst) in 1897 by Rudolph Dirks, later titled (after Dirks left Hearst) *Hans and Fritz,* and later yet *The Captain and the Kids.* Hans and Fritz were fiendish brats dedicated to breaking all things and to destroying all of Captain Katzenjammer's plans and projects; and the date of the first attested usage (1928), suggesting about 30 years of oral use before first attestation, supports the Morrises' assertion, for this comic strip was at the height of its popularity at about this time. Yet some question remains. Why, for instance, was it not *on the hans?*

These questions asked and these possibilities reviewed, there seems to be no firm answer; neither is there likely to be one.]

frugal   Sparing. Intent on making the most of what one has, avoiding expense or waste: *Yankee ingenuity was above all make-do frugality.* [And so the sense has shifted toward "miserly." At root, however, the word intended good husbandry and the *enjoyment* of the fruits of good husbandry. Ult. < IE *bhrug-,* a stem in words having to do with farm produce. With standard bh/f on passing into Latin → new stem *frug-* → L. *frux,* fruit; *frui,* to enjoy; *fructus,* enjoyment, product of labor, harvest. *Frieda left the farm because her husbandman was too frugally fruitless.*]

fungible   *adj. Law.* Interchangeable. (Bulk goods are fungible. A debt of a ton of anthracite is payable in full by any ton of anthracite of the same quality. If, on the other hand, I borrow Michelangelo's *David* as a party decoration and it vanishes while in my care, I cannot replace it with even three plastic madonnas: you—or the court—must set a money price on the missing article and I must pay it when I get my Social Security check. Money is always fungible: if I owe you $1,000, any legal tender in the amount of $1,000 will discharge my debt. I.e., I am not legally required to return the exact bills I borrowed from you.) *All of Zsa Zsa Gabor's husbands have been fungible.* [Ult. < IE *beug-*, to enjoy. With standard bh/f, and with a nasal infix, -*n*-, to L. *fungi,* to do, to perform, to fulfill an obligation. The sense shift seems to have been from "I enjoy" (the good I receive) to "you enjoy" (the good I return).]

NOTE. *Fungo* in baseball has never been explained. I have seen efforts to derive it from L. *fungo,* I do, I undertake to discharge an obligation. Having noted the suggestion, I undertake to believe the form remains unexplained.

furtive   Stealthy. [At root, "like a thie.." < L. **fūr,* thief, adj. form *fūrtivus,* like a thief. In an old Brit. university joke, *homo trium litterarium,* a three-letter man (the three letters being understood to be *f-u-r, fūr*).]

G

gadfly   1. Any fly (or other insect) that bites livestock, including people. But in the now primary sense, 2. A person who goads others to good purposes. (One could with etymological reason goad others to evil deeds, but the language convention has decided that gadflies shall provoke only to good ends, or at least to such ends as seem good to the goader.) 3. *Associated sense,* One who habitually probes and picks at complacent assumptions. [< OE *gad,* goad, point. (GOAD). The OE form remains in common use only in this fixed compound, but it is also in limited special use in mining, in which a *gad* is a special pick for breaking up ore. Though I cannot find the form listed anywhere else, the Reverend H. Percy Smith, *Glossary of Terms and Phrases* (London 1889), gives OF **gad,* a goad, a sting.]

gadget   A generic for any small mechanical device that does not fit into an established category. The term implies some sort of ingenious mechanical twist. A monkey wrench, for example, is too well established to be a gadget, but a number of newly developed devices for turning nuts of all sizes do qualify. *gadgeteer* One given to making and using gadgets. *gadgetry* 1. The suburban do-it-yourself man's workshop religion of gadgeteering. 2. Gadgets collectively. [Ult. prob. < Frankish **gaspia,* a buckle → OF *gache,* padlock, hook, metal staple for securing a padlocked hasp → Fr. *gachette,* trigger (and also, padlock, the catch of a padlock → dialect Fr. *gagée,* small mechanical device. The term did not become common in Brit. till late XIX (and soon Americanized) but probably developed among steam-engine mechanics in the early Industrial Revolution. Sc. *gadge,* gauge, cannot be overlooked and is probably of this time. P. *Slang* notes *gadget,* variantly *gadjet,* in Brit. nautical use by ca. 1855. And at about that time Robert Browning (1812–1889), drawing from whatever unknown source, used *gadge* to label an instrument of torture, probably intending some small device, perhaps a thumbscrew.]

HISTORIC. Those who share my collector's interest in spook etymologies will be pleased by one I found asserted in a 1977 French magazine. I have a photostat of the page but have mislaid the name and date of the magazine. A deficient footnotery, therefore, but this false etymology is worth recording if only because the restoration of the Statue of Liberty will almost certainly move one journalist or another to reassert it.

Frédéric-Auguste Bertholdi designed and began work on his colossus about 1874 with the thought of presenting it to the U.S. on the hundredth anniversary of its independence, but the cast parts (in 214 crates) did not reach Beddoes Island until June 1885 and the assemblage was not completed until Oct. 28, 1886, when President Grover Cleveland drove the last ceremonial rivet.

In 1884 final casting was begun by Gaget, Gauthier et Cie, and soon thereafter M. Gaget arrived in New York with three trunks full of maquettes of the statue for ceremonial presentation. These were eagerly sought and according to my lost-name magazine were soon dubbed *gadgets*—"Les petits 'gadgets' comme le dirent très vite les Américains par simplification en prononçant ce nom français."

This assertion of a post facto origin may be touchingly patriotic from a French view, but perhaps the French will settle for a remote French source some 800 years earlier.

gather ye rosebuds while ye may   *Carpe diem.* Seize the day, for it is fleeting. Make hay while the sun shines. [An old frozen poetic metaphor that achieved proverbial status. I am unable to fix its first use in English poetry, but the sentiment has precedent in most European languages.

Toward the difficulty of definition, gathering rosebuds may be said to mean the same as making hay, but the first is lightly delicate and the second bucolically lusty, the difference in tonality being critical. The father of a venturesome teenage daughter who is about to leave the house on a date with a dashing high-school athlete may spend substantial emotional energy in wondering whether the man is gathering rosebuds or making hay, and, categories aside, the possible difference weighs upon the fatherly mind.]

gendarme   [Fr. < *gens d'armes,* people (men) at arms.] 1. A French police officer. *Hence* 2. *In breezy arch usage,* An American cop. *But* *accurately,* 3. A member of a national militia serving on police duty. [The French gendarmes are distinct from the investigative police of the Sureté. They correspond more nearly to the Italian *carabinieri* and the Spanish *federales* as military forces on civil duty, usually living at home, but spending some time in barracks. In the U.S. most state police have regular duty periods of living in barracks.]

George *Aviation.* The automatic pilot. [In limited usage in USAF in WWII. Borrowed from RAF.]

German silver Now more commonly *nickel silver* An alloy of nickel, copper, and zinc in various proportions. [Neither silver nor German. This alloy was developed by the Chinese for inexpensive decorative work. Germans introduced it to Europe in 1840 and it accordingly became known in Great Britain as German silver. Then in WWI when "German" became a dirty word, *nickel silver.* This alloy, when high in nickel, closely resembles silver, is easy to work into shapes appropriate for inexpensive jewelry, and its durability makes it especially suitable for silverplated tableware. See also *ormolu.*]

ghost [IE *geis-* (Ger. *Geist,* ghost) is the base of many words having to do with fear and implying fear caused by an unnatural apparition. AGHAST, GHASTLY. Zero-grade variant, prob. suffixed *-d-* → Gmnc. *ghois-d-* → OE *gāst,* ghost. ME *gast, gost.*] 1. The visible shade of a dead person. In surviving early belief, it haunts the earth because, for some reason, it cannot rest. It was a common early belief (and so in *Hamlet*) that one who had died by foul play could not rest until his kin had avenged the death. 2. *Ext.* A haunting memory: *the ghost of one's youth.* 3. An elusive trace or vestige: *the ghost of a smile.* 4. One who writes for pay what another signs as his or her own work. Commonly *ghost writer.* 5. *TV.* A second (sometimes a third) shadowy image that plays about and seems to double the primary image. 6. *Printing.* A blurred secondary impression, especially in improperly coordinated color printing.

give up the ghost To die. [Now a cliché, but in primitive belief the spirit fled, or sought to flee, the dead body, and was believed to enter and seize any living thing. For this reason, early death rites involved the immediate blocking of all bodily openings.]

not have a ghost of a chance To lack not only hope, but the very ghost of dead hope.

ghost ship 1. A derelict ship found drifting at sea without a trace of its crew, or with a dead crew. 2. *In sailors' superstition,* A vessel, such as the mythical Flying Dutchman, doomed for some dark reason to sail forever with only ghosts for a crew.

ghost story A yarn dealing with revenant spirits and occult phenomena, told either in superstitious credulity or to move the reader or listener to dread.

ghost town *XIX Am. Western frontier.* An abandoned town, once a more-or-less thriving community, as a mining center abandoned when the ore petered out. Because of the hot, dry climate in many parts of the American West such towns remained remarkably well preserved many years later. But not all ghost towns were abandoned mining centers. Some once-established communities were abandoned when prolonged drought or a fissure in an aquifer caused the water supply to fail.

to ride the ghost *Archaic. Taxi driver's slang from the Great Depression of the 1930s.* To throw the meter and drive around without a passenger. [Cabbies were usu. assigned a cab on a daily basis and were required to register a daily minimum on the meter, failing which they might be refused a cab in future. To make up that minimum, drivers ran up the meter in this way, paying out of their own pockets in the hope that they might make up their losses on a better day.]

gimmick 1. *Late XIX Am. carnival slang.* A usually foot-operated device for controlling the spin on a gambling wheel. 2. Any trick device that gives the user a cheat's advantage. 3. Any advantage secured by trickery, as a card hidden up one's sleeve, or self-serving ambiguous phrasing in the fine print. 4. *Ext.* Any self-seeking and showy trick: *Hearst gimmicked up the art of journalism and made a yellow empire of it.* [Prob. (?) < earlier *gimcrack,* < ME *gibbercrak,* < OF *giber,* to act erratically/oddly; with *crak,* echoic of a breaking sound *(crack).* P. *Slang* glosses *gimmick* as Canadian carnival slang ca. 1920, but of Am. origin, anglicized ca. 1946 (prob. by GI transmission to the Tommies).]

gism *Am. slang.* 1. The male sexual ejaculate. 2. *By association.* Strength, vigor: *Norman Mailer used to be full of piss and gism.* [Origin unknown. I can find it listed only in Lester Berrey and Melvin Van Den Bark, *The American Thesaurus of Slang* (New York 1942). Yet it is a term known on every street corner and in every poolroom in the U.S.A. Berrey and Van Den Bark offer no attestation, even of the spelling, and I know nothing against such variant forms as *gyssum, gyss, jiss, jissim.*

To borrow a choice usage from Partridge, I will "trepidate" that it may, at deep root, be akin to *jazz,* earlier *jass.* (See *Browser's I.*) *Jazz,* in one clear line of descent, is < Fr. **jaser,* to banter, to engage in idle social give and take, and is so attested in mid-XIX Brit. use with no ref. to jazz music. In Creole, it seems to have become *jass,* intercourse ("sexual give and take"), and so to New Orleans XIX *jass house,* whorehouse; whence *jazz,* because jass houses were the first places in which black jazz musicians were paid for playing. If *jiss* and *jizz* were Creole or black Creole variants, they might underlie *gism.*

Robert F. Thompson, the brilliant master of Timothy Dwight College, Yale, and one of the few U.S. scholars with a firm knowledge of West African dialects, and especially of Ki-Konga, cites (in work in progress) the verb *dinza,* to discharge semen, to come. With d/dj/j and nz/zz this form may just possibly have been altered in black Creole to *jiss/jass/jazz* partly under the influence of Fr. *jaser.* Such speculation ranges beyond etymology, but slaves torn from their native roots and learning to mispronounce Creole —and their children distorting the word forms further—were certainly capable of such alteration.

I so speculate in the hope that someone familiar with black Creole may be able to supply an attestable note on *jiss, jizz,* for if these forms existed, *gism* (whatever its spelling) may not be far behind. Pending such a note (or notes) I can only say *da capo,* origin unknown.]

glee 1. Exultant merriment. 2. *Since XIV., now obs.* A musical accompaniment. 3. *Since XVII.* Unaccompanied songs for group performance, now with many variants. *gleeful* Merry, exultant. [At root, "in a mood to shout for joy." Ult. < IE *ghel-,* to call (out). Substantially unchanged in Gmnc. → OE *gellen,* to call out. And with regular shift of OE *g* to *y* → YELL. One may call out in exultation. As a trait of this bent species, one may yell with vindictive joy at the downfall of another. One may cry out merrily in the course of happy festivities. And music may also be said to "call out" to us. *Glee* was once the art of music, and early *gleeman* was common until replaced by *minstrel.* So XIV "Orgnes, chymbes, ech mannere of glee," may be rendered "organs, cymbals, each manner of music [or accompaniment]." And so, surviving:]

glee club A singing group once basically different from a choir in that it performed without musical accompaniment or with very little, though today glee clubs have made use of everything including minimum choreography. [At root, "music club." Though they often seem gleeful in the recent extended sense even when singing a dirge—as they are entitled to be if—and only if—they sing it well.]

glitch   1. *Computer jargon.* A computer error or malfunction. *Hence,* 2. *Ext.* Anything that goes wrong in a system. 3. *Further ext.* Any breakdown, snag, hindrance, pratfall. [I have been solemnly assured by various computer clickers that the word is a high-tech acronym derived from *G*remlin *L*oose *I*n *T*he *C*omputer *H*ut, though none of these knowledgeable specialists can give me a precedent for "Hut" as "computer programming center." The fact is that these boys and girls, more given to formulas than to language, amuse themselves by compiling "dictionaries" for the computer to print out, and that they have been frivolously inventive in this acronym, as in many other terms, failing to recognize that *glitch* is pre-computer Am. slang from Yiddish (see below). My friend William Whittington, an attorney of Greenwood, Mississippi, tells me that when he used *snafu* routinely for "system error," his secretary did not recognize the term, but seemed instantly to understand when he shifted to *glitch.*

Glitch < Yiddish *glitch* < Ger. *glitschen,* to slip, to slide (implies "and fall"). *Glitch* common in big-city Am. slang since late XIX. Leo Rosten, *The Joys of Yiddish* (New York 1968), defines the word as: 1. To slide, to skid. 2. A risky undertaking (that risks a fall). 3. Not kosher. Also, a shady business. All of these senses have carried over into Am. slang with the exception of "not kosher."]

go chase yourself   A term of contemptuous dismissal, rejection, incredulity: *When you need a friend in Manhattan, go Chase yourself.* [Am. First dating uncertain but common by late XIX. One of a wide range of similar derisive commands from "go jump in the lake" to more recent "go play in traffic," with such more flavorful related forms as "go shit in your hat (and pull it down over your eyes)," "go piss up a rope," and with a rhetorical flourish, "go take a flying fuck at a galloping goose." All such imply that the person addressed is stupid enough to do as ordered even when, as here, the command is impossible to obey. And so to the mythical phillyloo bird that flew in decreasing concentric circles until it disappeared into its own anus, at which point it became as extinct as Richard M. Nixon, and why would it want to stay alive?]

Gog and Magog   Shadowy biblical figures of evil. [Generic figures of evil, they have no specific history. In Ezekiel 38:39 Gog is said to be king of the dark and evil land of Magog, never geographically identified, a sort of biblical bogeyman's realm. In Revelation 20:7–8 Gog and Magog are said to be the unidentified nations whose enormous armies of evil will join with Satan to attempt to overthrow the Kingdom of God on earth. In his poem *Scyros,* Karl Shapiro uses them in this biblical tradition as figures of unclean purposes: "Gog and Magog ate pork / In vertical New York."]

HISTORIC. England long had its own confused version of this biblical legend. As the XV English printer William Caxton told that mysterious legend, Emperor Diocletian's thirty-three weird daughters all murdered their husbands. Punished by being set adrift in a charmed (or damned, if you like) ship, they washed up on the coast of England and married an unspecified number of local demons, giving birth to a race of evil giants that harried England until a party of Trojan heroes under Brute also washed ashore (all tides lead to England) and proved that they were still heroes by killing off these giants.

In Caxton's version, Gog and Magog were the last survivors, and were brought to London in chains before the palace of Brute. When London's Guildhall was built on the former site of the palace, Gog and Magog remained chained there to serve in eternal drudgery as porters.

Whatever the sources of Caxton's legend, medieval England was well aware of it. It is known that in the reign of Henry V (1413–1422), two huge, grotesque, wooden statues of Gog and Magog were raised outside Guildhall, remaining until they were destroyed in the Great Fire of London in 1666. In 1708 Richard Saunders carved new figures 14 feet high and put them on the original site.

But this legend was not restricted to London. Gog and Magog come together as a single lump in Gogmagog Hill, which rises a few miles southeast of Cambridge. Legend has it that combined Gogmagog was a single oafish hulk who loved a local nymph named Granta. Spurned, he changed into the hill that bears his name. Or Granta got rid of him by changing him into a mound of local real estate.

go-go, a go-go. à go-go, gogo   *adj.* 1. Aplenty. 2. Labels frenzied, festive, nonstop energy. 3. *Passé.* Of the latest fad in entertainment. [A passingly popular chic term of the 1950s and 1960s, fading fast thereafter. < Fr. nursery talk *go-go,* throat. Perhaps akin to gargoyle, Fr. *gargouille* (at root, "the throat animal"). But this is a promoter's coinage, more nearly an advertiser's catchword than an etymology. More or less specific to discotheques and to late-hours drinking places.]

go-go girl A girl, often naked from the waist up (and sometimes down), who gyrates frenetically on a pedestal or on a small stage, or in a gilded cage, or in the window of a go-go joint. Also, but only in loose ext. and by association with common "on the go," a swinger.

HISTORIC. I am indebted to Professor Julian H. Wülbern of San Diego University for the following account:

It all started innocently enough when a Scot named Compton MacKenzie published a novel called *Whiskey Galore,* 1947. Set in the Hebrides Islands, it narrates the plight of locals cut off from their source of whiskey by WWII, until a freighter loaded with 10,000 cases of the precious stuff is shipwrecked nearby. The rest of the tale concerns the antics of the islanders as they attempt to outwit HM Customs, the police, and the Home Guard to salvage the whiskey for themselves.

The novel was made into an internationally popular film in 1948 under the title *Tight Little Island.* When the film was dubbed for distribution in France, the pun in the title [on *tight,* secure, clannish, and *tight,* drunken] could not be translated, so its French title became *Whiskey à go-go,* roughly "Whiskey till you've got a snootful," or "whiskey galore."

So popular was the film in France that an enterprising Frenchman opened a Parisian bar called Whiskey à go-go, with the further innovation of dance music on recordings: the discotheque had been invented.

Within a few years such joints had opened in New York but by then there had emerged such new dances as the Twist [Note: Prof. Wübern's memory is slightly blurred here: the twist was a fad prominently associated with Chubby Checkers], the Watusi, and the Mashed Potato. These dances were so "far out" that the manager of a New York Whiskey à Go-Go hired girls to demonstrate them in scanty attire, creating an instant hit and giving rise to the term *Gogo Girl.*

By the summer of 1964 [and certainly before] there were gogo discos in San Francisco and the city was seized simultaneously by two crazes: the Republican Convention, and the innovation by designer Rudi Gernreich (his name means something like "glad to be rich") of a new look: toplessness. Gogo girls [sometimes called "bubble dancers"] began to appear topless and so, at least here in the West, *Gogo Girl* has since meant a female dancer naked from the waist up.

[Note. Rudi Gernreich never operated a gogo joint. He was a flash-in-the-pan fashion designer who won some titular press attention by extending the bare midriff to the neck.]

goose egg Nothing. Zero. [Am. XIX sports slang, originally with ref. to baseball in which inning-by-inning totals are posted on the scoreboard, a line of zeroes being taken for a row of goose eggs standing on end.

But why not simply *egg?* or some other sort of egg? *To get the goose, to get goosed* is, ultimately, to get nothing, and this association may have entered into the choice; but note, as lexicographers seldom do, that of all possible variants *goose egg* is the easiest to say.

The idiom is specific to Am. slang. A popular spook-etymology asserts that *love* in tennis (see *Browser's I*) is < Fr. *l'oeuf,* the egg. But in tennis scores the French say *zéro* for nothing, and French slang has never used *egg* for *zero.*]

Gordian knot 1. *Greek myth.* A knot so intricate none could untie it (see note). *Hence,* 2. An unsolvable problem that can only be dealt with by breaking the rules. *to cut the Gordian knot* To hack one's way through a subtle difficulty. [After Gordium, in Asia Minor.]

HISTORIC. The question of divine omniscience has always invited the folk mind and the young to probing suppositions. A standard boy's question used to be, and probably still is, "If God can do anything, can he make a boulder so big he can't lift it?" The Greeks held Zeus to be omniscient, but sometimes whimsically so. Zeus commanded the people of Phrygia to anoint as king the first man to ride up to his temple there in a wagon. This Olympian lottery fell to Gordius, a Phrygian clodhopper, whose first kingly act was to dedicate the wagon to Zeus. (The least he could do: has a kingdom ever been bought for less?) The city around the temple was thereupon named Gordium (in true clodhopper barter, God got the wagon and the clod got the city), and the wagon was attached to a post of the temple, secured there with the Gordian knot, said to have been fashioned with the art of Zeus or of one of his Olympian artisans.

In a later oracle, Zeus declared that whoever should untie the knot would conquer all of Asia. Alexander the Great (356–323 B.C.), on reaching Gordium and confronting the knot, simply took out his sword and hacked through it. Whatever the sources and significance of the early forms of the Gordian myth, it was clearly adapted after IV B.C. to the hero cult of Alexander.

gourmand . . . gourmet These terms are in many ways identical at their obscure roots, but a *gourmand* is now generally understood to be an epicure who is also a glutton and guzzler, whereas a *gourmet* is one with exquisite table standards but given to eating and drinking with some moderation. *Gourmand* came into XV English with the sense glutton-guzzler < OF **gormaunt, *gourmaund,* glutton. *Gourmet* did not come into English until XIX, < Fr. *gourmet,* a judge of good eating and drinking, < OF **gromet, *gourmet,* which had the specialized sense, "servant or apprentice of a wine merchant," and so the later sense "wine taster," hence, "man of a fine palate." It was probably introduced into English to distinguish a person of refined but moderate tastes from a high-living glutton. At obscure root, however, OF *gourmet, gromet* as the wine merchant's apprentice might readily have been taken by his master to be a shiftless guzzler and food-snatcher, while the apprentice, with the best to choose from, would be happy enough to put away (on the sly) a guzzler's plenty of his master's best.

graft   *n.* A bribe or bribes paid to a public official for a favor or exemption. ***grafter*** A public official who accepts bribes. *v.* To accept bribes for abuse of a public office. (In common understanding only the one who accepts the bribe(s) is said to graft: the briber is said *to pay (out) graft.*) [Am. NWD so stars the term without explanation, and no detailed account of the term is generally available. The one positive-sounding (but unattested) clue I can find is in Jim Tulley, "An Ex-Hobo Looks at America," 1920. Tulley mentions Josiah Flynt, late-XIX Am. hobo, and says he published "The Powers that Prey," adding, "which was directed against the New York Police and in which he invented the word *graft* as used in common speech today." Tulley does not explain Flynt's coinage but Flynt's basic metaphor would seem to be that of adding an extra fruit-bearing branch to a tree.]

granted—when I'm governor   A supposedly smart catchphrase reply to "I beg your pardon." [Am. 1920s to WWII, and since blessedly forgotten. Often used as a meaningless phrase to show the speaker has been around and "knows his/her stuff." But often as a rebuff. U.S. governors do have the executive power—rarely used—to pardon state prisoners, but the chances that the speaker will be elected to the governorship are at least remote. Hence, the extended sense might be, "OK, but go to jail and wait there until I become governor." Which would mean a life sentence, and beyond. Hence: "Drop dead!"]

grave: to have one foot in the grave   To be half dead; halfway to being buried. [One of many variant figures for expressing mortal decrepitude. In 1700 John Dryden wrote, "I am half seas over to death."

Ger. has *halbtot* and It. *mezzo morto,* half dead. And in Latin, *pabulum Acherontis,* food for the Acheron (Acheron was the legendary river the dead had to cross to reach the infernal regions). Though it alters the image, Am. *buzzards' bait* conveys the same essential sentiment.]

grease *n.* 1. *Root sense, but no longer primary.* Animal fat, especially rendered animal fat. 2. *By analogy, and now the primary sense.* A high-viscosity petroleum lubricant. 3. *By analogy.* Any jellied lubricant as pomade, Vaseline. 4. *Slang.* A bribe. (Because, like grease, it reduces friction.)

And corresponding verbs. Also *adj.* **greasy** And in slang, *all of them cops is greasy* = they are bribable.

greaser Pejorative word for a foreigner, primarily in the Southwest for a Mexican. [Implies that Mexicans are repulsively oily to the touch.] But also for any Mediterranean. Variantly, **grease ball** 1. A greaser. 2. An obese person.

grease monkey A mechanic.

grease paint Theatrical. Makeup. [< L. **crassus.* See *crass.*]

greased lightning An exuberant formula for expressing great speed: *He was mean as jail bread and faster than greased lightning.* [I am unable to date the expression, but will guess that it came into being as part of the language exuberance of the Jacksonian Age of the 1830s. Mark Twain's style is a rich inheritance from this Jacksonian American, and I have searched his works for "faster than greased lightning." I feel it must be there, but I have not come upon it.]

green-eyed monster Jealousy. [A Shakesperean image. Shakespeare uses green-eyed for jealous in *Merchant of Venice,* III.ii.110 and IV.iii.75, and also in *Othello,* III.iii.166. There is no previous mythological or folk reference to the figure of jealousy as a green-eyed anything; the image is from Shakespeare's metaphoric prop room and has become fixed in English idiom.

Would it have become so fixed had Shakespeare written "squint-eyed," or "yellow-eyed," or "dark-eyed"? The question is more important than the answer. The English-speaking people have found something memorably right and affective in this image and have therefore adopted it as idiom. Language does not follow rules of reason. It is and becomes by some sort of sequential native illogic we respond to. The memorable is what does not get forgotten.]

Gresham's Law   *Economics.* The declared principle, in brief, that bad money drives out good, i.e., that given two currencies of equal face value but of unequal intrinsic worth, the more valuable currency will be hoarded and only the inferior will continue in circulation. When, for example, ca. 1973 new U.S. "silver" coins began to be minted as "copper sandwiches," the true silver coins, in a dramatic demonstration of Gresham's Law, disappeared from circulation in a matter of weeks and could be procured only from numismatists at a collector's premium price. [The principle (and it does seem to work with the force of a law) was so named in 1857 by H. D. Macloud, who was under the impression that Sir Thomas Gresham had first formulated the principle in 1558. The essential principle had in fact been set forth by various earlier writers, perhaps most notably by the Polish astronomer Nicolaus Copernicus, in a treatise on currency reforms in parts of Poland in 1525, and earlier by the French monk Nicole Oresme, whose treatise *De moneta,* About Money, was written about 1360.

And so the principle that bad attribution also drives out good.]

Gridley: (You may) fire when (you are) ready, Gridley   Reportedly the command given by Admiral George Dewey to the captain of his flagship at the Battle of Manila Bay, May 1, 1898. [It has since become a catchphrase to indicate one's readiness to engage in any action. I once saw a cartoon in which the captain of the Harvard team used these words to let the Yale team know he was ready to receive the kick-off. (Or was it the other way round?)

My wife insists that these were the words I said to the preacher at our wedding, but she was in a state of triumphant excitement that might readily have induced error.]

grog   *n.* 1. Watered rum. 2. A generic name for strong liquor. Survives in (now rare) **grog shop** and (even rarer) **groggery** A saloon, a liquor store. (Cf. *Demon Rum* as a fixed name for alcoholic addiction, though rum has not been the most common Am. hard liquor since colonial times.)

But though *grog* seems to be passing from Am. use, there remains the common adjective **groggy** 1. *At root.* Befuddled by drinking grog (or some other hard liquor). *But* 2. (The present primary senses.) (a) Befuddled by lack of sleep. (b) Befuddled by a hard blow: *The challenger took a right to the jaw that left him groggy.* [XVIII Brit. Navy coinage. After Admiral Edward Vernon, nicknamed Old Grog. To combat drunkenness on the ships of his fleet he ordered that the daily ration of a cup of rum, originally of neat rum, be changed to rum mixed with an equal amount of water. By ca. 1730 the rest of the Brit. Navy had similarly watered its rum ration, and *grog* became the standard name for watered rum.]

HISTORIC. In the days before slickers and rubberized fabrics Vernon conceived a waterproof greatcoat for foul weather, and ordered it made of heavy grogram (grogain) treated with pitch and beeswax. It must have been warm and dry, but when he came on deck during a winter storm, the cold so stiffened the coat that the admiral could not move, not even to get out of his mummy case. He had to be carried below and propped up in front of a stove before the pitch and beeswax mollified enough to let him slip free of his invention. The tale of the old boy being carried below stiff as a spar ran titteringly through the fleet and he was instantly dubbed *Old Grogram,* whence *Old Grog.*

From 1739 to 1742 Vernon undertook the naval action memorably called *The War of Jenkin's Ear,* after the captain of a Brit. merchantman who had tried to trade with a port the Sp. claimed as their monopoly. He was stopped by a Sp. *guardiacosta* (coast guard), his cargo rifled, and one of his ears cut off by way of admonition. Nearly ten years later Parliament took notice of this national insult and sent Vernon with a fleet of six ships to teach the Spaniards better manners. Vernon started brilliantly, capturing and looting Portobello (now Panama City); but thereafter nothing much happened, and then this obscure action became absorbed into the War of the Austrian Succession.

But Vernon's presence in the Caribbean is still memorialized in American history. On his only trip out of the colonies, George Washington traveled to the Caribbean with his brother Lawrence. There the two young Virginia gentlemen were well received by the admiral, and developed such an admiration for him, that when George completed his great house in Virginia (after the death of Lawrence) he called it Mount Vernon, luckily preferring that name to Old Grog or Mount Grog.

gruesome   Horrifying, shocking, repugnant. [Obs. *grue,* horrible, survives only in this compound form. < ME *gruen,* to shiver (with horror). *Give your girl a gorgeous Gruen for Christmas—and watch her go into shock.* Akin to and perhaps derived from MD *growen,* to abhor, to recoil from. Something like gooseflesh is implicit in all these forms; and so too in the ult. root, IE *ghreu-,* to rub, to rub against, to grind (as if to roughen the flesh). GRATE.]

guerre: c'est la guerre That's how things are these days. [Fr., it's the war. Probably the commonest Fr. phrase of WWI by way of explaining (with a shrug) whatever was wrong or lacking, the effect being to dismiss all misfunction or malfunction as an inevitable result of the war. So into both Brit. and Am. by way of the military services, and immediately generalized into a formula for shrugging off all slings and arrows. *Pregnant again? C'est la guerre.*

There is also a reversal of this formula (with a variation). A Fr. marshal (whose name I once knew but have forgotten), on hearing of the Charge of the Light Brigade in the Crimean War (1854–1856), commented, "C'est magnifique, mais c'est ne pas la guerre," in effect, "A magnificent display of (wasted) valor, but it's no way to fight a war."]

guillotine A device for execution by beheading. It consists of a sort of bench to which a victim is strapped with his neck in line with the course of a weighted steel blade elevated on vertical rails. Down comes the blade and *chop,* you're dead. [From March 25, 1792 to the present the guillotine has been the official instrument of execution in France. It is named after Dr. Joseph Ignace Guillotin (1738–1814), who successfully urged its official adoption for humane reasons. Guillotin, however, did not invent this device. He was urging the use of what he called the *Louison,* after a Dr. Louis, who adapted it from devices long in use in Italy, sometimes for hacking up a victim by precisely prescribed bits and pieces.

And the fact is that if a state execution is ordered the guillotine is relatively painless, or at least instant, as our electric chair certainly is not in stewing a victim in his own juices, often for as long as several minutes before he is dead.]

HISTORIC. Guillotin's name became associated with this device because of his public advocacy of it before the French senate, but he seems not to have relished this use of the name, especially during the French Revolution, when thousands of heads rolled from it. To escape this monstrous association with gore, his children had their surnames officially changed soon after his death. Be careful where you leave your name.

guinea pig 1. A short, plump, short-eared, furry member of the rat family without an external tail, commonly raised as a laboratory experimental animal, and also prized as a children's pet. *Hence,* 2. A person used in laboratory testing. Sometimes *human guinea pig. Children are guinea pigs for the moral assumptions of their par-*

ents. [In the language laboratory this label wins special honors as a misnomer, for this creature is neither a pig, nor is it from Guinea in Africa. It is a rodent and native to South America. It is so called because it was first brought to England in XVIII by *Guineamen,* in effect merchant-slavers who put into Guinea for slaves to carry to South America and the West Indies before returning to England with goods picked up along the way, the last cargo before the eastward crossing being acquired with the proceeds of the slave traffic.

So "creature brought by the Guineamen"; and "pig" fancifully because the creature is plump and can be said to resemble a small furry pig more than it does a rat.]

gumshoe   A detective, either of police, or a private investigator. [Late XIX Am. slang. An attribution more legendary than real. Because detectives were supposed to sneak about silently on soft rubber soles. Crepe soles had become generally available by ca. 1880, but in my fallible research I can find no evidence that they were widely, or even commonly, used by detectives.]

H

hail *n.* A cry or shout. (1) Of greeting: *hail to you.* (2) To attract attention: *hail a cab.* 3. Of acclamation: *hail to the chief!* (And almost identically in Ger. *heil Hitler!*) And corresponding verb forms. At root, "health (and long life)." Ult. < IE *kailo-*, propitious, healthy (HOLY. HEAL. HEALTHY.) Via Gmnc. to OE *waeshaeil*, a drinking toast: "may you be healthy."

to hail from Come from, originate from. [As if, "from what place does your voice (identity) come?" In nautical usage a cry from the fog might be answered, "Where do you hail from?" (Where are you?) or cried to a passing ship in clear view the same question could mean, "What is your port of origin?" *That schooner hails from Boston.*]

hail fellow (well met) A convivial chap worth greeting and toasting. [Archaic, "hail, fellow, well met!" in which *fellow* means "peer, equal."]

halatious *Am. fad slang.* Swell. Great. Groovy. The max. Splendiferous. All that could be desired. [Since ca. 1965. Like most fad slang, this form is probably ephemeral, though halatious has firm historical roots in Yiddish *chalushus,* terrible, tragic, disastrous. Though not specifically a term of black English, the sense reversal follows a pattern established by such black English usages as *bad* for *good, mean* for *admirable, righteous* for *powerful* (including powerfully bad), and *outrageous* for *superlatively good. He is a mean bad dude,* for example, means he is powerful, not to be messed with, and therefore admirable—the opposite of a despicably subservient Uncle Tom. The formulas seem to be based on the assumption that self-assertion, even in evil, is admirable, proving that Negroes no longer have to cringe. The dominant recreational and social patterns of white youth have long been shaped by the blacks; here it is the black language pattern that has been adopted by the white would-be swingers.]

half cock The position of a gun's hammer when raised halfway. [In that position it is held by a safety and presumably cannot be fired by the trigger, though early guns often malfunctioned and went off half-cocked. First attested 1745 by OED. Later:] *to go off half-cocked* To act erratically and in an unforeseen way. [James Russell Lowell, *Bigelow Papers*, 1848, "Now don't go off Half-cock." And in Brit., "at the half cock." In Brit. slang ca. 1850 (P. *Slang*) *to go off at half cock*, to ejaculate before achieving a full erection. In Australian slang ca. 1888 and in Brit. dial. ca. 1835, *half-cocked*, slightly intoxicated.]

handsaw A young heron. [Archaic but fixed in the language by *Hamlet* II.ii, "I know a hawk from a handsaw" (i.e., I know one thing from another). The form is a dialect corruption of *hernshaw* < HERON; with *shaw*, little < OF diminutive suffix *-ceau, -sel*. Chaucer in XIV uses *heronsew*.]

handsome is as handsome does *Proverb.* In common use with some such sense as, "A fair exterior will not cover foul practice," or "Bad character cannot truly be masked by good appearance," or, perhaps more aptly, "It is our deeds speak us." As commonly in proverbial ambiguity, the sentiment leaves something in doubt. Lilith still has her charms in men's eyes, and handsome men can be empty shells as surely as Warren G. Harding was once president.

But this particular proverb has been confused also by the passing from English of ME *hende*, gracious, courteous, chivalric, gentle (in the root sense, for which see *gen-, Broswer's I*). So Chaucer, in the Friar's Prologue:

> Tho' spoke our host; ah sire ye should been *hende*
> And courteous as a man of your estate.

And so Malory, *Morte d'Arthur*, using the term adverbially: "Launcelot spoke . . . for to comfort that lady *hende.*"

Hende be as hende doth is not attested, but if this substitution be made, the original sentiment would be something like "True gentility lies in the deed rather than the appearance," an observation beyond argument but at some distance from the commonly understood sense of the surviving proverb.

hardshell [Am. XIX. A natural metaphor. As if "a hard nut to crack." Hence unswervable in one's point of view. But with an interesting variety of specific applications.] 1. A common label for Senator Thomas Hart Benton and the supporters of his 1850s hard-money policy. 2. Ca. 1870 and for the rest of the century, a conservative of the New York State Democratic Party. 3. *Still in common survival.* A strictly fundamentalist Baptist. 4. Generic label for anyone of adamant conviction.

harness bull　A uniformed policeman (esp. as distinct from a plainclothesman). [Am. XIX, now rare. A word play. *Bull* for cop was in early XIX New York City usage (large, beefy, powerful male presence). Bulls, of course, are not harnessed, but these bulls can be said to be when in their belted uniforms.]

heebie-jeebies　The jitters. A state of uneasiness. *to have the heebie-jeebies* To be nervously ill at ease. To be in a state of flustered anxiety. *it gives me the heebie-jeebies* It upsets me, flusters me, gives me the creeps. [A reduplication in which neither element has etymological precedent. Coined whimsically and popularized by W. B. DeBeck (1890–1942), originator of the once widely popular comic strip *Barney Google.* The strip, syndicated by King Features, continues as a popular feature under the title *Barney Google and Snuffy Smith* or sometimes simply as *Snuffy Smith,* drawn by Fred Lasswell.

As a guess only, I have wondered if *heebie-jeebies* might not have developed from the XIX Am. minced oath *holy jeepers!* (holy Jesus!) perhaps modified to *heepy-jeepers* and so to DeBeck's variant. If that evolution remains possible, it remains so without evidence, and the coinage remains securely DeBeck's.]

henchman　An assistant, underling, servitor. Now carries the sense "unsavory underling in evil," but earlier a trusted, loyal follower. [This compound locks in the only survival into modern English of OE *hengstmann,* groom, squire, < Gmnc. *hengst,* stallion. Stallions, be it noted, were prized horses and would be entrusted only to the care of esteemed servants. (Cf. *marshal,* now a high-ranking officer or parade or protocol official, earlier simply a horse groom.) In ME, and now obsolete, *henxman, henchman,* a ceremonial page to a lord (a post of honor).]

NOTE. Off Prince Street in Boston's North End, a bit north of the Old North Church, there is an alley behind the North Bennet Street Industrial School. I have not been there for almost 40 years, and anything may change, but it was then (and I hope still) called *Henchmans Place.* I have always treasured it as a possible address for a criminal gang's headquarters, or for a school for political wardheelers.

Hera   *Greek mythology.* The wife and sister of Zeus. The equivalent of Roman Juno (whose name is of unknown origin). [Gk. *hera,* earth, the earth. Cf. Ger. *Erde,* Earth; *Mutter Erde,* the Earth Mother, who would seem to be a variant descendant of the same lost Dawn Age myth.]

HISTORIC. The primeval God was Kronos (Gk. *Khronos,* time). Accounts of him are vague. Zeus may have sprung from his mind fully formed, and so, later, Hera, for there may have been no sexual principle to begin with. In some early manifestations, sex had reared its head, and his wife was Rhea, her name derived from *rhēo,* I flow, prob. a ref. to the waters of creation. In the most common surviving legend Zeus killed and ate his father and married his sister.

If Chronos is time and Rhea and Hera the waters and the earth of creation, then Zeus is certainly the Sun. Owen Barfield, *History in English Words* (London 1926), has commented brilliantly on Tiu (Tuesday) as the original chief god of the Teutons (at root, "the people who worship Tiu"). A simple thickening of the *T* to *Tz,* with an *s* suffix, readily yields *Zeus,* which in Illyrian was *Zeus pitar,* God the father, which is obviously akin to Latin *Jupiter.* These three survivals are clearly from a common etymological ancestor. All are traceable to the IE root *deiw-* or *deiu-,* meaning, among other things, "sky, heaven, god, sun."

No such speculation can be brought to exact references, but Hera certainly began her mythico-religious reign as a Dawn Age earth goddess.

heresy   In dogmatic creeds, the act of a professing member who makes up his own mind on matters of doctrine in defiance of established church pronouncement. [Gk. *haresis,* independent thinking, < *haireomai,* I choose for myself. Such choice would generally pass as a virtue among the Greeks. It was in late L. *haeresis* that independent thinking which differed from church pronouncement came to be classified as a mortal sin and a cause for excommunication.]

HISTORIC. Dante, writing in early XIV, took his categories of sin from Aristotle, but added to his infernal roll two groups of damned souls Aristotle would scarcely incline to condemn. One was the Virtuous Pagans (damned because they lacked Christ's redemption), and the other the Heretics, specifically the Epicureans, who asserted that the soul died with the body, thereby denying life after death (and implicitly the relevance of all church teaching, which is finally directed to the eternal life). Such independence of mind would have seemed admirable rather than sinful to the Greeks.

Hermes   The Greek god corresponding to Latin *Mercurius,* Mercury. [He was a major Greek deity, the son of Zeus by the nymph Maia, illusion, a daughter of the Titan Atlas. He is a figure of great power, inventiveness, and cunning. When a few hours old he escaped from his crib, found a tortoise, ripped off its shell, and strung cords across it, inventing the lyre. Later that day he stole the cattle of Apollo and ate two of them, which he spitted, but he so charmed Apollo with lyre music that he escaped punishment. When he gave Apollo the lyre, Apollo gave him the caduceus (from then on, his standard symbol). Among its other powers it brought luck to the bearer and transmuted all it touched to gold. Hermes became, among other things, the chief messenger of the gods, one of the gods of music, the explainer of the ways of the gods, the conductor of the dead to Hades, the patron of Greek chicane, cunning, and theft, and the patron of sea traders and merchants (which may explain their talent for chicanery). His name is akin to Gk. *hermeneuō,* I explain (all things).]

    hermeneutics The "science" of interpretation, now esp. of biblical texts. [In the primitive church *hermēnutae* rendered Scripture into the common tongue and explained its meaning. Also Gk. *hermēneutēs,* translator.]

    hermetical 1. *Now.* Sealed airtight and set apart. 2. *Earlier.* Sealed within mysteries known only to initiates (apart from common understanding). [Originally specific to alchemy, said to have been invented by Hermes, and impenetrable except to those schooled in the arts of explanation.]

hesitate   To falter, to hold back, to be indecisive, to be slow to act: *He who hesitates often has the pleasure of watching fools jump in.* [The root sense, which has receded from the word in English, is "to be frozen in place by terror, by the sight of some dread apparition." Ult. < IE *gheis-,* a root widely distributed, via Gmnc., in words having to do with dread. (GHASTLY.) Suffixed *-t-* → Gmnc. *gaistaz* → OE *gāst,* a ghost. (AGHAST.) Also OE *gaestan,* to scare. The OE stem *gheis-* with g/h → L. *haesum,* fixed fast in place, p.p. of *haer ēre,* to stick in place, to hang back → L. *haesitāre,* early with the root sense "frozen in place by a dread apparition," but later, simply, "to falter, to be indecisive."]

hick A country bumpkin. [Common in Am. since colonial times, but P. *Slang* first notes the term in XVII Brit. slang, first with the sense "country boob who is easy prey for city sharpers," and only later as simple "yokel." < *Hick,* in Brit. rural areas, a traditional nickname for Richard.]

    hick town A small town in the country. Where the hicks live. [Am. only, and recent. MMM's first attestation is dated 1924, but the context makes clear that the form was familiar by then. Prob. in oral use by at least 1900.]

hide one's light under a bushel To be modest. (Can mean, to be reticent about revealing one's great abilities. More commonly the practice of those who have no great candlepower to begin with: *Senator Kennedy keeps hiding his lack of light under a transparent bushel.* [No one knows the earliest date of this ancient image, but it must have been in common use when used in Matthew 5:15, "Neither do men light a candle and put it under a bushel."

    It is uncertain what Matthew meant here. No one knows exactly what measure a biblical bushel may have been, but it was almost certainly some sort of carrying basket, probably with open spaces between the basket weaving. Were a candle placed under an inverted bushel, the weave might allow the passage of enough air to keep it burning, but if the candle was much more than a minimal stub, it would almost certainly start a fire—which lights hidden under today's idiomatic bushel tend not to do.]

hijack To stop and rob a vehicle in transit, either removing the goods it is carrying or seizing and diverting the vehicle and goods. Now also *skyjack* To seize control of an airplane in flight, forcing it to fly to a destination chosen by the skyjacker(s) on threat of killing crew and passengers or of blowing up the plane. [*Skyjack* is, of course, a recent variant of *hijack,* for which all sources give "origin unknown." But:]

    HISTORIC. Our sense of the word has been primarily colored by gangsters of the Prohibition Era who regularly stopped and seized trucks carrying beer and especially hard liquor. Speedboats plying between the shore and supply ships waiting outside the two-mile limit were also sometimes seized in this way. I can find no instance in which trains were said to have been hijacked, primarily, I believe, because they run on tracks and cannot be diverted. A hijacking at sea is, in effect, an act of piracy. A hijacking now labels a similar act carried out on land. Our awareness of the term is from Prohibition Era gangsters, but despite the standard disclaimers by dictionaries the word has traceable maritime antecedents.

I am indebted to Professor David T. Ray, who traces the word to Chinese *hoi,* ocean; *ts'ák,* robber, whence the XIX Treaty Ports term *hoi ts'ák,* pirate. As a further confirmation Professor Ray cites the Sino-Japanese sea term *kaizoku* or *haizoku,* pirate, which is rendered by the same characters as *hoi ts'ák.*

It is not difficult to conjecture a line of transmission from this Far Eastern XIX term for pirate, through pidgin to nautical use, and so to the ex-Navy men who ran the rumrunner supply ships and the off-loading speedboats that rendezvoused with them. The OED Supplement dates the term from Prohibition Era American, as if to support this suggested line of transmission, though it does not mention it. But P. *Underworld* cites it in Am. hobo use in 1914 with the sense, "to rob men at night while they are asleep." This is a sense at least distantly related to an act of piracy, and again, though I cannot attest the line of transmission, it is reasonable to suppose that some former tramp-steamer sailors from the Far East turned hobos when beached and spread this term in its modified sense. Pidgin English, moreover, would readily account for the minor alteration in form from *hoi ts'ák* to *hijack.*

homogenized milk   [< Gk. *homos,* the same; *genos,* kin → Eng. *-genized,* made of one sort. The Gk. roots were combined in English with the sense "made the same (throughout)."] I cite the definition given by MMM, *Americanisms* (from the "Century Supplement"): "a trade name for milk which has been heated to 185° F. and forced by heavy pressure through a number of fine openings, the jets impinging upon a porcelain plate." For reasons I do not understand, this treatment keeps the cream from separating and helps to prevent souring. "We have homogenized society: that keeps the cream from coming to the top."—Robert Frost.

HISTORIC. The Century definition is dated 1909, and the process was developed about 1903. I, for one, find that dating surprising. Until ca. WWII, home-delivered milk commonly arrived in glass bottles with a half-cup, or cup, of cream on top. Some milk bottles were even made with a bulbous top that contained the risen cream. For makeshift homogenizing, one simply covered the bottle top and inverted it a few times, giving it a shake or two. It is my memory, subject to correction, that homogenized milk did not became standard until *after* WWII.

honeydew   An especially desirable, sweet, greenish melon with a smooth, relatively thin rind. [Gk. *mēlon* (see *melon*), of untraced, prob. Mediterranean, origin, became late L. *mēlon, mēlo,* which some, despite the long vowel, have confused with L. *mel,* honey, wrongly suggesting that *honeydew* is from this source. Go rather to the aphid, thou sluggard. Aphids (and some other insects) secrete on leaves a sweet, sticky substance resembling blotches of pale mildew. (*Mildew,* coincidentally, is at root, "honey-dew.") In English folk etymology this substance was called *honey dew* (sweet dew), the belief being that aphids caused it to condense from the night air. Until the late XVII and the arrival in Europe of West Indies sugar, small amounts of cane sugar were expensively (and rarely) available in Europe, largely for medicinal purposes, arriving at the Mediterranean by caravan from the Far East. Honey was the only generally available sweetener, and that, rare in proportion to the population. As a boy I chewed grass for its sweet juice. I have never licked leaves for their aphid-do, but it is easy to assume that Robin Yokel did so in earlier England to savor that touch of sweet.

In XIX Brit. tobacco sweetened with molasses was called honey-dew, a simple transfer name. And, by the same transfer, *honeydew* was applied to this variety of melon, which was not developed for general distribution until 1916.]

honorificabilitudinitatibus   The condition of being honorable at some length. [A whimsicality coined by Thomas Nashe, *Lenten Stuffe* (1599), as his effort to coin the longest word in the English language, and, a few medical technical terms aside, it is more than pseudotransteletelicatiously so.]

hooker   A prostitute, especially a streetwalker. [Often but wrongly said to be original Am. slang, and explained as a reference to General Joseph (Fighting Joe) Hooker who, as a corps commander in the Army of the Potomac, issued directives regulating prostitutes and soldiers who consorted with them. I am indebted to Walter Newman for citations from *London Labour and the London Poor,* published in England in 1857 by Henry Mayhew. The work consists largely of verbatim interviews with street people. In one interview Mayhew reports a whore as saying, "we hooks a white choker (a clergyman) now and then." And in another he records, "I've hooked many a man by showing an ankle on a wet day." Originally, therefore, a bit of Brit. slang from before the American Civil War, the term probably by analogy to hooking a fish; but the EDD also lists the Cumberland usage, "to grab, seize hold of," and the Yorkshire usage *to hook on with, to hook together* meaning "to associate with, to marry." And so much for Joe Hooker, who was not much of a general to begin with.]

horizon [Root sense: "dividing line (between earth and sky)." Ult. < Gk. *horos,* bound, limit; *horizein,* to divide; *horizōn,* line that divides earth from sky. L. *horizon* → OF *horizonte* → ME *horizon(te).*] 1. The line at which the farthest visible reach of land or sea seems to meet the sky. 2. *Astronomy.* Various imaginary planes extending to infinity from an observer's position on earth. (Astronauts must have a new definition of horizon as observed from their orbital position, but I am not capable of formulating it.) 3. *Metaphoric extension.* The outermost scope of one's wish to know and to master.

new horizons A new (effective sense, "enlarged") area of knowledge, experience. [Technically, of course, the horizon changes with every step one takes.]

beyond (over) the horizon 1. *Literally.* Out of sight beyond the earth's curvature. 2. A common figure for venturing forth into new areas of knowledge, experience, venture.

low on the horizon 1. Said of a ship or of some large object or natural configuration, part of which rises to view above the horizon, the lower part remaining below it and out of sight. 2. Said of a heavenly body that has just risen or is about to set.

horseshoe crab A spiny sea creature of the North American East Coast. It is not a crab but a curious evolutionary survival akin to the spider and the scorpion. It does, however, have a shell that in some ways resembles that of a crab, and it is found along the shore often among crabs. [First named (in colonial America) *horsefoot crab.* Folk names usually report nature accurately and vividly. Except for its long spiny tail this creature does resemble what a horse's hoof might look like if it were cut off the horse. Subsequent folk-naming has visualized the creature turned upside down, and in that position it does resemble a horseshoe, except for that tail. One primary use of the tail is to permit the creature to turn over again when chance—or idiom—has turned it upside down.]

horse's mouth: straight from the horse's mouth A figure for accurate information from an indisputable source. Now colloq. for information of any sort. Earlier for sports information and especially for inside information about an upcoming horse race. [P. *Slang* dates this sports and horse-racing sense from ca. 1830 Brit., but the earlier and original context was certainly horse trading, in which the seller traditionally lies about the merit, condition, and especially the age of the horse. The buyer must decide for himself on the horse's merits and condition but can determine its age accurately by examining its teeth, which grow and begin to wear down according to its age; and on this point, no matter what lies the seller may tell, a knowledgeable buyer may get accurate information straight from (an examination of) the horse's mouth.]

host: to reckon without one's host   To calculate one's tab for board and lodging, or for food and drink, without taking into account various items the host (innkeeper, publican) will remember to include. *To reckon* is, here, to calculate what one owes. *Host* is "mine host," the innkeeper or publican who provides services.

The idiom is first attested in *Blanchardyn and Eglantine,* a French work translated into English and published by William Caxton in 1489: "It is sayd in comyn [common] that who soever rekeneth withoute his hoste, he rekeneth twys [twice] for ones [once]." The quotation cannot mean that the customer computes his bill at twice what mine host charges, but rather that he will forget to include a number of items and must, therefore, recalculate the charges when he is given the host's accounting.

The idiom is, of course, faded, but remains within range of the literate. In Scarsdale today, I think it means that a guest at a party who goes to bed with the lady of the house, forgetting that the man of the house has an extensive gun collection and is a crack shot, is reckoning without his host. But this idea may be as archaic as Scarsdale, if not as entirely obsolete as the National Rifle Association.

hot walker   *U.S. horse racing.* A stable boy (now, commonly, also a girl) who holds a usually blanketed horse by the bridle and walks it to cool it off after a race or workout. Akin to an exercise boy/girl, but pedestrian rather than astride, and there to tend the horse rather than train it. Cf. the Western saying, *you look like you was rode hard and put away wet.* No trainer of thoroughbreds allows his horses to be put up after a hard ride until they have been hot-walked and rubbed down.

Hudson seal   Trimmed muskrat pelts dyed to resemble seal. [The Hudson seal is a late-XIX furriers' nonesuch. There is no species known as the Hudson seal and there is no sealskin in a Hudson-seal coat. Hudson seal is a durable, lustrous, and softly luxurious fur, but furriers decided that fashionable ladies would resist the skin of anything called a rat. They were probably right, though a muskrat is no more a rat than its fellow rodent, the squirrel. The Hudson seal, therefore, must be classified as a mythical semantic species.]

HISTORIC. The affective power of words is the basis of the advertising industry. Early canners found a sales resistance to *horse mackerel* and achieved wide market acceptance only when they renamed their product *tuna*. It has since been trademarked Chicken of the Sea. If we ever achieve a neoclassical age, we may yet find it called *abyssal ambrosia*.

The first canneries to market white salmon ran into a related form of market resistance until they announced on their labels "guaranteed not to turn pink in the can." No lie, but one more evidence that this species, having invented language, remains forever ready to be duped by it.

hunger [< IE *kenk-*, to burn up, to desiccate, to endure pain. (The sense shift has been from "any slow lingering deprivation/affliction" to "the pain of being denied food." ME *steorfen* similarly meant "to suffer long lingering pain and death for lack of food, water, or shelter, or under torture." So Chaucer, "Christe sterfed on the crosse." But when cities were "sterfed" under siege, the first thing to run out was food, and so *starve* came to mean "long lingering pain/death due to lack of food.") The form is from the IE root with k/h and k/g to the skeletal Gmnc. root *h'ng-* → OE *hungor*, which prob. meant to thirst as well as to lack food.] *n.* 1. The craving for food. The pain of being deprived of it. 2. Famine. "To kill with sword and with hunger" (Revelations 6:8). 3. *Ext.* Any strong craving: *to hunger for knowledge and be denied.* (And corresponding verb forms.)

strictly from hunger Wretched. Inferior. Fit only for panhandlers and gutter bums. *Hence,* Unworthy, despicable, to be scorned. [Dating? Prob. XX and prob into Am. via Yiddish, though all of starving Europe has had forms to express contempt of a person too feckless to wring food from the earth. It. *un morto di fame*, lit. "a dead-of-hunger person," expresses contempt for a worthless person. So Eng. *starveling* as a term of contempt. Uncharitable perhaps, but wherever food must be won by hard labor, the person unable to feed himself threatens those who just barely can, and accordingly invites contempt.]

hyperbole (pron. *hī-pûr'-b'-lē*) *Rhetoric.* A figure of speech based on exaggeration. [First element ult. < IE *uper-*, over, above (UPPER)

→ Gk. *huper,* over, above, beyond, in excess. Second element <
Gk. *ballein,* to throw, → Gk. *huperballein,* to throw beyond, over,
above, too far. The p.p. stem is *bol-,* whence *discobolus,* discus
throw, *diabolus,* devil ("one who throws across"—*dia-,* across—
probably "souls to hell"): *Graig Nettles threw a hyperbole to first
and another run scored.*]

hyphenated American   A common designation for an American of
relatively recent foreign origin. (Though how recent are Mexican
Latin-Americans whose ancestors were here before the Anglo-
Americans arrived?) [The term developed in late XIX as the children of the XIX immigrant hordes began to find a place in U.S.
society. Originally a pejorative arising from the fear and distaste of
Americans with colonial roots who thought of themselves as a chosen free yeomanry threatened by mongrel hordes. The sense varies
with the user's intent: some use it to mean a naturalized immigrant;
others, the children of immigrants. Though I was born in Boston
and grew up under New England schoolmarms, Robert Lowell had
me insistently categorized as an Italo-American, as I am sure the
Lowells will continue to think of my children for the next X generations—if the Lowells make it that long.

*At the Little Big Horn, Sitting Bull and Crazy Horse wiped out
the hyphenated Americans.*]

I

iatrogenic   *adj.* Arising from the healing process. *iatrogenic disease* Any illness contracted as a side effect of medical treatment or by medical neglect or malpractice. [Gk. *iatros,* healing, cure, medical treatment. In late scientific coinage with L. *gen-,* arising from. GENETIC.]

HISTORIC. With *nosocomial* (which see) one of the scare words of physicians and hospital administrators, whose malpractice insurance rates keep rising in anticipation of legal actions on *nosocomial* and *iatrogenic* claims. And though most Americans do not know the words, their payments for medical treatment and medical insurance are adjusted to their legal definition. Puerperile fever, for example, is commonly iatrogenic and fatal.

ice cream   Earlier *iced cream,* but the earlier term included chilled custards and sherbets, whereas the name today signifies a sugared and flavored cold food made from milk products containing about 12–14 percent butterfat along with nonmilk products, emulsifiers, etc. [Ice cream seems to have been a colonial Am. invention and the name a simple folk label. My father-in-law was a Missouri farmer and I have known a crock of milk from his Jersey cow, when set in the icehouse overnight, to produce an eight-inch cap of cream too thick to pour. When spooned out, say over blackberries, it did immediately as an "iced cream." In XIX U.S. however, ice cream was made by churning high-butterfat milk in a zinc container inside a tub of rock salt and ice that served as the refrigerant.]

HISTORIC. The still-operating firm of Breyers (see your local supermarket) claims to have been the first to make ice cream commercially, in Baltimore in 1866, and though it is well to be wary of commercial claims, this one seems to be accurate. By a bit before 1880 ice-cream parlors had become a standard feature of the American Main Street.

It is worth noting that the soda-fountain ice-cream parlor had much earlier precedent. In 1834 John March opened a new shop on Park Row, New York City, and advertised a soda fountain with champagne on tap. No ice cream was on sale, but those who did not want champagne could certainly order carbonated water, either plain or flavored. (And see note to *locofoco, Browser's I.*)

iffy   Chancy. Not securely predictable. [Am. The earlier form, prob. in use by at least late XIX, was something like: "Your plan sounds good, but there are too many *if*s in it." Wentworth and Flexner first cite *iffy* in *Time*, July 14, 1941, but it was almost certainly not a *Time* coinage. Prob. in use from ca. 1930.]

ilk   *Now used pejoratively.* Of that kind: *We don't want any of your ilk here* = We don't want any of your (bad) sort. [But earlier, in formal nomenclature, designated one whose surname was the same as that of his estate. *Shaw of that ilk,* Shaw of the Estate called Shaws. Surnames were rare in England until after the Norman Conquest, the first surnames then being only for landed gentry and commonly, though not always, after the names of their landholdings. The usage was based on ME *ilke,* the same, like, also; so *that ilke daye,* that same day, that very day.]

illegitimis non carborundum   Don't let the bastards grind you down. [Mock Latin. *Carborundum* is a U.S. registered trademark for an abrasive substance (CARBon cORUNDUM) used in grindstones and as an abrasive powder. P. *Catch Phrases* cites it as a WWII usage, and perhaps so in Brit., but it was in earlier and quite common use in Am. as an office or garage wallhanging or desk piece, and generally much approved by those who tended to do business under a sign that read "Think." (Poets, of course, favor the sign that reads "Create" or "Ideate.")]

immaculate conception   1. The Roman Catholic dogma, advanced since the late Middle Ages but not pronounced infallibly until 1854 by Pius IX, that the Virgin Mary was free of all taint of original sin from the moment of her conception. [Because she was a direct creation of God, and the first such since Adam and Eve, who share with her the distinction of being the only human beings so conceived.] 2. *In caps.* A common name for a Roman Catholic school. [Sometimes with odd results on the sports page, as during football season when a headline may announce, "Immaculate Conception Trounces Holy Name."]

implode   1. To collapse inward suddenly and violently, as a sealed glass vessel partially exhausted by a vacuum pump. (Early Edison light bulbs—into the 1930s—were such vessels, and imploded when broken. Certain phenomena, among them tornadoes, atomic fission, and collapsing novas, display at least some of the intricate characteristics of implosion.) 2. *Phonetics.* To sound a consonant by a sudden stoppage of breath. [In both senses the word is a *ricochet formation* (which see). It could not have come into being except as it bounced off *explode*, which is itself a metaphor adapted to the detonative sense in XVII. See *explode.*]

inchoate   *adj.* Incipient. At an early stage. Just beginning to get underway. [But at root an even more specific sense that may be rendered "hitched up but not yet plowing." Few words have a more specific root image. < L. *cohum*, the harness strap from the yoke of oxen to the forward point of the plow. Hence *in cohum*, hitched up. Whence L. *incohare*, variantly *inchoare*, to begin, or in the extended root sense "to hitch (oxen) in preparation for beginning (to plow)." *Cohum* is ult. from IE *kagh, kogh-*, to grasp, to attach (to), and with gh/h → L. stem *coh-* → *cohum*. There is something like the lovely specification of good poetry in such a word, making it what the XIX philologist Archbishop Richard C. Trench called "a fossil poem."]

incubus   1. A male fiend said to descend upon and to rape sleeping women. (Hence, because modesty once required women to be horrified by the pyscho-dramas of their wet dreams:) 2. A nightmare. 3. *Figurative ext.* Any troublesome great weight upon one's spirit: *The incubus of I.R.S. descends quarterly.* [< L. *in-*, on; *cubare*, to lie (with) → *incubare*, to hatch. INCUBATE. In medieval L. *incubus*, a demon of wet-dream nightmares; later the nightmare itself; any nightmare.]

HISTORIC. Despite the power of this demon, on which Freud and others have expatiated, and his taste for rape, he seems to have limited his etymological assaults to the missionary position. The female of his dark line was called a *succubus* < L. *sub*, under; CUBARE, at root, "(she) who lies under." Succubi shared the family taste for rape and also its adherence to the most traditional sexual positions. In late and medieval Latin *succuba* meant a whore. (Though if one may take the evidence of the illustrated cribs in the *lupinaria* of Pompeii, the working girls knew far more positions than their demon sisters.)

Succubate does not occur for egg hatching, though penguins, to protect their eggs from the ice, hatch them on their large webbed feet. If the feet contribute significant heat, which I doubt, penguin eggs might be said to be *circumcubated.* Bordellos regularly offer girls for circumcubating young heroes and middle-aged overreachers.

inertia [L. lack of skill, < *iners, inertis,* idle, sluggish, dull, cowardly. Ult. < IE *ar-,* to conjoin, to articulate, to put together. (ART.) So, with a neg. prefix, "lacking art, unassembled, fragmentary." Also, resistance to change, as in L. *vis inertiae,* lit., the power (force) of inactivity (which expresses resistance to social change even if it promises better things, if it involves the risk of trying something new.) And it was in this sense that inertia was borrowed in the new Latin of the Renaissance metaphysician.] 1. *Physics.* Resistance to change: the tendency of a body in motion to continue in motion in a straight line (or, add now, in orbit), and of a body at rest to remain at rest. (Thus both the hypothetical "irresistible force" and the "immovable object" are inertial. But in common use, as in the Latin:) 2. Sluggishness. The tendency to remain motionless. (In which the inertia of momentum is ignored.) But note: *He became inert when his jaw interrupted the inertia of Ali's right cross.*

inglenook 1. A corner by a fireplace. 2. *Hence, but loosely, if away from the fireplace.* A cosy retreat. [Rare in Am. Not entered in AHD, but coming back into general recognition as the well-advertised brand name of Inglenook Wine of California. (I hope the Inglenook Wineries do not store their wine by a fireplace to age. Let me assume rather that the name suggests we should drink the wine cozily around the fireplace. The second element, *nook,* corner, recess, cozy place. *Ingle* is easily confused with *angle* but is from Gaelic and Sc. *aingeal,* fire; hence, "fire (place) nook."]
      HISTORIC. Old fireplaces were commonly separate walk-in rooms that contained a firepit equipped for cooking with various grates, andirons, and hooks on which to hang pots, as well as a spit and some means for turning it. There was often a comfortable space on either side of the firepit, at least one of the walls of which was equipped with a rack for holding wet capes or mantles (whence *mantelpiece*). And commonly there were benches on either side of the firepit (and sometimes in front of it as well) where one might sit to toast oneself warm. In modest houses, of course, the dimensions were reduced; but at least one bench by the fire was a common furnishing.

in thing   Post-WWII slang for "that which is *in* fashion." Picked up and popularized by chi-chi advertisements for fad-everything:

> There was a promoter named Hugh
> Who promoted a dance called The Screw.
>   Disco by disco
>   From NY to Frisco
> He made it the in thing to do.

inwit   Consciousness, awareness, imagination, native perception. [All readers of James Joyce know the "agenbite of inwit." I pass on the complex pun of "agenbite," reserving the obvious guess on "achingbite." Archaic *inwit,* inner awareness and imaginative connection, as opposed to *outwit,* discrete information. Langland makes the distinction in *Piers Plowman,* XIV:

> With *inwit* and with *outwit,*
> Imaginin' and studie.

And cf. *mother wit,* native discernment, understanding.]

IO   In official record-keeping, especially in the armed services, stands for *initial only.* So, *Harry S. (IO) Truman.* In some areas, especially in Texas and Oklahoma, boys are named with initials only, as in R. T. (Artie) Bailey, and such a name would be recorded as R. (IO) T. (IO) Bailey. Conceivably J. Doe might be entered in a service record as *J. (IO) (NMI) Doe.* And of, course, there is *John Q. (IO) Citizen.* And see *NMI.*

   Purists insist that there be no period after a letter that is itself a name, but to leave the name as John Q Citizen is to invite confusion.

ipse dixit   It is spoken authoritatively, or as it might once have been phrased, "it is spoken authorially," i.e., from the source itself. [L. "He (himself, the authorial authority) said (it)." Translates the Gk. form *autos epha,* Himself spoke it, used by the followers of Pythagoras in dogmatic assertion of the master's text, they taking his words to be as indisputable as Scripture is to biblical fundamentalists. The Latin form has been in common English use since XVI or a bit before.]

iron   (pronounced *ī-'rn*) [At root, "the holy metal." Cf. the many legends of God-blessed swords, e.g. Excalibur, as part of the warrior mystique. And the first soldiery equipped with variously enforced iron swords did, in fact, hack down the last bronze-equipped opponents as if God were on the side of iron. Etymologically < IE *eis-*, rage, passion, religious frenzy or seizure. With an early dissimilation of *r* for *s* → Gk. *heiros*, holy ("god fervent"). HIERARCHY. And similarly → L. *ira*. rage. The original stem into Gmnc. prob. as *is-* and suffixed *-'rn-* → the successive OE forms *isern, isen, iren* → ME *yren, yron, iren* with first syllable pronounced as *ē* (as in *he*). The prob. XVI pronunciation was *ī'-ron*, the short *i* much like the earlier long *e*, and then *i'-ron*.] 1. The metal. 2. A symbol of strength and inflexibility. [Note that simple iron is vastly inferior to steel in strength, flexibility, and the ability to retain an edge, and it is also quite frangible, but retains its metaphoric quality for strength from its earlier superiority to bronze in weaponry in many idioms, some of which are self-evident, as **iron man, an iron constitution, in irons, to have many irons in the fire.** But also:

strike while the iron is hot Seize the opportune moment. But note that one does not strike with the hot iron. Rather, one strikes it, hammering it into shape on the anvil while it is still hot enough to be malleable.]

to iron out To make smooth. [To press with a hot iron.] But in ext. to solve a problem, to remove obstructions.

iron curtain The rigid line of demarcation between "Free Europe" and the Russian-dominated eastern bloc. [Coined by Winston Churchill in a speech delivered at Fulton, Missouri, March 5, 1946, where the then-former prime minister had gone to receive an honorary degree from Westminster College: "From Stettin in the Baltic to Trieste in the Adriatic an iron curtain has descended across the Continent." The term immediately passed into wide popular use. "Curtain" might seem rather flimsy for so impenetrable a barrier, but "iron" carries the idea of impenetrability, and "curtain" the sense "that which obscures and shuts out." In any case Sir Winston mouthed his phrase with such clangorous overtones that when China later excluded the outside world, that exclusion was, in some natural association, labeled the *bamboo curtain.* Language, finally, means whatever we agree that it shall mean.]

isthmus 1. A narrow strip of land connecting two large land masses: *the isthmus of Panama.* 2. *Ext. in anatomy.* (a) A narrow band of tissue connecting organs or parts of an organ. (b) A bodily passage between two cavities, as the Fallopian tubes. [< Gk. **isthmos* with sense 1 above.]

italic   1. *Printing.* A slanting type now used primarily to indicate emphasis or to set off foreign words and phrases, or sometimes quotations. 2. *In cursive or typewriting.* Words or passages emphasized by underlining. Commonly **in italics** Underlined for special emphasis: *The initials of Samuel Oliver Bryant should always be written in italics, preferably with an exclamation point.* (Underlining goes back at least to the Middle Ages as a means of indicating emphasis or a special case. It was probably by association that italic type came to be used for the same purposes, but not until the XIX.) [< new Latin *Italicus,* Italian. There was no Latin word for what in It. is now *Italiano.* As late as early XIV, Dante used *uno latino* for what is now *uno Italiano.* He did refer to southern Italy as *umile Italia,* low(-lying) Italy, but *Italiano* did not come into general use until late XIV.]

HISTORIC. In 1501 Aldo Manuzio, scholar and founder of the Aldine Press, issued an esteemed edition of Vergil, which he set in a slanting type in imitation of Greek manuscript cursive. Manuzio dedicated his many-volumed edition "to Italy" and by association the slanting type became known as *Italicus,* whence Eng. *italics.* Note that *all* of the Aldine Press text (like the sex life of Mae West) was set in italics.

itching palm   An immemorial idiom-metaphor for greed, the yearning to feel money in one's hand. The first English attestation is in Shakespeare, *Julius Caesar* IV.iii (1603), but the idiom must have been long current in spoken use. Cf. the Gypsy formula, "cross my palm with silver."

J

jake   *Obs.* A Prohibition Era (1920–1933) rotgut liquor in which the crudely distilled and often inadequately denaturalized alcohol was disguised by a liberal infusion of Jamaica ginger. Especially in the South, jake was the old toper's sneaky Pete. [A slurred condensed form of J(am)aic(a).]

jake leg A Southern generic term for the various "shakes," paralyses, impaired gait, and seizures caused by delirium tremens or by poisoning. The distillate vapors of moonshine alcohol were (and still are) commonly cooled through an automobile radiator, picking up cumulatively poisonous lead particles from the solder; but the base of jake was poisonously denatured alcohol. Jake remained a favorite of alcoholic derelicts and became available in a drinkable form with the relegalization of hard liquor, but the Prohibition Era death toll raised a scandalously high monument to public morality.

jamboree   A large, festive gathering. Now primarily associated with a large encampment of regional, national, or international Boy Scouts. [Origin unknown. The suggested derivation < Fr. *jambon*, ham, and the root sense "a large-scale hamming it up" is merely coy. The forms *-aroo, -eroo, -oree, -aree* are variants of the common agential suffix *-er*, and give boisterous slang voice to the sense, "having to do with." *To jam* is "to crowd together." There was a mid-XIX Am. form *camparee*, a large camp meeting; and that is one likely source of *jamboree*, the *b* being a modified survival of the *p*. Perhaps surprisingly (at least to me, and perhaps to the B.S.A.), MMM's first attestation (1864) is from card playing and labels a high hand of cards: "as, for example, the two Bowers, Ace, King, and Queen of trumps . . . which entitles the holder to count sixteen points." I do not know what game of cards is being discussed, but the holder seems to have a large festive gathering and good cause to celebrate.]

jig   1. Now a lively dance, old style: *An Irish jig.* 2. Sc. and into earlier
Brit. colloq. and thieves' cant: A trick or ruse. Whence surviving:
the jig is up The trick has been discovered—with the effective
sense, "Clear out! Scram! Beat it! Cheese it, the cops!" Alternatively, if used by a bobby who surprises a petty thief red-handed,
"I've gotcha!" [Sense 1 is of unknown origin, perhaps by way of
caper, "an act" as, a danced jig is a lively caper. Sense 2, also of
unknown origin, was once not only the country dance and the
music for it, but in XVI Brit. the singsong cry of street hawkers and
chapmen, and also what they sold. "Look to it, you booksellers and
stationers, and let not your shops be infected with such stinking
garbage . . . as the *jigs* of newsmongers." —*Pierce Penniless,* a work
unknown to me, quoted by Charles Mackay, *Lost Beauties of the
English Language* (London 1874).] 3. *In Am.* A bigot's sneering
name for a Negro. [Now obsolete, or nearly so. But not many years
ago when, in a poem about Hamlet (since discarded) I wrote "the
jig is up," a black friend wrote to accuse me of racial bigotry, as if
the jig is up meant "the nigger is awake." I assured him that
neither Hamlet nor I had had such a thought and apologized for
replying in black ink on white paper. This vanishing term from the
bigot's vocabulary is a shortening of *jigaboo,* a ridiculous label for
what the bigot takes to be a ridiculous person, or, in fact, nonper-
son.]

jimmies   Broken bits of chocolate rods about the diameter of spaghet-
tini used as a topping for ice cream, esp. for ice-cream cones. Now
more commonly called *sprinkles.* [Now rare, though once common, and one of the most neglected of Am. idiomatic terms. *Jimmies* is not listed in any Am. dict. I can find and the term is ignored
by both Mencken and MMM, yet the word was in common use in
Boston in the 1920s and beyond, when every soda fountain kept a
supply of jimmies to sprinkle on ice-cream cones. I can further
testify from positive memory that in an early Anthony Quinn
movie (late 1930s?) he ordered an ice-cream cone and added,
"Gimme lots of jimmies"—evidence that the term had at least
penetrated Hollywood. I can only conjecture that *Jimmies* was
originally a trade name, perhaps from as far back as ca. 1900, but
that it passed from common use before our dictionary makers took
note of it.]
   HISTORIC. I wrote to the National Candy Wholesalers Association of Washington, D.C., and was told that they have no historical
record of a candy product named *Jimmies.* A similar question to the
National Confectioners Association of Chicago, however, produced

the information that *Jimmies* are "chocolate decorative particles" and that they were first (and still) produced on December 31, 1944, by Just Born, Inc., of Bethlehem, Pennsylvania; and further that Just Born filed on February 16, 1966 to make *Jimmies* a registered tradename (registration no. 829,873), the application still pending according to the Association's files.

But Just Born enters the picture long after *Jimmies/jimmies* was in common use. I knew the term intimately from the very first nickel I clutched in my hand at the ice-cream store back in 1922 or 1923. On incomplete evidence, I can only guess that Jimmies was an early XX tradename that fell out of use sometime before WWII, and that Just Born, Inc., later picked it up and revived it because of its surviving recognition value.

And there is a postscript: on October 14, 1985 I stopped at a Howard Johnson's Restaurant in Massachusetts and saw for the first time in many years a sign offering *Jimmies* as an ice-cream topping. Our dictionaries and even our National Confectioners have forgotten, but Howard Johnson's remembers.

joey 1. A clown. [Brit. and Am. circus slang. After Joseph (Joey) Grimaldi, great Italian pantomimist–clown, 1778–1857. The fool in Italian pantomime was called *Giovanni,* shortened to *vanni,* and altered to *zanni,* whence English *zany* (see *Browser's I*). Joey was the son of a well-known *zanni,* made his first stage appearance at age two, scored a triumph as Punch in Dec.–Jan. 1800–1801, and went on to be celebrated as the King of the Clowns, scoring many triumphs in England and in other English-speaking countries.] 2. *Australian.* A young kangaroo. Also in limited use for a cub of various other animals. [If from joey for clown, probably because cubs of all sorts are given to ludicrous play-antics. But while this is a plausible guess, it depends largely on the dating of the Australian form, which I am unable to fix.]

John: dear John letter *WWII GI slang (but ah the pang!)* 1. A letter to a man in the armed services who thought his girl would be waiting for him only to be told she has found someone else. 2. *Ext.* Any kiss-off. (Cf. the now faded catchphrase, "If you weren't going to kiss me, why did you keep me standing on tippy-toes?") [*John* as a generic man's name. In the neurosis of war, boys tended to make rather too much of their pinup photo of the girl-they-left-behind-and-were-making-the-world-safe-for. The kiss-off was the letter that ran more or less to a set formula: "Dear John: You will always be in my thoughts. I cannot stop dreading what you are going through out there. I know we all owe you so much, and my most affectionate thoughts are with you wherever you are, along with my prayers for your safety; but I have met someone else, and before I knew it I had fallen in love beyond my control. Please forgive me and do not think badly of me. I will always remember you. Good-bye, sadly. /S/ Fifi."]

John: why don't you speak for yourself, John?   A catchphrase from colonial history. [As celebrated by Longfellow in his poem "The Courtship of Myles Standish," the evidence being that the phrase is Longfellow's invention, though based on Boston folklore. Captain Myles Standish, a warrior but shy in the presence of women, sent John Alden, a sort of lieutenant-governor of the Massachusetts Bay Colony, to ask the hand of Priscilla Mullins in the name of Captain Standish. She is said to have replied, "Why don't you speak for yourself, John?" John did, and they lived happily almost forever after, he living to be the oldest male survivor of the original Mayflower company of 1620, dying Sept. 12, 1687 at (about) age 88.] The phrase survives in extended contexts. In 1948 Adlai Stevenson, as governor of Illinois, greeted the delegates to the Democratic Convention so movingly, declaring party principles so persuasively, that he was chosen as the party's candidate. One newspaper reported that the party had said to him, in effect, "Why don't you speak for yourself, John?"

juggernaut   An awesome force that overruns and destroys anything in its path. [< Hindi, *Juggernaut,* "moving lord of the earth," one of the titles of Krishna.]
    HISTORIC. In an annual Hindu religious festival an enormous statue of Juggernaut-Krishna is drawn in procession on a huge wheeled platform, the faithful pushing it, straining to turn the wheels, and tugging at many ropes to pull it forward. Once it begins to roll, it is nearly unstoppable. It happens regularly that some of the faithful, tugging at the ropes, slip and are crushed under the enormous wheels. They obviously acquire great soul-merit in being so crushed by the god. It is even likely that some few choose to commit suicide in this way. These facts have given rise to the assertion that the Juggernaut ceremonial is a ritual of suicide, and certainly every sort of religious excess is recognizably human; but suicide is not an intrinsic part of this ritual, as it has been in historical times in, let us say, the mass suicides that have occurred periodically in Japan.
    Religious association and meaning aside, juggernaut (lowercase)

has become fixed in English to label any implacable destructive force: *The German juggernaut has twice crushed Belgium.*

julep   1. *In earlier English,* A syrupy sweet drink (rosewater, violet water) used primarily to disguise the taste of medicine. (Bear in mind that before recent encapsulation most medicines, however bitter, were prepared in powdered form to be swallowed [ugh!] with a liquid.) *But in Am. since colonial times,* 2. A mint julep, a mixture of bourbon, sugared water, crushed mint leaves (no stalks please), served over shaved ice. The julep is the ritual drink of the Southern states, served ideally in frosted silver goblets. Its preparation is a ritual, with the special point that since sugar will not dissolve in alcohol, it must be dissolved in the water before the water is added to the holy spirit of the bourbon. [At root, "rosewater." < Arabic *julāb,* < Persian *gulāb,* rosewater, a cosmetic mixture made by steeping rose petals, and also used in cookery when sweetened. In OF and ME *julep* the common sweetener was honey, though small amounts of Far Eastern cane sugar reached Europe expensively (by caravan routes) for medicinal purposes.]

jumping-off place   In the western migration after the Civil War, a last outpost of civilization before forging on into the wilderness. [The term was used as early as 1826 in the first MMM citation, with the sense, "the ultimate boondocks." So Flint, *Recollections,* "Being, as they phrase it, the 'jumping off place,' it is necessarily the resort of desperate, wicked, and strange creatures who wish to fly away from poverty, infamy, and the laws." But note that "as they phrase it" implies a long-familiar form; and in this sense there were jumping-off places in colonial times, as Fort Wayne, Indiana, for example. And the citation from Flint might describe Vinegaroon, later Langtry, Texas, where "Judge" Roy Bean opened his hanging saloon in 1882. But the evolved sense is as given above, and most applicable to such a place as St. Joseph, Missouri, ca. 1866–1870. There westward migrants could find wagons and supplies, make final repairs, and above all sign on a professional wagonmaster for the 2,000-mile trek to Oregon. Once they left the jumping-off place, they might forage for food and buffalo chips, and they might get limited help from remote army posts, but they were essentially on their own in a long, dangerous race before winter closed in.]

kangaroo Familiar Aussie variant, *roo;* and for a young roo, *joey.* The Australian marsupial mammal existing in several subspecies. The first Europeans to observe it (1770) were Captain James Cook and his naturalist, Sir John Banks. [An irregular among words. Perhaps at root, "the gawnose watt." Cook and Banks recorded the name as *kangooroo,* stating that to be the name given it by the aborigines; but see note.]

HISTORIC. As a language curiosity, the name has worked back from English into all the dialects of today's Australian aborigines, but no one who has studied their language(s) has located any pre-English word resembling *kangooroo* or *kangaroo.* The name is clearly the Englishmen's misunderstanding of some native form. Distorted into English, it has returned to aboriginal use as a (now) native word.

Cook and Banks reported a meeting with an unidentified band of aborigines on the east coast of what is now Queensland. Neither party, of course, could speak a word of the language of the other. The Englishmen pointed to this odd animal and asked its name, and received in reply something they heard as *kangooroo,* understanding that to be the native name of the animal. For all they knew the natives might have been saying "God knows what these queer-looking blokes are talking about." Language grows from anything. And everything.

kazoo A crude musical instrument, usually a tin tube with a paper membrane that vibrates when the player hums into it. [Developed in XIX Am. in what was then hillbilly music.]

kerchief In Am., more commonly, *handkerchief,* and sometimes *pocket handkerchief.* A piece of cloth, commonly a square and commonly of cotton or linen (though other fabrics, esp. silk, are also used), carried (now) by men in a pocket, by women in a purse, and variously used, primarily for mopping perspiration or for blowing the nose, though paper handkerchiefs have largely taken over the nose-blowing detail. Some are ornamented and worn in the breast pocket of a man's suit, variously folded and draped. Ladies' handkerchiefs are often frilly, embroidered, and lace trimmed, rendering them practically useless. From XVI into XIX Brit. fops wore large, lace-trimmed, usu. silk kerchiefs tucked into their sleeves (whence the addition of *hand* to form *handkerchief*). These ornate cuff-dandles were a favorite loot of starveling petty thieves, though the act of snatching one was once a hanging offense. [But all these variants are late. At root, "head covering." So OF *couvrechief, couvrechef.* I.e., a *babushka* (which see). *Couvre,* to cover; *chief, chef,* head. The Eng. form retains OF *chief,* altering *cou(v)re* to *ker.* The common, and late, *handkerchief* is, somewhat confusingly, "head cover for the hand."]

kewpie, kewpie doll   A chubby, elfin, originally winged doll with a fluffy topknot bound at the base. With uppercase *K,* a registered tradename for a doll once as popular as the still-surviving teddy bear. [The name is a commercialized "cute" variant of *Cupid.*]

HISTORIC. The doll was manufactured by a licensing agreement with Rose O'Neill, who died in 1944, long a great and gracious lady of Greenwich Village. She was a successful commercial illustrator especially given to flowing designs of winged, glowing, innocent creatures, Kewpie dolls having been based on some of her illustrations. The popularity of these dolls from early XX to WWII left Miss O'Neill with a comfortable income even after the market crash of 1929, and she continued her career as an illustrator almost to the day of her death, tending always to angels and putti.

kid   [Of unknown Gmnc. origin, as evidenced by Ger. *Kitzchen,* kid, fawn, kitten; and also *kitzeln,* to tickle. First attested in Eng. in XII Anglo-Norman legal document, but prob. into Brit. dial. use under Danelaw in IX–X < ON *kith,* young goat. The sense "human child" is from XVI colloq.] *n.* 1. The young of a goat. (Also, though rarely, the young of various wild animals, esp. of the antelope.) 2. *Slang.* A small child. [Though U.S. schoolmarms have scorned this use as illiterate and ignorant, it is a simple, indulgent metaphoric use, fondly comparing goat-kid and human-kid because of their boisterous antics, silly cuddliness, and general smelliness.] 3. The flesh of a kid as food. 4. Also the hide and the fine leather made from this hide. *adj.* Made of kidskin: *kid gloves. v.* 1. To deceive, tease, josh. 2. *Rare.* To have, to bear a child: *Mary is kidding again.*

to handle with kid gloves To take care of a matter tactfully, carefully. [Kid gloves have become an idiomatic symbol of delicacy, taste, tact, savoir faire.]

kidding n. Joshery, foolery, trickery, deceit. A subtly variable slang form. As a simple statement, *no kidding* = Honest, really, straight out. As a question = Do you really mean it? You're not trying to fool me, are you? As an exclamation of delight = Wow! Wonderful! And in many common variants Am. has: *I kid you not; who's kidding?* (as the hangman said); *don't kid a kidder;* and *who's kidding who(m), kiddo?* Also (now obsolete but pandemic from ca. 1900 into the 1920s) *I love my wife, but oh, you kid!*

kidney   1. Either of a pair of body organs of the abdominal cavity. The kidneys are essential to proper bodily chemistry, its water content, and especially to the excretion of urine. [The possible root sense is "abdominal eggs or testicles"; but the first element, now *kidn-*, is untraced. Earlier *kiden-;* with *ei*, egg, also testicle.] 2. Sort, type, temperament: *of that kidney.* [Shakespeare uses "man of my Kidney," *Merry Wives of Windsor* (1598). But the first OED citation is dated 1555. The idiom has never been wholly explained, but is almost certainly related to the theory of the humors (see *humor, Browser's I*) in which the secretions of specific organs determine one's character type. *Of that kidney,* however, has come to mean not only "of that temperament" but "of that sort / class / condition of being."]

Kilkenny cats   Legendary incessant squabblers. *Ellie and Peter Welt keep their marriage alive by fighting like Kilkenny cats.* [Kilkenny is a county in southeastern Ireland. In solemnly attested legend, two Kilkenny cats fought one another until there was nothing left but their tails. With typical Irish reticence, the tails stopped short of eating one another and wandered off quietly, each in quest of a cat it might wag. (And so the Welts, who have settled down happily to wagging one another.)]

Kilroy was here!   A piece of graffiti that somehow became a part of the GI psyche in WWII, and even before, for it began to appear on the toilet walls of camptowns by about 1940 when the first draftees were training for a war yet to come. Part of the game seems to have been, at least in those first years, to scratch this message on the most unreachable places; and though "Kilroy" may have begun as a particular man's surname, it soon became a generic announcement from the psyche, a way of saying, "Hey, world, I'm here!"

Carried to Europe, this unknown quantity spread to the Tommies and to other allies, even to those who did not speak English. After Normandy there was hardly a wall in a liberated town that did not assert Kilroy's passage. By then *Kilroy was here!* had come to mean something like, "We got here and we did it, by God!" Kilroy had somehow become the alter ego of the civilian inductee who took the world, the sad sack as the unknown liberator.

klutz   A worthless person. A dim-witted bungler. [Slang, but only so because the term came into Eng. from Yiddish. In a sense all Yiddish borrowings are relatively recent in Brit. and Am. (mostly within the last century). But also because an only lightly veiled anti-Semitism has taken Yiddish terms to be déclassé. Had this stem passed (for instance) into Fr. *closse* (as it did not), *closseur,* whence *closser* might readily have become standard English. The form is certainly of ancient lineage. < IE *gel-*, to cohere, to form into a lump or ball (GEL). With g/k → Gmnc. *kel-*, zero-grade form *kl'-*, with common Gmnc. *-z-* suffix → MHG *kloz,* clod, block, lump, whence Ger. *Klotz,* Yiddish *klutz,* these variant forms keeping the IE root sense but the Ger. and Yiddish extending it further to signify a cloddish, lumpish, blockheaded person.]

knight of the road   1. *In XIX Am.* A hobo, esp. one who chooses freedom from social commitment as a philosophy, as distinct from a mere tramp who wanders homeless as an outcast. 2. *In Brit. since XIV.* A highwayman. [So called in a pun on the order of the Knights of Rhodes, a militant order of knights and crusaders who did not return home but established themselves on the island of Rhodes as pirates and brigands. A properly weighted cross makes an excellent battle axe.]

Know Nothings   A mid-XIX more-or-less secret political party self-labeled the American Party. Founded in 1853 it was dedicated to the suppression of immigrants and naturalized citizens, its principles (or lack of them) based on the fear of the *mongrelization* of the descendants of colonial America by the new *immigrant hordes.* In public the Know Nothings advocated a 21-year residence as a precondition for naturalization. In private they proposed other, stronger anti-immigrant measures, but insisted that they *knew nothing* about such things when questioned about their means and aims. *know nothing* By about 1900 the Know Nothings had ceased to be a ponderable presence in U.S. politics, and their name, in lowercase letters, began to serve as a label for any insistently self-seeking superpatriot.

kraal   [Though often cited as a Dutch word, this form is properly Afrikaans and almost certainly < Portuguese (common in Afro-pidgin) *curral,* animal holding pen. CORRAL.] 1. *In Afrikaans.* A native settlement, the crude huts commonly clustered inside a stockade. *And also,* 2. A holding pen for livestock. [There is an obvious racial slur in this doublet.] 3. *In limited Am. use.* A pen for large sea turtles. [This use may be specific to Key West, whose Turtle Kraals are a well-publicized tourist attraction. Now a restaurant by the Shrimp Docks, it features richly stocked fishponds, a small bird sanctuary, and (until 1984) three kraals of giant turtles. Until shortly before WWII the kraals were used to hold boatloads of giant Caribbean turtles to be processed into canned turtle soup. The present tourist turtles are survivors of the soup cauldrons. It is not surprising that the original owners of this enterprise were from the Dutch West Indies.]

L

lamp: to smell of the lamp   To show signs of diligent (or merely academic) preparation in a written work. (Cf. *to burn the midnight oil,* essentially the same idiomatic metaphor, but implying diligent study rather than academic withdrawal from reality.) [Forms of the lamp idiom have been in use since at least ancient Greece, but among the Greeks implying only late hours of diligent study. Latterly, however, the idiom tends to imply bland academic theorizing to one side of practical engagement, a theoretic rather than a vital approach. *Ronald Reagan's speeches never smell of the lamp; it is hard to believe, in fact, that their texts have ever seen the light.*]

Latter-day Saints   A self-designation of the Mormons. [Their scripture, the *Book of Mormon,* is declared to be the history of an early, lost, holy people who lived in the true ways of God. This history of the early-day saints was inscribed on tablets of gold in an unknown language. In mid-XIX the Angel Moroni brought these tablets to Joseph Smith in Vermont and showed him how to translate them, taking the tablets back to their sacred storage place after each transcription. The resultant scripture informs Mormons what they must do in this latter day to strive for the purity and godliness of the saints of that earlier day.]

lavender, to lay (out) in lavender   To store away carefully, to preserve. [As domestic napery and linen used to be sprinkled with lavender *(herbe du lavenderie)* after washing, ironing, and folding. [In XVI, passingly, with the sense "in pawn," because Lombard pawnbrokers used to sprinkle fine linens with lavender to keep them fresh while in pledge.]

leap year   A calendar year that adds a twenty-ninth day to February to raise the annual total of days to 366; commonly in years divisible by four but not in centennial years unless they are also divisible by

400. The years 1600 and 2000, for example, are designated leap years, but not the years 1700, 1800, and 1900. [A firmly fixed English idiom since probably VIII, if we may judge by ON *hlaupjahr,* which is a simple transaction of the English term. Most Norse calendar terms are from English, and since the main interplay of English and ON occurred during the IX–X Danish occupation (Danelaw), the English term is probably earlier, though not attested until XII. (The original Nordic week consisted of the five days from Tuesday to Saturday that are named for Nordic gods. Under the influence of the Roman calendar a Sun-day and a Moon-day were added, this Roman influence reaching the North through Britain, a former Roman colony.)]

If we ask what the leap year can be said to leap, the idiom makes little sense. It does, however, have historical precedent. Medieval astrologers computed a 19-year lunar cycle, and for reasons beyond my ken, they deleted the last day of the last month of this cycle, calling that deletion *saltus lunae,* the leap of the moon. A deleted day every nineteen years is hardly the same thing as one added every four years, but both computations were calendar corrections, and with the lunar correction to hand as an example, scholars simply translated *saltus* as *leap,* and that idiom became locked into the language as if it made sense. (In German, be it noted, the term is *Schaltjahr,* "shift year" or "switch year," if that term can be said to make better sense.)

In the Romance languages the term is some variant translation of L. *annus bisextus,* bisextile year, as in Spanish *año bisiesto.* The term, however, needs explanation. The Julian calendar, adopted in Rome in 46 B.C., was the first in Europe to introduce a calendar correction by adding a day to February. It did not, however, add a February 29. Rather, it counted February 24 twice. By some reasoning that must have seemed natively clear to the Romans, February 24 was taken to be the sixth day before the kalends of March (March 1), as if February had 30 days. So designated, and counted twice, it was called *ante-diem sextum Calendas Martias.* Such is the base of the now securely established idiom in the Romance languages, though it probably makes no more sense to native speakers of those languages than *leap year* does to native speakers of English (and none to foreigners).

HISTORIC. The normal calendar year consists of 365 days. By astronomical measure, however, a year equals one complete orbit of the earth around the sun, the orbital period being calculated as 365 days, 5 hours, 48 minutes, and 12 seconds. This small discrepancy between calendar time and orbital time began, by millennial increment, to move the seasons out of calendar place, January 1 beginning to fall in the season of approaching spring. This seasonal precession underlies the various customs of *April Fool's Day* (for which see *Browser's I*).

In 1582, therefore, either as a work of Pope Gregory XIII or as one under his auspices, the Gregorian calendar introduced substantial corrections. Adopted later in Britain and the American colonies, it remains in use among us, its surviving imperfections tended by government astronomers who regularly adjust the length of Dec. 31 by a second or so to keep our year coincident with our orbit, and perhaps to assure us that no one need be early or late for his or her funeral.

Nor for the wedding. It is not possible to say when there developed the custom of permitting women to propose marriage during a leap year. There is an obviously apocryphal legend that St. Brigid proposed to St. Patrick during a leap year and that he rejected her on the grounds that he was already betrothed to his vows but paid her a forfeit of a kiss and a silk gown. St. Patrick, be it noted, was a fifth-century saint, and the concept of the leap year, or at least the idiom for it, could not likely have developed in Britain before VIII and probably a bit later. The story element of St. Patrick's forfeit suggests a date closer to 1200, for in 1228 the Scottish Parliament enacted a law imposing a fine on any man who refused such a leap-year proposal unless he could show that he was already betrothed:

> Ordonit that during ye reign of her maist blessed maiestie, Margaret, ilka maiden, ladee of baith high and lowe estait, shall hae libertie to speak ye man she likes. Gif he refuses to tak hir to bee his wyf, he shale be mulct in the sum of ane hundridty poundes, or less, as his estait may bee, except and alwais gif he can make it appeare that he is betrothit to anither woman, then he schal be free.

An absurd law. A fine of 100 pounds (though commonly less) was an enormous sum. And what if a milkmaid thought to propose to a lord? It is mind-boggling to think what a sum of fines a busy and ugly woman might occasion during a leap year! Yet the measure is worth noting as an early enactment of women's rights. Nor was it merely a parliamentary bouquet for Queen Margaret. Circa 1300, as I have read—though I have not seen the law—a similar one was passed in France, and about 150 years later, though only briefly, in the city-state of Florence. Perhaps the leap of *leap year* will turn out to be the leap into matrimony.

lecher   A sexually excessive person, implicitly a man. In the common practice of this species, a lecher works out to be anyone more given to sexuality than the person who uses the word. [And though the dead do not consent to be interviewed, the sense "sexier than I in ways of which I disapprove" is locked into the word, the root idea being disdain of cunnilingus (when engaged in by others). Etymological root sense: "a licker." Ult. < IE *leigh-*, to lick. With g/k → Gmnc. *leik-*, Ger. *lecken*, to lick. So *lichen*, plant licked off rocks by animals. The OE form was *liccian*, the two *c*s being pronounced as *k*s. But ME *lechour, lechur* is primarily from OF *lecheur, lechour*, which is separately from Gmnc. by way of Frankish. The OF verb form *lechier*, to be lecherous or to engage in lechery, had the generalized sense "to be sexually promiscuous."

In common though unrealistic assumption lechery was earlier assumed to be specifically a male disportment, barely conceivable as a feminine trait, and so the root sense *cunnilingist* (unless lesbians be taken into account, as our languages have not been moved to do). Today "lecherous woman" is an acceptable concept, as lust has ever been in fact: it is the legend that changes, not the species.]

leeway   1. *Nautical.* The distance a ship drifts off course downwind (or because of current). Also, later, room in which to maneuver downwind. 2. *Generalized ext. Brit. only.* The distance one has strayed off course because of wind or current: *He has a lot of leeway to make up.* 3. *In Am.* A margin for freedom of action. A permissible degree of freedom of action in a given situation: *If adolescents are permitted a little leeway they will yet manage to wreck everything as securely as adults have done.*

leman   (Obs. but known to readers of English poetry up to about XVI, and then revived as a pejorative poeticism by XIX Romantic poets.) A paramour, a mistress, an illicit lover, a concubine, a doxie. [But up to early XVI, without pejorative sense, a lover; and in earliest use in XIII, a man. So ME *leofman*, love(r) man, < OE *leofan*, to love. (LIEF.) Also with the ME forms *lefman, lemman*. Then specific to a woman in the senses given. The term had about expired by the time Shakespeare wrote his sonnets to the dark lady—which kept him from picking a leman.]

lemon   *Slang/colloq.* Anything that turns out badly *(his date/his marriage/his business was a lemon)* but now primarily a new automobile that is forever in need of repair: *The Ford Edsel was almost certainly the worst lemon in the history of Detroit.* [Lemon is, of course, an idiomatic symbol of sourness, and the term must have been influenced by such common slang phrases as *a sour deal, it turned sour, it soured on him*. But these are chance associations. This sense of *lemon* in Am. can be dated as arising in or immediately after 1910 (anglicized by 1919, prob. transmitted by WWI doughboys), and is a reference to slot machines, on which any combination that includes a lemon is a loser. The original phrase was prob. *to turn up a lemon*, to lose when playing a slot machine. Few idioms can be fixed with more precision.]

HISTORIC. There is some small confusion about the history of slot machines. One source declares that the first three patents for such a device were issued to Gustavus Schult in 1895. In 1896 a man named Leonhart seems to have developed a five-reel machine that spun poker hands. And there is, at the corner of Battery and Market Streets in San Francisco, a plaque (California Registered Historical Landmark No. 937) commemorating the invention and first manufacture of slot machines at 406 Market Street by Charles August Fay Bell in 1894, and the development of "the original three-reel Bell slot machine in 1898."

I leave the sorting out of these slight discrepancies to the seminarians of the Cathedral of Las Vegas. The point of etymological interest is 1910, when the Mills Novelty Co. began to produce slot machines with, for whatever reason, attached gum vending machines whereby, aside from gambling, the player received a stick of gum for each coin played. The flavors of the gum led to the use of the now-traditional fruit symbols: *lemon, spearmint* (soon replaced by *cherry*), *orange,* and *plum*. Combinations of these symbols in a row paid off in various multiples, unless the combination included a lemon, in which case the player lost. The symbols also included bars, now traditional, stamped *1910 Fruit Gum,* and three bars in a row signaled a jackpot payoff.

Lemon seems to have passed into idiom almost immediately, an evidence of the fervor with which the American psyche embraced the slot machine or "one-armed bandit."

let's get this show on the road   In any context: let's get going. Move it! [Ubiquitous since its WWII usage as a call to arise and take action, but also in earlier general use. It is tempting to say this was originally an exhortation by the manager of a theatrical troupe, exhorting it to be on its way to the next performance and to waste no more time in getting ready to hit the road. And though I can find no secure attestation, it probably was. But grant language the ability to take off and fly without being licensed by literal fact.

Consider *no skin off my nose,* said by many sources to have begun as a boxing term. And probably so if one thinks of bare-knuckle street fighting rather than gloved boxing (in which noses tend to get flattened but not scraped). Yet there are many situations in which noses can be skinned, and such one-to-one literal deriva-tion, unless securely attested (as this one is not) are at least chancy. Not that it's any drip off my icicle (of disputed Eskimo origin), nor hair off Matilda's balls (of unlikely origin), nor any barnacles off my keel (attributed to Shipwreck Kelly), nor any helium out of my balloon (attributed to the Goodyear blimp).]

linoleum A now rare, once ubiquitous floor covering, esp. in U.S. kitchens. Linoleum consists of linseed oil hardened by oxidation and mixed with ground cork. This slurry is then heat-sealed onto canvas or burlap in a process that impresses a colorful design on a slick surface. At room temperatures linoleum is flexible enough to roll gently, and it was commonly sold in rolls; but it becomes brittle when cold, and even when warm will crack if folded sharply. [Pat-ented in England in 1862 by British chemist Frederick Walton and given the registered tradename *Linoleum* < L. *lin(um),* flax; with *oleum,* oil. Linseed is flaxseed. Cf. OE *līn,* flax (LAWN), *līnsāēd,* linseed. A U.S. court has since ruled that linoleum has become a common noun (for a no-longer-common product).]

HISTORIC. Up to about WWII, when it began to be replaced by creosote tiles, linoleum not only decorated the U.S. kitchen but made it a dangerous place, its slick surface becoming treacherously slippery when wet. Any common spill could be dangerous, but a main peril was the contemporaneous icebox, in which the melt of ice commonly drained into a large basin placed under the ice compartment. If this basin was allowed to overflow, a thin, wet film spread across the linoleum, causing a slick on which only a figure skater could hope to keep his balance. Bone-breaking and some-times lethal falls were once a common side effect of Mr. Walton's once-capitalized, now lowercase linoleum.

Still offered for sale today is a product called *Congoleum* (Regis-tered Tradename). To my eye, it looks very much like the old linoleum, but I have been unable to learn its chemical difference, nor have I been able to trace this new name. And though I have seen this product on store racks, I have never been aware of it in use in any U.S. home I have visited.

loblolly *In Brit. dial. and colloq.* 1. A thick gruel (XVI). 2. A country lout. (One who lives on loblolly. XVII. Cf. Am. *beaneater* for Bostonian.) Also a lazy fool; one who lolls about stupidly. [Brit. dial. *lob*, 1. To boil. 2. To slurp; to eat noisily. And *lolly*, soup, broth, gruel. Now archaic or obs. in Brit., but the term was brought to the American colonies in XVII and survives in limited use in the southeastern states, sense "one" being an obvious ext. of the XVI Brit. sense, and sense 2 remaining as pure XVII Brit.:] 1. A mudhole. 2. A lout.

loblolly pine A southeastern U.S. pine. A splendid, straight, tall tree when allowed to grow, but commonly slashed young to make paper pulp. [Because the wood, when pulped, is cooked in a thick (and stinking) stew to be hot-rolled into paper when sufficiently reduced. Cf. Brit. dial. variant *lobscouse* < LOB; *scouse*, broth, gruel, stew.]

long hooding *Among Am. taxi drivers.* In answer to the radio dispatcher's announcement of a fare waiting at a certain address, the act of a cabbie who reports himself closer than he really is to the waiting fare. (Because the dispatcher routinely assigns the fare to the nearest cabbie.) [Whimsical, as if the responding cabbie stretched the hood of his car a few blocks to place himself near the waiting customer. The idiom is Am. and very recent but already widespread. Michael Pertschuk of the Advocacy Institute, Washington, D.C., writes me that he first heard this term in the autumn of 1985 in a Virginia suburb of D.C., and then heard it again a few days later in San Francisco. It is unlikely to pass into general slang, even transiently, for the term makes no sense except within the special situation of cabbies who hack radio cabs, but once that situation is known, it is an engagingly imaginative language turn. Cf. under *ghost,* the 1930s cabbie idiom *to ride the ghost.*]

loran [*LO*ng *RA*nge *N*avigation.] A navigational method based on pairs of radio transmitters, the master transmitter sending a constant signal which also bounces off a slave station, the two signals being received at microsecond intervals at any given point within range of the twin stations. The navigator is supplied with maps of, say, the Pacific marked with precomputed arcs that show all the points at which there will be a given differential reading. When the navigator repeats the reception from a pair of stations at approximately right angles to the original pair, he gets a reading on another set of precomputed arcs, and his position is at the point at which the two arcs cross. Loran navigation, when accurate, gives the navigator a position in a matter of seconds.

HISTORIC. Previous overwater navigation was by instruments, by visual sighting of islands, and by celestial observations at night. The business of shooting a three-star fix to compute a position within a triangle used to take the navigator about 20 minutes. In a plane, that is, he could only compute where he had been more than 100 miles back, projecting that line to an estimated present position, and starting the process over again after a short pause for a cigarette.

The loran network established over most of the Pacific by early 1945 gave the navigator his position in a matter of seconds *if his receiver was exactly calibrated.* In September 1945 I was a gunner on the crew of a B-29 returning to San Francisco from the Pacific. On our last leg in from Oahu our navigator took a loran fix that showed us to be north of the Aleutians when we were about five hours out of Oahu. Since the navigator, seduced by his push buttons, had forgotten how to shoot an old-fashioned star fix, the pilot took a guess at a course that would make a landfall on the California coast at least two hundred miles south of San Francisco, and then turned left. The idea of such a landfall is to hit far enough to one side to know in which direction to turn. Had he cut it too close and made it to land north of San Francisco before turning left, we might have wetted our feet in Canadian waters. We might in any case have wetted our feet had we not had the luxury of plenty of fuel. Like most technological miracles, loran has a spectral power for multiplying error.

lord and master   A long-established redundancy of the sort to which legal prolixity has long been addicted, as in the surviving phrasing of Latinate diplomas that grant "all rights, privileges, and perquisites thereunto appertaining." And though one might argue that rights, privileges, and perquisites are distinct terms, it would be a fine-spun argument, which could not negate the ancient legal tendency to duplicate terms.

Theodore M. Bernstein, *Dos, Don'ts and Maybes of English Usage* (New York, 1977), sees the source of this legal tendency in the double language of Britain following the Norman Conquest: "Sometimes redundancy in legal phrasing is a vestigial remnant [note: double phrasing?] of the Norman Conquest. . . . to the lowly worker in the fields a particular animal was a *sheep* in his Anglo-Saxon tongue, whereas to the conquering lord presiding at the table the flesh of that animal was mutton in his Norman-French speech. [sic] To insure understanding on all sides, some legal phrases included both languages. An example is *will and testa-ment,* in which the Anglo-Saxon and the Norman-French words are coupled to describe the same document."

Perhaps. But the Normans phrased law for their own convenience with little regard for the Saxons, and the examples leave some doubt. In XII and again in XIV (see *mutton, Browser's I*) sheep is attested as signifying a young animal, and *mutton,* a full-grown one. Yet Bernstein has a point. The coexistence of two distinct tongues in England certainly contributed to legalistic redundancy but only as a contribution to an already established tradition of legal self-importance. From the beginning, self-importance and self-seeking have been the basic curriculum of the law.

lord of creation   1. Man. [Based on Genesis 1:28–29, in which God is said to have given man dominion over all things on earth. But today this idiom means:] 2. An imperious swaggerer who expects all others to defer to him. (Which is not a pointless possible definition of humankind.)

loser: born loser   One who fails at everything, or is disaster-prone. [Am. Dating uncertain, but prob. XX and subsequent to common XIX *born leader* and *born to succeed.* The idiom could be argued to be applicable to an able person whose best efforts are nullified by bad luck, but in common usage it implies a generalized incompetence.]

loving cup   1. In various church services a bowl, commonly of silver or gold-plated silver, from which all communicants drink wine in turn (or in some Protestant denominations, grape juice, or cream sherry) on the sacramental assumption that trenchmouth for one is trenchmouth for all in equal gift from the hand of God. 2. *Now rare and all but unknown to the young.* Such a cup, commonly deeper and with two gracefully sweeping symmetrical ears, engraved and presented as an athletic trophy. Athletic loving cups were once commonly of sterling silver or heavy plate or, as an economy measure, of pewter.

HISTORIC. Athletic loving cups once attempted the simplicity and grace of a well-turned urn. They were aesthetically commemorative. They have been almost universally replaced by garish trophies that consist of cheaply standardized statuettes mounted on a plastic mishmash of neo-neon Las Vegas lobby architecture. Today there is not a trophy case in an American school or college that is not a monument to the bad taste of the Athletics Department.

lunch   Midday meal. In Manhattan, the food one orders for the sake
of appearances while one consumes the essential three martinis. [In
late XVI, thick piece, hunk, or slab of food. Perh. < Sp. *lonja,* a
slice; but more likely < Sc. *lunch,* a hunk of bread, cheese, a slab
of meat. ODEE notes *luncheon* < *lunch* in XVII by analogy with
punch-puncheon, trunch-truncheon; but the XVII sense was a
snack between breakfast and the noon meal. (*Snack* came into Eng.
in late XVI < Du. *snacken,* to eat furtively—as in snatching food
from the pantry when no one was watching.) *Luncheon* survives
as perhaps a shade more genteel, but lunch became the common
form in XIX.]

free lunch 1. *In Am. XIX saloon custom,* An array of cold cuts,
cheese, sausage, boiled eggs, and sliced bread available free to
drinking patrons. 2. *Common ext.* Something for nothing: *Sooner
or later country girls discover there is no free lunch in New York
City.*

out to lunch 1. *Literally, of a working person,* On one's daily
lunch break. 2. *Common Am. slang,* Not present mentally. *Non
compos mentis.* Not all there (on the mental job). Addled (as if one's
wits were off duty). [I lack a secure dating and can only guess that
this idiom developed in post-WWII U.S.]

$\mathcal{M}$

macabre   Grim, gruesome, ghastly, having to do with death and decomposition. ***danse macabre*** The dance of death. [The *danse macabre* was a common subject of medieval illuminators and later painters, an allegory of wild dancers (life) presided over and finally led away by a dancing-master skeleton (death). The *danse macabre* was intimately associated with the riotous festivity of Europeans seizing their last pleasures at the time of the various great plagues. *Macabre* is a largely unexplained Fr. alteration of *Maccabée* (see below).]

HISTORIC. Among other plagues, the Black Death (bubonic plague) that swept Europe in XIV carried off as much as two-thirds of the population. Bone fires (crematorial bonfires) burned everywhere. The still living reveled wildly in near-certain expectation that they would be carted off to the bone fires tomorrow or the next day. When the plague passed there came a time of great prosperity, the one-in-three survivors inheriting the goods and property left by the dead (as much of it as the crown did not seize). [A note on social improvement: is there anything 230 million Americans can do that 76 million might not do better?]

But this plague revelry had precedents in the medieval morality play based on the apocryphal second book of the Maccabees, in which it is recorded that Antiochus IV required all Jews to worship his Greek gods. Judas Maccabeus and his followers refused and endured especially protracted tortures toward a slow death.

In various versions of the medieval morality plays Death calls great crowds of all sorts of people to him, and each argues for an extension of his life. (Solomon was believed to have pleaded so on his deathbed and to have been given a fifteen-year extension, and that legend may be one source of this motif.) In the obvious moral of the morality play, however, Death always won and led the crowd into the shadows like a pied piper.

The Maccabees, though enduring insufferable tortures, were always given a prominent role in this disputation for a life extension. It is not clear why they would want such an extension in order to endure more torture, but the pious saw it as their desire to go on worshipping the True God at all costs—a thumping moral as long as someone else is enduring the suffering. So from death and the torture of the resolute Maccabees, the unprecedented corruption to Fr. *macabre.*

macadam   1. Now almost universally understood to mean a road surfaced with asphalt tar, or similar material. *hit the macadam Slang.* To go along the road ["hit" it with one's feet]. 2. The material used in such road surfacing. *But at origin,* 3. A method of road building by putting down and tamping successive layers of variously sized crushed stone. Named after the developer of this method of road building, Scottish engineer John Loudon MacAdam (1756–1836). Since most of his road building occurred in late XVIII and early XIX, macadam roads were developed almost a century before what we now call a macadam surface came into common use on roads and streets. Be it also noted that macadam roads were originally for horses and steel-rimmed wagon wheels that would have cut deep into early asphalt surfaces. Until at least 1930 the asphalt used in road surfacing tended to be so soft, especially on hot days, that one could actually leave footprints in it. Carriages and heavy wagons would have rutted it in short order—which is why so many XIX city roads and streets were covered with *cobbles,* which see. What happened was that *macadam* became generic for a road. Thus, when most roads became tar-covered, the sense shifted to the tar as the most prominent feature. So, too, *to macadamize (a driveway),* to cover it with (hot, rolled) asphalt.

madstone   *Am. folk-belief.* An unspecified and unidentified stone believed to have the power to draw the infection from the bite of a rabid or venomous animal. [Whence the name, as if "mad (dog) stone." Of Am. origin but with precedents in ancient medical and alchemical belief that ascribed healing virtues to various stones. *Jade,* for example, derives its name from Sp. *piedra de ijada,* stone of the iliac (side), because such a stone worn on one's side(s) was believed to cure kidney ailments. The OED's first citation in Am. use is dated 1864, but if Life Books (see below) is correct, Abraham Lincoln used the term in a familiar way ca. 1857, and it must have been in Am. folklore from at least early XIX.]

   HISTORIC. Abraham Lincoln believed in the efficacy of madstones. *The Life [Magazine] Treasury of American Folklore* reports that Lincoln's son Robert was bitten by a dog [ca. 1857] and that

"Lincoln took the boy to Terre Haute, Indiana, to have a madstone applied to the wound. To a friend he explained [source of quotation not given] that he had 'found the people in the neighborhood of those stones fully impressed with the belief in their virtues from actual experiment.' "

Life does not say, and I have been unable to learn, what passed for a "madstone" in mid-XIX Terre Haute. Robert did recover and went on to sit out the war on General Grant's staff (Lincoln did take care of that boy) and, further, to become corporation counsel for the tyrannical George M. Pullman Company. Since Robert lived, and since there was then no cure for rabies, it follows that madstones do no serious harm in treating the bites of nonrabid animals.

Maine: As Maine goes so goes the nation   A once-common, still surviving, but faded political assertion that Maine's vote in a national election foretells the national result.

HISTORIC. The saying began as a Republican campaign slogan in the presidential election of 1840 when William H. Harrison, a Whig, solidly defeated the incumbent Democrat, Martin Van Buren.

At that time, because of the wintry blasts of November, Maine's election was held in September. Its returns were in, therefore, about six weeks before those of the rest of the country, and Harrison supporters could not resist making a slogan of their clear victory there.

When the Republican Party succeeded the Whigs, Maine was long known as a "rock-ribbed Republican state." Maine now votes in November, and the state is no longer solidly Republican, but the slogan continued in use for some time, almost as if it were a political axiom. And so it was—in years when Republicans won the presidency; which is to say, a self-evident truth that is true about half the time.

Main Street   1. *Literal.* The principal, usually commercial, thoroughfare of many (perhaps of most) U.S. small towns. [Working from faulty memory, I can think of no major city that is now or was earlier centered on a Main Street. There must be an exception I have not thought of, but Main Street associates immediately with the small town.] Hence, 2. *Transfer sense.* The life, manners, and more or less jingo assumptions of the U.S. small town. [Fixed in popular use seemingly forever by *Main Street* (1920), a wildly popular novel of small-town American life, by Sinclair Lewis. *Babbitt,* a slightly later novel about a small-town businessman, was once also in wide general use to describe a way of life *(Babbittry, he's a Babbitt at heart),* but has largely passed from use as Lewis has lost his once-central position in recent American letters; though *Main Street* seems to survive.]

majority 1. The greater number. 2. Legal adulthood or voting age [at which one ceases legally to be a "minor"]. 3. The military rank of major (corresponds to naval lieutenant-commander). [The rank at which one technically ceases to be a junior officer. In all senses the form is < L. *mājor,* greater, < IE *meg-,* great. MEGALOPOLIS. MEGALOMANIA.]

To join the majority In Greek and Latin, and thus known to the English-speaking literate (though now rare). To die. [The assumption, at least somewhat questionable, was that there were always more people who had died than were alive at any one time.]

the silent majority Perhaps the shrewdest political rhetorical scam in American history, an invention of President Richard M. Nixon, in which he implied that most God-fearing, true, cherry-pie Americans were not vocal about their deep fundamental beliefs, but that all who had nothing to say were uttering their silence in fervent support of aforesaid R.M.N., and God bless him two or three times. An equivalent might be to hold an election and to count all votes not cast as being in one's favor.

maraud To roam in search of plunder. [Now commonly implies a lethal attack. A U.S. jet fighter-bomber was called the *Marauder,* and its specialty was death and destruction. But at root in OF, almost certainly as an echoic rendering of a tomcat's growl-and-purr; *maraud,* tomcat (conceived as a prowler; from a mouse's-eye view, a lethal one) → *maraud,* a vagabond, a wandering rogue (eager to snatch and snitch what he could) → *marauder,* to roam in search of plunder. Into English in XVIII, but though Bailey lists it in 1721, Johnson (1755) ignores it.]

mark *Am. criminal slang, but now common in general slang.* The person selected as a criminal's victim. [Today, *mark* can mean person to be killed (cf. *he's a marked man*). But more commonly, since about 1910, person to be robbed. Earlier, from about 1885, specific to the person a confidence man selected as his victim.

All senses follow from post–Civil War hobo slang *mark,* an in-group sign made by hoboes at or near a house to indicate that the occupant was known to give food or money. And this coded system is ultimately traceable to the signs and symbols once left by Gypsies

to advise later-arriving Gypsies. But *Gypsy sign* in non-Gypsy slang
is a curse and not akin to these scouting marks.]

HISTORIC. The hobo tradition is today on the wane in the U.S.
but was more or less thriving until about WWII. My friend Harry
Crews, the marvelously freakish novelist, spent a year on the road
in the 1930s and found at the approaches to small towns an elaborate system of marks to show what a bum might expect there, from
"thirty days" to "easy pickings." These marks, he assured me, covered basic information in considerable detail, were rarely noticed
by local residents, and were placed where any experienced bum
would be likely to see them as he approached the place.

maroon *n.* The color, dark brownish red. *adj.* Of that color. [< Fr.
marron, chestnut; It. *marrone* < an unknown common root.]

HISTORIC. Spook etymologists have established as a false derivation that the color maroon derives from the battle of Marrone in
Italy, an engagement so bloody that the ground was dyed maroon.
A number of sources have mentioned this false derivation, and it
is at least popular enough to be the wrong answer requested by a
popular TV quiz show in February 1985. And since the ultimate
derivation of Fr. *marron*, It. *marrone* is unknown, the door is open
for spook etymologists. Yet there is no etymological doubt that the
name of the color derives from the name of the chestnut. As for the
now-forgotten battle of Marrone, it is an ancient cliché of battle
chroniclers to say the ground was dyed red or that the rivers ran
red at the scene of the carnage.

marquee *Am. since XIX.* The rigid canopy over the entrance to a
theater. Also, but rarely, a similar structure above the main entrance to other public buildings. The vertical sides of theater mar-
quees commonly bear illuminated signs announcing the theater's
offerings (rarely the name of the theater, which is commonly bla-
zoned in lights above the marquee). [From Fr. *marquise*, wife of
a marquis. This fem. form was mistakenly taken as a plural, whence
this theatrical form, wrongly conceived to be the singular. Note,
however, that in Brit. a *marquee* is a tent at a fair, either an individual small vendor's tent or one resembling a large circus tent used
for group gatherings. The obvious association is with an officer's
tent pitched near a field of battle, usually with some pomp and
pretension and with his shield and colors displayed—a reasonable
paradigm of a theatrical announcement.]

marzipan   A confection of sugar (earlier, honey), a moistener, and almonds pounded into a paste to make small festive delicacies. Prob. in XVIII, with the general availability of New World cane sugar, this paste began to be pressed into molds in the form of cherubs or seated lambs, especially as an Easter treat. [The name is by a long series of confused associations, at root, "the seated king," hence, "the seated Christ, i.e., Christ enthroned." In early It. these honey-almond candies came in a small box festively decorated with an image of Christ enthroned. Still earlier *marcipane* was a small dry measure, and still earlier a small measure of weight. The chain of associations is, therefore, weight → measure → container → decorated container → contents.

    The name was further confused by association with early It./medieval L. *Marci panis,* St. Mark's bread, a festive bread traditionally prepared for the Feast of St. Mark, April 25.

    But at root Arab *mauthaban,* seated king, this name given to a small coin after the image stamped upon it; whence medieval L. *matapanus,* a Venetian coin stamped with a figure of Christ enthroned. This image was then transferred to the box (above) in which the early honey-almond-paste confections were packed, especially as an Easter sweet. When it became customary to mold this paste into Easter figures, the seated lamb was the primary figure, never the image of Christ enthroned—for what Catholic child could eat the head of Christ? It is all but certain that the Arabic root was lost in emergent Italian, largely replaced by the association with St. Mark's bread. So may all eat festively while engulfed in the mystery.]

mathematics   *n.* The branch of learning that investigates quantity, magnitude, form, rate of motion, and the real and hypothetical relations of all these, computing by number, symbol, and various sorts of graphic projection. *adj.* **mathematic** Now more commonly *mathematical.* [At root, "learning." < Gk. *mathēmatikos,* scholarly, given to learning. Hence, given to the study of mathematics. But the Greeks were never accomplished *mathematicians* as we understand the word, at least as compared to the Arabs. They could hardly count much beyond 10,000 (see below, *myriad*). The Greek *mathēmatikos* studied logic, philosophy, and in an approach to our present sense of the word mathematics, excelled in geometry. Hence, a good root sense of the word might be argued to be "geometer."]

matrimony 1. Marriage. 2. The condition of being married. 3. The marriage ceremony. [L. *matrimonium* had the present senses. (Also *matrimonia,* a married woman.) The suffix *-mony* has the various senses: 1. Allotted portion. (ALIMONY. PATRIMONY.) 2. Condition of being. (CEREMONY.) And 3. Functions as an abstract noun ending. (TESTIMONY.) It is ult. < IE *mens-,* measure, and akin to *-ment* as in *management,* the condition of being taken in hand or the act of so doing. The first element is L. *mater,* mother, combining form *matri-*. By all etymological reasoning L. *matrimonium* and Eng. *matrimony* should mean "motherhood." But the two conditions remain at least commonly connected.]

HISTORIC. In most societies matrimony has been conceived as the putative maiden's rite of passage from virginity to sexual serviceability and so, by first causes, to motherhood. But though daddy has his own connection to the concept, the same reasoning would make his involvement *patrimony.* I know of no explanation for this strange survival, but let it illustrate how readily native speakers accept long-established absurdity in word formation. So firmly is *matrimony* established that I have been able to find no lexicographer who has even questioned the propriety of the word.

mausoleum 1. A stately tomb. 2. A palatial memorial containing various ornate tombs. 3. An upgraded name for whatever the local undertaker uses for dead storage. [At root, "(place/shrine) of Mausōlus." He was king of Caria in Asia Minor, on the Aegean. Upon his death in 353 B.C., his wife Artemisia ordered the erection at Halicarnassus of a palace of death that was admired as one of the seven wonders of the world. English has adopted the Latin form of the word which derives from Greek *Mausōleion,* (place) of Mausōlus. Cf. the same form in Eng. *atheneum,* which is the Latin form of Greek *Athēnaion,* place (temple) of Athena.]

maven (Rhymes with *raven.*) An expert, especially in minor matters, as *herring maven,* a *feinschmecker* who has, or pretends to have, special discernment in judging the quality of fine smoked fish. [< Yiddish *meyvn* with sense given, < Hebrew *mēbhin,* wise man (the label applied half-ironically). Though sufficiently common in Am. colloq. as an adopted Yiddishism, *maven* has been ignored by most of our more popular Am. dictionaries. I once had a moment of triumph when I made *maven* in a game of anagrams, only to be challenged and to find the word was not listed in the miserable dictionary Richard Wilbur had chosen as the arbiter for his feloniously rigged game. I had to give him back his silly *main* and lose my turn to boot, but he certainly lost his soul in that engagement. I attest that he did.]

May Variantly *Mae*. A common feminine given name. [The common association is with *Maia*, an ancient Italic earth and fertility goddess. But in no particular conflict with this ancient source, May as a girl's name and as the name of the month is also associated with OE *maeg*, girl, sweetheart, maiden. OE *g* was often unvoiced and commonly disappeared in later English or was changed to *y*. *May*, as a girl's name, is in one sense, sweetheart; and May, the month of sweethearts (in this limited English association).]

May and December A long-established idiomatic figure to label an old man with a young wife or mistress; as applicable in this liberated age to an old woman with a young husband or lover. [I believe this figure, a natural metaphor, to be of considerable age, but cannot locate an earliest, or even early, pre-Chaucerian usage. Note that *January and December* would allow for a greater age disparity, but *homo loquens* knows his metaphors: May suggests the full bloom of youth as opposed to the hoary old age of December. January would put two coldnesses back to back. Or it might suggest that old December is a child molester. The point of metaphor is emotional rather than mathematical accuracy. The point of this one is the contrast between full-bloom time and sere time.]

MCI The official, though otherwise unused, designation of the Kansas City International Airport.

HISTORIC. Air travelers who wonder why their tickets and baggage checks to Kansas City are marked MCI may be interested to learn, as I was, that MCI stands for Mid-continent International, a name assigned when the first major Kansas City Airport was in the planning stages. The mid-continent designation was contested by St. Louis and Omaha, and local boosters avoided it, all road signs and local public mention labeling it KCI.

In the early 1970s a new airport, also locally known as KCI, was built some miles out in the prairie, the old airport becoming known as MKC, for Missouri Kansas City, or simply as the Downtown Airport. To the confusion of travelers, however, MCI remains the official designation in the Federal Aviation Administration's Official Airline Guide, and it remains so labeled on airline tickets, in the computers, and on baggage checks.

meerschaum 1. *In most common usage,* A smoking pipe highly prized by some but requiring such care, especially in the breaking-in process, that it may be said to own the owner. 2. The mineral, sepiolite, from which such pipes are made, a white, claylike, hydrous magnesium silicate, $H_4Mg_2Si_3O_{10}$.

HISTORIC. The technical name sepiolite is $<$ Gk. *sepia,* cuttlefish (see *sepia*) because this mineral, found on seacoasts, was believed to be a wad of decomposed cuttlefish cartilage. It was also believed to be a solidified form of sea foam, whence Gk. *halos hakhnē* and L. *spuma maris,* foam (exhalation/spume) of the sea. Aphrodite (as Venus on the half-shell) was believed to have taken form from sea foam. In another association, therefore, the mineral might have come down to us (though it did not) as *Aphrolite* or *Aphrodilite,* stone of Aphrodite (and to have had a legendary career as an aphrodisiac).

As it happened, the ancients found no use for the stuff, which remained a simple curiosity until XVIII German craftsmen began to carve it into highly prized pipes and cigar holders said to give a sweet smoke, and notable for its ability to absorb nicotine and tobacco tars, whereby it started white and turned to a rich warm brown. So delicately absorbent is the stuff that pipe afficionados wear white gloves during the breaking-in process, because perspiration and body oils would be absorbed as a disfiguring stain.

Ger. *Meerschaum* $<$ *Meer,* sea; *Schaum,* foam, is a simple translation of the Gk. and L. names. Because these pipes have been a Ger. specialty for almost three centuries, the Ger. form is known to pipe smokers of all languages, but there are also: Sp. *pipa di espuma de mar;* It. *pipa di schiuma;* and Fr. *pipe en écume de mer* —all meaning "pipe of sea foam." Eng. has simply adopted the Ger. term.

megrim (pron. *mē'-grim*). Commonly, ***the megrims*** Low spirits. The blue funk. [Attested by OED 1633. A XVII citation gives it as a term meaning the staggers (in animals). John Jamieson, *Etymological Dictionary of the Scottish Language* (4 vols. London 1879–1882): "A whim; a foolish fancy . . . prob. an oblique use of the English term denoting 'disorder of the head.' " But the immediate base is OF *migraine,* migraine, which, via late L., is an alteration of Gk. *hēmikrania,* lit. "half the cranium," with effective sense, "headache in half the head." Cf. *splitting headache.* The Gk. form minus the first syllable and with k/g → *migraine.* The sense connection between headache and mental depression is obvious, the Sc. sense being, as noted, "oblique." *I get the megrims, the fantods, and the mulligrubs at the very mention of reality.*]

melodrama   1. *Now.* A stylized dramatic presentation in which a simplistically overacted heroine is ruthlessly beset by a ditto villain but is saved for a final declamatory clinch with a ditto hero. 2. *Ext.* Any sensationalized account of conflicting but essentially simple motives: *The melodrama of the Bishop Hall murder trial.* 3. *But at root.* A usually romantic stage play with songs and an orchestral accompaniment: *Italian opera is melodrama in all senses.* [< Fr. *melodrame,* coined < Gk. *melos,* song; *drama,* a stage action, < *draō,* I do. Robert Southey, English poet laureate from 1813 to 1843, seems to have been the first to convert Fr. *melodrame* into what one would suppose to be its inevitable Eng. form, if anything in language can be said to be inevitable.]

melon   Any of the many varieties of vine- or tree-growing large fruits with a relatively hard rind and a juicy pulp in which the seeds are located. [The ult. untraced origin is prob. common Mediterranean. In Gk. the form was *mēlon,* meaning either "apple" or "tree-borne fruit." (L. *malum* has this same double sense. Fr. *pomme* means apple, but also any fruit, as in *pomme de terre,* potato.)

This stem was compounded in Gk. with *pepon,* gourd → *melopepon,* melon ("gourd fruit"). And in late L., by back-formation, *mēlon, mēlo* (not to be confused with L. *mel,* honey, which has the short vowel sound; though this confusion has tempted some to explain *honeydew,* which see, erroneously). In late XIX Am. colloq. *melon* came to mean a special bonus; akin to *windfall.* Whence:]

to cut the melon Originally *to slice the melon* To distribute profits among insiders in a venture (now can include employees). Originally with some implication of ill-gotten gain, but now implies a bonus-distribution from a good year's profits or other lucrative return. [Am. First attested by MMM in Chicago *Daily News,* Sept. 16, 1911: ". . . 'deals' and 'melons' and 'extra dividends' and 'inside buying' which were distributed through Wall Street in 1906 and 1909." The use of quotation marks would seem to indicate that all these terms were specialized and new. No specific origin can be attributed, but it is easy to imagine a farm situation in which workers, especially after a hot day, were allowed to regale themselves by slicing up a watermelon or two. White bigots created the legend that Negroes went into uncontrollable raptures when they were eating watermelon, and even made watermelon eating a derogatory racial cliché (so much so that many blacks are still sensitive about being served watermelon), but who doesn't relish a good juicy melon, especially one that has been cooled in the spring, especially on a hot day? (And who doesn't like bonuses?)]

mercy [L. *mercēs,* merchandise, trade goods, pay, reward. < obscure Italic sources, perh. Etruscan, hence of untraced origin. In church L. influenced by *miserere,* to pity, to have compassion ("to make a gift of a good thing in Christian love to one in need"). So *mercēs* took on the Christian sense, "God's compassion toward man, not because he earned it, for we are all miserable sinners, but as a gift of grace from the Divine Love." And thence to the sense, the gift of kindness from mortal to mortal. All non-theological senses are by analogy, as "to throw oneself upon the mercy of the court," not because one is innocent, but begging an unearned kindness.] 1. Kindness and compassion. 2. The disposition to show kindness and compassion.

HISTORIC. The word survives in both its original sense and its acquired Christian variants. Sp. *mercador,* merchant, shopkeeper, dealer in wares. It. *merce,* merchandise. But note also Sp. *merced* with the Christian senses, gift, favor, grace. But also functioning in *merced de agua,* a free distribution of water, and *merced de tierra,* a land grant, these gifts being mundane rather than of the spirit. The interplay in Christian preachment of *mercēs* and *misericordia,* along with *gratia,* is at the root of Fr. *merci,* thanks, and archaic Eng. *gramercy,* great thanks.

meretricious 1. Whorish. 2. *Ext.* Cheap and gaudy, sensationalized: *the meretricious patriotism of Senator Joseph McCarthy.* 3. Unprincipled, self-seekingly deceptive: *meretricious advertising claims.* [The last example is closest to the root in L. *merēre,* to earn money. But this (more-or-less neutral) verb was soon associated with the noun *meretrix,* a whore (one who offers sex for money), whereby *merere* acquired as one connotation "to earn money in unsavory ways." At one time in the corruption of Rome even ladies of noble family whored, becoming known as the *meretrices honestae,* the noble whores. *Merit* is also from *merere,* though with a different connotation. (And between one connotation and another what is a merit *raise?*—an acknowledgment that one has whored faithfully for the company?)

Between connotations I once heard a Boston politician in oratorical flight salute a colleague for "years of meretricious service in city finance." I suspect he used the word accurately, but more accurately than he knew.

See also *emeritus,* a retired professor who keeps the title he has earned by years of either meritorious or meretricious service to collegiate intellect.]

merit   *n.* 1. Superior character: *a man of merit.* 2. Superior quality: *this wine has merit. v.* To earn, to deserve a good; to be worthy of a reward. [IE *(s)mer-,* to share, → L. *merere,* to earn, deserve a share (implicitly in Latin "of good"). P.p. *meritus;* substantive *meritum.* But also in Latin *demerere,* with the identical sense, the prefix *de-* functioning with the sense "of," whereas now, in *demerit,* it functions with the sense "away from, opposite to." Shakespeare uses the word in the old sense (*Othello* I.ii) when he has Othello use *demerits* for "high aristocratic qualities of birth, ability, valor":

> I fetch my life and being
> From men of royal siege; and *my demerits*
> *May speak unbonneted,** to as proud a fortune
> As this that I have reached.

(*May speak as an equal. One removed his hat in the presence of a superior.)

Bailey gives: "to DEMERIT, to do a thing worthy of Blame, Punishment, etc.," but also, "to deserve well." As a noun, however, he gives for *demerit* only "that which makes us worthy of Blame or Punishment." Samuel Johnson's *Dictionary* (1755) gives *demerit* as the opposite of merit, but notes, "Anciently . . . merit, desert." It would follow that *demerit* underwent a sense shift from merit to its opposite in XVII. Today a *demerit* is always and only a mark *against* one's merit. (Modern *demerit* might have taken form as *emerit,* but that form was preempted by *emeritus* to label one who retains in retirement a title earned in long, faithful, or at least tolerable, service.)]

Mesopotamia   An ancient kingdom extending northwest from the Persian Gulf between the rivers Tigris and Euphrates, now part of Iraq. [At root, "between the rivers," < Gk. *mesos* (combining form *meso-*) between; with *potamos,* river. *Pittsburgh is mesopotamic.* And cf. *hippopotamus,* in literal Gk., "river horse," < *hippos,* horse; with *potamos.*]

(I have been asked a number of times if the Potomac derives its name from the Greek, and the answer is no. Had the name a Greek source it would properly be Potamic. The Potomac derives its name from obscure Algonquinian sources that probably meant, "place where the tribute is brought." If that is an accurate rendering, the river was named in a prophetic dream that the IRS would raise its mansions there.)

metaphysic   1. *Prob. the primary common sense, long distorted by history.* The study of the supernatural, the arcane, the ectoplasmic. 2. *At root.* Scholarship [As based on *scholar* < Gk. *skholē*, man of leisure (with time for philosophical inquiry). See *scholar, Browser's I.*] Specifically, the philosophical inquiry into first causes, ontology, and teleology. [< Gk. *meta,* after; *phusikē,* physics; specifically the *Physics* of Aristotle. In medieval collections of Aristotle's works, the *Physics,* his inquiry into the nature of the apparent world, was commonly placed first. After it came his books on the origin, development, and ultimate cause of that world, along with his inquiries into the nature of knowledge itself (epistemology). For scholars who had labored to grasp the *Physics,* these later books were an even greater challenge; for nonscholars all such stuff, including the *Physics,* seemed abstrusely beyond the natural reaches of the world. Whence:]

   metaphysical school, metaphysical poets An early XVII school of English poets—Herbert, Crashaw, and dominantly Donne— whose works were marked by vividly specific imagery elaborated by seemingly fantastic intellectual leaps to noumenal abstractions. T. S. Eliot called John Donne "expert beyond experience." [And if 'experience' is taken to mean the commonly observable data of this world, Eliot comes close to fixing the gist of this distorted word in "other-worldliness." Medieval scholars were much given to parsing the revelations of "the life beyond," and they, along with self-mystifying alchemists (see *alchemy*), commonly thought of themselves as metaphysicians, or they were so labeled; in consequence this label has acquired its popular sense as a designation for supernaturalism, occultism, and ectoplasmic spiritualism. And note that there is no university Department of Metaphysics, neither at M.I.T. nor at the Harvard Divinity School, though that term might at times reasonably label the administration of either institution.]

mew   1. *In hawking.* A cage for molting hawks. [Ult. < IE *mei-*, to change, → L. *mūtāre,* to change. MUTANT. COMMUTE. MUTUAL. The cage is named after its function: "place in which hawks molt (change)." But extended by association:] 2. Any cage for hawks. 3. *Further extended.* Any birdcage, coop. 4. *Brit. only.* A secret hiding place. [Because falconers put molting hawks in quiet, remote places.]

mews (Plu. form used with sing. verb.) *Brit. only.* A street designation, as if *court, lane, place, circle.* [Few words have had so many sequential senses. A mews is now a lane lined by small apartments. Earlier, an alley behind a row of residences. The stables (mews) were once located along it. So Charing Cross Mews, London, once the site of the royal stables; in medieval times the place where hawks were caged for falconry.]

miasma 1. Stinking mass of air, early associated with swamps and their decomposed matter. [Swamp air was anciently believed to cause diseases, whence *malaria,* lit. *mal aria,* bad air; and the ancients attributed malaria to the "poisonous" air rather than to swamp mosquitoes. But recent medicine has borne out the theory of disease resulting from or being aggravated by atmospheric pollutants.] 2. *Ext.* Any stinking air: *the miasmal exhaust of diesels.* 3. *Further ext.* A figuratively nauseating atmosphere or utterance: *TV commercials are the rec. room miasma.* [Ult. < IE *mai-,* to dirty, to defile, to profane. With suffix *-l-* in Gmnc. → OE *māl,* spot, blemish (polluting particle). MOLE. But with suffix *-n-* → Gk. *mainein,* to defile, to dirty; and related *miasma,* pollution, polluted thing. Revived by Renaissance alchemists as if a Latin form.] As adj.: *miasmal, miasmatic, miasmic.*

misprision *Law.* 1. Misconduct, esp. by neglect in the administration of a public office. [Most swearing-in ceremonies call for an oath containing some such phrasing as "I solemnly swear to undertake the duties of this office to the best of my ability." Misprision need not be criminal in intent; it may constitute simple neglectful avoidance of one's sworn duties.] 2. Failure to take proper pains to prevent a crime, or to report to the authorities a crime of which one has knowledge. [Same sense of neglect of one's public duty as a citizen. This misprision is hard to prove at law, but if I know you are drowning in my swimming pool (into which I happened to push you—accidentally of course) and I do nothing about it, that is at least in part a misprision. Or in a clearer instance:] *misprision of treason In Brit. and Am. law.* The failure to report treasonous acts of which one has knowledge. [Even when one does not participate in the treason, one becomes an accessory by the act of concealing it. If in doubt about the teacher who makes you study Russian history, students, turn him or her into the FBI just to be safe, but do so before the final exam you are sure to flunk. < Anglo-Norman (the legal language of England from XII to about XV) *mesprisioun* < OF *mesprendre,* to take wrongfully, to seize wrongfully, < L. *praehendere,* to take/seize wrongfully before (the law). "Marriage is the misprision of sex." —*Le Mari coupable,* by Malgré Lui.]

Molly Maguires   1. An Irish secret society formed in 1843 to oppose evictions by agents of the great landlords. Sometimes called terrorists, they did their best to terrorize the terrorizing agents. [The name is a generic for Irishman, female in form because the members of the society sometimes disguised themselves as women, the better to ambush the evicting agents.] 2. *In Am.* An Irish-American secret society of eastern Pennsylvania coal miners who, from 1865 to 1875, fought against the oppression of company towns, harsh work rules, and industrial police in sometimes bloody ambushes and clashes.

month   One of the twelve divisions of the modern calendar year. A month corresponds crudely to a lunar cycle. [IE *me-*, measure, to measure. Extended form *men-*, → L. *mēnsis,* month. Gmnc. variant *mon-*, month, moon → OE *mōnath,* month, ME *moneth.*]
    HISTORIC. Our calendar is called the Gregorian calendar after the reforms instituted by Pope Gregory XIII, originally named Ugo Buoncompagni (1502–1585). In early Roman times June was the sixth month, followed by September [< L. *septem,* seven], the seventh month; October, the eighth month [L. *octem,* eight]; November, the ninth month [L. *novem,* nine]; and December, the tenth month [L. *decem,* ten]. The errors in this calendar moved the dates of festive and religious observance far out of their normal seasons. In Imperial Roman times July [named for Julius Caesar] and August [after Augustus Caesar] were introduced between June and September, but the "numbered" months retained their names as if there had been no interpolation. This insertion of two months still did not bring the calendar into correspondence with the solar year. By XVI the cumulative error had precessed the New Year almost to April 1 (see *April Fool* in *Browser's I*), and the Gregorian reform was undertaken. The calendar is now in clumsy but approximate correspondence with the period of the earth's orbit around the sun, but scientists still regularly add a second to each expiring year to bring the New Year into accurate correspondence with the period of the earth's orbit. (A second a year is a one-minute error

every 60 years, and the accretion of that error over the millennia would once again move our traditional dating out of its traditional seasons.)

The first six months of the year are named after Roman deities and observances as follows:

January It has 31 days. L. *Januarius mēnsis,* the month of Janus, the two-headed god who faces in opposite directions. He was associated, among other things, with doorways and gates (coming and going). The full reasons for naming the first month after him are lost in dim time, but clearly a new beginning is also a time for looking back.

February It has 28 days normally, 29 in leap years. L. *mēnsis februarius,* month of the festival of purification, < *februa,* an ancient festival, possibly of Sabine origin, held on Feb. 15.

March It has 31 days. L. *Martius mēnsis,* month of Mars. In his earliest form he was *Mawort,* an Italic deity who became the god of war and who may have been so from the beginning, but who was also earlier a god of agriculture. The ancient assumption, lost in time, may have been that land had to be conquered and defended before it could be tilled.

April It has 30 days. L. *Aprilis mēnsis,* month of Venus. Her Greek name is, of course, Aphrodite. If *aprilis* is conceived as *aphro-ilis* the connection becomes evident. The linkage is probably through lost Italic or Etruscan or Sabine sources.

May It has 31 days. L. *Maius mēnsis,* the month of Maia, an obscure Italic earth goddess. The IE stem of her name is *meg-,* great. She is, therefore, "the great (earth mother)." In English, however, the feminine given name May, though it may derive from this source, is as likely from OE *maeg,* sweetheart, maiden. (See *May.*)

June It has 31 days. It is the sixth month, and the last to derive its name from the old-time (Roman) religion. L. *Junius mēnsis,* month of Juno, chief goddess of the Romans. She was the wife and sister of Jupiter, as Hera, her Greek manifestation, was the wife and sister of Zeus. (And cf. the Egyptian dynasts, who continued this godly dispensation in their marriage customs.) The name *Hera* is at etymological source "earth." She was, therefore, or at least began, as the earth goddess or earth mother. At root, the name Zeus means, among other things, sky: hence, the marriage of Heaven and Earth as a concept of creation. The name *Juno* is of unknown origin, but she almost certainly corresponds to Hera in all essential attributes.

moon calf 1. A congenital idiot. 2. A lout. 3. *Rare if not obs.* A monstrosity, animal or human (as for example a two-headed calf in a freak show). 4. *(And even),* One who moons about witlessly, esp. a young love-smitten oaf. [These are the senses to be found in modern dictionaries. The first three are weakened extensions from a seemingly forgotten root sense; the fourth is a merely random association.

In demonic folk belief a moon calf was not even a monstrous deformity but a formless dead blob forced from the womb unmade by the lunatic influences of the moon, not so much a stillbirth as a shapeless malignancy in the very fabric of all nature. A related belief had it that bear cubs were regularly born as such shapeless blobs and were licked into shape by their mothers (see *lick into shape*). Both beliefs are rooted in a black-magic view of malignant forces of unreason and chaos that stalk all life, such omens as the moon calf being signs from the deep source of all horror.

Etymologically *calf* here does not mean "newborn bovine" but "swelling of the flesh," this sense surviving in "calf of the leg"; and this is the sense of the IE root *gelebh-*, to swell, a swelling of the flesh. In skeletal form this root is *g'l'bh'-*, which with g/k and bh/f, prob. in Gmnc. → OE *cealf* (in which *c = k*), the senses being in historical progression: 1. swelling; 2. fetus; 3. the newborn of a cow.]

morning glory 1. The folkname of the common garden vine whose colorful flowers open wide in the morning and then close in the heat of the day. 2. *Ext. in XIX Am. sports slang.* An athlete who begins a game or a contest with flashes of brilliance and who becomes lackluster as he tires. 3. *Generalizing ext. from preceding.* Anyone who performs in this way in any context: *The official flower for the fiftieth wedding anniversary should be the morning glory.*

motor *n.* A mechanical device for converting energy into thrust and motion. [L. *motor,* agential form of p.p. *motus,* moved, of *movere,* to move. The related form *locomotion* came into XVII Eng. with the sense "ability to move (oneself)," the prob. antecedent being Thomistic *in loco moveri,* to change one's position in space; and this sense survives in medical *locomotor ataxia,* lit. "power to move not in order," a syphilitic disease of the spinal cord that impairs the ability to move, commonly degenerating into paralysis. But since the first steam railroad (Wales, 1804) *locomotive* has become specific to the drive engine of a train.]

NOTE. I have seen efforts, especially in WWII technical manuals, to distinguish between *motor* (stationary mechanism) and *en-*

gine (mobile mechanism), but the distinction remains blurred. Electric motors are usually fixed in place because connected to a power outlet, and *engines* do not commonly move about, carrying their power source with them. But a locomotive is driven by an engineer, a motorist drives an engine-powered car, there are single- and multiple-engine planes, but the notable Ford plane of the 1930s was called a *trimotor* or *tri-motor,* and the Ford Motor Company manufactures engines. On electrified railroads, morever, the *engine* is an electrical *motor* that moves along the wire that is its power source. The development of vehicles powered by storage batteries, atomic power, and such fuels as frozen hydrogen will likely blur the possible distinction further. For the present one can only note that it is fixed usage to say *steam engine* (never *motor*) and *electric motor* (never *engine*).

mousse   *Cookery.* 1. A light, whipped, chilled dessert made with egg whites, whipped cream, flavoring, and often gelatin, often mixed with fruits. 2. An aspic of fine chopped meat or fish, sometimes with cream. [Fr. *mousse,* froth, foam. Prob. < L. *mulsa,* fermented honey or the wine made from it (mead), < *mel,* honey. (And note Fr. *mousseline,* in various forms, a sheer stiff muslin or rayon fabric, Eng. *muslin.*)]

mulct   *n.* 1. *Now rare.* A legally imposed fine or penalty to be paid in property. *v.* To impose such a penalty at law. *But also,* 2. To take by fraud, deception: *Time mulcts us all.* [ODEE cites this as "a purely Italic word." Cf. *amerce.* Both are from common Mediterranean sources without IE precedent. To L. (prob. via Etruscan?) as *mulctare,* variant of *multare,* to fine; substantive *multa* (survives in Italian), a fine. One is tempted to associate *multa* with L. *multus,* much, but no sound etymological connection can be asserted.]

mumbletypeg   Earlier *mumble-the-peg.* Variantly, *mumbledypeg* A boys' game of throwing a knife into the ground competitively from many different positions on the fingers and other parts of the body, the loser being required to pull with his teeth a peg driven into the ground. (If the peg is driven in hard, he must of course eat dirt.) [The earliest form, attested 1627, was "mumble the pegge," but cited then in a list of long-familiar boys' games, indicating a much earlier origin. OED says it is called in Scotland *knifie.* EDD cites *mumble* as widely distributed in Sc., Irish, dialects of the northern shires, and also Am., with the senses: 1. To gnaw or chew without teeth; 2. To munch, to gnaw. (The penalty peg is commonly driven into the ground by a stated number of blows with the knife handle. If driven deep, it may require sense one, to mouth the dirt aside, before the teeth can grasp it.)]

mumpsimus   *n.* An old fogey so fixed in long-established error that he will not accept correction. *adj.* Persistently and insistently ignorant. [The form is a nonsense corruption of liturgical *sumpsimus,* we have received, the whole phrase being *quod in ore sumpsimus,* what we have in this hour received.]

HISTORIC. The story is much told, perhaps most recently by Robert Graves in *Impenetrability,* of an old parish priest who had been reading *mumpsimus* for forty years, perhaps from an incorrectly copied missal, and who refused, when his error was pointed out, to change his old *mumpsimus* for any new-fangled *sumpsimus.* But the story is an old priests' joke that goes back at least to ME, and probably earlier. Brewer points out that in 1545 in a speech from the throne, Henry VIII said, "Some be too stiff in their old mumpsimus, others be too busy and curious in their sumpsimus."

murder   [IE *mer-,* variantly *mor-,* death, to die; also, to rub out, to mar. (MAR.) So in L. *mors,* death; *mori,* to die. MORTAL. MORIBUND. In Gmnc. prob. suffixed *-thr',* as deduced from OE *morthor,* murder. ME *murther, mordre.*] 1. The felonious taking of a human life, as distinct from battlefield killing, legal execution, and to some extent from assassination. (And note that Am. criminal slang *to rub out,* to murder, revives one IE root sense.) 2. Am. slang. Indicates enthusiastic approval: *The new Stones album is pure murder!* Also used as an exclam. of enthusiastic approval: *A. How was your date? B. Murder!* Also to indicate an ordeal: *That final exam was murder!* In extended verb senses: *She murdered that song!* i.e., she rendered it poorly. And more formally, *Malice murders (destroys) reputations.*

myriad   1. *Archaic.* The quantity 10,000. 2. *Poetic.* A large indefinite number. *adj.* Countless. ("Beset by myriad woes, I weep, / Insomniac of countless sheep." —X. Tempore.) [IE *meu-,* damp. A root that functions in many words having to do with swamps, wetness. An extended form of this root was *meug-,* and that with a common g/k → L. *mucus,* mucous. MUCOUS. Via *meu-s'-* in Gmnc. → OE *mos,* bog ("mossy place, wet place"). MOSS. And also MOIST, a special evolution from L. *mucus.* Suffixed probably *-ro-* → *meuro-* → Gk. *murios,* beyond all count. (This sense is almost certainly by association with the endlessly teeming life forms of great swamps.)

Then, curiously, the plural of *murios (murioi)* came to mean 10,-000, as if that number expressed the plural of countlessness (as in a sense—see below—it did for the Greeks and Romans).]

HISTORIC. Both the Greeks and the Romans tended to go vague when the count reached 10,000. Any higher count tended to be expressed by something like "countless as the sands, the blades of grass, the stars in the sky" (though on the clearest night no more than 3,000 stars are visible to the naked eye from any point on earth).

In Roman practice an overlined letter-numeral expressed a thousand times more. Thus $\overline{V}$ = 5,000. And thus $\overline{M}$ could be said to equal 1 million, a thousand thousand, but in practical fact the Romans had no accurate notion of so large a number. And how, for that matter, does one even go as far as to multiply MDCXLI by CCCXIX? Our classical ancestors had many talents, but no real theory of numbers.

Not until about X–XI, when arabic numerals crossed the Mediterranean—bringing with them the magic of zero and its shadow in the sidewise eight of infinity—was there a real beginning of European mathematics.

If, at a conservative guess, *meu-* and extended *meu-ro-* had come to express "countlessness" by about 2000 B.C., the vagueness of that concept dominated European mathematical thinking for at least 3,000 years before arabic numerals began to free European mathematicians from the bog in which their languages had mired them.

narcotic   *adj.* 1. Inducing stupor. 2. Of addictive stupefacient drugs. *n. Plu. only.* 1. Any addictive, stupefacient or hallucinogenic substance subject to legal control or prohibition. 2. The class of all such substances, especially heroin and, today, cocaine. [Gk. *narkōtikos,* benumbing, < *narkē,* numbness, stupor. The stem *nark'* is not to be confused with Gmnc. *nar, nahr,* corpse (see *narwhal.*) The senses "stupefied" and "dead" are sufficiently alike to suggest that there may be some connection between Gmnc. *na(h)r-* and Hellenic *nark',* but if so it is at a depth no one has been able to trace.]

narwhal   Also *narwhale, narwal* An arctic whale of the species *Monodon monoceros* ("single-tooth single-horn") with a pale gray dorsal surface, the males of which have a long, thin, spirally grooved tusk (an adapted tooth of unknown function), after which it is sometimes called the *unicorn whale.* [At root, "corpse whale" (because of its pallor) < Norwegian and Danish *narhval,* < ON *nāhvair,* < *nār,* corpse; with *hvair,* whale. To the best of my knowledge the Gmnc. root *nah(r)* survives in English only in this compounded name.]

naulum   *Obs.* In Greek burial practice, a small coin placed in the mouth of the dead to pay for the passage across the River Acheron on Charon's ferry. See *pennies on the eyes* (of the dead). [*Naulum* is the L. form of Gk. *naūlos,* passage money, < *naus,* ship. NAUTI-CAL. ASTRONAUT. Akin to the once-common, now obs. *naulage,* 1. Passenger's fare on a ship. 2. Charge for shipment of cargo. And 3. *By association.* A ship's cargo.]

neat   *Obs.* A domesticated bovine. (Survives only in) *neat's foot oil* An oil derived from the hooves and shinbones of cattle, once in common use for treating leather. (But now rare except in craft work, having been replaced by other oils, and therefore prob. in limited survival even in this combined form.) [Ult. < IE *neud-*, to make use of, enjoy the good of, needed thing. (NEED) → Gmnc. with d/t → skeletal stem *n't-* → OE *nēat*, domesticated bovine.

The root sense might equally be rendered, "thing of value." So taken, IE *neud-* echoes the sense of IE *peku-*, wealth as expressed in heads of cattle. (See *peculate, peculiar, pecuniary* in *Browser's II.*) Before bars of metal (later made into coins) became a medium of exchange, one's wealth was expressed in livestock (as the Masai of Africa still do). Many of the first metal bars and coins were stamped with a bull's head in memory of what was once the only wealth. *Neat* is a word that has virtually disappeared from the language, but it provides a telling clue to the survival of old concepts in deep language memory.]

nice guys finish last Sportsmanship is fine but winning is better. Good losers get that way by being losers: winners get that way by playing as hard and as dirty as need be. [This baseball saying, since generalized to any tough competition, from business to war, was coined by Leo ("The Lip") Durocher and became practically his logo as a hard-driving, umpire-battering, dirty-tricks major-league manager. In a stormy career as manager of the New York Giants from 1948 to 1955, he won a pennant in 1951 (his second as a major-league manager) and the World Series in 1954—definitely not by gentlemanly sportsmanship.]

niggard n. *Rare.* A miser. *adj.* Miserly. (But the more common adjectival form is *niggardly.*) [The first element, *nig*, miser < Swedish dialect *nygg*, miserly. Into limited Eng. use under Danelaw (IX–X) with the form *nigon*, prob. < ON *hnōggr*, miserly. The later Frenchified form (found in Chaucer) is *niggard* with the common pejorative Fr. and Eng. suffix *-ard*, as in *bastard, coward, drunkard, stinkard*. (This unexplained pejorative is akin to Ger. *-hardt*, able, and English *hardy.*)

This word is now sometimes, but irrationally, suspect as a racial slur, by late association with the bigot's *nigger*, though it evolved long before American racial oppression and discrimination.]

ninepins (Plu. in form but takes sing. verb as in "Ninepins is an obsolete game.") A lawn bowling game in which the target is a rack of ninepins. [I cannot find ninepins listed among current games, nor can I find any rules for this game, nor how the pins were set up. It was, though briefly only, a simple variant of tenpins as played on a bowling green. That game was so popular (see the legend of

Rip Van Winkle), esp. among the Dutch settlers, that their lawmak-
ers banned "lawn bowling at tenpins" as an addictive waste of time.
The addicts, thereupon, evaded the law by removing one pin and
calling the basically unaltered game ninepins. The official morality
was specifically numerical and was evaded by the numbers.]

ninety-nine and forty-four hundredths percent pure   Pure indeed.
About as close to lily-white as one can get in this world. [After the
advertising slogan adopted in mid 1920s by Ivory Soap. I haven't
the slightest notion what the slogan means, except that the stuff
contains 56 hundredths of a percent of certified impurities, possibly
noxious, but a sustained national advertising campaign fixed this
slogan in the public mind as a useful catchphrase, and it survives,
though Ivory Soap began to vary its logos about 1960.]

NOTE. The missing 56 hundredths of a percent is a token understatement and is somehow more effective than 100 percent might
have been. It is certainly more effective than the blatantly 110
percent effort the Vince Lombardis of this world orated as a goal
of effort, perhaps persuasively where football players are con-
cerned. But except among jocks, even a touch of understatement
seems to work more effectively in English than does loud overasser-
tion. "Anything more than the truth would have seemed too
weak." —Robert Frost.

nit   1. The egg of a louse. 2. *Ext. by association.* A louse. (I have noted
some dictionaries that say "a young louse," and I suppose lice do
hatch young, but who thinks to compute their ages?) [With only
slight and obvious modifications the word and sense have remained
the same for about 8,000 years. Lice, it is clear, were early ancestral
associates. < IE *knid-*, louse egg. With the *k* silenced and with
d/dt/t in Gmnc. → OE *nite*, same meaning. Perhaps akin to, or
influenced by, IE *nizd*, nest (see *nasty, Browser's II*), the original
sense of which was "(bird) sit-down place," and by association "egg-
laying place."]

nit-picking The act of being fussily laborious about trivial details. Also verb, *to nitpick*, and agential, *nit-picker*. [This usage is
Am. and recent. I cannot find an exact dating but will trepidate that
it came into general use in the 1950s.]

NMI   In official record-keeping, especially in the armed services,
stands for "no middle initial. So *Jack (NMI) Frost.* (See *IO* for
"initial only," which is a companion form.) I have known men,
especially from Texas and Oklahoma, whose given name consists

only of an initial, as J. Hanks, and this name would be rendered as J. (IO, NMI) Hanks. (But give the computer another generation or two and we shall all be on the record by social (in) security number.)

no runs, no hits, no errors   1. *Baseball scoring.* An official summary, (a) For an inning in which nothing much happened, (b) For a complete game in which nothing much happened. (No errors is all good enough, but no hits neither wins games, nor gives the fans much to watch. A hitless team could, to be sure, put one or more batters on base with walks—which do not count as hits—and a series of those, or compound errors by the opposing team, could produce a game-winning score; but the result is usually a dull game, and no way to progress toward a winning season. Thus: 2. *In general usage.* Lackluster. Faultless but futile. (And so the once-popular comic epitaph for an old maid: "Lived a virgin, died a virgin. No hits, no runs, no errors.")

nosocomial   *adj.* Of a hospital. **nosocomial disease** A disease contracted while being treated in a hospital for something else. [< Gk. *nosos,* disease; *nosokomeion,* a place set aside for the sick or wounded. (Sometimes applied to slave quarters.) But to render the term as "hospital" would be an anachronism, for nothing in ancient Greece corresponded to the modern notion of a hospital. Wounded soldiers might be tended in a *nosokomeion,* but the term might better be applied to a leper colony, a place for the isolation rather than the treatment of the sick.]

HISTORIC. Hardly a common Am. word, though every hospital administrator has on his desk stacks of reports on nosocomial problems and knows it as a scare word that troubles malpractice insurance. A hospital, unfortunately, is a germy place, hence a likely one in which to become infected. And though most Americans do not know the term, they pay tribute to it in their medical insurance rates. (See also *iatrogenic.*)

not unlikely   Sort of likely but maybe not. [Double negatives of this sort were not unheard of before FDR's New Deal rhetoric, but it is not undocumented that this form became not unusual because of FDR's not unlavish use of it in his not unlengthy presidency. The form is, of course, a political straddle. The person addressed must guess for himself what is likely, unlikely, and not unlikely; the speaker may later interpret his meaning to suit what he sees in his not unconsiderable hindsight.]

novaculite A dense, extremely hard, siliceous stone used for whet-stones and hones. [At root, "razor stone," < L. *novacula,* razor, which is at root "the honed (scraped) thing." Via a complex evolution < IE *kes-,* to scrape. (Zero-grade form *ks-* with a nasal suffix to some such form as *ks'no-,* with common k/h → *hs'no-,* and → *(s)no-;* suffixed LITE, stone: a speculative series.)]

NOTE. *Novaculite* is, as far as I can determine, the only survival in English of Latin *novacula.* For some reason, this common Latin label did not pass into English usage. In XIX and early XX, many gentlemen stopped for a daily shave with a ritual of hot towels, blather, and bay rum at a barber shop called a *Tonsorial Empo-rium,* which might as floridly have added *and Novaculatory Acad-emy.* The language chose to eschew this flourish, but one touches upon a central mystery in asking why a language evolves one form and not another. Why for example English *uncle* from the middle of L. *avunculus,* maternal uncle, and not *atry* from the middle of *patruis,* the paternal uncle and a personage of rather more impor-tance in the patrolinear Roman gens (clan)? *Atry* might be argued to be as logical as uncle, and even to be a more significant title of respect; but such an argument would only prove that logic is not the essence of the language process.

nunnery Literally, of course, a convent, but in common Elizabethan slang, a whorehouse. [Students are generally familiar with Hamlet's rejection of Ophelia's love with the directive "get thee to a nun-nery" (*Hamlet* III.i), but will do well to recognize that his real career guidance was not simply to a life of solitary prayer but to more immediate social interactions. Shakespeare's audiences would certainly have registered the pun.]

O

obstreperous   *adj.* Voicing loud opposition. Heckling. Protesting vigorously. [The sense "noisy in opposition" is specific to the word. < L. *strepere,* to be noisy; prefixed *ob-,* against. Cheer leaders might be said to be *streperous for* their team, and a purist might argue for *the streperous play of happy children,* but the language convention has not endorsed this form. (Cf. *ept, ruly, couth, mune,* all of which are merely artful without their various neg. prefixes.) Children at streperous play become obstreperous when told to do their homework.]

off-islander   *Nantucket localism.* Anyone from anywhere other than Nantucket. [Primarily, of course, a mainlander from the U.S. (called on Nantucket "the continent"), but the real distinction is between Nantucketers and everyone else in the world.

A popular movie about the invasion of Nantucket by the crew of a grounded Russian submarine was given the Hollywood title *The Russians Are Coming.* It was based on a novel by Nathaniel Benchley, the title of which—in native idiom—was *The Off-islanders.* Had the invaders been Martians or day trippers from Wood's Hole, they would equally have been *off-islanders.* So in Utah all non-Mormons, including Jews, are *Gentiles.*]

Old Harry   The devil. *to raise the Old Harry* To have a helluva time, to raise the devil. *by the Lord Harry* By the devil. [Though not firmly attested, prob. < *Old Hairy,* the devil conceived as hirsute and bestial. Hyamson has pointed out, "In *Leviticus,* 7:7, the Hebrew for 'Hairy Ones' is translated 'devils.' "]

onyx   A gemstone variety of chalcedony commonly decorated with intaglios. [At root, "claw stone" or "fingernail stone," because it is a dark stone commonly with pale striations said to resemble the moon (lunette) of a fingernail or the horny claws of predatory animals. < Gk. *onyx*, claw, fingernail, hoof; and by later association, the name of this stone. An Amerind bearclaw necklace might well have passed as onyx among the ancient Greeks.]

opium The inspissated and variously treated sap from the unripe seed pods of a species of poppy. Opium is by itself a narcotic and also a base for morphine and heroin. Laudanum, a popular drug of XIX Am. and the commonest ingredient of the medicine man's cure-alls, is simply an elixir of opium. Opium has a long history as a narcotic smoked in a special pipe and as an oral painkiller or *opiate.* [< Gk. *opos*, sap (of tree or other plant). The diminutive affectionate form *opion* is, lit., "dear little sap/juice," and also the name for opium, a sufficient indication that it was in some use among the ancient Greeks as a narcotic. And nearby Turkey was, until recent intense government efforts to stamp out drug trafficking, one of the principal world sources of opium. Opium was, of course, included in early *materia medica,* and it must have been at least a secret addiction of some Greek physicians, as cocaine was once in common use among XIX U.S. physicians.]

ormolu An alloy of copper and zinc, sometimes with a small amount of tin. Developed in XVIII France it was widely used for elaborately shaped, chiseled, and chased decorative mountings on furniture, many examples of such furniture surviving as prized antiques. The alloy resembles gold and can be worked in fine detail. Gilded brass and even copper have been called ormolu and used for similar work but they tend to tarnish—as does ormolu to be sure, but more slowly. [At root, "milled gold," prob. because the French artisans who developed this alloy thought that name more salable than "fool's gold." Coined from Fr. *or,* gold; *moulu,* milled, p.p. of *moulere,* to grind. (MOLAR.) Akin to *moulin,* mill.]

orthodox Conforming to the traditional authoritative view in religion, morality, and social behavior. [Gk. *orthos,* straight (ORTHODONTIST); with *doxa,* opinion. In mod. slang *straight,* labeling an orthodox, work-ethic life-style (not of the swinging, narcotic, dropout subculture), is an exact return to the Greek sense of *orthos.*]

oysters "R" in season A traditional fish-market and restaurant slogan announcing that oysters are for sale in months whose names contain the letter *R.* Those are the months from September through April. Oysters are not generally on sale in the "*R*-less" months of May, June, July, and August. These are also the summer months in which oysters of the northern hemisphere spawn.

HISTORIC. I am not on sufficiently intimate terms with oysters to know whether or not spawning reduces their delicacy. The R months are also months of colder water, and temperature may have something to do with the taste of oysters. I am sure that a spawning oyster, if not at peak flavor, would yet be edible. But oyster fishing has long been government-regulated in the U.S., and they simply are not taken in non-R months. Why interrupt romance?

$\mathcal{P}$

padlock A portable lock designed to fit through a hasp (as opposed to one fixed in place in a door or gate). [An obscure and redundant form. ME *pad,* lock; with LOCK. From XIII, *pad* also meant "toad." (Origin in doubt.) MD *pad* meant "path," and *paden,* to tread a path; hence possibly toad as "thing found along a path." And just possibly *pad* came to mean padlock because of the whimsical notion that it looks like a toad in one's hand. But with these speculations noted all remains (redundantly) in doubt.]

paint the town red To go on a riotous, or at least festive, spree. [Little is known about this XIX Am. idiom. It seems to be akin to *there'll be a hot time in the old town tonight* and *to set the world on fire.* The sense is clearly to redden by setting afire rather than by covering with red paint. My temptation is to look for a source in the wild sprees of trail herders on reaching a Western town, perhaps with a precedent in the orgies of killing, looting, raping, and burning when guerrillas hit the towns of Bloody Kansas. Yet MMM does not attest its use until 1884, and then in the Boston *Journal:* "A spectrophotometric study of pigments, by Professor Nicolls, is recommended to young men who intend 'to paint the town red.'" It is an arch joke but it uses the idiom as a familiar one, and a lag of something like 25 years between first usage and attestation would take it back to the 1860s, and possibly to Bloody Kansas. Many Massachusetts abolitionists settled in Kansas, and others sent arms and money to support the Free Staters. The Kansas and Western frontier origin is, therefore, plausible, but cannot be asserted from the known facts.]

pajama game 1. The pursuit of casual bed-raggling. The sport of swingers. [And this is the generally received sense since the popular Broadway play *Pajama Game,* adapted by Richard Bissell from his novel titled *7 ½ Cents.* But earlier:] 2. *New York City garment* *industry,* The business of manufacturing and distributing pajamas. [*Game,* business. As in Seventh Avenue slang *rag game,* the garment industry.]

palestrian   Having to do with wrestling. [Gk. **palaiein,* to struggle, to wrestle; *palaistrōs,* a wrestler. → L. *palaestra,* wrestling arena, wrestling floor. A word looking for a press agent who can popularize *palestrian palace* for "wrestling arena," and therein stage tag matches billed as a *pandemonium of palestrian pachyderms.*]

palomino   A prized saddle horse, golden or tan in color, with a light blond to white mane and tail. [The name is Tex-Mex Spanish from Sp. *palumbes,* ring dove, wood pigeon, *palumbinus,* ring dovelike; at root, therefore, a folk formation meaning "horse that resembles a ring dove," but though folknaming is usually sharply accurate in its observations of natural resemblance, this one evades me. The ring dove is especially distinguished by a *black* half-circle on the neck, and a white band on the wings (the one possible point of resemblance to the palomino), but it is not notably buff-colored. In any case, and whatever elusive resemblance prompted this name, the etymology is certain.]

pan dowdy   *Sthrn. cookery.* A deep-dish fruit pie baked with sliced fruit, sugar, spices, and a thick crust. [Some dictionaries give *pan dowdy* specifically as an apple deep-dish pie, and *apple pan dowdy* is commonest; but I have had a peach pan dowdy, and certainly some Southern housewife has ventured on pear pan dowdy. AHD glosses as "origin unknown," and some of the connecting forms are in doubt, but the EDD gives *dowl,* to knead (hurriedly), *dowler,* a cake or dumpling made in a hurry, and at least one substantial connecting form is obs. Somerset dialect *pandoulde,* a custard.]

paper bag: he couldn't punch his way out of a paper bag   *Catchphrase.* A formula of contempt for a weakling. [Am. early XX, anglicized during WWI.]

NOTE. The force of language can be independent of literal fact. Few things are easier than to punch a hole in a sheet of paper if it is stretched tight. I clearly remember, however, a TV gag show in which a champion boxer of the USMC was placed in an oversize paper bag to try to punch his way out—and couldn't. The host of the show assured the viewers that the bag was made of ordinary bag paper, though in a specially ordered large size. Yet the champion boxer could not punch his way out of it. He might as well have tried to put his fist through a wind-wafted piece of newsprint, or to punch a hole in air: no matter how hard his blow, the paper simply yielded before it. And yet, despite all wasted force, language asserts its own, and a man who can't punch his way out of a meta-phoric bag remains a hopeless weakling.

parapet 1. A more-or-less chest-high stone course atop the walls of a castle or other fortification, designed to protect soldiers who fire over it. 2. A similar wall along a rooftop or balcony, designed to keep people from falling off. 3. At ground level, a similar wall or embankment from behind which soldiers may fire while partially protected. [At root, "breast-high (protective wall)," < Gk. *para*, alongside of (PARALLEL); but common as a prefix with the sense "protection from" (PARASOL). The second element is a clipped form of It. *petto*, breast.]

parfleche 1. Undepilated rawhide, esp. buffalo hide, used for heavy robes and moccasin soles. [Also used in making various articles of plainsman's gear, but *parfleche*, as Bernard DeVoto specifies in "Across the Wide Missouri," referred to the hide itself rather than to the article made of it.] 2. *As an exception to DeVoto's specifica-tion,* A large wallet or backpack of parfleche equipped with straps for carrying food and other items on the trail. [At root, "arrow deflector." < French-Canadian *parer*, to parry; *flèche*, arrow. (FLETCHER) Common first in voyageur use in early XIX, then into Plains use ca. 1830. Buffalo hide, esp. in a double thickness, might be an effective shield against arrows, and this fact could be the explanation of the root sense; but voyageurs and plainsmen were not much given to carrying shields. The root sense is more probably based, therefore, on the fact that a buffalo-hide back-pack could be useful in stopping arrows fired from behind.

The term, now practically archaic, has been replaced by *raw-hide* but remains notable, for its root reference still has some point in stressing the special toughness of buffalo hide, and it remains indispensable to accurate historical narration.]

parish 1. In various churches, esp. the Roman Catholic, a diocesan subdivision that has its own church. (The parish corresponds roughly to an incorporated community within a county.) 2. In Loui-siana, following from its French-Catholic origins, the equivalent of what other states call a county. 3. In Great Britain, a civic, adminis-trative subdivision of a shire corresponding to the area of an Anglican church parish. *parochial adj.* Of or concerning a parish. [At root, "(area) around my house." < Gk. *para,* alongside of, around; with *oikos,* house, < *oikeō,* I dwell. (The *eco-* of *economy* is an altered form of *oikos.*)

Parishes are historically specific to religiously homogenous communities, as in Catholic Europe before Protestantism. There are, for example, no Methodist parishes because the Wesleyans began as small, scattered dissident groups within the established Anglican parishes of which they were not a part.]

parody   The imitation or reperformance of a work in such a way as to ridicule the original. [< Gk. *para,* alongside of (PARALLEL); with *ōdē,* song → *parodia,* a (mocking) singing (to one side of the original). The Greek orator Demosthenes (the real or legendary pebblemouth) was renowned as an expert at demolishing orations by seemingly repeating them literally but with inserted ludicrous touches.]

part: till death us do part   A standard part of the marriage vows. [But the sense of *part* is ult. < IE *per'-,* share → L. *pars,* portion, *partire,* to divide. So the senses of the stem *part-* are, 1. A share, a sharing. 2. To divide: *to part one's hair.* And also, to go away, to depart.]

HISTORIC. This part of the marriage vows was earlier "till death us depart," with the sense "take us from each other," for marriage is temporal, there being in heaven (and in alternative destinations) neither marriage nor giving in marriage.

R. C. Trench, XIX Anglican archbishop of Dublin, records that *do part* replaced *depart* in the 1662 revision of the Anglican Prayer book because, as he says without explanation, "Puritan divines objected to the form as it then stood."

(Let me suggest, for the celebratory divorce service of Ste. Polyandra the Conjugatrix, a further revision, to "With all thy worldly goods I thee depart.")

passion pit   A drive-in theater. [Am. post WWII. The first drive-in theater opened in 1953 (in the new postwar prosperity that made cars available to large numbers of teenagers), and such theaters had become common by 1960. *Pit* (as if from *orchestra pit*), the place where cars parked next to the audio hookups to hear the sound; *passion,* the necking that went on in the cars in lieu of watching the movie. Not everyone who goes to a drive-in movie is screenstruck.]

pathos [< Gk. *pathos,* at root, feeling, but with the early associated sense, suffering. The L. infinitive is *pati,* same senses; and the p.p. *passus* is the base of COMPASSION.] *n.* Feeling, compassion. (See *bathos.*) *adj.* **pathetic** 1. *Root sense.* Marked by strong feeling. 2. *Ext.* Arousing pity, compassion: *a pathetic story* 3. A general pejorative for an unsuccessful, inept, stupid person: *he has made a pathetic mess of his life,* or simply, *he's pathetic* = he is below compassion. [A curious sense inversion; as if his failure was so pitiful that it would be a waste of time to pity him, whereby what is expressed is scorn. Cf. Italian *morto di fame,* lit. a (person) dead of hunger (which should elicit pity) but in effect, an utterly worthless person, one not even capable of winning bread from the world, and therefore to be scorned, for what good is a man who cannot win bread? This pattern of reversal is native to the folk mind, especially in cultures in which hunger is a presence and starvation a constant possibility.]

pathetic fallacy Esp. in literature. 1. The attribution of human feelings to inanimate objects: *the cruel sea, the reluctant river, the self-delighting mountain.* 2. The attribution of human feelings, reasoning, actions to animals: *the wise old owl, the merciful squirrels.*

pedigree A record of ancestry. [< OF *pié de grue,* crane's foot. Because in genealogical diagrams the line of descent from ancestors *A* and *B* are commonly obliquely drawn with a vertical to descendant *C,* the figure resembling a letter *Y,* and this figure, sometimes upside down, was fancied to resemble the print of a crane's foot in soft earth.]

peg: not move a peg Not move at all. Stand fast. [This idiom is rare. It was my impression that I had never encountered it, but I must have met it at least once when I read *Huckleberry Finn,* though I passed over it without noting it. Huckleberry says when the steamboat knocks him off his raft and he wanders to the Grangerford house, "a lot of dogs jumped out and went to howling and barking at me, and I knowed better than to move another peg."

I am indebted to Tom Shine of Redding, California, for this citation, and for another, dated 1929, in a recording called "Pinetop's Boogie Woogie," in which the pianist, Pinetop Smith, gives the following instruction to dancers doing the boogie-woogie: "When I say stop, don't move a peg! When I boogie-woogie, I want you to shake that thing."

I can find nothing recorded on the sources of this Am. idiom, but I will trepidate that it falls from "to take (him/it) down a peg," or "to put it up a peg." Peg, here, for a point in a series of gradations, as a high-jump bar is raised or lowered. A peg up or a peg down would therefore equal the least gradation of motion up or down. Not to move so much as a peg, it seems to follow, would be to move not at all.]

Pekingese   *Adj.* Of Peking, China, its people, dialect, customs, cookery. *But as a n.,* A silky-haired, snub-nosed, pestiferous toy dog once popular in Peking, now much favored by doting American dowagers (or so type-cast in Hollywood's hermetic legend). [From the earlier adjectival form *Pekingese dog,* and also rarely, *Pekinese dog. Paregoric* (see *Browser's I*) similarly became a n. in XVIII following the earlier adjectival form *paregoric* (soothing) *elixir.*]

pelican   Labels various large, web-footed, warm-water, marine birds that plunge from the air to scoop fish with their large, long bills, the lower halves of which have expandable pouches for storing and carrying what they do not eat at once. [L. *pelicanus* < Gk. *pelekanos,* pelican (also, woodpecker) < *pelekus,* ax; lit. "ax-bird."]

HISTORIC. In tropical and subtropical ports, pelicans commonly wait for fishing boats to come in, to scavenge discarded fish or parts of fish. In Key West they line up next to the people on the pier, and I have seen children reach up to pet them, a bit afraid of what they might do if they jabbed with that beak, but I have never seen them do so.

The pelican was a favorite creature of medieval bestiaries in which it commonly appeared as a symbol of Christ because it was believed (with no basis in fact) to peck its own breast in order to feed its young with the blood that flowed forth.

peninsula   A long, narrow land mass projecting into a sea or a large body of water. (Peninsular Florida is distinct from the Panhandle. Italy is a peninsula: Denmark, a smaller one; Norway and Sweden make up the great northern peninsula of Europe.) [At root, "almost an island." L. *peninsula* < *insula,* island; prefixed *pen-* < *paena,* almost. The prefix is perhaps most common in Eng. *penultimate* (L. *paenultimus*), commonly rendered in courses on language and prosody as "next to last" (with reference to a syllable), but more properly, "almost last." "Next to last," to speak strictly, would be rendered in English by the cumbersome *proxultimate* < L. *proximus,* next to, nearest to.]

pennies on the eye (of the dead)   No one knows the exact beginning of this burial custom. It could not have developed much before 1500 B.C. for lack of small coins before that time. (In *Browser's II,* see *peculate, peculiar, pecuniary.*) The Greek practice was the *naulage penny,* a coin placed in the mouth of the dead to pay the soul's fare for crossing the River Acheron on Charon's ferry (see *naulum*). Lacking the fare, the soul would be left to roam homelessly, neither in this world nor in the next, and would certainly return to haunt those who had neglected it.

Naulage, fare for a passage on a ship or ferry (< Gk. *naus,* ship), is rare but survives in standard Eng.

At some time, probably in the Middle Ages, the single mouth penny was superseded by two pennies, one on either eye. The dating of this altered custom is uncertain. It was always a pagan ritual in clear opposition to church teaching, which established its own spiritual and material fees for this transition.

Despite hazy and long-abandoned practice, those coins remain to living metaphor. In a WWII poem titled "Scyros," as a dark prophecy of FDR's death, Karl Shapiro wrote:

> With coins on either eye
> The President came by.

And in the 1960s Beatles album, *Revolver,* there is a song called "Taxman," in which the dead are sardonically advised to declare the pennies on their eyes. The obscure practice has faded, but its memory survives in idiom.

pension   The one functioning sense in Am. is regular payments made to a person who has retired from work or service because of disability or age. [At root, "payment." Fr. *pension,* It. *pensione* is a sort of boarding house (house at which one pays to stay). < L. *pendere,* to weigh (whence *pound* as a unit of currency). P.p. *pensus,* weighed; *dispensus,* weighed out, paid out (DISPENSE).]

HISTORIC. Samuel Johnson added to his definition of *pension:* "In England it is generally understood to mean pay given to a state hireling for treason to his country." But when the crown offered him a substantial pension in general recognition of his learned cantankerousness, he accepted it. If U.S. Social Security payments are a pension, they may be understood to be a lifetime of payments one cannot live long enough to recover even if the fund is not bankrupt, and which one must pay taxes on, perhaps as a partial return of capital.

people [L. *populus,* people, the population. (Of obscure, perh. Etruscan origin.) OF *pople, peuple;* ME *peple, poeple, people.*] 1. Human beings in general. Whimsically, *I confused my dog by peopling him.* 2. All the persons of a given ethnic or national group: *the Irish people; primitive people(s).* 3. Persons of a given group or class: *professional people.* 4. Gregarious ones: *Con men are real people people.* 5. Kin, or kith and kin: *my people.* 6. *As a form of address.* All of you who are present: *All right, people: settle down and listen.* 7. The electorate: *the people's choice.* [The term has antecedents in L. *vox populi, vox Dei,* the voice of the people is the voice of God. In more literate times, the L. was commonly abbreviated *vox. pop.* The L. saying did not imply that public opinion was always right and good, but that (in Republican Rome) it was, more or less, law, and therefore absolute (or presumably so). That state of affairs did not last long. The later Romans threw away the difference by declaring the emperor to be divine. Brewer points out that when the people dethroned Edward II and chose his son, Edward III, in 1327, the archbishop of Canterbury, preaching at the coronation, took the L. phrase as his text. The implication seems to have been that Edward II's divine right as king had been superseded by *vox. pop.*—which was, in any case, a fait accompli.]

the little people 1. *In Irish folklore and superstition.* Leprechauns and other small supernatural beings native to dark woods, bogs, and Irish whiskey. 2. *In Am.* The commonality. (a) The masses as distinct from officials and power brokers. (b) *Pejorative.* All those who are conceived to be less important than "our kind" and who should, therefore, take orders from us: *those people.* (c) *Among do-gooders.* The same masses, powerless but possessed of human dignity, and therefore worthy of the reforms we intend to bring about (whether they like it or not).

good people Persons and classes approved by us. *bad people* All others. *those people* Persons not like us and, therefore, unworthy. (We just don't want their kind here. Why don't they go back where they came from?)

period *n.* 1. A more-or-less discrete span of time: *The twentieth century has not had many periods of peace.* 2. A conclusion. The end of something. (a) The point beyond which there is no more to say: *That is my last offer—period.* (b) A dot used as a punctuation mark to indicate the end of a sentence (and so used also after an abbreviation). 3. *Grammar.* A sentence (a statement ending with a period): *William Jennings Bryant spoke in ringing periods before dying as* *a question mark.* [L. *periodus,* cycle (of time, events), < Gk. *peri-odos,* a circuit. And so most dictionary glosses, but the Gk. could also be rendered as "by roundabout roads, through many windings." < Gk. *peri,* about, around (PERISCOPE); with *hodos,* road. Cf. *synod* < *hodia,* plu. of *hodos,* prefixed *syn-,* the syncopated form of *sym,* with, by. *Synod,* a church council to which ecclesiastics come "(from afar) by (many) roads."]

pert *adj.* 1. Saucy, unrestrained, forward, impudent. 2. These same qualities but interpreted indulgently as simple vivaciousness, especially in a child or hoydenish girl. Hence, jaunty. [At root the opposite of what genteel moralists once meant by "a decent reticence," especially in a child or a social inferior. < L. *apertus,* open (but with the special acquired sense "not veiled in the proper forms of respect and reticence"). → OF and ME *apert;* and note old-style Eng., from Fr. *malapert,* impudently open/forward, i.e., ill-bred. But the primary Am. sense now seems to be sense 2 above.]

pheasant A widely various, usually brightly colored game bird and gourmet delicacy about the size of a chicken. [Aside from various show birds valued for their dazzling plumage, the prized wild pheasant of North America is now the Siberian ringneck. The name, however, is < Gk. *phasianos* (It. *fagiano*), bird of the Phasis. The Phasis is a river of Colchis, the ancient kingdom on the Black Sea to which Jason is said to have sailed in the Argo in quest of the Golden Fleece. As with many plant and animal names, the exact creature intended by Gk. *phasianos* is not known; the word may have labeled some species of grouse or partridge. Etymologically, however, the Siberian ringneck served to an Am. gourmet retains its billing as "the bird of the Phasis."]

picayune *adj.* 1. Petty, mean, cheap. 2. Trivial. *n. Formerly,* A Spanish–New World silver coin worth half a *real.* It was the smallest silver coin and was worth 6.25 cents. (A piece of eight, roughly the equivalent of the later U.S. silver dollar, was worth 8 *reales.* Roughly, therefore, though with a much higher purchasing power than that sum would now represent, the *real* was worth 12.5 cents. Note that it was not, as has commonly been asserted, the smallest available coin, but the smallest silver coin. In early XIX in and around New Orleans a nickel was called a picayune—which, one may suppose, is close enough.)

　　don't be so picayune Don't be so mean and cheap.
　　not worth a picayune Literally, not worth 6.25 cents; but in

effect, not worth much. [The term is Creole < Fr. *picaillon,* a small copper coin worth about a farthing, < Provençal **picaioun,* a small coin. The second sense, "trivial" *(picayune gossip),* is reflected in the New Orleans newspaper *The Picayune,* which, with a proudly asserted Creole flavor, might serve as a translation of *The Tattler* (not because it sold for a picayune or nickel: at its founding newspapers commonly sold for 2 cents, and sometimes for 1 cent).]

pickpocket cant   Thieves' cant has always been a specialized jargon that allows members of the in-group to converse without being understood by outsiders, and even to discuss a prospective victim in his hearing without letting him know he is about to be victimized. There have been a number of early dictionaries of thieves' cant, all making the sales pitch that a gentleman who learns the cant may become aware of the thieves' intention in time to save his property or even his life.

Inevitably, too, specialized cant tends to pass into generalized slang, thereby losing its earlier encoding. It must then be replaced by new terms. Cant, therefore, is usually local and ephemeral. Early Brit. thieves' cant, for example, used many terms borrowed from Romany. Brit. rogues have worked out a limited thieves' alliance with the Gypsies, who arrived in England in late XV. *Shiv,* knife, *pal,* brother, *bajour,* bag of money (whence bajour game, *badger game*) and *posh* (misunderstood by British rogues to mean "money" though it means "half" in Romany) are fair examples of a once-dense cant that became generalized into common slang, thereby requiring replacement terms. Among pickpockets *dip* is an example of a term that lost its cant purpose by becoming generalized, whereupon it was replaced by *shot.*

This is a note on Am. pickpocket cant, as an example of the genre. It is derived from a Los Angeles *Times* report, March 8, 1982, on Oscar O'Leary, a retired Los Angeles police officer who specialized in pickpockets. He is reported to have made over 2,000 arrests while on the force. In retirement he continues to nab pickpockets as a hobby.

dunnigan A pickpocket who lacks class. In speaking of Sam the Spear, a princely sort of dip, or shot, O'Leary says, "Sam is not like the sleazy dunnigans who work toilets, or the dips who grift with squealers" (for *squealer,* see below). [*Dunnigan* remains unexplained; prob. the name of a notable sleaze among dips.]

squealer A baby carried by a pickpocket as a means of distraction.

stall A pickpocket's confederate whose duty it is to create a distraction while his partner "spears" a wallet. ("Distraction," says O'Leary, "—that's what it's all about.")

spear n. A pickpocket. v. To pick a wallet. [In XIX hobo slang *to spear* was "to be successful in mooching, begging, or stealing something." Almost certainly a metaphor borrowed from spear fishing.]

hooking Stealing. [But this is an old slang term, long in general slang, and therefore not useful as cant. And the same may be said of:]

grift One's racket. One's way of turning a dishonest dollar. [Originally carnival slang, an alteration of *graft.*] *a grift sense* A feeling (O'Leary calls it "an instinct") for knowing whose pocket can be picked. When the dips apply the term to O'Leary, they mean he can look over a crowd and spot the working pickpockets.

tool The working dip who picks a pocket or a purse while his *stall* creates a distraction. Also called a *wire.*

mark Another term that has been generalized beyond cant-usefulness. [See *mark* as a separate entry.]

feet, on its feet Said of a wallet when it is standing on end in the pocket.

whiz The practice of picking pockets. *on the whiz* Out plying the pickpocket's trade. *guys on the whiz* Pickpockets, esp. those out plying their trade.

[Curiously, O'Leary does not give the cant terms for wallet, purse, roll of bills, watch, bangle, or other items a shot on the whiz might spear; nor the term for the confederate to whom the shot passes the grift so that he will be clean if O'Leary nabs him. The cant term, I am told, is *drop,* but in any case O'Leary's grift sense will have made the drop and he will already be collared by a partner who got the eye from O'Leary.]

piepowder   1. A vagabond, a wandering rogue. 2. A vendor who travels to local fairs to sell his goods. *piepowder court* Also *court of piepowders* 1. A local tribunal for dealing with rogues and vagabonds. 2. The court (the lowest in the judicial hierarchy) for overseeing the management of local fairs. [Brit. only and obs., but a lovely example of the British way with foreign words and phrases. Most immediately < Fr. *pied poudreux,* dusty foot, though the earliest attested form (1267) is the legal L. *pepoudrous.* The term was variously attributed to all wanderers of the dusty British roads. The *piepowder court* dealt with charges against vagabonds but more usually supervised matters at local fairs, itself sitting dusty-footed in the fairgrounds. Though low in judicial rank, these courts sat at a time that theft was commonly a capital offense. Since fairs could only be held by royal license, and since they were important to the local economy, piepowder courts were vigilant and peremptorily stern in dealing with cheating merchants and thieving rogues.]

pigeon [Ult. < IE *pip-*, peep (echoic of the peeping of fledglings) → L. *pipere*, to chirp, *pippio*, young bird, fledgling, squab → OF *pijon*. (Cf. *widgeon*, by way of a similar OF evolution from L. * *vipio*, crane, heron.)] 1. A bird of the family Columbidae, the principal U.S. species being the lithe, clean-lined racing pigeon, and the squatter, heavier common city pigeon (also called *rock dove*), an urban vermin that smears the ledges and sills of city buildings with its disease-bearing droppings. 2. *Slang.* A dupe, an easy victim (because pigeons, though they survive as a prolific species, are easily snared as individuals).

As common birds, pigeons are idiomatically available for various comparisons: *pigeon breast* An abnormal projection of the sternum caused by rickets. *pigeon-toed* An abnormal bone condition, often the result of rickets, that causes the toes to point inward. *pigeon-hole n.* 1. A small nesting cubicle in a pigeon loft. [Most U.S. city pigeons are descendants of birds that nested in similar small hollows weathered in the soft chalk of the White Cliffs of Dover.] 2. A similar small cubicle for filing documents, usually above a desk. An essential part of the old rolltop desk. *v.* To file papers in such a cubicle. Sometimes implies to file and forget; to file away as an inactive matter.

pigeon-livered Variantly *lily-livered* (Both forms now rare, being largely replaced by *chicken-hearted* or simply *chicken.*) Cowardly, unmanly, lacking in aggressiveness. [So Shakespeare (*Hamlet* II.ii): "it must be/That I am pigeon-livered and lack gall/ To make oppression bitter." Shakespeare's "pigeon-livered" is without a specific precedent I can find, but survives today in an ancient idiomatic symbolism in *doves and hawks,* pacifists and militants. *Liver* is from the old theory of the *humors (Browser's I)* and the related theory that certain organs spur specific emotions.

In Eng., for instance, the heart sometimes denotes the seat of compassion *(have a heart),* but as often the seat of courage *(take heart).* In the Romance languages and in most of the languages of Europe the heart is specific to compassion, the liver being the seat of the aggressive, warlike disposition. (Note harsh masculine *animus,* emotional set against; and the softer feminine *anima,* soul.) In It., for instance, a man of courage and aggressiveness is *un fegatone,* literally, a man of large liver (from *fegato,* liver; with majorative suffix *-one*). Eng. idiom comes close with *a man of stomach.*

This courageous aggressiveness is due to the fact that the liver secretes bitter black bile (Shakespeare's gall). It is the reputed lack of black bile that makes pigeons gentle and dovelike. Similarly the absence of this black "humor" makes the coward's liver lilylike.]

piggy bank   In typical form, a child's slotted ceramic receptacle for coins, now almost invariably in the shape of a pig. The common assumption is that the coins cannot be removed until the (filled) receptacle is smashed, but most children know that coins can be shaken out of the slot, especially by sliding them along the flat blade of a knife. The slot is not only essential for inserting the coins (and sneaking them out) but to allow the escape of hot air when the receptacle is fired in the kiln. [The pig shape, now long standard, is, however, an accident of word association. In early Brit. dial. of unknown origin but listed by the EDD as still current in Sc., Irish, and Northumberland dial., *pig* signified a ceramic container, an item of crockery. So the Sc. proverb: "Where the pig's broken let the sherds [shards] lie." EDD also cites *pigwife,* a woman who sells crockery at a street fair; also, *pig-ass,* an ass used to draw a cart filled with crockery. (The potter's donkey?)

But the most interesting survival is in the popular British pub name, *The Pig and Whistle.* (Cf. surviving Am. slang "in the pig's whistle," a minced form of "in the pig's ass.") This pub name is a corruption of earlier *Pig and Wassail,* in which *pig* signified a ceramic mug for drinking beer and *wassail* signified wine drinking (from a glass); hence, at root, "The Mug and Glass."]

HISTORIC. I do not know when these ceramic coin containers became a child's toy. I will guess that it was in XVIII with the emergence of an affluent mercantile class whose children had small coins as a common possession (and note that this dating corresponds with the first regular schools for children of this class). But by XVIII the earlier common sense of pig (ceramic article) had receded, though the word survived. I will further speculate, accordingly, that potters, influenced by word association, made these ceramic containers in the shape of the pig, a custom they have ever since retained.

pike   Short for *turnpike,* which see.
   to come down the pike To arrive from some far place; hence, to happen unexpectedly. Cf. *to appear from nowhere* or *from God*

knows where. So, to an old friend reappearing from far off after a long absence: *Well, look what just came down the pike!* (Because *pike* always signifies a highway, never a local road. What comes down the pike, therefore, is coming from a distant place.)

piker A tight-fisted person. A cheapskate. (And note that *cheapskate* is at root "a cheap shit," < OE *scittan,* to shit, the *c* functioning as a *k.* Piker is also derogatory.) [Origin in dispute. In post-Civil War XIX *piker* had some currency in Am. with the sense "tramp" (one who wanders the highway/the pike). Such a person would be more likely to beg or cadge (or steal) than to be lavish with money. *Piker* for *tramp* is now archaic. I would trepidate that it survived with this sense shift from *tramp* to *cheapskate,* but I can find nothing to attest the connection.]

pin [An intricate evolution from IE *pet-,* to rush by, the sense early associated with, first, the flight of birds, and, second, feathers. The sense "speed" in the pure stem survived, via L. *petere,* to rush toward, to assault (IMPETUOUS, IMPETUS). Suffixed probably *pet-ro-* and with p/f and t/th → Gmnc. *fethro-,* feather. But this sense association must have occurred in IE rather than Gmnc., for the same sense occurs in suffixed form *pet-na-* which underlies L. *penna,* feather, and *pinna,* quill.

The Eng. sense of pin as a metal fastener is by association with the barb of a feather and the nib of a cut quill ("sharp, firm object"). Probably because wooden pegs serve in some of the ways metal pins do, we have *belaying pin, thole pin;* because they resemble such a peg, though they do not do the work of one, we have *bowling pin, rolling pin;* and because it fastens somewhat in the way a metal pin does, we have *clothespin.*

In ME, for reasons I cannot trace, pin also had the secondary sense "leg" (perhaps because legs are what one rushes by on as a bird does using its feathers?), and this sense survives in *underpinning, to be weak on one's pins;* and in the fight fans shout, *knock him off his pins!*] n. 1. *Most common sense today.* A small, pointed wire fastener with a head: *common pin.* 2. The same but with a metal extension that places a metal clasp over the point: *safety pin.* 3. *The primary sense until mass-produced late-XIX common pins.* A large metal fastener with a more-or-less elaborate, sometimes jeweled, head: *hatpin, stickpin, tiepin.* 4. An ornament or badge fastened to one's clothing by means of a device resembling a safety pin: *fraternity pin. v.* 1. To insert pins, as in dressmaking: *pin up a hem; pin together a rip.* 2. To attach something, usually to fabric, with a pin: *Mother, mother, mother, pin a rose on me; pin the tail on the donkey.* 3. To fix in place. And note special sense in wrestling, which is "to fix an opponent's shoulders to the mat and hold them there long enough for the referee to count to three." 4. *Collegiate.* (a) To make someone a member of a fraternity or sorority (by affixing the fraternity or sorority pin more or less ritually). (b) What a male undergraduate does when he gives a girl his fraternity pin as a sign that they are engaged, or at least "going steady." (And today, I suppose, a coed might similarly pin her boyfriend, though it was never done in my day.)

to pin down 1. To fix precisely in place. 2. To identify exactly. *pinhead* A dolt.

not care a pin To care little if at all. *not worth a pin* Worth little if anything. [I lack firm attestation but believe these idioms must be no earlier than late XIX, for only then were common pins mass-produced. Earlier handmade pins tended to be valuable. See *pin money,* below.]

pinball The idiocy that preceded video games, an electro-magnetic game played with a steel ball that scored fantasy points by striking various electro-magnetic bumpers or "pins."

firing pin The steel point of a trigger system. It fires the cartridge in the chamber by striking the primer load that detonates the black powder.

on pins and needles Restless and nervously expectant of some anticipated good or evil.

pinup girl WWII GI slang, and after. 1. A photo or graphic rendition of a naked or seminaked voluptuous woman as the wall decoration of GI sex fantasies. 2. A photo of the soldier's girl posted in this way. 3. A woman, especially an actress, prominently endowed to play a role in such fantasies: *Betty Grable was probably the featured pinup girl of the WWII wet dream.*

pin money The money available to a woman for incidental items of adornment.

HISTORIC. Women of any social standing have traditionally had such incidental money reserved to them. In the ancient covenant a woman brought to her marriage a dowry that became the property of her husband (and so, more or less, did she). In Greek that dowry was called *phernē*. But she also brought *parapherna,* lit. "things outside the dowry" (PARAPHERNALIA), which remained aside from her husband's overall ownership. The U.S. farm wife traditionally gathered eggs and churned butter to sell at the general store, and this *butter-and-egg money* was hers to use as she pleased, her form of pin money in a tight economy.

Pin money can be said to be the first traditional grant of

woman's rights. The concept, however, once involved rather more than we understand by the term. Common pins, now the cheapest item among a dressmaker's supplies, were not mass-produced until late XIX. Earlier handmade pins were scarce and costly, and "pin" once implied a hatpin or a stickpin, an often elaborately wrought article more nearly an item of jewelry than a small wire fastener. From early times, moreover, "pin" was used as a generic for all the small—and often expensive—items of cosmetic and costume jewelry (and even of jewelry) a lady of social standing might take to be necessary. ODEE cites a will dated 1542 in which a lady's pin money was secured by an annual endowment: "I give my said daughter Margaret my lease of Kirkdall Chirche . . . to buy her pinnes withal."

pink¹   1. A flower of the genus *Dianthus* [At root, "double flower" < L. *di-*, two, double; with L. *anthus*, modification of Gk. *anthos*, flower. The name, unknown to Rome, is taxonomist's new L. of late XVIII.] This genus includes carnations, garden pinks, wild pinks, and the cultivated small white-blossomed groundcover called moss pink. [Note that pinks are not necessarily, though commonly, pink in color. Pink, as "the finest flower of excellence," was familiar in XVI England, and is so referred to by Shakespeare. Prob. in late ME use as a flower name (not yet as a color) from MD *pinck(e) oogen*, in which *pinck(e)* is "small" and *oogen* (akin to Ger. *Augen*) is "eyes." In XVI Shakespeare *(Antony and Cleopatra)* does mention *pink eyne* as a medical affliction, but in earliest English usage pink had not yet become "a pale red color" and MD *pinck oogen* is a simple poetic folknaming of this flower as "small eyes." Compare English folknaming of the *daisy* as "eye of day/day's eye."

(To complete these flower-designations, *carnation* is, at root, "flesh-colored flower," ult. from It. *carnagione*, a Renaissance painter's term for the treatment of flesh tones, especially the pink-and-white flesh of female nudes. I have been unable to learn if deep red carnations had been developed by ca. XV, but it is fair to assume that female sitters did not come in that shade of red.)] 2. The color of pink *Dianthus* flowers, a diluted red verging toward white. *Hence.* 3. A Communist sympathizer. ["Pale red," as distinct from Red-red, though in right-wing usage anyone to the left of Barry Goldwater passes as a pink, or in more scornful variant, a *pinko.*] 4. In plu. only. *pinks* The near-khaki gabardine trousers with a pinkish cast worn by Army officers in semidress uniform. 5. *Primarily Brit. but also in Am. fox hunting.* The bright pink coat worn by fox hunters, traditional since early XIX.

pink-eye The common name of an acute contagious conjunctivitis. [Because its commonest symptoms are inflamed (pink) eyelids and pupils. As evidence that this medical folk-term came after the MD folkname of the flower, note again that Du. *pinck(e)* meant "small" with no reference to color.]

pink elephant A nonesuch now firmly associated with the hallucinations of *delirium tremens.* [I believe, but cannot attest, that the association is Am., since late XIX. It might have been inhibited in Brit. by the earlier idiom *to see the elephant,* to see (and know) the world, prob. < Fr. *avoir vu le loup,* to have seen the wolf, with the same sense.]

pink lady A cocktail made of gin (or vodka), grenadine, egg white, and lemon or lime juice, and shaken with shaved ice. Sickening stuff. [Because the grenadine syrup gives it a pink cast, and because the resultant froth is associated with ladies; though after a few of those that ain't no lady but a barfly.]

in the pink In glowingly perfect condition. Fine and fit. [*P. Slang* dates this idiom from early XX, but by XVI in the language of flowers the pink ("finest flower") had come to stand for excellence/perfection.]

pinkie, pinky The little finger. [As above, < MD *pinck(e),* small. And this, insofar as I can determine, is the last survival in Eng. of the MD adjectival sense, *pink* in Eng. having come to mean the color. Note that the dim. ending makes the finger, lit., "a small-smally."]

pink² *v.* 1. To prick, to pierce. [XIV. < Low Ger. *pinken,* to peck. Prob. into Eng. via Du.] 2. *In XVI.* To work holes into cloth in an ornamental lacelike pattern. Also to finish cloth with a decorative scalloped edge.

pinking shears Cloth scissors that cut a serrated edge, which inhibits raveling. (Most commonly used for trimming the folds of inside seams, but as an economy measure. A fine seamstress finishes the inside seams with fine stitches.)

pipeline 1. A major water conduit, especially one that runs cross-country as distinct from the water mains under city streets. 2. A long-distance conduit for transmitting oil or natural gas from the well to main distributing points: *the Alaska pipeline.* 3. Any source of regular supply across a considerable distance: *The Vietcong had a pipeline into Russia.* 4. Any source of regular and essential information from somewhere else: *What Ed Koch needs most is a de-*

pendable congressional pipeline. 5. *Surfing.* A surf running so high that the crests arch over and beyond the surfer, enclosing him as if in a large-bore tube. Especially *The Pipeline,* a surfing area on the northern coast of Oahu. [A pipeline is dangerous because if the surfer falls off, as he is eventually likely to do in a pipeline, his heavy board may loop the loop and come down on him hard enough to dent even a surfer's skull. In the nature of such skulls, however, that danger is part of the challenge of riding the pipeline.]

pixie, pixy   *n.* 1. Elf, fairy, sprite. 2. An elfin person, esp. a fay girl. *adj.* **Pixieish, pixyish.** [< obscure Celtic sources surviving in southwestern Brit. dial. variants *pisky, pisgy,* elf, elfin.]

pixilated   1. *In present Am. slang,* Befoodled by the alcofluence of incohol. 2. *Earlier Am. and Brit.,* In a bewildered state, as if in an elfin trance. Whimsically incoherent or bemused. [< *pixie* (as if led astray by a pixie spell). And so in Brit. *pixy-led* (XVIII). The EDD also gives the forms *Pixy-laid, Pixy-laden. Pixilated* is prob. the Am. colonial variant of the latter. MMM reports, without giving a reference, that the first written use of the form was in Marblehead, Massachusetts, in 1848. A likely guess, therefore, is that the Am. variant was in oral use by, or before, ca. 1800, for everything takes at least fifty years to get to Marblehead (and seldom, if ever, gets back).]

plagiarism   The act of stealing another's work or idea and claiming it as one's own. The term commonly implies the stealing of someone else's writing to pass off as one's own, but one could plagiarize from another person's laboratory research, or a musical score, or almost any other original work. And note also: "The second *autobahn* murderer was a plagiarist who had read the newspaper account of the first murderer's M.O. and thought, 'Gee, I'd like to do that to some girl!' " (Fletcher Pratt, *True Crime*). [At root, "(brain) child stealer." < L. *plagarius,* sea raider, plunderer. < *plaga,* net; hence, at root, "one who seizes things in his net." *Plagarii* commonly stole children to sell as slaves.]

plum   1. The fruit and the tree. [< L. *prunum,* plum; *prunus,* plum tree. The unexplained shift pr/pl occurs commonly from L. to the Teutonic languages, and also in medieval L. as written in England.] 2. *Figurative ext.* A good thing. A special prize. "He stuck in his thumb / And pulled out a plum / And said, 'What a good boy am

I!" [Perhaps from *sugarplum,* i.e., a goody.] 3. *Brit. slang, now obs.* The sum of £100,000. Also, one who possesses such a sum. (Sometimes spelled *plumb.*)

HISTORIC. The now obs. sense "100,000 pounds" was common in XVIII. *The Clandestine Marriage,* by the XVIII playwrights George Colman the Elder and David Garrick (III.ii), has: "My brother Heidelberg was a warm man—a very warm man, and died worth a plum at least. A plum! Ay, I warrant you he died worth a plum and a half." But though this sense is not clearly attested before XVIII, there was likely precedent for it, as above, in "Little Jack Horner" (XVI). *The Annotated Mother Goose,* by William S. Baring-Gould and Ceil Baring-Gould (1962), explains the rhyme by "a persistent legend" that identifies the original Jack Horner as Thomas Horner:

> a steward to Richard Whiting, last of the abbots of Glastonbury Cathedral. At the time of the dissolution, when Henry VIII was taking over all the church property he could get his royal hands on, the abbot is said to have sent his steward to London with a Christmas gift intended to appease the king, a pie in which were hidden the deeds to twelve manorial estates. On the journey Thomas Horner is alleged to have opened the pie and extracted one deed—that to the fine manor of Mells (a plum indeed!). There his descendants live to this day.

Allegation said to be from persistent legend does better for a Mother Goose jingle than for royal Henry's eager sense of audit, but the legend, however distorted, establishes that *plum* must have been in more than poetic use for an especially good thing, and even for the equivalent of what we would call "a millionaire's estate."

(And see *cheat, Browser's II,* for a further note on pilferage from the crown.)

point in time   Now. Then. At this/that time. [A now pandemic infection of robotic English. "Bear in mind that at that point in time we were under an ongoing imperative to preserve deniability." —Ron Ziegler, R. M. Nixon's press secretary, referring to the Watergate mess of 1970. In translation from Federalese: "We were lying like hell then, but had to leave ourselves a way to deny it, in case we were called upon to defend ourselves." Ziegler was mimicking the boss's vocabulary. If Nixon did not originate this form, he used it so regularly that it became part of his voice print. Any TV or nightclub comic who used it in the early 1970s was recognized to be impersonating or referring to the president, though by now it has become a generalized illiteracy and has lost that immediate personal illiteracy and has lost that immediate personal identification. Or is it simply that at this point in time Richard M. Nixon has been lost as a point of reference?]

HISTORICAL. The Ziegler comment, which I copied word-for-word into my notebook from a newspaper account, is worth noting as something like an ultimate achievement of double-talk Federalese.

police   *n.* 1. Local (urban) law-enforcement agents as a class. 2. *Ext.* Armed-service units charged with enforcing regulations governing orderly behavior of military personnel: *military police,* and commonly *M.P.s. v.* To clean (up), to make and keep things neat and orderly. (Especially in the substantive *kitchen police* or *k.p.*, enlisted men not classified as cooks but assigned the work of helping cooks prepare food—by peeling potatoes, for instance—and of cleaning up after them, mostly by washing and scrubbing and hauling garbage.) [At root, "(force) of the city," one of the many branchings from IE *pel(e)-*, citadel, fortress guarding a city. Variantly, *pol-*, the form in which this basic stem is widely dispersed in European languages. Note that the forces of a citadel not only protect it but are charged with maintaining physical as well as social orderliness.]

HISTORIC. In *Browser's I* see IE *bhergh-* for a related root, beginning by meaning "high" (with a first reference to high ground as the most defensible site for a nomadic camp, and later with reference to high walls defending a lowland city, hence with the late-evolved sense "settled community." PITTS*burgh,* HAM*burg,* CANTER*bury, borough, bourgeois*).

Pol- varies only in form, confirming identically to the root sense "that which defends a city," and hence, "city." So Gk. *polis,* city. (ACROPOLIS, METROPOLIS.) So also *politēs,* citizen of a city-state. (POLITICS; and from the same base POLITE, urbane, having big city manners, not boorish.) So *politeia,* the orderly relation of a *politēs* and the *polis. Police* is one of many cousins in this family of words. And note that It. *polizia* means both "law-enforcement agency" and "cleanliness." POLISH.

policial   *adj.* Of the police or police methods. ["The policial eyes . . . policial modes of action" (Poe, "The Purloined Letter"). A true nonce word. Ignored by OED and AHD but listed in the Unabridged Webster's International, 3d Ed. and there almost certainly culled from Poe. As precedent for this adjectival formation, many nouns ending in *-ice* or *-ices* become adjectives by adding *-ial* after the *c:* office/official; solstice/solsticial; artifice/artificial; superfices/superficial; and, variantly, justice/judicial. Nevertheless, except in Poe's usage in this one story the word seems not to occur. It seems never to have won the approval of the Eng. language convention.]

HISTORIC. The word is spoken only by C. Auguste Dupin, Poe's brilliant forerunner of Sherlock Holmes. Dupin is almost flawlessly bilingual, yet not entirely native to Eng., speaking it, so to speak, intellectually rather than idiomatically. Is "policial" a brilliant minor touch of characterization by Poe to show that Dupin forms his words by reasoning from rules rather than idiomatically? Or did Poe himself think of it, wrongly, as a standard Eng. word? (There is no answer to these questions.)

Policial remains not only a true nonce word, but a double ghost word. Though many have read "The Purloined Letter," many of them have never seen the word because so many editors and type-setters (those of the widely read Knopf edition of Poe's work among them) have "corrected" this ghost out of existence by making "po-litical" of it, which is, of course, nonsense.

politic *adj.* 1. Of political organization: *the body politic.* 2. Astutely prudent. 3. The same merged with shrewd, self-seeking experi-ence. [Gk. *politikos,* of citizenry, < *politēs,* citizen, < *polis,* city. ANNAPOLIS. Ult. < IE *pele-,* citadel, a fortress defending a settled community (city-state); hence, the community itself.] (See in *Brow-ser's I* the entry for IE *bergh-,* at root, high—in early times high ground selected for a nomadic band's camp, with later shift to "high" walls defending a settled community. *Bergh-/berg* is a Gmnc. evolution; *pele-/polis,* Hellenic, but the different roots have functioned in the same way, Pitts*burgh* and variant Canter*bury* being etymological doublets of Anna*polis.*)

politics n. 1. What ambitious office-holders and office-seekers practice in the generalized absence of statesmen (who must also dirty their hands at times). 2. *Ideally,* The more or less necessary mismanagement of public affairs. 3. A particular view of how affairs might be better mismanaged: *His politics are money-conservative.* *politico* Pejorative term for a politician. [< It. and Sp. *politico,* political, a politician. In these languages the term is not inherently disdainful, except as all men tend to distrust politicians as insincere and self-seeking. In the common It. shrug-phrase, *la vecchia, sporca politica,* the old, dirty (game of) politics.]

political machine 1. A more-or-less boss-dominated political organization. 2. *In common use.* The other side in any political bickering.

political science A self-seeking ha-ha term for the study of the history and operation of politics. [When garbage men became sanitary engineers and sent their sons to college, those aggrandized sons could hardly call themselves professors of Political Studies; not when they could dub themselves *scientists* (of the least scientific subject in the curriculum) and defend their adopted label by insisting that they used "scientific" mathematical analysis and polls as a base. I will grant them about 10 percent of their argument, but will insist that Political Studies is a more accurate category. Ask any man who has married a Domestic Scientist.]

poltroon A coward. [The opposite of an active, valiant man, but at root "like a baby or cub." It. *poltrone*, coward, < *poltro*, colt, < L. *pullus*, a cub, chick, young of an animal. Young animals are rarely formed in the ferocity of the full-grown male of the species, but they do tend to be active, whereas It. *poltrone* implies "unmanly sloth," as witness the fact that it is also used to signify what we call an easy chair, an overstuffed seat of inaction.]

pooped *Slang.* Heavy with fatigue. Too weary to go on. *I'm pooped* = "I'm worn out/exhausted." In slang, "I'm drag-ass." [Brit. slang has used *poop* in a variety of senses: in nursery usage (also in Am.) *to poop* is "to defecate." (Whence common Am. *visiting poop*, a VIP, i.e., "a big shit"—but also influ. by old nautical *poopdeck*, high stern deck, officers' country.) In XVII Brit. slang, *to poop*, to coit (also to fart); and *poop-noddy*, sexual intercourse.

But despite these surviving shitty (and in Brit. sexual) associations, *pooped*, dragged down by fatigue, has a respectable nautical history from at least early XIX and prob. earlier. So *pooper*, a great wave or sea that breaks over the stern of a ship, dragging her down by the stern (not necessarily to founder, but at least to stagger and wallow under the weight of water as if heavy with fatigue). So, at root, *a great sea pooped the ship*, a great sea broke from behind making her stern-heavy.]

pop goes the weasel "That's the way my money went. / Pop goes the weasel." —Popular drinking song since early XIX, perhaps late XVIII.

The reference, I am persuaded, is to the hatter's tool called a *weasel,* which, as I understand it, was a large wooden shaping device with spokes used in molding hats.

Through XVIII and into most of XIX craftsmen were expected to supply their own tools. (The idiom *to get the sack* is based on the fact that when a man was fired he was given a sack in which to carry away his tools.) The most essential tool of the hatter was his personal *weasel,* for without it he could not work. Hatters were also said to be notorious drunkards, perhaps to rinse from their throats the mercury fumes that eventually left them with *the hatter's shakes.* A thirsty, unemployed hatter who pawns ("pops") his weasel might end up with enough change for a night's drinking, but with no way of finding employment when he sobered up again. When the weasel goes pop, therefore, just about everything else does. And that's the way his money (and prospects) went.

posthumous   *adj.* After death. [Lit., "after burial." < L. *humus,* earth, clay; *humare,* to bury, to inter. Ult. < IE *dhghem-,* earth, soil. The aspirated skeletal root is *h'm-* → L. *humus; and variantly* → *homo,* man ("creature of mortal clay"). Prefixed L. *post,* after, ult. < IE *apo-,* away from (APOGEE), here with the sense "away from (after) in time." The form first arose in late XVI, the first OED citation (1591) using *postumous* to label a child born after the death of its father. In 1661 the form *posthumous* labeled works published after the death of the author. And these senses survive, but in most common Am. usage, labels an award, most commonly a military decoration, made after the death of the person so honored.]

pounce   *n. Obs.* Powdered resin of the sandarac tree. In the days before blotters and quick-drying inks it was sprinkled onto a newly written page to dry the ink. [The term may have some survival in arts and crafts. As far as I can determine, powdered sandarac resin is no longer commercially available, leaving the word as an obs. label for what no longer exists. The form is < Fr. *pouce,* pumice; a curious sense transfer, for pumice is black and not absorbent, and the absorbent pounce is red.]

HISTORIC. Not, as noted, a current word, but when, in a period film, an actor or actress is shown writing with a goose-quill pen and then sprinkling and shaking the page with powder from a desk cannister with a salt-shaker top, the word-curious may be pleased to know that what is being sprinkled is an imitation *pounce*—an imitation because the real thing is not commercially available, and because anything will do for Hollywood's imitation of reality.

pow-wow 1. An Amerind ceremony with dancing and incantations led by a medicine man who invokes the gods. 2. A ceremonial council of Indians. [These seem to be the original senses of Algonquinian *pow-wow* or *pow-waw.* The arrival of the white man gave rise to the new sense:] 3. A more-or-less ceremonial palaver between whites and Indians. *And* 4. *In the language of the whites.* A more-or-less formal discussion meeting, a negotiation between two sides, or among more than two.

proscenium *Theater.* The stage. [Root sense, "in front of the scenery." In Greek theater it was bounded by the rear wall (*skēnē,* scene) and the *orchēstra,* the forward place in which the chorus danced. < Gk. *orchēomai,* I dance.] *proscenium arch* The opening, traditionally arched but often squared, in which the curtain rises or opens laterally to reveal the inner stage. The forward space between the curtain and the orchestra pit of the modern stage is called *the apron.*

proscription 1. *Since XVI.* The formal act of posting someone's condemnation at law. (On the western U.S. frontier a common equivalent was a Wanted-dead-or-alive poster. If apprehended by the law the posted person would be put to death after short ceremony. Until then he was denied all civil privileges and could be seized or killed by any citizen.) 2. *Since XVII.* A formal, posted denunciation, prohibition, or interdiction. 3. *In the original Roman practice.* The legal act of declaring a person or persons to be stripped of all rights of citizenship and to stand condemned. [At root, "formal public writing/writ." L. *proscriptiōnem,* < *scribere,* to write; prefixed *pro-,* before (the public); hence PROCLAMATION.]

HISTORIC. In the bloody unrest that followed the assassination of Julius Caesar, the triumvirs Octavian, Antony, and Lepidus were proscribed by the Senate, and with them Cicero, who had been deeply involved in politics. Cicero fled but was killed in Caieta on Dec. 7, 44. As an evidence of Roman sincerity in politics, Cicero's head and hands (the head from which all those orations had sounded, the hands that wrote them) were displayed on a rostrum in the Roman Forum, probably one from which he had orated. (See *rostrum.*)

protest (As *v.* with accent on second syllable; as *n.,* on the first.) 1. *Undisputed primary sense in Am.* To object to, to speak out against, to declare one's disapproval: *protest meeting.* 2. *But at root, and still commonly in Brit.* To declare openly, publicly, solemnly.

(This sense surviving in Am. in:) *to protest one's innocence* (which is not to object to the fact that one is innocent, but to testify, as if under oath, that one is not guilty). [< L. *pro-*, forth; *testari,* to speak in witness of, to testify. In *Browser's I,* see *testify* and its relation to *testicles* as witnesses to one's manhood. And so *detest,* to stand in witness against (at root to denounce from the bottom of one's balls).]

prothonotary warbler   also *protonotary warbler* A small songbird of the southeastern U.S. with a yellow head and breast and light gray wings. [Am. prob. late XVIII, early XIX. I have been unable to identify the person who first so labeled this bird but must guess that he was a gentleman birdwatcher well acquainted with the hierarchy of the Roman Catholic church, or possibly of the Greek Orthodox church; and that this bit of ecclesiastical whimsy associates the bird's coloring with the ceremonial robes of protonotaries, as the cardinal is so named by association of its coloration with the red robes of Roman Catholic cardinals. It may even be that the naming of the cardinal suggested a similar sort of naming for this warbler in the contagion of whimsy.

The form is from late L. *protonotarius,* first secretary. In the Vatican the college of twelve apostolic protonotaries is charged with recording all the solemnized acts of the curia. In the Greek Orthodox church the *prothonotarios* is the first secretary of the patriarch of Constantinople.

This bit of fanciful labeling puts a heavy charge upon so small a bird. I have been told but have not been able to verify that the ceremonial robes of the church officials are gold and gray, approximately the coloration of the bird. There is, of course, the additional fact that apostolic prothonotaries chant (sing) when they march in procession. I doubt that these warblers move in processional alignment, but whimsy is not a Q.E.D.]

psalm   (the *l* is silent) A sacred song, a hymn. [< Gk. *psalma,* song sung to the accompaniment of a harp or similar instrument; < *psallein,* to pluck, to play the harp.]

HISTORIC. The modern Eng. sense of the word is now firmly associated with the Songs of David; so much so, in fact, that it would now seem bizarre to refer to Homer as a psalm singer. Yet Gk. *psalma* is at root a rhapsode's song, the work of the ancient tribal minstrel who rose at campfire meetings and, strumming his harp or lyre, sang of the mythico-religious origins of his people. Homer and David were equally descended, each in his own way, from this ancient figure.

Psaphon   Perhaps one of the most obscure figures of Greek mythology. He is said to have spent his time training birds to cry Psa-PHON! Psa-PHON! Psa-PHON! (or PSA-phon! PSA-phon! PSA-phon!) and then turning them loose to cry his name to all mankind and to the gods of the upper air.

The Greeks must have seen in his behavior an act of overweening foolish pride for which the gods must have punished him by decreeing the extinction of the only species of bird capable of pronouncing his name. Despite his failure and his resultant obscurity, Psaphon must be credited with the first large-scale name-recognition advertising campaign in history and might very properly be enshrined as the presiding spirit of Madison Avenue ad agencies.

Nor can I resist this opportunity to propose to the language the word *psaphonic* Of advertising (implying that it is for the birds).

Pullman   1. A railroad sleeping or parlor car. (But commonly specific to sleeping cars only. The earlier *Pullman coaches* are now commonly called *parlor cars. Pullman Hotel Cars* briefly, in 1885, combined sleeping quarters with food service, but were superseded almost at once by dining cars never called Pullmans but *dining cars* or *diners.* The first Pullman diner, called Delmonico after the famous New York City restaurant, was built in 1886.) 2. *Formerly,* A large suitcase. [The name was by association: the sort of suitcase one took on a long trip in a Pullman.]

Pullman, Illinois Founded 1880 on the outskirts of Chicago as a showcase company town. Now part of the City of Chicago, but established as a separate municipality wholly owned by the Pullman Company. Workers there were made to accept low wages, and to pay high rents for company housing and high prices at the company stores, with the local police serving as company police to quell labor unrest.

Pullman porter A Negro attendant (bed maker, shoe shiner, baggage handler, wake-up man, kow-tower, and general servitor) on a Pullman. From the start, Pullmans were staffed with Negroes, partly because they could be expected to be servile and to accept low wages for exhausting working conditions. The Pullman Company was ever ready to squeeze cheap labor. Yet even under harsh conditions, a Pullman job was an early form of emancipation for many Negroes who found on the railroad their escape from the fields, and wages and working conditions that, though harsh, were better than almost anything else available to a late-XIX Negro. Above all, these Pullman jobs permitted a wholly new experience of the world for the far-traveling porters.

They were invariably called *George.* [After George M. Pullman. But the title was less than honorific. It was, in effect, a variant of the pejorative "boy"; as if a short form of "Hey, you, George's boy!"]

HISTORIC. All these terms derive from the name of George M. Pullman, one of the ruthless industrial barons who built the network of late-XIX American railroads. But Pullman left more than his name upon the land. From him stems the institution of the American *diner* (see *Browser's I*). As noted above, Pullman built the first car to be exclusively (and ornately) equipped as a diner in 1886. In the early XX, retired dining cars, and work cars once used for feeding work crews, began to appear on sidings by railroad stations as cheap, quick eating places, later spreading away from the stations. Some of today's diners are elaborately glossy and sprawling affairs, but still retain traditional architectural touches reminiscent of railroad cars, especially in the construction of their entrances and of their windows.

Pullman also left his mark on the now hardset U.S. habit of beginning restaurant meals with a salad, a custom that surprises most Europeans, especially when they must fight off waiters and waitresses whose fixed national compulsion it has become to snatch away the unfinished salad when the main course is served—or before. In most of Europe, and in America before Pullman, salad was a side dish to the main course, or a separate course after it (to freshen the palate).

Because of limited space in the dining car's kitchen, George the waiter was instructed to serve the customer a preprepared salad to munch on while awaiting the main course. Fred Harvey's restaurant chain, long intimately connected with the railroads, was the first to spread the habit wide. Harvey died in 1901, but the chain he founded survives, and first at Fred Harvey's, and then generally, salad began to come first.

The new custom is the salad bar, to which the customer goes at his pleasure and prepares his salad himself. It is now possible, therefore, to have one's salad at any point in the meal, even with or after the main course. But one who takes his salad late in the meal must be prepared to face charges of subversion for a departure from the established order of Pullman-Harvey.

Punch[1]   In commonest form, a hand puppet in a once wildly popular street show of Neapolitan origin. Punch traditionally wears a black eye-mask and a white smock. He has an enormous hooked nose, a vile temper, and a squawky voice in which he is forever arguing with his wife, Judy. [Neapolitan *Policinella, Pulcinella* is based on *pulcina,* chick, perhaps with ref. to a hook-nosed, diminutive, squawking guinea cock. Before he became a hand puppet he was portrayed by a human actor in XVI Neapolitan farce, and some authorities even refer the name to Paolo Cinella, an actor said to have played the role. He is also said to have once been a poultry dealer. Dozens of ingenious sources (including Pontius Pilate) have been advanced more or less plausibly.

Once Pulcinella became a hand puppet he became popular in France by ca. 1600 and in England by late XVII, his name there being modified to *Punchinello* and then to *Punch.*]

Punch[2]   A British humor magazine founded 1841 and still a favorite of Britons and of U.S. anglophiles who pretend to understand the humor as part of their quaint mental posture. [The magazine logo, still carried on its masthead, is a drawing of Punch.]

pleased as Punch 1. *Originally,* Vaingloriously self-satisfied. 2. *In loose ext.* Very happy indeed: *I was as pleased as Punch when Sandy Martin dropped in, for I was not at home.*

pup   And the tender dim. form, *puppy* 1. A young dog. 2. Also the young of other canines, and also of such creatures as the seal or the whale. (But *puppy* is generally used only for the young of the domesticated dog.) 3. *Loosely.* A small boy: *Not since Hector was a pup.*

puppy love Can label the whole-souled adoration of a small child, but is generally specific to adolescent infatuation, or to the juvenilized raptures of the chronologically older. Puppy love is sweet, intense, and foolish in ways that emotionally developed old dogs and bitches are expected to have outlived. [Ult. from IE *pap-,* baby, the root being echoic of the sucking sound made by a nursing infant. Hence, at root, "little creature that goes 'pap-pap-pap.'" PAP. PABULUM. PUPPET. POPPYCOCK. PUPIL.]

pyx   *In the communion service.* 1. The polished metal cup that holds the consecrated communion wafers, esp. in Catholic communion services. 2. The covered container in which the pyx is carried for giving communion to the sick, or to those about to be executed. [See *box.* < Gr. *puxis,* a small, lidded box, once commonly of boxwood, for storing small valuables. L. *pyxis* retains this sense, but also signifies "cash box." (In earlier England, samples of newly struck gold and silver coins were placed in a small chest to be assayed before the issue was released, and this chest was once called the *pyx.* And *pyx* once labeled the box that held the ship's compass before the binnacle was developed. These senses, now obs., follow directly from the Gk. and L. senses.)]

Q

quaestor *Ancient Rome.* A nonlegislative public official whose functions varied from one period to another. In all variations the quaestor had something to do with finances and the general management of civil and military expenditures. He was a sort of comptroller inspector-general with police powers. [At root, "he who asks questions." < L. **quaerere,* to search, to ask, to look into. QUESTION. INQUISITOR. QUEST. The *quaestor* has no etymological descendant in English officialdom, but if you go to Italy and misbehave there you may be taken to the *questura* (roughly the equivalent of a U.S. police station) and there be asked hard questions by a sort of police sergeant called *il maresciallo,* the marshal.]

quagmire 1. Boggy ground, seemingly solid because covered by light vegetation (in this, unlike quicksand), but yielding under the weight of a person or animal. If the quagmire happens to be shallow, one is simply mired. More commonly it is deep enough to swallow one whole. 2. *Figurative ext.* Any situation from which it is difficult or impossible to extricate oneself: *Stuart Wright disappeared from view in the quagmire of my logic; or so I will attest.* [Mire is evident. The first element *quag-* survives in English only in this fixed combination, though with g/k it underlies *quake.* Perhaps from Du. *quabbe,* wetness. Ult. < IE *gwebh-,* to dip into, to sink (obviously implying wetness) → Gmnc. base *kw'b'-.* I cannot account for the b/g shift to quag. As a curious cognate, the IE stem rendered *(gwe)bh-* and with hypothetical suffix is the base of Gk. *baptein,* to dip, to sink; whence theological *baptize.* And so from baptism to the quagmires of theology.]

quality Originally of the greatest merit, ability, enabling power. Then, in Latin, with a sense shift to "degree of merit"—from which *good and bad quality* have followed from the original sense, "highest worth/ability." Hence with the sense, "a trait, a characteristic."

237

But the original sense, "best, most able," survives (from Elizabethan English) in Southern colloquial *quality folks* or simply *the Quality, persons of quality,* the social elite, the figures of a conceptual timocracy (i.e., rule by those of superior merit, however defined). [What might be called "an immigrant etymology." Originally Gk. *poien,* to make, to create, to be able to do (POET). (And so *onomatopoeia,* at root, "the power to make up and assign names to.") Ult. < IE *kwei-,* to amass, to build, to create. Thus the participial substantive of *poein, poiotes,* enabling power to do, to make.

Then, because L. had no corresponding word, Cicero translated *poiotes* as *qualitas* < *qualis,* of what kind; and instantly the sense shifted from "highest creative ability" to "degree of ability, more or less."]

quango   *Brit. only.* An acronym for "*Q*uasi-*a*utonomous *N*on-*g*overnment *O*rganization."

HISTORIC. Acronymic word formations were rare in English until FDR and the New Deal. The very word *acronym* was not coined until the mid-1930s. By the beginning of WWII acronymania seems to have seized the government and the Am. language, the infection then being spread to our British former cousins, and beyond.

I have as little notion of Brit. government as I have of the holy mysteries of cricket. I can only guess that a *quango* is an extra-governmental agency established and financed by the government. In any case *quango* must mean something to the British, enough at least so that they would understand a London *Sunday Times* headline of November 18, 1984: "Thatcher Prepares Another Squeeze on 1,680 Quangos." The story explains that the new government has cut at least 600 but that 115 have sprung up in their place, "mostly advisory and judicial bodies but including nationalized industries."

The story adds that, "The finances of quangos are notoriously vague," that closing some of them down has saved over £600 million a year, and that the Tory M.P., Sir Philip Howard, lists as his hobby "hunting quangoes." Whatever quangoes are, they seem to be a rich game. One of them, the Manpower Services Commission, spends £1,069 million a year.

quasar   1. *Recent radio-astronomy.* A very distant starlike celestial body that emits intense light waves or powerful radio waves, or both. 2. *Advertising promotion.* A catchy high-technology name applied to TV sets today (and other electronic devices tomorrow) to suggest intense brilliance, as of the projected image, and powerful audio reception. (Quasars, to be sure, do not receive but transmit, but in advertising hoopla the connotation is all.) [A recent coinage from *quas(i)-(stell)ar* radio source.]

Queen of the May   1. In the old English festival a maiden crowned with a wreath of flowers, gaily bedecked, and chosen to preside as the symbolic reigning spirit of the May frolic and dance around the Maypole. Hence, queen for a day. 2. *Simple ext.* A girl whose head has been turned by tinsel pretensions: *she thinks she's Queen of the May* = she acts as if she were really a reigning beauty.

HISTORIC. The traditional English May festival and Maypole dance is from an immemorial druidic spring rite. All ancient spring rites were fertility rites in which a young and flowering virgin was an obvious symbolism of spring's rebirth. For ritual purposes a putative virgin would do as well as a real one, but in early tribal practice, and in the later rigid caste system of rural England, there was every likelihood that the festival's virgin queen was in fact a virgin. What can one get away with in a tribe or a small town?

quincunx   *n.* An arrangement of five design elements, four forming a square with a fifth in the center. *adj.* **quincuncial** So arranged. [A standard word but rare, more's the pity, for it is useful, and firmly specific, and the quincunx is a common design arrangement. The spots that mark a five in dice, for instance, are a quincunx. (And note that my definition took sixteen words to say what this one word means. Compare the awkwardness of saying "one who amasses money not for any good it can do but for the obsessive urge to hoard it," when one could have said "miser.")

< L. *quincunx,* five-twelfths, < *quincus,* five; *uncia,* a twelfth part. In Roman coinage an *as* was a copper coin worth 12 *unciae,* ounces, and the *quincunx* (quincuncially stamped with five dots) was a sort of Roman halfpenny worth five-twelfths of an *as.* The calculation becomes a bit confusing, but the Romans were never notable mathematicians.]

quip   1. *Earlier.* A sarcastic remark. 2. *Now.* A short, witty remark; commonly a barbed one (whereby the earlier sense still functions in part). [< XVI *quippy,* a sarcastic remark. Almost certainly < L. *quippe,* which with a sarcastic or ironic force understood, may be rendered "Indeed!" or "Say you so!" or in modern slang, "Oh, yeah?" < L. *quid,* what. Ult. < IE *kwo-,* the base of many relative

and interrogative pronouns (WHAT, WHY, WHO, WHICH, WHENCE).
The form of these pronouns is directly from the IE base *kwo-*, with
k/h to Gmnc. hypothetical stem *hwo-*, as evidenced in OE *hwaet,
lo!* (WHAT), which explains why the *W* of these pronouns is still
aspirated in the proper pronunciation *hwat,* though *wat* is becoming increasingly common in Am.]

quote *n.* Standard short form for *quotation.* *v.* To repeat someone
else's speech or writing verbatim with an acknowledgment of the
source. (To do so without acknowledgment is plagiary.) [< L.
quotus, a given number in a series. In later church L. *quottare,* to
cite Scripture by chapter and verse. Cf. ME and through XVI,
quoth he, quod he, he said.]

quotient *Maths.* The result of dividing one number by another. [<
L. *quoties,* how often? how many times?]
    intelligence quotient Commonly *I.Q. Psychology.* A measure of
intelligence determined by dividing chronological age by tested
"mental age." So called because the result is a quotient that measures relative intelligence. The result is usually expressed by multiplying the quotient by 100.

R

radar   A device for detecting objects not in sight and for determining their location, altitude (if any), heading, and speed by transmitting focused radio waves and tracking their echoes on an electronic screen. A relatively advanced (though by now seemingly primitive) radar system was an invaluable secret weapon of Britain in WWII, for it made it possible to detect approaching German bombers well in advance and to concentrate fighters for maximum defense. Newly refined radar has been successfully tuned to get a return blip from the moon. It can also be used for aerial mapping and it is, of course, invaluable for aerial navigation and for airport traffic control. [An irregular acronym devised by the British, who developed radar: *ra*(dio) *d*(etecting) *a*(nd) *r*(anging device). Above all, now that the war is over, it is a new common palindrome.]

ragamuffin   A *tatterdemalion* (which see). An implicitly dirty child dressed in rags. [And now often used indulgently and fondly for a messy, clothes-destroying but lovable child. At origin, however, the name of a fiend, *Ragamoffyn,* mentioned in *Piers Plowman* (1393). The grotesque name did not imply an indulgent view of the fiend, but followed from a medieval tradition of making up grotesque-gargoyle names for lesser devils. (See note to *flibbertigibbet.*)

Since the name has not been turned up in any earlier work on fiends, it seems likely that Langland invented it. The first element of the name cannot fail to suggest "ragged." Some ingenious efforts have been made to show that *ffyn* is a corruption of "fiend," and that the name means something like "ragged my fiend," but any speculation is possible where there is no evidence.]

railroad flat   Primarily in Northern and Eastern U.S. big cities, a tenement apartment in which the rooms are arranged one behind the other (like railroad cars on a train), making it necessary to pass through each room in turn when going from front to rear of the apartment, thus utilizing all of the interior space, though at some cost to bedroom privacy. [Cf. *shotgun house,* the sthrn. equivalent. Dating a touch uncertain, prob. very late XIX. Sthrn. *shotgun house* was roughly 20 years earlier.]

reentry 1. *In standard English.* In any sense, the act of coming back in. 2. *In the now-primary space-age sense.* A space vehicle's reencounter with the earth's atmosphere and its potentially dangerous friction. [First in limited theoretical use by science-fiction writers even before WWII; then in the 1950s in the calculations of scientists who planned space flights; then in journalistic use; whence into general usage in this specialized sense, following the reports of the first manned space flight (a single orbit in less than two hours) by Soviet astronaut Yuri Aleksevich Gagarin, April 12, 1961.]

reeve (*Obs.* until revived by Faulkner in the title of his novel, *The Reivers.*) 1. *In feudal England.* An estate steward or overseer. [Earlier *grieve.* So Allan Ramsay's *Scottish Proverbs:* "Too many grieves hinder the work"—in effect, "Too many cooks spoil the soup."] 2. *Also in ME (when England was still substantially feudal).* An officer of the shire or parish. [*Sheriff* is just one language step beyond *shire-reeve,* which is, at root, shire-steward; < OE *ge-refa,* a local lord; the form cognate with Ger. *graf,* a count. (*County* is, at root, domain of a count.) Ult. < Gmnc. stem *grave-,* a designation of rank as count or baron. LANDGRAVE, WALDGRAVE, MARGRAVE.]

(Nautical *reeve,* to pass a line through an eye or a pulley or around a post—and to fasten it—is of separate but lost origin.)

rhinestone A small, faceted, glass "diamond" affixed variously, often in intricate patterns, as glitter on a woman's gown or on theatrical costumes. [Named after the place of origin, in Fr. *caillou du Rhin,* little pebble of the Rhine, because these glitters were first made in Strassburg, which is on the Rhine.]

rhombus *Geometry.* An equilateral parallelogram. It has the sides of a square but no right angles. If drawn standing on one apex it resembles a diamond. Also *rhomboid* A similar figure but with no two adjacent sides equal. (Think of a rhombus as a "squashed" square, and of a rhomboid as a "squashed" rectangle.) [Via L. *rhombus* < Gk. *rhombos,* the geometer's label for such a figure; but at earliest root, a *bull-roarer,* sometimes also called a *magic circle,* probably one of the oldest of child's toys, a slat twirled on a string that is said to make a sound like the roar of a bull when twirled rapidly. The less-usual name *magic circle* refers to the seemingly magical properties of this toy in giving off such a sound. These senses are implicit in the IE root *wer-*, to turn. (VERTIGO—so labeled because it seems to make the head whirl.) This root suffixed and modified to zero-grade, prob. by way of *w(e)r-embh-* → *wrembh-* → Gk. *rhombos*, the whirly-toy; and only much later borrowed by geometers to label their specific four-sided figure.]

HISTORICAL. There is a fascinating historical puzzle here. As a boy I made bull-roarers by splitting a cedar shingle and attaching it to a string for which I bored a hole in the thick end; always the thick end because the force of the twirling would cause the string to cut through the cedar of the thin end. I seem to recall that a slat no more than two or three inches wide seemed to produce the most satisfying noise. Greek boys would not have had available to them the split cedar shingles so common in the house-building 1920s in America. They must have used some sort of slat somehow split and whittled or ground flat. Could it be that they found a small diamond-shaped whirler threaded near one apex to give off the most satisfying bull roar?

History and poetry (once much the same thing) are mute on the shape of early Greek bull-roarers. In the hope that there might be a clue in science, I have written to a number of physicists to ask if a diamond would be an ideal shape for producing the "bull roar" when twirled fast enough to perturb the air. I have not found any physicist who is prepared to say yes or no.

Yet, on the assumption that geometers are precise men, can we suppose they would borrow the name of a randomly shaped slat to label so precise a figure as an equilateral parallelogram? There is no doubt that this piece of nomenclature went from the boys' toy to the geometric figure. The mystery is *why?* Since, as noted, history is mute on this point, I welcome information from any physicist who has wandered so far afield as to be reading this note.

rhubarb   *Baseball.* A noisy dispute between a manager and an umpire, sometimes with players joining in, sometimes in fact with players from both sides joining in, always with some nose-to-nose shouting, arm waving, kicking of dust, and slamming of hats to the ground, but stopping short of any physical contact, since any act of touching is grounds for expulsion from the game. [Am. Certainly in use by 1890s, prob. from at least 1875. Origin and derivation unattested, but probably from a theatrical practice in Brit. use since Shakespeare's time. When the play calls for a crowd scene for which no lines have been written but in which some hubbub is needed, the actors have traditionally been directed to repeat over and over "Rhu-bar-bar, rhu-bar-bar, rhu-bar-bar," and this repetition by many voices does excellently to reproduce the background sounds of a crowd. The line of transmission from the theater to baseball need not strain credulity. It is even possible that the carnie alarm signal "Hey, Rube!" (a signal that local yokels have discovered that they have been cheated and are ready to become physical about it) may have reinforced the theatrical tradition in formulating this baseball idiom.]

ricochet formation   In the inevitable process by which language gives rise to language, a word or phrase called into being by another, without which it could make no sense.

In the days of the Irish bogtrotters *hayburner* might have labeled (but did not) a night rider who set fire to ricks, crops, and animal shelters. It became late XIX Am. slang for a horse, but only after the locomotive (the iron horse) had been commonly classified first as a *woodburner* and later as a *coalburner.* The (noniron) horse could only then be conceived to "burn" hay as its motive fuel.

In computer talk *hardware* came to label the physical mechanism of the computer, and *software,* its programming, tapes, discs, and printouts. Input was the obvious third element, and input had, obviously, to come from the human brain. In context, therefore, this third element acquired the ricochet label *wetware.*

Explosion (see *explode*) is a metaphor drawn from the Roman theater, at root a loud, sudden, derisive audience outbreak. In XVII this metaphor was first extended to the idea "detonation." Later something like (but not exactly like) detonation was observed, the phenomenon of a violent, sudden, loud collapse; and this, by ricochet formation, was labeled *implosion* as if "an explosion inward" (which it is and is not, though enough so to suggest the ricochet term).

riddle   *n.* 1. A conundrum. 2. A puzzling or enigmatic thing. *v.* To put forth a conundrum. 2. To speak in an enigmatic way. *to riddle out* To find the answer to a conundrum or to a perplexing problem. [A complex evolution, best discussed in the following note on related words:]

NOTE. The IE stem is *ar-, are-,* to conjoin, to fit together. Variously suffixed in Greek and Latin, that is the base of ARISTOCRAT, ARM, ARMADA, ARMATURE, ARTICULATE. A common sense of all these words is "something that has been put together (in an orderly way)."

The variant reduced form *'re,* suffixed *-dh-* in Gmnc. → OE *raedan,* to advise; *raed,* advice, counsel. So the early Eng. name *Ethelred,* noble counsellor, < *aethel,* noble; with *raed,* counsel. So *King Ethelred the Unready* of England (978–1016). His name, a long-standing source of amusement for schoolboys, signified "noble adviser unadvised (or ill-advised)." True or not, rumor had it that he murdered his brother to gain the throne. He therefore had difficulty winning the support and counsel of his lords. *Ready,* therefore, is of this word group, its root sense being, "prepared for action by wise counsel and consideration."

Another development from this root, with the prob. Gmnc. form *redaz,* signified condition of being, relationship. This is a survival of the IE root sense, "way of fitting together, conjointure." It is the source of OE *raeden,* condition, relationship; and this form survives as the suffix in *kindred* and *hatred.* Variantly, this stem produced OHG *rat,* council of state ("a condition of social being"), as in Ger. *Hausrat,* a state council that met in the king's house (castle). And so Ger. *raten,* to advise, to guess.

And so around the circle to *riddle,* from OE *raedels,* an unexplained form meaning "opinion"; akin to Ger. *raten,* as is visible in OE *raedan,* to guess, to decipher. The OE form survived as ME *redeles,* which was incorrectly taken to be a plu. (cf. *pea* from earlier *pease,* also wrongly taken to be a plu. and, so to speak, "singularized"). The later ME form, therefore, became *redel,* also *ridil,* whence modern Eng. *riddle.*

But *read* on. For the ancestral Gmnc. form took a new sense from the arrival of Runic writing, which probably reached the Teutons by overland trade routes from the Black Sea about A.D. 300. Writing, previously unknown in the Northland, appeared to be a magician's mystery. The few wise counselors who could carve and decipher runes were viewed as Merlins of arcane knowledge. They were simultaneously *readers* and *riddlers* of the mystery.

Compare *glamor (Browser's I),* a variant via Sc. of "grammar." A grammarian originally signified one who could read—and who therefore had access to secret books of magic. Sc. *gramour, glamour* signified the working of magic spells. Sir Walter Scott used the word to label the enchanting spell cast by women of great beauty, whence its present sense in English. Its history illustrates the same connection between literacy and arcane wisdom (for the few who are *ready* to *read* the *riddle*).

ring finger Counting the thumb, the fourth finger of the left hand, the one next to the little finger (see *pink, pinkie*). It is the finger on which the wedding ring has traditionally been placed since about the first century of our era (because in the medical belief of the time, based on an obscure earlier Egyptian assertion, that finger is connected directly to the heart by a special nerve, called by the Romans *vena amoris*).

HISTORICAL. In pious legend special symbolisms were assigned to various fingers. The thumb of the right hand, for example, was said to represent God the Father; the second finger, God the Son; the intermediate index finger, the Holy Ghost. Many priests, accordingly, made the gesture of benediction with these three fingers joined (and Brewer notes that this tradition survived into Anglican practice).

From the little I can learn of first-century Roman anatomical theory the *vena amoris* did not have a second branch from the heart to the corresponding finger on the right hand but was specific to the *pronabus sinistrus*. In any case the left has long been the traditional side of lesser honor, the lower side in protocol, and the woman as the inferior partner in a marriage (Women's Liberation should note and strive to remedy) wore her pledge on the lesser side.

robber baron 1. *In European history,* Any of the feudal lords who robbed and killed or enslaved travelers passing through their territory. *Hence* 2. One of the financial pirates of XIX America who amassed enormous wealth by exploiting natural resources and the workers with the connivance of corrupt public officials. [Popularized as a term of American history by Matthew Josephson as the title of his book, *The Robber Barons,* a history of such financial pirates as John Jacob Astor, Commodore Vanderbilt, J. P. Morgan, Jay Gould, and other rapacious lords of laissez-faire economics.]

rock-ribbed Firm. Immovable. [Maine has a coastline of submerged, low, granitic mountains, irregular, but firmly and forbiddingly fixed, at least in contrast to the shifting sands of the geologically emergent coastline one finds from Cape Cod south. XIX Am. oratory fixed on that rock-ribbed coast as a standard figure for rugged firmness of character.] *rock-ribbed Republican* The standard designation for a person of unwavering Republican conviction. (Also *staunch Republican,* these two modifiers being by now idiomatically out of place when applied to Democrats.) [The Republican Party was founded and named in 1854, Maine becoming traditionally the most solid of Republican strongholds. By association with its unalterable shore line, therefore, first the Maine Republicans were said to be rock-ribbed, and then the merely maniacal ones.]

HISTORIC. And so Maine remained (see *as Maine goes, so goes the nation*) as long as its considerable French-Canadian population ignored "Yankee" politics. By about WWII, however, the French-Canadians had become politically sensitized, largely by the labor unions and their Catholic church affiliations. So sensitized, and overwhelmingly Democrat in their views, they found they outnumbered the Republicans and proceeded substantially to staunch them, rocking their ribs not only in Maine but in Vermont and New Hampshire.

rolling *Narc. slang.* Distributing drugs. "the police believe it was a house they were rolling (selling drugs) out of," Detroit *Free Press,* Oct. 17, 1985. [Certainly from *rolling along,* moving. This usage may be local to Detroit, for when I checked with newsmen in other major cities, none had heard it. It is, in any case, likely to be transient crim. cant.]

rood *Poetic archaic.* 1. The true cross. 2. A crucifix. 3. Any cross. [Ult. < IE *ret-,* post → prob. Gmnc. stem *rod-, rodd-* as suggested by OE *rod,* post, cross, and *rod* as a linear measure (now 16.5 ft., but the length of the OE measure is not precisely known). *Rood* has some specialized survival in Brit. as (a) a variable linear distance from 5.5 to 8 yds., (b) a land measure of 40 square rods, about 0.25 of an acre.

The vertical member of a cross was, of course, a post. There is no evidence to indicate when OE *rod* sprouted a cross-member in what by the sixth century had become a sacred symbol. One earlier side sense of OE *rod,* however, was "perch," and the rood, as one may say, was historically perched upon. But if this sense was once the connective, it has long since receded from the word.]

root *v.* 1. The act of swine in digging with their snouts in search of food. [Ult. from, and already visible in, IE *wrōd-,* which had a double sense, to dig and to gnaw, whereby one must assume the stem was already specific to swine. Via Gmnc. → OE *wrotan,* to root like swine.] 2. *Sports.* Commonly *to root for* (a) To cheer loudly, enthusiastically, and necessarily mindlessly for one team or another. (b) To encourage and support: *I'd root for death over Reagan, but that would only leave us Bush.* [Am. It cannot be shown beyond a doubt that sense 2 derives directly from sense 1, but loyal rooters regularly express their enthusiasm with a swinish intensity, if with less purpose than seems to motivate pigs.]

rostrum   A platform for a public speaker. [At root, "bird's beak." And then by obvious association, the pointed, ornamented, ramming prow of a war galley.

The form of the word is readily traced to IE *rad-*, to gash, scrape, gnaw, whence the zero-grade stem *rod-* → L. *rōdere*, to gnaw. RODENT. The same stem suffixed prob. as *rod-(s)tro-* → L. *rostrum*, beak of a bird. Today we do not seem to associate gnawing with pecking or with the tearing of predatory birds, but it is easy to understand how the Romans or their Italic ancestors must have done so. But if this much explains the form of the word, the sense is from late association:]

HISTORIC. At some time before 100 B.C. the Romans mounted in the Forum as trophies of victory the cut-off prows of Carthaginian ships. Such prows were called *rostra* because they resembled the beaks of birds. As these Carthaginian trophies weathered away the Romans replaced them with prows cut from captured pirate ships. Aside from their symbolic vaunt, these prows provided convenient platforms that Roman orators might mount in order to address the Forum crowds.

Cicero (see *proscription*) spoke from rostra in the Forum. When he was proscribed by the Senate following the assassination of Julius Caesar, he fled Rome but was hunted down and killed, his head and hands being hacked off and returned to Rome to be displayed on a rostrum. It was a poetic barbarity—the head that had spoken there and the hands that had written the speech were returned to testify from probably the same rostrum from which Cicero had harangued the crowds—a Roman homecoming.

runt   A disparaging term for an undersized person or creature. *runt of the litter* 1. The smallest, hence weakest and least competitive, member of a litter. The one most likely to be pushed aside in the competition for the mother's tits, hence underfed and least likely to survive unless taken up as a pet and separately nurtured. 2. The metaphoric equivalent in any human grouping: *As often as not the Pulitzer Prize in poetry has gone to the runt of Erato's litter, if not to the already dead.* [The most likely source is Du. *rund,* an undersized ox (and therefore not worth much as a draft animal). *Rund* is a specialized derivative of IE *ker-*, horn, horned head. Akin to Gk. *keras*, horn. Speculatively: into Gmnc. with k/h and zero-grade form *hr'-*, suffixed *-n-* and extended → Eng. horn; but also suffixed *-nd-* → Du. *(h)rund*, runt.]

S

saddle tramp   A homeless cowboy wanderer who rode about between short stints as a ranchhand (when work was to be had) and who turned his hand, at intervals, to whatever foraging, pilfering, or outright banditry might keep him alive. In effect, a tramp on horseback. A pejorative term for the legendary lone rider of the epic mythology of the Westerns; the hero riding off into the sunset, the saddle tramp into whatever dirty tricks might keep him alive and in whiskey. [Am. wstrn. from ca. 1875, by which time the West had been fenced in and riders of the range were no longer pioneers but bums, often in flight from a Wanted poster.]

sally lunn   So in some cookbooks, but more properly *Sally Lunn* A tea muffin made of butter, milk, flour, baking powder, whole egg, and salt, and baked in a greased muffin pan for 30 minutes at 400°. [The name is attributed most commonly to Sally Lunn, an XVIII girl who sold prized baked goods from a cart through the streets of Bath, England. I have not searched the local archives and cannot attest this derivation definitively, but she is mentioned in many sources and her name (or legend) survives in modern Bath.

HISTORIC. *Sally Lunn* or *sally lunn* muffins, with one or another local variation, have been popular in parts of the U.S. South, where a persistent spook-etymology has it that they are French in origin and that their name derives from Fr. *sol(eil) et lune,* sun and moon, so called because they are brown on top, as if tanned by the sun, but pale as the moon on the sides (as any muffin would be when baked in a greased muffin pan at 400°).

As in most spook etymology, this explanation is ingenious and even seemingly simple, but it falters on the fact that *sol(eil) et lune* does not occur in French with anything like this sense, nor in any early Creole form of French Louisiana. Short of mathematical certainty, the honors beong to Miss Sally Lunn of Bath.

Saltire

saltire   Also *saltier Heraldry.* An *X* (St. Andrew's Cross) on a shield.
It is formed by crossing a bend with a bend sinister (the bend
sinister or bar sininster indicating a bastard lineage). [Hardly a
common Am. term and obs. except in heraldry. Ult. < IE *sel-,* to
leap, whence L. *saltare* and OF *saulter, sauter,* same sense. (AS-
SAULT. SOMERSAULT.) But then ME *sawtire,* a cattle-guard device
in a fence. Essentially what we call a *sawhorse* or *sawbuck.* It keeps
cattle in (not sheep), but a nimble person can skip over it lightly by
placing his or her hands at the points marked *X* in the illustration,
and a less nimble one can clamber the upper *V* with little difficulty.
Sawtire has long been obs., but it remains as a good example of
folknaming (sometimes called folk etymology).]

sandal   Footwear. A sole variously attached to the foot by straps or
thongs. [OF *sandale* < L. *sandalia,* plu. of *sandalium;* the form
only slightly modified < Gk. *sandálion,* which is the dim. form of
sandalon, sandal. And there the etymological trace stops. There
was a remote Lydian god called Sandal, and AHD suggests that
Lydian *sandal* (unattested) may have meant "the shoe of Sandal";
but the suggestion amounts to little more than woolgathering
where there are no bushes, for almost nothing is known of Sandal,
and nothing in the misty record specifies footwear. Except for the
winged sandals of Hermes, in fact, Greek mytho-religion has almost
nothing to say about the footwear of the gods and goddesses, who
in any case saved on shoe leather by walking on air.

(Not akin to the fragrant sandalwood of Asiatic origin, named
via Arabic *sandal,* the name of this tree and wood from cognates
in Persian, Urdu, and Sanskrit.)]

scalp [Etymology uncertain. Perhaps akin to ON *skalpr, sheath, leather sheath; hence "sheath of skin over the skull."] n. The skin covering the skull. v. 1. To cut away the skin and hair from the top of the skull of a dead or wounded enemy's skull for display as a battle trophy. (Scalping is commonly but not always fatal. A number of victims of scalping have survived, with interesting hairlines to be sure, but still matching sistole to diastole about one-to-one.) 2. *Theater and public events.* To buy tickets to popular events at box office prices in order to sell them at inflated prices. 3. To cheat outrageously.

    scalper 1. One who lifts scalps as war trophies in the manner of many American Indians. 2. One who practices verb senses 2 or 3 above.

    scalp lock Among American Indians, a tuft of hair on an otherwise shaved head to serve as a handle in taking a scalp—an act of proud defiance, as if to make it easier for an enemy to take one's scalp (if he can get close enough and live).

    HISTORIC. Hollywood seems to have accepted and to have built into the dialogue of bad movies the misinformation that it was the British who first taught Amerinds to take scalps. The British, as part of their everexpanding civilization, did once pay bounties for enemy scalps, as did the French during the French and Indian Wars, but the practice was native. Archaeologists have found pre-Columbian human remains showing that not only scalps had been taken as trophies, but also hands and feet.

Scaramouch 1. The standard stooge of Italian low comedy and pantomime. A braggart and poltroon, he is forever being beaten by Harlequin. (Fans of the Three Stooges—and, Lord knows, there are today fans of everything—will readily recognize Curly the Skindome as the Scaramouch of that still-popular buffoonery.) [< Italian *scaremuccio*, skirmish → Scaremuccio the stooge, because he is the recipient of all blows.]

schmo A more or less pitiful dolt. A born loser. [< *schmuck* (which see), of which it is a minced form. "Not a Yiddish word but a Yinglish invention," according to Leo Rosten, *The Joys of Yiddish* (New York, 1968).]

schmuck *Slang.* 1. A pitiful, clumsy dolt. 2. A loathsome one. A cheap prick (see derivation). [An intricate evolution < IE *(s)meug-*, damp, slimy, → Gmnc. *smug-*, slippery, → OE *smok*, shirt (thing slipped on), → MHG *smuck*, clothing. (SMOCK). Hence Ger.

Schmuck (rhymes with *hook*), decorative clothing (earlier, and now:) ornament; hence, embroidery, jewelry. Then into Yiddish as a minced form for *penis.* (Because genital references are strongly taboo in Yiddish, *schmuck* was half-whimsically adopted, as if to call the penis, especially Daddy's, "the family jewels," which is also a common whimsicality in English. Thus the two senses derived from Yiddish are: 1. A pitiful prick; 2. An offensive one.

Then, because the taboo carried over into Am.-Yiddish (Yinglish), *schmuck* was often altered to the less offensive *schmo,* which is not properly Yiddish.]

seltzer   1. Originally a naturally effervescent spring water with a high mineral content. [< Ger. *Selterser Wasser,* Selterser water, after the waters of the springs of Nieder Selters (Lower Selters), near Wiesbaden, in Germany. 2. *Loosely.* Any carbonated water. And so especially as a St. Louis localism. (In local usage there, *scotch and soda* means—perish the thought—"scotch and ginger ale"; one must ask for a *scotch and seltzer* to get what is known elsewhere in the United States as a "scotch and soda.") 3. Especially in New York City, and perhaps only there, tapwater charged in the bottle with bubbles much larger than those of commercial club soda, and served through an attached siphon-top.

HISTORIC TRIVIA. The 1978–1979 *Manhattan Yellow Pages* lists (under "Beverages") only Seltzer Unlimited of 249 West 18th St. as specializing in "Home and Wholesale Siphon Delivery." There may be still in operation in the other boroughs two smaller companies, but Seltzer is far from being an unlimited business.

Before WWII New Yorkers, esp. those of German and German-Jewish origin, prized the large bubbles of seltzer water served through a siphon attached to the bottle. Those preferred large bubbles, however, require an especially strong bottle with its own siphon top, and the Czech factory that once monopolized the manufacture of such bottles stopped producing them ca. 1938 when the Nazis took it over. New York seltzer distributors are limited by the number of pre-Hitler bottles still available for refilling, and also by the fact that only two charging machines, their capacity reduced by age, remain operational in the area, with a third that is no longer functional standing by to be cannibalized for a limited number of spare parts. As the old bottles are lost, broken, or made into lamps, and as these last charging machines give up the ghost, the New Yorker's traditional seltzer water (which I will call a nostalgia rather than a delicacy) will be replaced by club soda and by commercial nonsiphon-top variants falsely labeled as seltzer water.

senile   1. Old-mannish. Of a man in old age. 2. *Loose but common ext. (see anile).* (a) Of old age. (b) Of the deterioration accompanying old age: *senile dementia.* 3. *Geology.* Approaching the end of a cycle of erosion. [L. *senilis,* like an old man, < *senex,* old man (SENATOR). *Anile* is specific to the old age of women, though increasingly senile is in common use for old age without regard to sex.]

sepia   1. A color ranging from dark yellowish brown to medium olive. 2. An ink or pigment of this color originally from the protective fluid of the cuttlefish. 3. An ink drawing, wash, or painting in this color, characteristic of earlier schools of art. 4. Also *sepia print* A brown-tinted photograph of a sort common in XIX photography. And many early photographs, because of imperfect fixatives, fade to a sepia mist after long exposure to light: *Even under the neons of Washington, Senator Sam Ervin throws a sepia shadow, as if from a world photographed long ago and faded.* [At root (ref. to Sen. Ervin intended), "rotten." < Gk. *sēpia,* cuttlefish, < *sēpein,* to rot. (And, from p. p. stem, SEPTIC.) Because cuttlefish ink was supposed to cause things to decompose, it was, and still is, a common marinating fluid in Gk. cooking. Sp. *calamare en su tinta,* squid marinated and cooked in its own ink, is a survival. And see *meerschaum,* technically *sepiolite,* because once believed to be a decomposed and wadded mass of cuttlefish cartilage.]

Septuagint   The first translation of the Hebrew Old Testament into Gk., said to have been made in the third century B.C. at Alexandria by 70 (or 72) scholars who worked for 70 (or 72) days. [< L. *septuaginta,* seventy. Understood in speaking of this Gk. Bible as *The Seventy.*]

HISTORIC. It is probably true that in the third century B.C. the scholarly Ptolemy Philadelphos ordered a translation of the Old Testament for the community of Alexandrian Jews who had lost the Hebrew tongue in generations of living abroad, and who wished to understand the words of their Scripture. Whatever the exact facts, the project was opposed by the rabbis of Jerusalem, who clung to the law that the Holy Books were sacred only in the original Hebrew and were not to be rendered into any "lesser" tongue.

The naming of this work arises more from legend than from fact. One pious legend had it that Ptolemy had his 70 (or 72) scholars locked in 70 (or 72) separate cells for 70 (or 72) days, each working on his own Gk. version, and that at the end of that time every version agreed to the letter. More commonly it is said that this assembly of scholars collaborated and produced their version in that many days. The facts seem to be, however, that this first seminar rendered only the Laws into Gk., the translation of the prophetic books continuing only a century later, and of the Psalms and other writings, later yet.

Whatever the legend-obscured facts, the *Septuagint* had a profound influence on later Christian theology and on the intellectual life of Europe. University studies were long for holy orders only, though nonclerical "gentlemen" attended later universities more or less negligently for a social "pass" degree. Up to about WWI the basic curriculum at Harvard and Yale was Hebrew, Greek, and Latin, and prescribed courses for the application of the Scriptures these languages made available. The *Septuagint* is still one of the three basic subjects in denominations that demand a learned clergy, and that training continues to influence the sermons delivered from America's more scholarly pulpits.

sequin A small, shiny disc originally sewn as a spangle on a woman's gown, now sewn or glued on theatrical costumes as well. Originally in gold or silver; now common in any color that glitters. [XVII Eng. *sequin* < Italian *zecchino* < Venetian *secchino*, a coin, < *secca*, the Mint of the Venetian Republic, < Arabic *sikkah*, the die used in stamping coins. Root sense, therefore, "stamped disc." The Venetian *secchino* was not perforated, but coins have long been used as costume jewelry, often as buttons but also worn in chains as an ancient Gypsy motif.]

sequoia The giant *Sequoia gigantea* or the closely related redwood, *S. sempivirens,* of California. They are the largest and oldest trees known to forestry. [What is not generally known is that they are named after a late-XVIII, early-XIX part Cherokee variously called Sequoya, Sequoyah, or Sikwayi and also as George Guess, the name of a white trader he claimed as his father. Having received an education in English, he devised a syllabary for rendering the Cherokee language, his principles being later used for rendering other Amerind tongues. His Indian name was given to this genus of trees in 1847 by Stephen Endlicher, a Hungarian botanist. I do not know Endlicher's connection with the half-Cherokee, but no man's name has been attached to a more magnificent life-form. Let us at least be grateful that Endlicher chose the Indian name, or we might otherwise have found ourselves in the Geogus National Forest.]

serendipity   The act of making a surprisingly happy discovery while looking for something else. There can be an isolated act of serendipity, but at origin the term implies the habit of making such discoveries. [After the mid-XVIII fairy tale by Horace Walpole, "Three Princes of Serendip," whose titular heroes were forever making such happy discoveries by the way. Serendip is the old name for Ceylon, now Sri Lanka. But the word *serendipity* does not occur in the fairy tale itself. Walpole coined it a few years later in a letter dated January 28, 1754.]

serge   A twilled cloth, either of worsted or of worsted and wool, once commonly used for men's suits. [A much-traveled name. L. *serica lana*, silky wool, → OF *sarge*, ME *sarge, serge*. L. *serica* < Gk. *serikos*, silken, < *Sēnes*, the Chinese (at root, "the silk people"). In botany *sericeous* describes a plant covered with silky hairs. If there was once a twilled ("two-thread") cloth woven of silk and wool (and there probably was not), later serge was, as above, of wool or wool and worsted, though present technology is capable of strange synthetic blends. L. *serica lana* did not imply that silk was used in weaving this cloth, but rather that it had a hard finish that gave it a silklike sheen, and pure serge suits become notably shiny, especially in the pants, when well worn. Eric Partridge, *Name into Word* (New York, 1950), notes, "In XIX . . . there was a material called *silk serge,* a silk fabric twilled like serge."]

shillelagh   (In Am. commonly pronounced *shi-lā'-lē,* but ask any professional Irishman and be ready to fight over the answer.) A stout Irish walking-stick-and-cudgel of oak or blackthorn, the national head-splitting club of festivally bloody donnybrooks. (Bear in mind that under feudal law woodcutting was so severely regulated that such a heavy club would be per se illegal unless it were passed off as a family heirloom. Even then the almost mandatory possession of a shillelagh was a bold vaunt.) [After the forest of Shillelagh, renowned for its choice stands of hardwood, named after the town it borders in County Wicklow. For a note on feudal woodcutting restrictions see *hook or crook, Browser's I.*]

shivaree   1. A raucous wedding-night carouse, often ending in a bride-stealing riot but starting as a mock serenade to the newlyweds. 2. Any raucous country nightfest with music and booze. [Sthrn. regional < Creole < Fr. *charivari,* a raucous wedding-night festival. Via L. *caribaria* < Gk. *karēbaria,* hangover, from *karē,* head; with *barus,* heavy (BAROMETER).]

shoot the wounded   Or in the full and playfully rotund formula of friendly poker players at their weekly game, *Slam the gates of mercy, shoot the wounded, and sink the lifeboats!* A common hyperbolic assertion of determination to compete relentlessly. [The form *shoot* cannot have been much before 1500 and was probably later, its elaborations much later; but the ruthless military imperative is immemorial. The most recent literary reference to this custom of killing one's own wounded comrades after a fight occurs in Hemingway's *For Whom the Bell Tolls,* when the Gypsy guerrilla leader prepares to kill his wounded junior, partly in mercy, to keep him from falling into the hands of Franco's Fascists, and partly in self-defense, because the wounded man would reveal secrets under torture.]

HISTORIC. History abounds with accounts and legends of defeated forces that made compacts to kill one another rather than be taken as slaves. Shakespeare's "Or to take arms against a sea of troubles and by opposing end them" is ultimately a reference to early Irish warriors: most battles were fought on beaches, and defeated Irish warriors (or at least many of them) swam out to sea, carrying all their gear, to drown rather than be taken and enslaved. Arabs developed a reputation for their ingenuity in torturing surviving wounded soldiers, who would gladly have begged their fleeing comrades for a merciful quick execution. The formula has been playfully generalized, but its military history is horribly literal.

shotgun house   *Sthrn.* A house in which the rooms are aligned one behind the other with no interior hallways. [Sthrn. Am., prob. ca. 1880. So called, perhaps, in the violent whimsy that a shotgun blast through the front door would pass through each of the rooms in turn and hit the rear door. Or perhaps because the rooms are arranged one behind the other like the shells in a shotgun. The northern equivalent was (and still is) the *railroad flat* (which see), this style being common in tenement apartments in northern cities, rare in northern houses.]

HISTORIC. This total utilization of interior space at some expense to privacy seems to have developed from the one-room shack in the South. When these began to be divided into separate rooms, they consisted of a porch, a bedroom, and a kitchen. With greater elaboration they progressed to sitting room, bedroom, bedroom, dining room, kitchen. Some remodeled shotgun houses added a verandah along the length of the building with outside doors into each room, but with the disadvantage that the inner rooms then had three doors, one from the outside and two for passing through.

sibyl 1. *Capitalized.* A feminine given name. 2. *In ancient Greece.* A prophetess who spoke in tongues. [Gk. *sibulla* is prob. < *dios boulē,* the will (sending) of God; in Doric dialect *Sios bolla,* the sending of Zeus; hence *sibulla* is, at extended root, "she who speaks what Zeus sends her to say."]

HISTORIC. In stripped fact the *sibulla* was a temple hysteric with a talent for "coming through" (in gibberish) when prompted by the priests, probably after eating or drinking some hallucinogenic substance. The priests thereupon interpreted her "holy" gibberish for a fee, the suppliant went home hugging a probably unintelligible message, Zeus seems not to have entered any overt objection, and the priests pocketed the offering. So may we all be served. The wonder may well be in the fact that the priests, at least to some extent, must have believed that their mumbo jumbo was in the true service of god.

Sisyphus *Gk. myth.* The central fact of his surviving legend is his eternal punishment, which consists of striving endlessly to roll a great boulder uphill only to have it roll back and over him, whereupon he must forever start over. Thus a paradigm of endless laborious futility; perhaps a myth-figure of the American taxpayer. *Sisyphean adj.* 1. Like Sisyphus. 2. Of never ending, self-undoing, self-defeating labor: *Our Sisyphean national debt.*

MYTHO-HISTORIC. Sisyphus is the Gk. version of the ancient folk story–myth of the crafty man. The pattern of the tale occurs in practically all cultures, clearly suggesting a Dawn Age origin. A common version is of the man wily enough to outwit even Death. In what is probably the older Gk. version, Death came for Sisyphus, who managed to bind him in chains, and no one died until Ares, the specialist in death, came and set his collector free. In a second and probably later version, the dying Sisyphus ordered his wife to omit the ritual sacrifices to the dead. He then complained to Hades, king of the Underworld, and was given permission to return to Corinth to punish her. One might ask: Once safely in hell, who would want to return to Corinth? In any case, Sisyphus made it back, and once there simply remained until he died of great old age.

I will speculate, too, that in Greece, his early legend was blurred with those of various Titans. Prometheus stole fire from heaven to bring to Earth and was punished by being chained to a rock to which an eagle (the bird of Zeus) descended every morning to eat out his (self-regenerating) liver. Tantalus stole nectar and ambrosia from the table of the gods and was "tantalized" by eternal thirst and eternal hunger in the presence of an unreachable great plenty. Sisyphus baffled the will of the Gods by tricking their collector, and suffers a similar eternal and self-repeating punishment. All other details of his legend are incidental accretions.

Siwash An Indian of the northwestern U.S. Pacific coast and southwestern Canada. [< Fr. *sauvage,* savage. The Fr. designation probably corrupted by the neighboring Chinook to something like *Sawash* or *S'wash* and further altered to Siwash *(sī'-wash)* by non-French white settlers.

To the French, of course, all Amerinds were *les sauvages.* The specification of the name to this tribe was prob. in ref. to their primitivism, for the Siwash have been known from the beginning for the crudity of their means and for their ability to rough it, taking off on long treks across barren country in all sorts of weather without provision or shelter and subsisting on roots, grubs, and earthworms. Hence, the Northwest regional verb:] *to siwash* To rough it. To handle back-breaking work by brute force.

HISTORIC. Northwestern lumberjacks built Skid Roads for hauling logs (see *Browser's I, Skid Row*). Not all trees could be felled conveniently close to such a haulway, however. Some logs had to be dragged across broken ground by main force, and this process was called *siwashing.* At intervals, the lumberjacks left standing a trimmed tree to which they could attach block-and-tackle gear for this work, and these trees were called *siwash poles.*

I'd die for dear old Siwash! Obs. Through most of the first half of XX a standard burlesque of the collegiate's rah-rah cry. From *good old Siwash* A mythical small college, the setting of a long series of popular humorous short stories published in the *Saturday Evening Post* by George Fitch (1877–1915) and collected in two volumes, *Big Strike at Siwash* (1909) and *At Good Old Siwash* (1911). [If Fitch was using the name in its root sense, "Siwash" implied primitivism. And his fictional campus was hardly a center of high culture. Fitch declared that he had made the place up for fictional purposes. He had, however, been a student at Knox College in Galesburg, Illinois, and the publicity people at Knox still claim that it is the original good old Siwash. I do not know the campus well enough to make a point-by-point comparison with the stories. Having once visited Knox, I would not label it as Primitive Academy, nor am I sure why it would want so to label itself.

I do not know how *Siwash* got from the Northwest to Galesburg. Fitch was born in Illinois. Call it cultural diffusion. How did the Bowery get to be Skid Row?]

skeleton 1. The total of bone and cartilage supporting the bodies of vertebrates. 2. This structure when laid bare by dissection or decay. 3. This bone structure as a grinning figure of death. 4. *Hyperbolic ext.* An emaciated person: *a living skeleton.* 5. *Technically,* The hard external carapace or bony or chitinous covering of various invertebrates, and also of such vertebrates as the turtle, but more accurately called the *exoskeleton.* 6. Any internal supporting framework. [But the root sense is "mummy." < IE *skel-*, dried out, → Gk. *skeletos,* mummy. So in obs. Eng. up to XVII *skelet,* mummy.]

skeleton crew A minimum work crew left in a plant not to run it but to maintain it. Aboard a vessel, a minimum crew left aboard (or put aboard) a disabled ship, not so much to sail it as to keep it from being claimed as an abandoned ship.

skeleton at the banquet A memento mori to remind revelers how all feasting ends. [Plutarch writes in the *Moralia* that the Egyptians always displayed a skeleton during their festivities, but Plutarch probably meant a mummy rather than what we call a skeleton.]

skijoring *Winter sports.* Tow-skiing behind a horse (and, now, behind a snowmobile). [<Norwegian *skigjöring,* literally, "ski-doing," in which the skier was towed by a horse guided by an experienced rider (or else!). Introduced into Minnesota ca. 1900 and enthusiastically taken up for cross-country and shorter races. Now locally popular in various winter resort areas.] Also *to skijor, skijor racing.*

skin [< IE *sek-*, to cut. BISECT. Zero-grade form *sk-*, suffixed *-n-* → Gmnc. *sk'n,* whence ON *skinn.* The root sense would appear to be "thing cut from the body," as in flaying.

(The metathesized form of Gmnc. variant *sekt-* is the basis of hypothetical OE *scittan,* to shit, though it is attested only in *bescat,* beshat; and there, too, the root sense is "thing divided from the body."

Language has only a limited number of metaphors for the

human condition. In late XIX when tramp steamers began to ply the Far East, they signed on many Malay sailors called Lascars, who spoke only pidgin English at best. Most Lascars worked as firemen, stoking and hauling ashes. Since their pidgin had no word for "ashes" they named them "shit belongum fire." Across 2,000 and more years, and halfway around the world in their distinct language groups, the Lascars and our OE language ancestors came up with the same language metaphor.)

But ON *skinn* seems not to have entered English except in ME under IX–X Danelaw.] *n.* 1. The outer layer of an animal or human body; the hide of an animal, the epidermis of the human animal. 2. *Ext.* The outer layer of most things, as the rind of fruit, the covering of an airplane's air frame, and even a surface layer of pond scum. *v.* 1. *In what is prob. the root sense.* To flay. 2. *In general.* To remove the outer layer of most things. 3. *Special sense in automotive body work.* To replace the outer covering. [When I ripped the right front door off my car by massaging it with a hydrant, several repairmen told me that rather than replace the whole door they would skin (i.e., replace) the torn outer surface.]

skin deep On the surface only. *skin dive* A scuba dive. So called in contradistinction to earlier deep-sea diving in a heavy weighted suit with a screw-on helmet connected to a long trailing air hose. Rubber suits are now common in deep diving or in cold water, but early scuba diving involved little more than swimming trunks. One dived, that is to say, in one's skin. *skin flick* A pornographic movie. (Because the featured wardrobe is the actors' skin.) *skin game* A swindle. (Because the victim is, so to speak, flayed.) *skin pop Narcotics slang.* The act of injecting drugs. *skin tight* Clinging closely to body contours.

to skin alive 1. To flay while the victim is still alive; from the days of tribal savagery to the higher savagery of the Middle Ages, live flaying remained one form of torture. [And with godly precedent. The legendary Phrygian flute player Marsyas challenged Apollo to a musical contest. Defeated, he was flayed alive for his presumption. To be more precise, he was not exactly flayed alive (his skin removed from him) but pulled out of his skin by the power of the god, though it is doubtful that Marsyas was in any condition to recognize the difference.] 2. *Hyperbole.* To chastise or punish severely: *When she finds out I lost my shirt my wife will skin me alive.*

skin the cat Child's play. To leap up, seize a parallel branch with both hands, and then to come to a sitting position on the branch by passing one's legs between one's arms and over the branch with a vigorous twist. (Fancifully, as if flaying a cat—or a rabbit—by pulling the hide over its head.)

get under one's skin 1. To irritate, annoy. (As does a splinter or a boring insect.) 2. To become obsessed by: *"I've got you under my skin"*—popular song. (Like an unremovable subcutaneous irritation.)

thick-skinned Imperturbable. Also **thin-skinned** Easily annoyed.

by the skin of one's teeth Just barely. (A biblical metaphor: Job 19:20, "My bone cleaveth to my skin and to my flesh, and I am escaped with [i.e., "by"] the skin of my teeth.")

gimme some skin Black English formula of greeting. 1. *Earlier,* Shake hands. *But now,* 2. Slap my palm (with one or both hands in whatever position is offered) in lieu of a handshake.

sky   The apparent atmosphere, especially in its changes. "Red sky at morning, sailor take warning. Red sky at night, sailor's delight."—Nautical adage. (Strictly speaking, we have only one atmosphere, and hence only one sky, but note how readily we pluralize, as in *clear skies tomorrow, under lowering skies,* for a word is not simply a thing defined and set; it functions within the associations of our nervous systems, and those associations prompt us to think of each weather shift as a separate sky. In this case, moreover, these associations are implicit in the root:) [Ult. < IE *(s)keu-*, to cover, to hide. OBSCURE. The root sense seems to be opposite to our natural associations with the "openness" of *sky.* One evolution from this stem has been, in fact, Gk. *skytos,* animal hide; whence, dropping the *s,* CUTICLE. But in widespread Gmnc. use this stem functioned in words for *cloud, shadow.* So OE *sceo,* cloud (read the *c* as a *k*); whence ME *skye,* but with the deep root sense "cloud-way," in which connection compare *Beowulf's* "whale-way" for *sea.*]

skycap An airport redcap, now only rarely wearing the red cap of the porter's trade. **sky diving** Parachute jumping for sport. **sky-high** Very high. (a) Exorbitant: *his prices are sky-high.* (b) Very drunk: *he finished the pitcher of martinis and was sky-high.* **sky-jack** To hijack (which see) a plane. **skylight** A roof window. **sky pilot** A preacher. At origin a military or naval chaplain. (He charts the heavenly course.) **skyscraper** A soaring commercial building of the order made possible by XX steel-girder construction (beginning in late XIX). [Familiarity has dulled our sense of this coinage as a stunning image from late folk poetry.]

the sky's the limit There is no limit. *to the skies* Limitless. Limitlessly. *out of a (the) clear blue sky* Unexpectedly. [Folk origin. The image is of lightning on a clear day.]

blue-sky laws Laws aimed at preventing securities frauds. [Aimed at regulating transactions in stock schemes someone described as having no more basis than so many feet of blue sky.]

HISTORIC. Piecemeal state laws regulating securities exchange began to appear ca. 1850. Kansas enacted the first comprehensive blue-sky law in 1911 and it was upheld by the Supreme Court in 1917. In 1933, in reaction to the disastrous market crash of 1929, FDR's Securities Act established national regulation of securities. Hoover had almost a full term as president following the Crash but seemed unable to conceive of regulation. By 1933 every state except Nevada had some sort of blue-sky law, but the Securities Act of 1933 established the first uniform national regulations.

sleeve   [IE *sleubh-*, to slip, to slide. Prob. *sliub-* in Gmnc., whence, with b/f → OE *slif, slēf,* sleeve ("thing slipped on"), ME *slefe, sleve.* Few words have so substantially retained their form and sense over so many millennia.] 1. The arm covering of a garment. 2. *Mechanics.* A casing, usu. tubular, into which a mechanical part slips.

sleeve coupling A metal tube that joins two other lengths of tubing by being secured over their butted ends.

to have an ace (or something) up one's sleeve To have a deceitful and dishonest trick in reserve: *Richard Wilbur plays anagrams with a shrewd head up his sleeve. nothing up the sleeve* All open and above-board. With no hidden tricks. (A common formula of the stage magician's performing patter.)

to laugh up one's sleeve To laugh at someone derisively while hiding one's laughter. [In use by at least XVII, at a time when gentlemen's costumes had sleeves ample enough to conceal one's face, commonly with a large handkerchief in the cuff. It was also a time that a derisive laugh might elicit a challenge to a duel. Whether in courtesy or caution, it was as well not to deride openly. The same sense, but with an altered image, was common in related languages. In It. *ridere sotto i baffi,* to laugh under one's moustache; in Ger. *sich ins Faustchen lachen,* laugh into one's fist; in Fr. *rire sous cape,* laugh under one's cloak (lapel?) or *rire dans sa barbe,* laugh into one's beard. And *laugh into one's beard* and *laugh into one's cape* were in Eng. use in XVI.

roll up one's sleeves To prepare to set to work.

shirtsleeves Lit., the sleeves of a shirt, but widely used as a symbol of the working man, laborer. [The elegantly dressed wear more or less elaborate coats; the laborer get down to shirtsleeves.] *back to shirtsleeves* Said of a working family that made money and then lost it, its descendants going from formal wear back to shirtsleeves in x generations.

slogan   A word, or more commonly a phrase, intended to produce a conditioned reflex more or less apart from any paraphrasable content; hence, an advertising catchphrase or political rallying call. [At root, "a battle cry": "St. George and the dragon for merry England!" was a slogan. So, too, the Marine sergeant's cry at Belleau Wood in WWI, "Come on, you sons of bitches: you wanna live forever?" Both meant the same thing to the troops about to attack. < Gaelic *sluggh-ghairm,* a call to the (embattled) host. The form and sense have been much altered, but the essential sense remains "Hooray to the death for our side!"]

snake: had it been a snake 'twould have bit you   It's right there in front of your nose. (Said to a person looking for something right in front of him and in plain view, though he has not yet focused on it.) [I first became aware of this ruralism as a favorite of my Missouri-born-and-bred father-in-law, taking it at first, therefore, to be a midwesternism; but I have since noted it in widespread usage. It is, in fact, a simple variant of Brit. *if it had been a bear it would have bit you.* P. *Catch Phrases* attests it in Brit. use by at least 1633 (and still current). Partridge's dating may explain why this catchphrase is not much used on the East Coast, the first settlers having come to the original colonies before the Brit. precedent was widely established in Brit.]

soap   [The substance is named at root from the method of making it by straining through a sieve. Otherwise, except for a vowel alteration, the word is unchanged from IE *sip-,* sieve, to pass through a sieve, thing strained through a sieve.] 1. Basically, and with many later refinements and additives, a cleaning substance made by straining fats and oils through a sieve, with the result usually formed into water-soluble cakes. 2. *Colloquial.* Flattery. (But in Am. more commonly:)

   soft soap Flattery. [Am. ca. 1830. P. *Slang* says it was anglicized ca. 1860. The Am. form may be a variant of Brit. *soft sawder* (prob. "soft sawdust," and prob. a ref. to sawdust strewn on the ground in country wrestling to soften the falls; or alternately to sawdust used in plumping out a scarecrow or an effigy, as flattery may be said to work in either way); but Brit. *soft sawder* is uncertainly attested and may be later than the Am. form.]

no soap A term of flat-out rejection (curtly and with no flattery). [Am. only. Exact dating uncertain, but prob. soon after the preceding, for this is a ricochet term and could not make sense except by bouncing off the established *soft soap.*]

Soapy Sam A generalized disparaging nickname for any unctuous person, whatever his first name. [Originally applied disparagingly, ca. 1860, to the notably unctuous Samuel Wilberforce (1805–1873), bishop of Oxford from 1845. In common Am. use until about WWII, but rarer since with the passing of strongly Anglophiliac earlier America.]

soapbox 1. *Literally.* A shipping box in which grocers once received many of their packaged goods. [Not necessarily a box containing soap, but since soap is heavy, the boxes containing it were especially sturdy. The soapbox also became a generic for any such wooden box. The term began to fade when various sorts of cardboard began to replace wood in such shipping cartons, but it still raises a nostalgic echo of earlier days when wood grew on trees and was used unstintingly.] 2. A speaker's platform. [In earlier America, when men were clearing forests to open fields and to build towns, the commonest object in the landscape, especially in the Midwest, was a stump. No man was ever far from one, and any man who wanted to make a speech needed only to take a step or two to mount the nearest one. Thus, *to take to the stump,* to run for political office, a peculiarly Am. idiom. In late XIX and into XX, however, stumps became rare in our cities. Union organizers, political aspirants, and every sort of idealist or crackpot who wanted to address a crowd commonly carried a sturdy soapbox to the park or the street corner and used it as a speaker's platform, as earlier Americans had taken to the stump. Thus, **to get on one's soapbox** 1. To take to the podium. *But* 2. *In a generalized ext.,* To make a speech. To have a lot to say. To berate at length: *Every time Jiggs comes in late Maggie gets on her soapbox.*

soapbox derby An annual competition originally for boys 11 to 15 and now also for girls, the first five of whom entered the finals in 1971. Sponsored by Chevrolet, this much-publicized competition begins with nostalgia for the good old days (up to ca. WWII) when every American boy put wheels to a soapbox and made a go-cart (only because manufacturers were not turning out plastic marvels that look like spaceships—which Daddy couldn't have afforded in the second place). Somehow this primitive home-manufacture of a box on wheels has been inflated into something like the genetic code for American know-how, as if the technological future of the U.S. is secure as long as the soapboxes continue to roll down the ramp. The competition has now even become international, with college scholarships for the top nine finalists, war bonds for all who compete in the annual roll-off in Akron, Ohio, and lesser war bonds for winners of local elimination trials.

Today's soapbox cars are expensive aerodynamic and suspension projects in which the young adolescent is supposed to learn the technology of the future by watching Dad build his crate. But watch out for the all-out competitive American Dad: several winners have been disqualified when it was found that Dad had hidden some sort of forbidden thrust device in the soapbox. No sort of cheating can now be invented, but it is readily inherited.

soap opera *Radio and television.* A serialized mock-epic in which a more-or-less fixed stock of actors gives two dimensions to an in-depth rendition of romance, intrigue, and life's generalized mortal assumptions at heart-tug in the damp souls of chambermaids and lonely housewives, whichever comes first. Once a daytime spiritual narcotic, the soap opera has made it to the prime-time soul of America in such semidramas as *Dallas, Falcon Crest,* and *Dynasty.* [*Soap* as a generic for the accompanying commercials; *opera* for larger-than-life melodramatics; but the label is certainly adapted from *horse opera,* for a Western film; so called because the horses, as the best actors in the cast, get all the starring roles.]

solace *n.* Consolation. (As comfort is a condition of pleasurable being, solace is whatever brings one more or less comfort—which see; in root sense, strengthens one—in grief or misfortune. And corresponding *v.*) [At ult. root, IE *sel-,* happiness, to be happy, to find favor. Via Gmnc. → OE *saelig,* happy; with collective prefix *ge-, gesaelig,* all happy, which was said of the pure and innocent and of the souls of the elect in heaven. To the folk mind, however, it must have seemed foolish, or at least impractical, to be *gesaelig* all day, and so, with a slight vowel modification and a standard shift of g/y, *saelig* became *silly,* as if to say, "Be blessèd on your own time, but right now there are pigs to slop."

So, in one remote cousinly sense, to solace is to make silly-happy. But the form of the word is from the L. evolution in which IE *sel-* became variantly *sol-* → L. *solari,* to console, to stay, to comfort; *sōlācium, sōlātium,* comfort; OF and ME *solas.*]

something else   [Am. Mod slang, since ca. 1960.] A rare thing. *Equally implies,* 1. Strong approval: *Susan and George Garrett gave a party that was really something else.* 2. Strong disapproval: *Those high-school party crashers are really something else.* [The form had ample precedent in earlier Am. *that is something else again,* that is a horse of another color, that changes things substantially, that alters the case. And also, in latter XIX, *something* or *really something,* a notable, a truly notable, thing. Also XIX Am. sthrn., generally diffused by sportswriters and commentators, *he is some kind of football player,* he is really a notable football player.]

soup strainer   A moustache, especially a bushy one that hangs down over the mouth. [XIX Am. jocular. As if in eating soup one had to strain it through such lip-shrubbery.]

spa   1. A resort at which one "takes the waters" of mineral springs, drinking them and bathing in them. 2. The mineral spring itself. 3. *Boston regionalism.* What is now called a convenience store, but with a soda fountain, hence "watering place." [< the place-name *Spa,* a renowned watering place in Belgium.]

sphincter   Primarily the muscle that opens or shuts off the bodily passages of excretion. (But a word of triumph. In a game of anagrams played at Key West, I had made the word *richest,* only to have Richard Wilbur turn up a *p* and steal my word by making *pitchers;* whereupon, to prove the ultimate triumph of good over the forces of evil, I turned up an *n* and stole my word back from him by making *sphinctre. Deo vindice.*) [Ult. < IE *spei-,* to grow strong, to thicken. Probably suffixed *-gg-* in Hellenic, which in Gk. is pronounced *ng* (cf. Gk. *aggelos,* messenger → L. *angelus,* angel. ANGEL.) → Gk. *spiggein,* to compress, to strangle, *sphiggtēr,* contractile muscle.

The word may be related to *Sphinx,* < Gk. *sphigx* (with *g* as *n*), a totemic idol associated with Boeotia, but ultimately from untraced Dawn Age religion.

I cannot think of an English word in which the stem *sping-* functions, but It. has *spingere,* to squeeze, and *spingere la mano,* to clasp (shake) hands in greeting or farewell.]

sphinx   1. A polymorphic figure of myth-religion, usually represented as having the body of a lion and the head of a man, though sometimes the head is of a hawk or ram. It may be the survival of a Dawn

Age religious animal-totem-deity, and the man's head may be a late adaptation to partially anthropomorphic beliefs. [Conjecturally, the name is akin to Gk. *sphiggein,* to bind, to strangle (see *sphincter*), and was associated in Greece with Boeotia, so Gk. *Sphigx,* Boeotian *Phix,* sphinx. 2. *Capitalized.* The monumental stone Sphinx of Giza in Egypt, having the body of a lion, a human head with an enigmatic smile (perhaps the effect of erosion in the desert sandblast), and the breasts of a woman. 3. An enigmatic person or a symbol of enigma. 4. A monster of Thebes in the form of a winged lion with a human head. Sometimes called the Enigma of Thebes.

the riddle of the Sphinx The Theban Sphinx lurked in wait for strangers and put to them the riddle, "What walks on four legs in the morning, on two legs at noon, and on three legs at night?" It then devoured all who could not answer. Oedipus replied, "Man. In the morning of his infancy he crawls on hands and knees, in the noon of his prime he strides on two legs, in the night of old age he totters along with a cane (a third leg)." Thereupon the frustrated Sphinx, having exhausted all the comic material available in Boeotia and with no hope of finding more there, is supposed to have strangled (sphinctered) itself in its rage.

spoils *Now always in plu.* The prizes/loot taken by the victor in a battle: *the spoils of war.* [IE *spel-, sp'l-,* to tear off, break off, to split, → L. *spolium.*] 1. *Prob. the earliest sense.* The skin off an animal (ripped from its body). 2. Arms, armor, and other loot taken from the bodies of the enemy dead after a battle. → OF *espoillier,* to plunder, to despoil; ME *spoilen.* In a separate association with "body" and "dead body," It. *spoglie* (a plural used for a sing. object, but also in the singular as *spoglia*), a corpse; and *spogliare,* to undress. **spoils system** *In XIX U.S. politics (now somewhat modified by civil service but still in effect in appointed offices),* The standard practice by newly appointed "ins" of firing all appointed officials of the other party in order to appoint their own supporters: *to the victor belong the spoils.*

HISTORIC. It was common practice after a battle for the victor to strip the enemy dead of arms, armor, bits of money, jewelry, and any other valuables. Small items probably disappeared into the pockets of the soldiers, but after one battle Hannibal was said to have sent to Carthage 30 bushels of signet rings hacked from the fingers of the Roman dead—a fine round figure of speech, since no one knows the size of a Roman bushel.

Trophy is a related term, at root, < Gk. *trophein,* to turn, *troph-*

ē, turning point. It was the custom to pile the spoils at the point at which the defeated enemy turned and ran.

squash The North American plant and its fruit. [From an Algonquinian (Massachusetts) word that has been rendered in transliterated distortion *askootasquash,* of which *askoot* is an unknown element, and *asqu,* plant, with *ash,* inanimate plural ending. As with many derivatives from Amerind originals, the distortions outreach etymology, though the shortening to *squash* is clear and simple. And there is attested in the records of the earliest settlers the confirming anglicized form *squantersquash* (which, to speculate further, may be the ultimate source of *winter squash* for those varieties, such as the acorn squash, that can be stored for long periods).

To further the confusion, Roger Williams, founder of the Rhode Island Colony, referred to squash as vine-apples and wrote that they were tasty when eaten raw.

I can make no comment on the eating habits of early Rhode Island. Charles Earle Funk, *Horsefeathers* (New York, 1958), gives the form as *asquutasquash,* a sort of melon (gourd), and says that the Indian word means "that which is eaten raw," but nothing supports that translation, and whatever "melon" Roger Williams may have had in mind, no one has identified among the flora of New England any squash or gourd that could be called tasty when eaten raw (though hunger is a mighty spice).]

squirrel The usu. arboreal rodent (the *dormouse,* which see, is a squirrel, but not primarily arboreal). [At root, "shadow tail." < Gk. *skia,* shadow; *oura,* tail, → Gk. *skiouros,* shadow tail; a bit of ancient folk poetry visualizing a squirrel sitting in the shadow of its own raised tail. (See also *ascian* under *antipodes.*) The stem *oura* also occurs in *cynosure; see Browser's I.*]

to squirrel To hoard. [Because squirrels hoard nuts and acorns in tree hollows as winter food.] *squirrelly, squirrely Am. slang.* Crazy. Not right in the head. [By association with *nuts,* common slang for "crazy," as in "he's nuts."]

USELESS KNOWLEDGE. Squirrels are equipped with cheek pouches for carrying nuts and acorns to their caches and have a powerful instinct against shedding these pouched nuts before they reach their chosen hiding place. This instinct makes it easy to trap a chipmunk (the name is of Am. Indian origin) by placing nuts in a glass milk bottle. The chipmunk can pop through the neck. Once it has filled its pouches, however, it cannot get out. So strong is its instinct that even with its pouches full and more nuts in the bottle it will starve to death sooner than let go its mouthful. It is a pointless trapping, since the chipmunk cannot be had without smashing the bottle, and is likely to be badly damaged when it is smashed. Luckily, this bit of knowledge is all the more useless in that few things are as rare today as glass milk bottles.

stadium (The traditional plural, from L., is *stadia,* but *stadiums* is now more common in Am.) 1. A traditionally oval, now sometimes domed, construction of tiers of seats around a field for sports. 2. *In ancient Greece.* A usu. semicircular open stone structure with tiers of seats above a track for foot races and other field events. [L. *stadium,* < Gk. *stadion,* the name of sense 2, above, and also a Greek measure of distance between 606 and 607 English feet. *Stadion* was a fixed Greek linear measure, after earlier *spadion,* the length of the race track at Olympia. The structure is thus named for the track. (It seems to follow that the 606–607-ft. 100-yard dash was the classical event, for there must have been longer tracks for other events.) But *stadion* is also the neuter form of *stadios,* fixed, unalterable, applied to this track with the sense "officially standardized distance."

    Stadia, the L. plural of *stadium,* survives as the name of an optical device for measuring linear distance. (In surveying, *stadia rods* are used in such measurement.) And *stadium,* now obsolete, or at least obsolescent, has served in medical usage with the sense, "a fixed stage in the development of a disease" (prob. by analogy with heats in a race).]

stalactite/stalagmite *Geology.* Reciprocal limestone formations found in caves as the result of the dripping of lime-rich water over millions of years. Stalactites are iciclelike forms pendant from the ceiling of a cave or forming downward along a rock face. Stalagmites build up from the floor at the point on which the stalactite drips. In time the two forms can join, but if the stalactite drips into water or across a considerable windy space no distinct stalagmite will form. [New Gk. ODEE first attests stalactite in XVII; stalagmite, not until XVIII, perhaps because the first observers did not note the reciprocal relation of these forms, or perhaps because the first *stalactites* to be so labeled had not developed corresponding *stalagmites.* The assignment of terms is arbitrary in that the Gk. roots are equally applicable to either form. < *stallassein,* to drip; *stalaktos* (adj.), dripping; *stalagma,* a drop of liquid. (To remember which is which, associate the *c* of *stalactite* with *c*eiling; the *g* of stalagmite with *g*round.)]

stark naked   Entirely naked. Bare-ass naked. [Influenced by but not derived from *stark*, severe, rigid, cruel, which is from OE *stearc*, rigid, not softened in any way. The original was *start naked*, < ME *stert naked* < OE *steart*, tail. Ult. < IE *ster-*, stiff, rigid (as are the tail feathers of most birds). *Start*, in this sense, has fallen out of English use except for its survival in the name of the *redstart*, a small, gray European bird with red tail feathers. Thus, though modified by *stark*, the root sense is tail naked, ass naked, which, generally speaking, is as naked as one can get short of flaying.]

state's evidence   1. Properly all the evidence presented by the prosecution. But 2. *In common use since at least mid-XIX.* Testimony for the prosecution given by a criminal accomplice in return for mitigation of his sentence (and sometimes to escape an indictment). Also the criminal who thus turns on his accomplices. [These second senses are by a common confusion with the standard idiom *to turn state's evidence*, to testify against one's criminal accomplices in return for judicial lenience.]

stereotype   1. The same as *cliché*, which see. 2. *Printing.* A metal plate first developed by French printers in late XVIII. A stereotype sets printer's copy, usu. for a single page, by pouring a molten lead-compound into a matrix of plaster of Paris, ceramic clay, or papier-mâché. [Late-XVIII Fr. *stéréotype*, coined from Gk. *stereos*, solid, hard; with *type*. By late XVIII most handset type was of a harder metal than the alloyed lead used in stereotyping. The name can only make strict sense as a reference to the entire rigid plate of stereotype or cliché, in contrast to the more adjustable pages of handset type locked into wooden frames.]

stigma   (plu. *stigmata*) [Gk. *stigma*, plu. *stigmata*, a sting, a prick. Also a tattoo mark. Early associated with the marking of slaves. (In Jewish custom slaves were marked by holes drilled in their earlobes. So, too, Anglo-Saxon slaves had their ears *drilled*, which was earlier *thrilled*, whence *thrall*, *to be in thrall to*, *enthralled*.) < Gk. *stizein*, to prick, to stick, and by ext., to tattoo. Ult. < IE *steig-*, sharp. STAKE.] *n.* 1. A metaphoric mark of infamy, blame, reproach. [Note. The mark of Cain is often referred to as a stigma, but it did not so function. Genesis 4:15 says that the Lord put the mark upon Cain to protect him from the wrath of any man who might kill him.]

2. (But earlier, and surviving in Brit. criminal law into early XVII) A mark branded upon a criminal. (See *clergy, benefit of, Browser's I.*) 3. *Loosely,* A disfiguring birthmark: *The stigma of having been born a human being.*

stigmata By long religious association the plural has become specific to the scars of the wounds of Jesus, especially of the nail holes, and especially of those through the palms.

HISTORIC. Various saints and holy men have experienced lesions and bleeding in this pattern, rejoicing in their stigmata as a sign of grace. There is medical evidence of hysterically induced bleeding through the skin. Religious fervor is probably capable of such hysteria, the wounds of Jesus suggesting a pattern. St. Francis rejoiced in having achieved the stigmata. Nikos Kazantzakis suffered stigmata at a time of religious fervor when he lived as a hermit. Periodically overcome by lust, he reports, he would journey to a town in search of a whore but found that before he could sin his palms would begin to bleed, and that they did not heal until he returned to his solitary retreat. He called it "saint's disease."

to stigmatize 1. To label a person as evil, guilty, or base. 2. *Earlier.* To brand as a slave or a criminal.

stomacher An ornately beaded, jeweled, or embroidered short garment once fashionable, esp. as women's wear. It extends from about the neck and chest, over the midsection, and even down to the knees. Also a jeweled upper-body ornament such as a spreading necklace covering the upper chest. [In neither sense does the term have much to do with "stomach" as we now understand the word. At root, "of the throat (and upper chest)," the downward extension over the midsection and beyond being simply an incremental extension as one fashionable woman after another sought to make her garment longer and more ornate than the other such garments at the same party. Circa 1620 Frans Hals painted a Dutch lady wearing an elaborate stomacher that extended from an elaborate ruff around the neck to about mid-thigh in what was in effect a decorative apron.

From Gk. *stomakhos,* which labeled not belly but *throat, gullet,* implying "below the mouth, < *stoma,* mouth. ("Stomach" in Gk. was *gaster.*) The word is commonly misunderstood because the Eng. language has caused the stomach to sink from its Gk. altitude.]

story A level, floor, or flight of a building. (In Am. the ground level counts as the first story, in Europe the stories [Fr. *étage,* stage; It. *piano,* level] are counted from what Am. calls "the second story."

So It. *primo piano,* second story). *second-story man* A cat-burglar. One who breaks into upper-story apartments, usu. through a window. [Each level, flight, stage, is called a "story" in Eng. because imposing medieval and Renaissance manors and castles had stained-glass windows, the windows on each level depicting a sequence (story) from the Bible, the life of a saint, or the great family's history. Each level of windows, that is to say, told a different "story." And the same was done with tapestries hung on the walls at each level.]

street   *n.* 1. In common specification (not always observed), a paved thoroughfare with curbs and sidewalks and lined at least on one side by buildings. 2. The paved area of such a thoroughfare: *go play in the street during rush hour.* 3. The thoroughfare and those who live on it as a community: *the people on my street. adj.* 1. Fit for use in public: *street clothes.* 2. Found on the street(s): *the street scene.* 3. Near the street: *street floor.* [< L. *strata via,* paved road. (STRATUM) Whence It. *strada,* but with the sense "open road," a paved way in a city being a *via.* The cognate forms, Ger. *Strasse* and Eng. *street,* are, however, specific to the city.]

     street Arab/urchin/waif A homeless child. *streetwalker* A prostitute who works streets and public places, as distinct from a house whore, call girl, etc. *street wise* Shrewd in coping with the life of the streets.

     it's on (all over) the street Police and crim. It is widely known/ rumored.

     SEMANTIC NOTE. Leslie Dunkling, in the *Guinness Book of Names,* writes that the British are content to have their houses on "roads, avenues, lanes, groves, drives, closes, places—anything but streets." He cites a British builder whose customers canceled orders for houses on learning they would be on a "street" address. The aversion to a street designation is less common in the U.S. Yet real estate developers label their tract roads as courts, terraces, drives, places, circles, lanes, and avenues, generally avoiding the designation "street." If they are sensitively keyed to buyer preferences, as they must be to stay in business, it seems the American middle class would sooner live on Swampstink Circle than on Paradise Street.

string   [The current central sense is "thread, cord," but < Gmnc. *strenk-,* tight, narrow, strong; whence OE *strang,* powerful, tight, strict (cf. Ger. *streng(e),* strict, severe). From same root, OE *streng,* string. Via Gk. *strangalē,* halter. The same root functions in *stran-*

gle, which should do for tight enough and narrow enough.] 1. With many variants, a thin line of twisted threads. 2. A stringed instrument (though the "strings" are not of spun threads). 3. Anything conceived as connected in a straight-line series, or a curving one: *a string of beads, of horses.*

apron strings Traditional metaphor of female dominance: *tied to his wife's/mother's apron strings.* [First OED citation is dated 1542. Also *apron-string hold/tenure,* tenure of property through one's wife and only during her lifetime (1642).]

stringer Am. journalism. One who serves as a part-time correspondent for a paper published elsewhere: *As an undergraduate at Brown, W. T. Scott was the campus stringer for the Providence "Journal."*

second stringer [Prob. by analogy to a "string" of horses, tethered together on same rope.] A reserve second best, as a member of a second team used to play against the first team in practice sessions and to serve at need as a substitute for a first-string player. *second string n. Music.* A violin or other stringed instrument tuned low as an accompaniment to the lead instrument(s). *adj.* Of the second-string class.

run a string Billiards and pool. To make a series of shots. [The playing count was originally kept by sliding counters (beads) on a wire (string) above and to one side of the table.] *run the string* To make enough consecutive shots (slide enough counters) to reach the game-winning number.

pull strings To manipulate secretely. (As a puppeteer manipulates his dolls.) *on a (the) string* Subject to control. Obedient.

string along 1. *Intransitive.* To go along with another/others (as a horse in a string of horses). 2. *Transitive.* To lead, to control. Implies deceitful means: *She has been stringing him along for years.* [Prob. by association with fishing and the act of reeling in (stringing) a fish once hooked.]

string up To kill by hanging. ("String" is a colloq. for "rope.")

sundae   A dish of ice cream variously or singly topped with chocolate, nuts, fruit preserves, sweet syrups, marshmallow, whipped cream, and the like. [The name is a variant spelling of *Sunday* (cf. such commercial usages as *nite klub, Krisp-E Krunchies Me-'n'-U Luncheonette*), and the common entry in our standard dictionaries, omitting even this much, dismisses the term with "origin unknown." Yet a great deal is known.]

HISTORIC. H. L. Mencken, *The American Language, Supplement I* (New York, 1945), has a two-page essay on *sundae* suggesting a possible coinage in the 1890s by George Guffy, who operated an ice-cream parlor in Manitowoc, Wisconsin. There is, however, evidence that the term, so spelled, was in use at the time in both Ann Arbor, Michigan and Ithaca, New York. Mencken also suggests that the name may have derived from the once popular evangelist Bill Sunday, but he was a professional baseball player until 1890, did not become a traveling evangelist until 1896, and did not become nationally popular until about 1910 (he died in 1935).

Soda fountains had carbonated waters and various syrups for flavoring. Almost inevitably someone tried topping ice cream with one of these sweet goos, and the more festive serving was born. Mencken implies, a bit vaguely, that Guffy found these concoctions attracted customers but that they were more expensive than plain ice cream, and that he therefore served them only on Sundays. (So why couldn't he charge a nickel more?) Mencken obviously never ran a store. Nor does he mention that once-common (and still-surviving) practice of stopping off for an ice-cream treat after the long, dry work of Sunday-morning salvation.

This note falls short of a definitive etymology, but I submit that it is more to the point than an evasive "origin unknown."

svelte *adj.* Lithe, willowy, graceful. (The opposite of short, squat, dumpy.) [Ult. < IE *wel-*, to bend, to coil, to be pliable, → L. *vellere*, to pull, to pull up, to uproot, to pluck; *e(x)vellere*, to extend, to dra.v out. It. *svelto*, long, slender (suggests a withe, a supple thing); whence OF and ME *svelte*.]

sylph *In common Am. usage,* A lithe, slim, graceful girl. *sylphlike* What every American female from 12 to 92 is commanded to be by the advertising industry. [New L. There may be some precedent in Gk. **silphē*, an insect, the name variously applied, without positive surviving identification, to a moth, a grub, a beetle. The late coinage is prob. the work of Paracelsus, XVI Swiss alchemist and self-promoter, who is said to have coined it from L. *"syl* (vestris nym)*ph*(a)," forest nymph. In XVII with the acquired sense, "fairy, a being that inhabits the air," esp. in Fr. *sylphide.*

For *Paracelsus* (Aureolus Philippus, born Theophrastus Bombastus Hohenheim, 1490–1541), see *Browser's I.*]

syringe A glass tube with a plunger and hollow needle used to inject or to withdraw body fluids. A hypodermic needle. [< Gk. **surinx*, a shepherd's reed pipe.] Some form of syringe was in medical use by the late Middle Ages and was labeled in medieval L. *syringa.*

Narcotics addicts inject liquefied forms of their drug with a syringe. Presumably they then hear the pipes of Pan, though as the music fades Pan once again turns out to be "he who inspires *panic*" (see *Browser's I*).

Syringa, the mockorange bush, is so named because its hollow stems were once used, or are said to have been used, for shepherd's pipes. The thought is too nonsensical for anything but legend, but branches of this bush may once have been used in making pipes.

tabloid A newspaper of approximately half the common page size. [Tabloids have traditionally offered strident headlines, sensational stories, and photographs as lurid as the censor would permit. They are nevertheless a commuters' boon, for on crowded buses and trains they can be opened and read without sticking the corners of the page into the next passenger's eye. The name came out of an old war of registered tradenames and had to be cleared by a court. It was originally applied to tablets of patent medicine.]

HISTORIC. Entrepreneurs of XIX Britain and the U.S. began the commercial ballyhoo that has now become the advertising industry. H. G. Wells's *Tono Bungay* (1909) is the history of a XIX entrepreneur who developed and promoted a patent medicine called Tono Bungay. Whatever the (doubtful) merits of the stuff, the novel is a readable account of one man's success in achieving name-recognition of a product through advertising ballyhoo.

Tabloid was such a coined and registered tradename (1884) of Burroughs, Wellcome, and Company, a British pharmaceutical house. At a time that medicines were commonly sold as "powders" in small paper envelopes, B. W. & Co. compressed many of its products into tablets and promoted them as *Tabloids,* the name passing into common usage for "compacted thing." (Cf. lowercase *kleenex* for any paper handkerchief and *kodak* for any camera, though *Kleenex* and *Kodak* are zealously guarded registered tradenames.)

By ca. 1890 *tabloid* ("compressed thing") had become common for a half-sized newspaper, and despite an action filed by B. W. & Co. to protect its tradename, the court held that the name was protected only as it was applied to medicinal tablets.

Cadillac, long an asserted standard of excellence in what is left of the U.S. automobile industry, is such a tradename and cannot be used legally by another automaker, but there is a *Cadillac* cat food, since no one is likely to confuse the automobile with ground fish guts. (Though for that matter the containers may be of better metal than is currently to be found in a number of General Motors cars: when the front bumper of my new Oldsmobile 98 was clipped in a parking lot, it turned out to be $250 worth of aluminum so thin that I broke off the projecting piece simply by flexing it twice.)

tang [In various senses, "a sharp, piercing thing." Root image, "point of a thorn, of a sharp (snake's) tooth, of an insect's stinger." So ON *tangi,* ult. < IE *denk-,* to bite, to sting. Into ME under IX–X Danelaw as *tange,* the root sense generally extended to label sharp sensation rather than the point/sting of such sensation, but surviving somewhat altered in:] 1. A (sharp?) projection of a metal tool (a knife, a chisel) which is encased, usu. in wood, to form a handle. 2. A sharp sensation of taste, smell, feeling: *the tang of sharp spices.* Sometimes labels a slight, sharp sensation: *a tang of salt in the sea breeze . . . of autumn in the air.* [Note that if the readily aphetic initial *s* be restored and the vowel be slightly modified, *tang* emerges as obviously cognate with *sting.*]

tatterdemalion A ragamuffin. [XVII. The first element is self-evident. All etymologists have cited OF *maillon,* swaddling clothes, and have been stopped there by the fact that "swaddling clothes" does not seem apt, and that the root sense "tattered diapers" is unlikely.

So is the dating. The term developed in English at a time that the Grand Tour and a long stay in Italy were prescribed for British gentlemen of fortune. I suggest that one should look to It. *maglia* (pronounced almost exactly like the Fr.—and many earlier forms were spelled with two *l*s to enforce the *ly* sound as in *million*), the word meaning in old It., shirt of mail, later undershirt, and also what is called in Am. an athletic jersey. The root is L. *macula,* spot. It. *maglia* and OF *maillon* are both, in a sense, things that become spotted. By association they are knitted or woven things, as a shirt of mail is, in a sense, woven.

Granted this It. *maglia* with the common majorative form *maglione,* big shirt, the root sense "tattered undershirt" is powerfully implicit. That sense has precedents in such earlier established forms as *raggamuffin* and *rag tag and bob tail.* The dating conforms to the British macaroni's habit of returning from the Continent with affected tags of Italian. And the sense conforms beyond question, whereas OF *maillon* was almost five centuries in the past by the time this form developed.]

'tec A de*(tec)*tive. [Late-XIX slang, primarily Brit. Now obs.]

teriyaki   A Japanese form of shish kebab, the skewered, sometimes identifiable vegetables alternating with pieces of marinated meat, fish, or seafood, broiled over an open fire. [At root "flame broiled," or even, one might argue, "sunburned." < Jap. *teri,* flame (but at root, sunshine); *yaki,* to broil.]

Thanksgiving   The Pilgrims celebrated their first year of survival in the harsh New World with a harvest feast and prayers of thanksgiving for their survival. Their descendants continued to observe the day (traditionally the last Thursday in November), but it was not an official national holiday until Lincoln so proclaimed it in 1863, more than 200 years after its first observance. Sarah Josepha Hale (1788–1879), best remembered as the poet who wrote "Mary's Lamb" and as an early feminist, is commonly credited with having first urged that Thanksgiving be made a legal holiday. (Earlier Benjamin Franklin had proposed that the turkey, and not the eagle, be proclaimed the national bird, but he did not propose what has since become its officially nationalized feast day.)

that's all she wrote   *In any context,* There is no more to say: *Once Nixon got the order to release those tapes, he knew that was all she wrote.* [Dating insecure. I believe this formula first came into use in WWII. It certainly became common then, and it persists. If that dating is accurate, I believe it is a ricochet term from the *dear John letter* (see *John: dear John,* above) of WWII GI slang.]

think tank   The confined arena of the *brainstorm* (which see). In the myth-metaphor of government, corporations, and even academia a panel of designated experts pooling their knowledge to analyze and project problems and methods; as if the best available managerial and research talent could be mashed into a fermenting vat called *input,* achieving there that uncertainty called progress. [The idiom follows from FDR's *brain trust,* which see, but did not come into common use until soon after WWII.]

tic dollaroo   A spasm of facial neuralgia. [Early-XX Am. Now rare. A corruption of Fr. *tic douloureux.* At about the turn of the century a Fr. physician in the U.S. (or was there an invasion of them at the time?) made the *tic douloureux* into a fashionable disorder among East Coast society matrons, some of their husbands thereupon contracting the disease from them. (Some of the fashionable diseases of the preceding century had been, less specifically, "sinking spells" and the terrible omnibus "wasting disease.")]

ticky-tacky   *n.* Shoddy stuff. *adj.* Shoddy, cheap, inferior. [Said to have been coined by Malvina Reynolds (prob. in the 1930s, since she was born in 1900), but it was obs. at birth and grew up in its first image, being less a coinage than a more or less artless reduplication of *tacky,* with *ticky* as the echoing element. Except that the reduplication introduces a possible noun sense, the "coinage" adds nothing to the meaning of *tacky.* I have been unable to fix the attribution to her flat-out, but as coinages go it is a *wishy-washy.*]

tike, tyke   A term of endearment for a small child, earlier, especially for an untidy, mischievous boy. [But the word has come a long way through less favorable senses to its present indulgent connotations. Ult. < IE *digh-,* she goat (shaggy animal); with d/t and gh/k in Gmnc. → ON *tik,* bitch, vixen. In XIV, mongrel cur; also, disreputable man. In XVI (Shakespeare) "base tike" and "bobtail tike" or "trundle tail." Tyke, Tike, or variantly Tige, has long been a common Eng. name for a dog. The pejorative sense receded in XVII, the senses "shaggy, worthless, lovable, clumsy pet" becoming associated with "messy, mischievous, lovable, clumsy child" (cf. *kid* for *child*) and more recently with, simply, "lovable small child."]

tilefish   A choice food fish marked by a crested head and a bluish body with yellow spots. It was first taken in colonial times from a bank about 80 miles southeast of Boston and was later found at various banks in the northerly Atlantic. It is a highly desirable catch with an average weight of about 10 pounds, though now rarely on the market. [Am. colonial. AHD misexplains its name as "influenced by Tile, from its tilelike spots"—whatever a "tilelike spot" may be said to be. Clearly there was no etymological precedent for this name, since the fish was unknown in Brit. waters. All the "lexicography" about "tilelike spots" aside, and whatever its first colonial name may have been, I will suggest that its present name is a corruption of its XVIII genus name *Lophotilus,* the second element *tilus* having been anglicized to *tile.*]

tinhorn   *n.* A low, flashy, fraudulent person. *adj.* Cheap, disreputable, low. [Earlier (mid-XIX) *tinhorn gambler.* But not, as often supposed, because a tin horn is a shoddy musical instrument when compared to a real trumpet. The ref. is to a gambler who ran a usually hard-pitch, low-stakes chuck-a-luck game. In this game the dice were twirled (and manipulated) in a metal cylinder (the tin horn). In the pecking order of XIX gambling establishments, faro and roulette rated high, with chuck-a-luck and the tinhorn gambler at the bottom of the scale. Hence *tinhorn* for a low, sleazy person.]

tissue [IE *teks-*, to weave, woven. (TEXTILE, TEXT, TEXTURE.) → L. *texere*, to weave, p.p. *textus*. With x/s → It. *tessuto* (the inserted vowel is typical of It. phonetics), cloth, fabric; and also OF *tistre*, to weave, p.p. *tissu*, woven. And so ME *tissu*, but with the sense, fine woven light fabric, gauze, and esp. cloth of gold (the term used in general as the opposite of coarse homespun). The root sense has more or less receded from the word, though all surviving senses are extensions of it:] 1. *Biology.* Bodily cellular matter, either: (a) A layer or cluster of cells similar in appearance and function; or (b) The total of soft body cells: *blood, bone, and tissue.* 2. Any fine-spun network: *His character was a frayed tissue of lies patched with money.* 3. Soft, absorbent paper, usu. layered, for use as disposable handkerchiefs and as kitchen and toilet wipes. This last is commonly *toilet paper,* though the delicatesse of ad agencies prefers *toilet tissue.*

tissue paper A fine, crinkly paper, not notably absorbent, used as protective layers and inner wrappings for delicate fabrics. [Because first used in protecting cloth of gold (as above, ME *tissu*); hence, "cloth-of-gold paper"—in the days that fine filaments of real gold were used in such majestic fabrics.]

toilet *In Am.* A toilet bowl or the room in which it is placed. (With many variants from the blunt to the uneasy, among them: *john, crapper, Chic Sale, shithouse, W.C., watercloset, potty, the facilities, the necessary, little girl's (boy's) room, comfort station;* and see *basement* in *Browser's II.*) [But in Brit., and in more or less elegant Am. into early XX *to make one's toilet* was to wash, comb, apply cosmetics, and dress fashionably. This sense survives in common Am. *toilet water* for cologne and *toiletries* as a vender's categorical word for colognes, perfumes, and cosmetics. The present fixed association with "place for bodily excretion" is by association with the fact that the room(s) to which milady retired to "make her toilet" also had a water closet, or earlier a pot.

At origin Fr. *toile,* a cloth, *toilette,* a dim. form for the more-or-less ornate cloth of ladies' dressing gowns, and also for a similar cloth used to cover a dressing table. But in Am. the forms and the sense are:]

go to the toilet Relieve oneself bodily. **down the toilet** *Recent slang.* Gone, lost (as if flushed down the toilet bowl). **toilet humor** So-called wit and jokery based on bodily excretion. (And there continues to be a market for so-called novelty items related to these bodily functions, as ash trays in the form of toilet bowls and ceramic turds fixed to the bottoms of beer steins. See Karen Horney on anal retentives and anal expulsives as personality types. See the Recording Angel for the original blueprints of the human nervous system.)

top: sleep like a top   To sleep soundly. [The first clear OED citation is dated 1693 (Congreve), " 'Tis but well-lashing him, and he will sleep like a top." But the expression is of proverbial age. A top appears to be motionless when at full spin: does this figure, then, conceive of sleep as a rapid spinning of dreams while one is apparently motionless? Akin to Fr. *dormir comme un sabot,* also of proverbial age and also now a cliché. The Fr., however, is more nearly akin to our *sleep like a log* (wooden thing dead to the world). *Like a top* is now no less cliché but has a bit of a hum (snore) to it.]

torpedo   1. *Naval.* (a) A self-propelled, cigar-shaped, explosive missile launched from a submarine, boat, ship, or plane and (if all goes well) designed to run underwater at a preset depth. (b) *Archaic.* An underwater (moored) mine, or a floating one. 2. *Railroading.* A small explosive charge set on a rail to be detonated by the wheels of a train as a danger signal. 3. *Fireworks.* A toy cap wrapped in a twist of paper with some small stones that set off the cap when the device is hurled against a hard surface. 4. *Oil drilling.* An explosive charge dropped into a hole to clear an obstruction. 5. *Crim. slang, and generalized.* A gang killer, a hit man, a thug. 6. *Capitalized.* The genus name of fish capable of emitting a powerful electric shock. Also called numbfish, electric ray. [< L. *torpēdō,* numbness, stiffness (TORPOR) < *torpere,* to be numb, stiff. Ult. < IE *ster-, (s)ter-,* stiff. (STARK.)] Altered in the new L. of XVIII taxonomists to serve as the name of the fish genus, as if "(the fish that produce) numbness, stiffness." All later senses are an extension from the new L. name of the fish ("explosive thing that numbs, stiffens").

damn the torpedoes—full speed ahead! Now a proud U.S. slogan of intrepidity and applicable in many contexts: *Preacher. Do you, Susan, take George to be your lawfully wedded husband? Susan. Damn the torpedoes—full speed ahead!* [From the command attributed to Admiral David Glasgow Farragut at the Battle of Mobile Bay, August 5, 1864. A fantasy Roman studying Am. might have understood him to mean "Damn my stiffness(es)—sail on and attack!"

But many U.S. students have been as badly confused by understanding "torpedoes" to mean the sort of missile fired by U-boats, in which case Farragut would have been more foolhardy than brave. He meant torpedo in the archaic sense "floating mine." These presented some danger but not sure disaster. Farragut was taking what is called "a calculated risk." He knew such devices often malfunctioned, and even that they were likely to after having been corroded by salt water. Expert riflemen at the rails could detonate some of them at a safe distance. Others might be fended off by boat hooks. And any that did go off near his hull might cause damage but not sink the ship. The fact that his ship came through is evidence that the risk was well taken. Nothing in this impugns Farragut's bravery, but students must be told that he sailed against the dangers of old-style and often-defective floating mines, not against a fan of modern naval torpedoes (which would almost certainly have numbed his hopes and knocked him stiff).]

travesty   A ridiculous burlesque, esp. the act of presenting buffoonishly what might more properly be taken with greater gravity. [At root, "absurdly and grotesquely overdressed, clownishly and absurdly disguised." Akin to *transvestite,* one who dresses "across" the line of sex, esp. a man who does himself up as a woman; and the language reserves some scorn for such behavior. But travesty is most directly from It. *travestire,* which can mean to dress as a transvestite, but has the primary sense, to disguise buffoonishly, to present in a ridiculous guise.]

trek   *n.* 1. A long, plodding journey. 2. *Ext.* Said of anything long and drawn out: *I went to the meeting of Let's Reform Everything and suffered through a trek of declarations.* (And corresponding verb forms.) [A mid-XIX Du. borrowing by way of Afrikaans. Du. *trek-kên,* to draw, to drag, to drag out. (Prob. < L. *trahere,* to draw, to pull; p.p. *tractum.* TRACTOR. EXTRACT.) In Afrikaans *trekken* took on the primary sense, "long, slow migration of settlers by ox-cart," and the extended sense, "migration of animal herds." The word came into Eng. in books and articles about Boers in XIX Africa and in books about African wildlife. The root sense remains "drawn by a slow, plodding draft animal." Cf. Du. *trekshuit,* a canal or river barge drawn by draft animals on the bank. (On the Volga, this chore was once reserved for the Volga boatmen, who did not know the word *trek,* but who lived in its essence.)]

triptych   Allowing for later nonreligious variations, a hinged, three-paneled icon, usually shaped like a Gothic arch, the panels hinged to either side being half-arches. The central panel is often mounted on a pedestal, but when not so mounted, the icon can stand free as an altarpiece or a home shrine when the side half-arches are set at an angle. The triple panels are thus both a practical arrangement and a pious evocation of the Trinity. (See also *diptych.*)

trite *adj.* Of a cliché or stereotype. Of a fixed phrase, mental process, or pattern of behavior so long overused as to have lost conscious intention: *For lack of a more definite feeling, I love you truly with a heart that is trite and true.* [At root, "worn away, rubbed away, eroded." As in MacLeish's "Ars Poetica," [A poem should be] "Dumb / As old medallions to the thumb." < L. *terere*, to rub, to wear away; p.p. *tritus* (DETRITUS). Ult. < IE *ter-*, to turn, to twist, to rub.

Trophonias *Gk. myth.* The greatest of the Gk. oracles. He stands as an all-but-forgotten figure of prophetic power, probably eclipsed in our memory by Cassandra, who also had the gift of foreseeing everything that was to come, which was always so disastrous that none would believe her. Is that a psychic image-portrayal of the human condition? Trophonias also speaks for the sadness of all human futures in the now obs. but apt archaic idiom *to have visited the cave of Trophonias* To be sad. (Because he foretells all, whereby all humankind is left to feel desolate in the knowledge of what surely lies ahead.) It is a dark view of human fate. It says we cannot stand very much reality and therefore fantasize what we know to be untrue. Hardly a platform on which to run for the office of Santa Claus, but the dark view does present itself at times, and Trophonias (and Cassandra) stand available to dramatize it for us, thanks to the ancient Greeks.

tryst 1. A lovers' appointment. 2. The place of their meeting, and the meeting itself: *Irving Klompus has been keeping a lifelong tryst with the first dollar he ever cadged.* [The word has become more or less specific to the meeting of lovers, whence in loose usage it has come to imply a secret meeting. The root sense, however, is trust, and though since XIV the word has been used for "appointed meeting," the essential sense has been "appointment faithfully made and faithfully kept."

In XIV *triste*, a carried-over OF form, was also the appointed station of a huntsman or beater (a position of trust). The unusually complex evolution is ult. < IE *deru-*, solid, firm ("like a tree"). The zero-grade form *dru-* occurs in many words having to do with trees. Gk. *drus*, oak, esp. the red oak, sacred to the gods. Suffixed

-wid-, to see, to know → dru-wid- → Druid, "one who knows about trees and their indwelling spirits." And from the same root L. durus, firm, hard. Also, in Gmnc., with d/t → ON treyste, trust. (TRUST.) So the old huntsman at his triste faithfully beat the game toward the hunting lords.

The word has come a long way to label what Mary Jane does when she sneaks off under the trees with Billy to beat the bushes.]

turbot (pronounced tur'-b't) Labels a group of European flatfish (and similar North American fish) prized as a delicacy. [Second element, bot-, akin to the last element of halibut (see butt- in Browser's I). And cf. archaic buttwife, a fishwife who sold flatfish. First element tur- is at root "spiny" < IE (s)tern-, thorn, thorny. → Gmnc. thurnu, thorn → OE thorn, thorn. The s survives in early Scandinavian sterbut, but not in old Swedish tornbut, both labeling this fish.]

turnpike 1. A main highway. Originally and still commonly, a tollway. In U.S. usually a transstate tollway, often as a link in the interstate highway system. But many transstate highways between major communities, original tollways, have retained the turnpike designation though they are now free roads. 2. Archaic. A tollgate. [At root, turnspike, ME turnepike, because the gates were equipped with revolvable spike barriers turned by the toll collector to permit passage. Pike is ult. from IE (s)peik-, a stem associated with a bird's beak; whence L. picus, woodpecker; pike, a long infantry spear; and spike. And see spic-and-span in Browser's I.]

tyrant 1. An oppressive and merciless despot. 2. Weakened ext. Any dictatorial person: His boss is a tyrant. [Gk. tyrannos, king (at a time, of course, that monarchs were absolute). So Gk. Oedipos Tyrannos or L. Oedipus Rex equally mean Oedipus the King. But the Gk. form early acquired the sense "usurper of a throne," and by association "merciless oppressor," for usurpers, always in some doubt of their claim to divine right to rule, tended to be relentless in suppressing all opposition, real or imagined. Into XIII Eng. tyrant with this sense, "merciless oppressor," as distinct from king, absolute monarch; though both terms labeled absolute power, the language convention established tyrant as a pejorative term and king as a neutral one. (And note that Oedipus was in fact a usurper, having come to the throne by killing the king, his father, and marrying the queen, his mother.)]

U

ultramarine   1. The stone lapis lazuli. 2. The color, deep blue. [By late association with *ultraviolet, ultramarine* is commonly understood to mean "very deep blue." Lapis lazuli is, in fact, a blue stone, but more nearly azure that cobalt-violet. The name *lapis lazuli* means, at root, "the azure stone."

But whatever disagreements might arise about its exact color, the name *ultramarine* is not a reference to color. It is a L. folkname "from across the sea," < from *ultra,* beyond; *marina, mare,* sea. Because this valued stone does not occur naturally in the Italian peninsula and had to be brought to Rome from overseas.]

HISTORIC. In archaic Eng., this color was also called *Saunders blue,* as if the dye were the product of someone named Saunders. He is, however, logofictive, briefly ghosting the English language as an ectonymic rendering of OF *cendres blewes,* blue ashes, to label the color *ultramarine.* Hardly a matter of the now-living language, Saunders the nonexistent dyer remains, though obscurely, as a choice example of the easy disregard with which the British have traditionally slovened foreign words and phrases.

ultramontane   In shifting historic context (see historic note) a varying reference to papal authority. [Root sense, "beyond the mountains" ("beyond the Alps" being understood). Hence in shifting context, depending on the side of the Alps on which the speaker finds himself, either "papal/Italian" or "nonpapal/non-Italian." Cf. *cis-alpine* and *transalpine,* the senses of which also shift with the position of the speaker. (*Cis-* < L. *cis,* on this side; cognate with Fr. *ici,* here—and where is that when the speaker is *there?*)]

HISTORIC. In late-medieval It. usage *i fideli ultramontani* referred to Catholics of northern and western Europe who accepted papal authority in most temporal matters as well as spiritual ones. (As one example of temporal authority, the shunning of an excommunicate king.)

In the early Renaissance various Fr. kings and high church officials worked to move the seat of the papacy to France, and did establish it at Avignon from 1309 to 1377, a period Italians referred to as the French Captivity. Fr. *ultramontagne* came into use on the return of the papacy to Rome, with the pejorative sense, "on that (the Roman) side of the Alps." Local variants of the term came into use thereafter in all the Romance languages (except It.), and in Du. and Ger., entering Eng. in late XVI (following Henry VIII's break with Rome) at first with the pejorative sense, papist; then gradually as a more neutral designation (often with an uppercase *U*) for one who looked to Rome for spiritual authority.

In this sense Irish Boston may still be said to be Ultramontane not only spiritually but in such social matters as legalized abortion and contraception (though the local view on this last point tends to be more honored in her breech than in his observance, inasmuch as many Catholic pharmacists still refuse to stock condoms).

umpire *In law or sports,* A third party appointed to adjudicate between two opposing sides. (In the Am. language convention this official in baseball is an umpire, but in most other sports, the referee, i.e., the person to whom decisions are referred.) [A simple but much-traveled word. At root, L. *non par,* not of the pair (of matched contestants, i.e., the third man in the field). In OF, especially with reference to dueling, the man on the field who is not dueling. He was called the *nonper,* the one not of the pair of contestants; also the *nonpar* or unequal/uneven/odd man; and also the *nonpeer, peer* being an equal. With *non-* syncopated before *p* → *nomper* and variantly *noumpere.* Then nonced (nunnated) in ME, initial *n* dropping from the word to attach itself to the article, i.e., shifting from a *noumpere* to an *oumpere,* with later alteration to *umpire.* See also *au pair.*]

underdog The weaker of two contesting parties. [Though now received as if it were an ancient and inevitable idiom, it did not develop until mid-XIX in Am., being first attested in 1876 in the title of a song, "The Under Dog in the Fight," by David Barton. I trepidate that the ref. is to the losing dog in such a fight because he might well find himself on his back under the winner, at which point, though he might squirm free and upset the other dog, the chances are that he is exposed and about to have his belly ripped open.]

HISTORIC. Animal combat was a long-established country

"sport" in England, but it traditionally pitted dogs against other animals, as in bull baiting, bear baiting, badgering, and other variations. In the Am. colonies and in XIX U.S. such contests were overwhelmingly dog-eat-dog.

under God The Ike-onology of the Pledge of Allegiance. Schoolchildren will have forgotten by now that these words were not in the original Pledge of Allegiance, but were inserted by executive order during the Eisenhower administration, 1953–1961, despite the reasoned opposition of civil libertarians, for in effect, this interpolation requires a religious affirmation from a nonbeliever who may be as loyal and dedicated a citizen as anyone.

I propose that the words be stricken or replaced by "in the universe." Those who see the universe as a godly creation are freely permitted by this phrasing, and so are those who puzzle at that star show as a scientific unanswerable. Both sorts can be loyal citizens, despite the once-common and tawdry assertion that there were no atheists in foxholes.

underground railway [The name is fanciful: *underground* for "covert"; *railway* for "means of transportation" (usually at the bottom of wagonloads of farm produce or by night hikes from one hiding place to the next).] Before and during the Civil War a network of secret routes established by abolitionists for smuggling slaves to freedom in the northern states, and thence, often, to Canada, because hunters of fugitive slaves might track them and legally demand their return to their southern masters.

unwritten law A survival of the ancient, firmly fixed blood obligation to revenge a slain or offended kinsman who is left in no condition to avenge himself. [The necessary insanity of modern law has decreed that the courts and the penal system will deal with murderers, rapists, and the like, but the ancient blood-motive runs deep. In the rather recent past a man was disgraced in himself and in his clan if he failed to avenge a blood-wrong. And in this name juries in our time have acquitted men who acted upon the unwritten law, especially in cases where a man murders a man he finds in bed with his wife. In the ancient unwritten law the man also had a patrilineal duty to do in the wife he had brought into his clan and who had offended its honor, but in a latter-day reversal of sentiment, few men have gone free after killing the wife in this tournament of motives.]

upper ten (thousand)   The extreme national range of New York's social *four hundred* (the number that could be accommodated in the ballroom of Mrs. Astor's XIX New York City mansion. See *Browser's I*). [Nathaniel Parker Willis (1806–1867) once wrote that the power and wealth (and hence the high social position) of the U.S. was concentrated in the hands of 10,000 persons. It may yet be (or in the hands of even fewer), but the upper ten is now passé, as is the four hundred, and though money talks, the once-revered concept of social position, like the old gray mare, ain't what it used to be.]

usufruct   *Law.* The right to use and enjoy the property of another so long as such use does not damage or alter it. The long-established custom of free passage across another's land is a usufruct; also, if long established, the right to gather firewood or windfall fruits from the land of another; and these usufructs remain a legal claim upon the property even when it has changed hands. [At root, "use and enjoyment (of the fruits of)." In full legal L. form *ūsus et frūctus* or *ūsus fructesque*. In Anglo-Norman legal terminology until XVI the frenchified form was *usufruit,* later latinized.]

uxorious   *adj.* 1. Overly fond (but who measures what constitutes an overage?) of one's wife, esp. in being sexually drawn to her. 2. *Loose ext.* Wife-dominated. Overly submissive to her. Dotingly henpecked. [The term is properly applied only to husbands. It is not to be confused with (rare) *uxorial,* of a wife, befitting a wife.

Both terms are < L. *uxor,* wife. The L. form is < IE *euk-,* to become accustomed to; with *suesor-,* sister, female relative. Modified stem *sor-,* whence *euk-sor-,* whence L. *uxor.*

The sense evolution is social. In the patrilinear Roman clan *(gens),* the wife was required to leave her natal family and to go live with her husband's. Thus, at root, the *euk-sor-/uxor* is "she who must accustom herself to this other family." Only so can she be properly *uxorial,* whether or not he is *uxorious.*

Those who need a role model for the uxorious husband may fairly fix on Charles Bovary, the doting and ultimately destroyed husband of Flaubert's *Emma Bovary.* It may also be noted that in the tradition of chivalric–romantic love, European gentlemen were swooningly submissive to the maidens they courted, though few persisted to the point of *uxoria* once the ideal wench had been wedded and bedded.]

𝒰

Veronica And sometimes, though redundantly, **the True Veronica**
The holiest of Christian relics, an ample kerchief said to be marked
with the image of Christ's face. It is stored in the Vatican, and to
avoid the fading effect of light, it is displayed only on the rarest and
most sacred occasions. [< L. *verus*, true; with Gk. *ikon* image, icon.
In L. *iconicus*, imagelike. Hence, "the true image."]

HISTORIC. Little is known of St. Veronica. She is probably a
pious myth associated with this relic. As Christ was bearing the
cross to Calvary, she is said to have wiped the blood, sweat, and
tears from his face, whereupon the kerchief was forever after
marked with an image of his face. Unless she blotted more than she
wiped, the image would have been smudged, but miracles are
where one finds them.

Veronica A feminine given name, probably derived from St.
Veronica, but also clearly akin to Gmnc. **Berenikē.*

veronica 1. A plant with, usually, blue flowers. [The reason for
giving this name to this plant is unknown.] 2. *Bullfighting.* The
dramatic pass in which the matador stands motionless and draws
the bull by him, slowly passing his cape over its face as it charges
by with its horns almost grazing him. [Because the cape is said to
wipe the bull's face much as St. Veronica's kerchief wiped the face
of Christ. Death risk readily invites the pious to religious comparison.]

vest: close to the vest (chest) In secrecy. Keeping one's own counsel
and letting nothing be known to others. [Am. XIX. From poker. If
a player holds his cards close to his vest when he looks at them, no
opposing player or kibbitzer can tell what he is holding.

But though the immediate form is from poker, the basic metaphor is old. It. *in petto,* with (or close to) one's bosom, is the same
metaphor. When the pope has decided to elevate a churchman to
the college of cardinals but has not yet announced the elevation,

even to the chosen man, that man is said to be *un cardinale in petto.*

If only one could conceive royal flushes *in petto* and bide one's time for opportune announcement!]

vignette [OF and Fr. *vignette,* < It. *vignetta,* little (grape)vine, a small, delicate ornamental illumination in the body of a hand-printed text or a marginal decorative scroll. Into Eng. ca. XV as *vinet,* curling leaf-and-scroll tracery in an illuminated manuscript.] 1. *Since XVII.* A delicately curlicued leaf-and-tendril design in the margins of a printed book, or between chapters, or in the endpapers. 2. *XIX, perhaps by association with emergent photography.* An etched (usually steel-plate) head-and-shoulders portrait at the front of the book; later anywhere in it. 3. *Ext.* Any head-and-shoulders portrait—oil, etching, wash, or drawing—that diffuses into a cloud of color or shadow around the edges. 4. *Further ext., now prob. the primary sense.* A literary sketch or anecdote aimed at catching an essence in brief—as distinct from a fully detailed and formed novel, memoir, biography.

𝒲

wagon [OE *waegen,* a usu. four-wheel horse-drawn conveyance. With common muting of *g* → *wain,* a two-wheeled farm conveyance. Ult. < IE *wegh-,* to carry (convey in a wheeled vehicle) → L. *veho,* I convey, *vehere,* to convey, to carry on a wagon, barrow. VEHICLE.] 1. A horse-drawn, wheeled flatbed, with or without sides. 2. *Automobile.* [By analogy to "large, roomy vehicle."] A style of automobile designed to carry both passengers and a limited quantity of goods, often with more than two rows of passenger seats, the rear seats usu. made to fold down and provide a flatbed for goods loaded through a rear door. Sometimes two rows of rear seats fold down. *station wagon, ranch wagon, beach wagon, estate wagon.* [But note that *Wagen* in Ger. is a generic term for automotive vehicle. *(Volkswagen.)* And also Fr. *wagon-lit,* railroad sleeping car; lit., "bed wagon."]

    hitch your wagon to a star Folk poeticism. Aspire to high achievement. *to fix one's wagon* 1. To render inoperable, as if damaging a wagon axle or wheel. [*Fix* as in "I'll fix you" = "I'll do you a damage." 2. To do one an injury. (Can mean to kill but usually implies only to cause trouble for someone.) *go on the wagon* To give up hard liquor. (To go on the [water] wagon.) And similarly, *to fall off the wagon* Having forsworn alcohol (having gone on the [water] wagon), to fall from one's resolve and go back to drinking.

walk *v.* To move along one step at a time. (In walking one foot is always touching the ground. Running begins when both feet are periodically off the ground at the same time. In jogging, one simulates the motions of running, commonly raising both feet from the ground at the same time, but in a slower, more deliberate way, with shorter steps. Race walking, often faster than most jogging, requires that one foot touch the ground at all times.) *n.* 1. A distance covered by walking: *It's a long walk to town.* 2. The act of walking: *Let's take a walk.*

to walk all over one 1. To abuse, to trample, to abase (to treat another as if he were dirt under one's shoes). 2. To defeat crushingly and effortlessly: *Immaculate Heart walked all over Holy Name*. *to walk away with* To win without real exertion. Similarly *to win in a walk* Same sense. *to walk out on* To abandon unceremoniously. *walk-up* An upper-story apartment in a building without an elevator. *walk-around money* Pocket money for the normal expenses of moving about town. *walking on air* Elated. (Cf. Shakespeare, *Sonnets*, "I grant I never saw a goddess go. / My mistress when she walks, walks on the ground.")

walkie-talkie, walky-talky A portable radio receiver–transmitter used in pairs or sets tuned to the same frequency for communication between persons working together within a limited area. Technology keeps increasing the range, but such devices are basically for communication within a few miles.

walking delegate Now rare. In early days of union organization an officer from central union headquarters who traveled around to locals for inspection and liaison.

water: of the first water 1. *In common usage*. Most excellent. 2. *Jewelers' terms, with ref. to a gem*. Of the highest purity and luster. [This usage dates to early XVII in English but with precedents in most European languages, jewelers tending to be an international breed. The ultimate source is almost certainly Arabic *mā*, which has the cluster of senses "water, sheen, splendor, purity," literally "of the purest water," but used by Arabic diamond dealers as a quality of fine gems. *Judge Rocksoff is a drip of the first water*.]

weather The condition of the atmosphere at a particular time, esp. with reference to temperature, humidity, precipitation, and wind condition. [At root, and with the factual accuracy characteristic of folknaming, "what the wind does." Ult. < IE *we-*, echoic of the *wheee* sound of a strong wind. Suffixed *-d-* in Gmnc., prob. *wedram* → OE *weder*, weather.]

wham bam, thank you, ma'am Also *whim wham, thank you, ma'am* And other variants, including the sometimes attached *as the rabbit said to the bunny*. To the extent that this established fad phrase means anything, it is about a sexual "quickie" in which the male jumps on, discharges, and walks away. (a) *Jocular*. A pillow-talk acknowledgment by the male by way of thanks for a good lay. (b) *Same, but as the females protest at having been had without tenderness, as if,* "Is that all I get?" (c) *Macho indifference*. So now you've been had, baby, and good-bye. (Cf. the common macho slogan since ca. 1900, *"Find 'em, fool 'em, fuck 'em, and forget 'em."*) [Prob. originally rhyming slang in black Eng. Clarence Major, *Dictionary of Afro-American Slang* (New York 1969), gives *bip, bam, thank you ma'am* in black use by 1895.]

whiffletree   A centrally pivoted horizontal crossbar to which the traces of draft animals are attached for pulling a wagon or farm implement. [The replacement of draft animals by machines would long since have driven this term into obscurity but for its survival in the slightly child-naughty campfire song:

> The old gray mare went poop on the whiffletree
> Poop on the whiffletree
> Poop on the whiffletree.
> The old gray mare went poop on the whiffletree
> Many long years ago.

The song remains popular in campfire singing, but I wonder if today's children know what they are singing about. I am certain that I heard one Boy Scout group about seven years ago singing about the "weevil tree."

The form is ult. Gmnc., variantly *whippletree* and *singletree,* a corruption of earlier *swingletree.* All forms and variants are either from: 1. IE *sweng-,* to swing, or 2. IE *weip-,* to swing, to sway, prob. ult. echoic of the swishing sound a rod makes in *whipping, whiffling, whiffing* the air. (Cf. baseball slang, *to whiff,* to swing hard and miss the ball, causing the air to whiff-swing-swish.)]

whingding   Variantly *wingding* [A disputed etymology. Prob. a reduplication based on *ding* (< Ger. *Ding,* thing; DINGUS) with *whing* or *wing* as a rhyming element into which one may read any significance at one's own pleasure.] [*P. Slang* attributes *whing ding* to a 1946 Toronto newspaper article on Canadian adolescent slang, but *wing ding* was certainly in earlier use at least in USAAF slang (see below).] 1. A frenetic, wild party. A bash. 2. A raging fit: *He threw a real whingding when his wife left him.* 3. *Crim. slang.* A seizure, a fit. Especially one feigned in order to avoid work, win special treatment, or to support a false claim for insurance compensation.

HISTORIC. In WWII USAAF, by association with *wing,* the Air Force equivalent of a regiment, with various senses based on "wing-thing," as, at one extreme, a wild drunken party at headquarters, or at another, a massive air raid carried out by the entire strength of the wing. As far as I know, these senses are now obs.

white eye   *In the Eng. of the Western Indian after the Civil War.* A white person. [The term was sometimes used pejoratively, but only in the context of ill feeling for the white invaders of Indian territory. At root, it is a neutral observation that the whites of the white man's eyes are notably less pigmented than are those of the native Americans.]

white man's burden   A smug assertion of the moral duty of imperialist Europeans to bring technology and civilization to backward peoples whether they wanted it or not, and over their dead bodies if need be, as long as the imperial profits justified the moral effort. [A phrase popularized in late XIX by various apologists for Imperialism, and perhaps most prominently by Rudyard Kipling. Such is the power of catchphrases that many missionaries actually went forth to do good (or to impose their ideas of the good on ignorant natives), but they seldom refused to have tea with their well-dressed countrymen who were exploiting the natives.]

white slavery   Organized prostitution in which ignorant girls are lured into houses of prostitution in which they are kept captive, or moved from one house to another in the ring under the coercion of strong-arm whoremasters until they are discarded as too old for the trade or eliminated for disobedience. [Black girls could also be "white slaves," though most were white.] The name is from late-XIX organized vice, primarily as a way of distinguishing it from the then recently terminated "black slavery" of the South.

White Slave Act A once-popular name for the Mann Act, proposed by Congressman James Robert Mann (1856–1922). The act was passed by Congress in June 1910.

HISTORIC. The Mann Act provided heavy penalties for transporting a girl across a state line "for immoral purposes." Though well intentioned, it did nothing to stop the interstate trade in prostitutes, for the girls under the power of a criminal syndicate were so thoroughly intimidated that they would, when ordered, go to an out-of-state house on their own with no need "to be transported." The law instead came to be applied abusively by blackmailers (including crooked cops) who entrapped men from, say, Connecticut who took a girl into New York City and checked into a hotel with her. The enforcement of the Mann Act became so predatory and pointless in the 1920s that even Congress saw its error and repealed it. Reformer phrase thyself.

whites of their eyes, don't fire till you see the   Now a generalized catchphrase applicable to many contexts in which one is called upon to stand fast and wait. After a command issued by General Israel Putnam at the Battle of Bunker Hill (actually of Breed's Hill), June 17, 1775. What Putnam said to his partially entrenched troops as the British advanced up the hill was, "Men, you are all marksmen —don't one of you fire till you see the whites of their eyes." The American language, informed by an epigrammatic sense superior to Putnam's, has reduced his original command to its essential and most memorable elements.

whitlow   A discolored, commonly whitish, pus-producing swelling in the terminal joint of a finger or thumb. Also called a *felon*. It commonly, but not always, occurs next to a fingernail. [The etymology is a bit obscure, but *whitflaw, whitflow* is attested in XIV and seems to be a folk contraction of *white-flaw*. The loss of the *f* is attested in XV but not explained. The resemblance to Ger. and Du. forms, while inconclusive, suggests that the term may be of foreign origin but folk-modified.]

widow's weeds   The widow's traditional black mourning dress. [OE *woed*, garment, survives only in this fixed formula.]

wind: take the wind out of one's sails   1. *Nautical.* In the days of sailing ships the act of one ship, in a race or in maneuvering for battle position, of coming up on another between it and the wind, thus causing the ship so "wind-shadowed" to lose power, speed, and maneuverability. 2. *Simple ext.* To come up against another in such a way as to cause him to falter in his declarations. Sometimes defined as "to give another pause," but the act of taking the wind out of one's sails causes a slowing down, not a dead stop.

windfall   1. *Lit.* Anything blown from a tree, especially fruit or branches. 2. *In idiom.* Any unforeseen and more-or-less substantial stroke of good fortune: *windfall profits.*

HISTORIC. Fruit grown on an estate belonged to the lord of the manor. Peasants might gather for themselves some of the fruit that fell before it rotted, and for them, such pickings (or nonpickings) were a windfall; but the lord's windfall was primarily timber. From some time in XVII and into mid-XIX, landowners were forbidden to cut down great stands of trees, especially of oak, these being reserved to the Royal Navy for building ships. Such lumber was accordingly at a premium, and a landowner who wanted to build or to enlarge his house, though he had great stands of timber, was obliged to import lumber expensively from abroad. If, however, a storm blew over a stand of great trees, the lord had windfall rights to cut and mill those trees. The original idiomatic windfall, therefore, was an unforeseen supply of valuable lumber.

wire [There was nothing in the experience of Aryan man to correspond to the many forms of what we call wire; hence there was no IE word for it. The adapted root is *wei-*, to twist, twisted thing, supple thing (WITHE). And early wire was of fine, twisted filaments. In Gmnc. *wei-r-* → OE *wir*, the reference being to threadlike metal rods or webs used in filigree work. So the sense, "slender metal thread." So Shakespeare, *Sonnet* CXXX, "If hairs be wires, black wires grow on her head." (Note, as part of the figure, that black wires were not known in Shakespeare's day, but only wires of gold, silver, and perhaps fine copper.)] 1. A metal strand of a certain gauge, normally supple, earlier normally woven or of a single drawn filament, only extruded in recent technology. (If approaching the size of a cable, sometimes called *wire rope*.) 2. *In XIX and since.* The line used to transmit telegraph signals. Hence, a telegram. Ext. to a wireless telegram, and more recently to electrical wires (but *power lines;* and a cable message is called a *cablegram*): *He has an open wire to the West Coast. Now if only he had something to say.* 3. *Horse racing.* An established metaphor for the finish line. [In years of searching I have come on no clue to this usage. Wire, of course, was never used at the finish line, and tape is used for foot races. Dating and origin unknown.]

down to the wire On the last stretch. Nearing finish line. [As above, primarily from horse racing.] *get in (just) under the wire* To complete something at the last possible moment. [Origin? Dating? Root sense?]

high wire The tight (or slack) rope walked by circus performers.

pull wires To manipulate from behind the scenes. (As if working marionettes?)

hot wire 1. The positive wire of an electric circuit; the wire delivering the electric charge, as distinct from the ground wire. 2. *Crim. slang.* A wire used for jumping the ignition switch of an automobile. *to hotwire* To jump the ignition of a car, boat, plane, usually with intent to commit grand theft.

livewire 1. Same sense as hot wire 1. 2. Any line charged with electrical current, especially a fallen powerline throwing sparks and releasing possibly lethal current. 3. An active or hyperactive party-goer, masher, supersalesman, or generalized eager beaver. (He shoots forth sparks of dynamically assertive stupidity.)

wired (for sound) 1. *When said of a building or area,* Equipped with a public address system. 2. *When said of an undercover police agent,* Rigged with a hidden device to record or transmit conversations, as with a felon the investigator is seeking to trap.

wise apple   A shrewd person. (Implies practical canniness rather than deceit.) [Commonly assumed to be a variant of *wiseacre,* variantly *wisecracker,* implying "false, flippant, would-be sagacity," though at root *wiseacre* is < Gmnc. *wiss,* Ger. *weiss,* wise; with Gmnc. *sago,* sage (akin to Ger. *sagen,* to say), whence *Weissager,* soothsayer, which means, if the roots speak sooth, "one wise enough to foresee the truth," though in the diminished English form *wiseacre,* a specious wisdom is implied.

But I am indebted to Mr. Walter Newman for a citation that indicates a different origin for *wise apple,* which is implicitly "truly shrewd." John F. Adams, *Guerrilla Gardening* (New York, 1983), mentions the *court pendu plat* apple (short, hanging, flat apple?) as among the oldest apples known. He adds, "In England the variety is commonly called 'the wise apple' because it blooms so late that it misses the spring frosts." That should be shrewd enough to bake into a pie to set before the king's English, and certainly points to an origin distinct from that of *wiseacre.*]

wisdom tooth   The third molar. [So called because it tends to appear at some time between the seventeenth and twenty-fifth year, at which time one may not be exactly ripe in wisdom, but at least beyond the baby years in which other teeth develop. Wisdom teeth commonly pose problems that require extraction, and if wisdom is to be won only through pain, earlier dental practice had its contributions to make to mankind's wisdom.]

witches' sabbath   1. A regular business meeting of witches and their satanic chief executive, usually in the dark of the moon. [*Sabbath* because the pious thought of such doings as corresponding to their church services ("Remember thou keep holy the Sabbath"), but in reverse, a black Mass of evil in supplication of the devil as lord.] 2. *Ironic ext.* Any convocation of gossipy women: *The ladies of Christiansville held a witches' sabbath in the ruins of Pamela's reputation.*

workaholic   Jack, the dull boy. One addicted to work to the exclusion of all else. [Post WWII Am. A variant portmanteau word combining *work* and *a(lco)holic,* the latter in the sense "compulsive drinker" or, in slang, "juice-head, juicer."]

wrong side of one's face: to laugh on   To weep. To grieve. [A Sc. idiom. Brought into Eng. by Sir Walter Scott, *Rob Roy* (1817). An excellent example of an idiom that makes no sense though it has the endorsement of the language convention, through which everyone seems to understand that "wrong side/to do something on the wrong side" somehow equals the opposite of doing it on the right. But try to explain to a foreigner which is the wrong side of one's face. Perhaps you may want to tell him it is the side you fell out of the left-footed bed on.]

Xanthippe The type of the shrewish woman. [After Xanthippe, the shrewish wife of Socrates. He may have turned philosopher in self-defense, probably after driving her to irascibility by his endless questioning of everything, and probably by being too abstract to be any good in bed. In any case, philosophy, like Washington, D.C., is full of famous men and the women they married when they were too young to know better.]

xenon An inert, colorless, odorless gas found in elemental form as a trace element of our atmosphere. [Gk. *xenon,* neuter form of *xenos,* stranger. The gas was discovered in 1898 by Brit. scientists Sir William Ramsey and M. W. Tavers, who so named it because it combines with no known element, remaining a stranger to all chemical bonding.]

HISTORIC. In new Gk. the base *xeno-* or *xen-* has been made to serve many functions unimagined by the ancients. In botany *xenia* is the hybrid that results when a plant of one strain is infused with the pollen of another. It is made, so to speak, to "receive a stranger"; < Gk. *xenia,* hospitality (the reception of a guest or stranger). In geology a *xenolith* is a rock fragment or intrusion foreign to the igneous mass in which it is found.

In less specialized usage a *xenophobe* is one who is hostile to strangers, especially to those of other national, cultural, or racial characteristics; and a *xenophile* is one who relishes and seeks such differences.

And so toward a definition of American family life in the late XX, *xenogenesis* will do for the process whereby we produce children out of all relation to their parents even as genetic malfunctions.

𝒴

yard¹   A tract of land, esp. when enclosed: *yard of a house, barnyard, prison yard, railroad yard.* [In this sense, ult. < IE *gher-,* to grasp; ext., to enclose (prob. with first ref. to an animal pen), → suffixed *-d-* in Gmnc. to OE *geard,* enclosed land, garden (GARDEN), and with almost standard shift of g/y → ME *yard(e).*]

yard²   1. A unit of linear measure in U.S. and Britain, 3 ft., .9144 m.; or of area, 1 sq. yd. equaling 9 sq. feet. 2. *Nautical.* A long, tapering rod slung at an angle to a mast for securing the spread of a sail. [In this sense, ult. < IE *ghasto-,* rod, staff, walking stick; variantly *ghazdh'-* → probable Gmnc. form *gazdaz* → IE *g(i)erd,* rod, measuring rod, and once again with g/y → ME *yerde, yarde.*]

the sun is over the yardarm It's time for a drink. [But though the import is clear, the idiom is complex. 1. In Brit. maritime or naval service, by XVII, signified "it is noon." At noon the sun is overhead. A confusing idiom: when the sun is dead over the yardarm it is dead over everything else in the ship. A *yardarm,* moreover, is simply one end of the yard, and there are likely to be many yardarms on a ship, unless it has been seriously damaged by a storm. A more logical idiom might have been "over the yards." Language, however, is coded not to logic but to a language convention, and for whatever reason one cares to adduce (I would guess rhythm and sound values), seamen came to pack their illogic into this idiomatic bag. 2. An officer and a gentleman did not drink before noon. In traditional usage, therefore, the expression came to mean, "time to go to the wardroom for the first drink of the day," whence, by association, "time for a drink (whatever time it happened to be)." 3. In common shore usage among salty or merely seacoast tourist types, this expression is commonly used to signal the 5:00 P.M. (or whenever) cocktail hour: *Roger Fredland came into view waving a whiskey bottle bright as the sun above the yardarm.*

Y chromosome   *Genetics.* The chromosome that determines masculinity. Eggs carry an *X* chromosome that determines feminity; the spermata carry an *X* and a *Y*. If the fertilized egg picks up an *X*, the result is a female; if a *Y*, the resulting individual *(XY)* is a male. [Arbitrary designation.]

UNHISTORICAL. Isaac Asimov is the only phenomenon in nature that is forever capable of rushing in to fill its own constantly expanding vacuum. On no urging whatever, he is also forever prepared to celebrate narcissistic genetic manipulation to the tune of "Home, Home on the Range":

> Oh give me a clone, a clone of my own
> With the *Y* chromosome changed to *X*.
> And when we're alone, I'll call her my own
> And we'll look into matters of sex.

His rendition is a matter to be recorded among the terrors the human race must recognize in order to flee, else he may continue with the slightly superior verse (with which I have provided him):

> Clone, clone of my own,
> Where no mere interloper can play.
> Where never is heard a discouraging third,
> And it's me and my ego all day.

(It is, of course, "I and my ego," but for the occasion I composed in Asimovian.)

you bet!   An Am. colloq. formula of hearty agreement, willingness. Also *you betcha!* or simply *betcha!* (So a gas station attendant, told to "fill 'er up," will sometimes reply with one of these forms to express hearty willingness to oblige.) [I cannot find a secure attestation or region of origin. Neither can Wentworth and Flexner, but they guess-date it from ca. 1870. Similar and prob. earlier forms meaning, at root, "it's a sure thing," but also used to express hearty affirmation, are: *(you can) bet your ass (on it), . . . your boots, . . . your bottom dollar, . . . your (sweet) life.*]

you can take that to the bank   Said of a proposition, offer, statement, promise. Signifies absolute face-value negotiability, good enough as collateral in the opinion of any prudent banker. [Am., dating uncertain; prob. XX with ample precedent in XIX (and earlier) *his word is his bond*—as certain as cash.]

yuppie   The young urban professional as a social class within the changing scene. [The one certainty about this now-common (and probably transient) term is that it is an anagram for *Y*oung *U*rban *P*rofessional (whatever that means), the form modified to conform with ca. 1960s *hippie,* and ca. 1970s *yippie.*]

HISTORIC. Nothing about the shifting fad allegiances of the young can be said without gross generalization. The flower-child *hippies* (from *to be hip,* to be aware) identified the profit-motive middle class as *the Establishment* and chose to reject it while living out of its garbage cans, and on square-dad's tax dodge. Their declared faith was *to drop out* (of the establishment), *turn on* (to drugs and hallucinogens for "mind expansion"), and so to *tune in* (to the Universal Allness, largely by way of meditation). They also declared, as the first article of their "social revolution," that anyone over age thirty was *the enemy* (because corrupted by "Establishment values").

Inevitably, then, as time runs, the hippies turned the thirtieth milepost and found they had become their own earlier declared "enemies." Most of them also found that life in communal pads, in shared poverty, often sustained by simple begging, was a bore. Today even Allen Ginsberg, quondam poet and high priest of the hippies, has trimmed his beard and replaced his priestly toga with a three-piece suit and tie to look like a Wall Street customer's man. Many of the most radical of the hippies followed the same course, taking jobs in the establishment they had shunned, and finding in themselves a taste for the good things a regular paycheck can buy. In their new ambivalence, they began to call themselves *yuppies.* In general, they seemed disposed to raid the establishment without cleaving to it in their souls. Many shaved and cut their hair conformably and wore the three-piece suit during business hours, and became swingers at night, wearing wigs and mod outfits. They were, I will venture to say, the cocaine generation and closer to the philosophy of Hugh Hefner's *Playboy* (in essence, let's grab for all the goodies—but be cool about it) than to their earlier Zen.

The next wave or two of the young, lustrum by lustrum, seem to have been attracted to the "Playboy grab," without having been earlier conditioned to the intensely held tenets of the flower-child. They tended to live-in "marital" arrangements, expensive living, and the disco, in which they performed a ritual resembling the dance of death of the Plague years, always arising the next morning to be briskly efficient in their business offices. I can only venture my undemonstrable conclusion that these young people have buried in their psyches a dark conviction that the Omega Bomb is on its way and that life must be seized on the run before all goes blooie.

But that sense of things seems to have faded again into a new style that includes formal marriage and the responsibility of rearing children. The latter-day yuppie seems to have turned into a theorist of child rearing, hot for every new educational experiment and intensely articulate at PTA meetings. The disco and its dance of death still flourish to be sure, but young yuppie parents seem to be professorial in their family planning. And—if the bomb does not go off—who knows what comes next? The parental yuppie even gives signs of having forsworn cocaine and even marijuana. Are we tending toward a new intellectualized establishment? Recording Angel, please hold the question for later discussion.

POSTSCRIPT. As these notes were being prepared for press, the Florida Evening (TV) News came up with the ricochet term *buppie,* *B*lack *U*rban *P*rofessional. (Perhaps *guppie* is next, an acronymic from *G*eriatrically *U*seless *P*erson *P*assing *I*nto *E*ternity.)

zeppelin   [After Count Ferdinand von Zeppelin (1858–1917), the German general who invented this flying cigar.] A rigid, powered, lighter-than-air airship first built ca. 1900, and for a time in WWI a dreaded German air raider.

HISTORIC. Zeppelins were huge craft with massive metal frames and a considerable ship's crew. Because they could fly higher than the planes of WWI they enjoyed a certain safety despite their relative slowness, their great bulk, and their consequent vulnerability to winds. In the early days of WWI several zeppelin raids terrified England, but a series of disastrous crashes moved the Germans to discontinue their use in war.

In the 1930s Germany instituted a transatlantic passenger service to New Jersey with the massive zeppelin von Hindenburg. Helium, however, was then produced in commercial quantities only in the U.S., and since the government refused to export it on grounds of national defense, the Hindenburg had to depend on highly flammable hydrogen gas. On May 6, 1937, while attempting a mooring at Lakehurst, New Jersey, the hydrogen of the Hindenburg was ignited by a spark of static electricity, resulting in a spectacular air disaster, after which zeppelin travel was abandoned. Technology is always more complicated than I can keep track of, but I believe all subsequent lighter-than-air craft have been balloons or blimps.

Zouave   [< Arabic *Zouaves,* the name of a mountain tribe of Algerian Berbers. Now, a soldier dressed in a uniform resembling that worn by the Arabic *Zouaves.*] 1. *Beginning in 1831.* Labeled two battalions of rigidly disciplined, fierce infantry of Zouave tribesmen recruited by the Fr. in Algeria and noted for their precision drilling and for their brightly multicolored uniforms worn with a tasseled fez, a sash, and baggy ankle-length knickers worn with short leggings. 2. *In the mid-XIX Fr. army.* A number of regiments of regular Fr. infantry whose training and uniforms were modeled on those of the Algerian Zouaves. 3. *In the Am. Civil War.* A regiment of New York firemen formed in the Union Army and given for purposes of unit pride distinctively colorful uniforms in subdued imitation of the Algerian and Fr. Zouaves, though those uniforms were soon abandoned as being cumbersomely impractical on Civil War battlefields.

HISTORIC. I know of no U.S. troops now rigged out as Zouaves, but these cock-a-strut plumages continue to turn up here and there in the uniforms of drill teams and marching bands, especially in Shriner parades.

zymurgy   The process and art of fermentation, the mystery on which all wineries, breweries, distilleries, and sipenseries of the spirits are based. [A late formation based on Gk. *zumē*, leaven, ferment; *-ourgia*, working (ERG, ERGON). Commonly implies the working of a skilled art, as in metallurgy, or an arcane one, as in thaumaturgy. Here, of course, with both senses functioning. And certainly, though neglected, a word that should be enshrined in the litanies of Zymeturgians and Lushian Templars.]

HISTORIC. What is the proper last word in the Eng. dictionary? Samuel Johnson settled unimaginatively in 1765 for *zootomyl,* which he defined as "Dissection of the bodies of animals." The language has found reason to reject his offering. The AHD reaches for *zyzzyva,* a coined name for a weevil, but cannot explain the coinage. Others close on Zyrian, a Uralic language. The *Random House Dictionary* even offers ZZZ as the sound of snoring. Perhaps. And a true browser will pause for anything. But language should shape the mind, and for the true tonic resolution, let this work step up to the bar and raise the last glass to sacred zymurgy, the art and means of the preserving grace.

SUPPLEMENT

Since the publication of *Browser's I* and *Browser's II,* I have turned up additional information about a number of the terms there discussed. The entries in this supplement expand, modify, and sometimes entirely supersede the earlier ones.

accolade   1. An expression of honor, praise, approval, esp. one uttered more-or-less formally in public. 2. A more-or-less formal embrace of welcome and respect. 3. *At root.* The essential last rite in dubbing a knight. Hence, *to receive the accolade* 1. To be elevated to knighthood. 2. *In loose ext.* To be (publicly) honored, elevated. [At root, "(act of getting it) in the neck." < Fr. *col,* neck, L. *colum,* collar, prefixed *ad-* (*ac-*), to, at, in.]

HISTORIC. The root sense has been confused by Fr. *acolare,* to embrace around the neck. In dubbing a knight the accolade was a ritual tap (blow) on the neck or shoulder, symbolizing the last insult or injury the bachelor would be required to bear servilely as a person of no rank. The blow was immediately followed (often with an embrace) by the words, "Arise, sir knight," which signified "arise elevated to noble degree (and henceforth free to defend your honor from all insult or injury)." The ritual became encrusted with many additions and variations, but the accolade remained the last insult to which the new knight would have to submit meekly.

affidavit   A written declaration sworn to before a notary public or other official by a witness who cannot appear in court. In the case of a deathbed declaration, it may be sworn before a clergyman or lay witnesses who sign the document to attest that it is a faithful copy of the dying declaration. If accepted by the court, an affidavit can be entered in evidence in lieu of a present witness.

(But note that technology changes all. Tapes of TV interviews in which deponents are sworn before a notary or officer of the court —in effect, audiovisual affidavits—are commonly accepted in evi-

307

dence.) [At root, "sworn on one's faith." < L. *fides,* faith; *affidavit,* he has sworn upon his faith. U.S. law now permits civil affirmation in lieu of a religious oath, but the act of swearing by Judeo-Christian sacred sanction is still standard.]

alibi [A legal term running together L. *alius,* other, with *ubi,* where, *ibi,* there; hence "elsewhere"; ext. "evidence introduced to show the accused was elsewhere at the time of the crime and therefore could not be guilty of it." (Not relevant when the defendant is accused of conspiracy or of commissioning another to commit the crime.)] 1. The root sense, as above. 2. *In Am. since early XX.* (a) Any excuse: *Late again: what's your alibi this time?* (b) *Further ext.* A witness to one's innocence: *Jim is my alibi that the train was late.* (c) *Further ext. as a verb.* To testify to one's innocence: *Jim will alibi me.*

Alibi Ike A fast talker who is forever ready with a self-exonerating excuse for whatever went wrong, none of which is ever his fault. [Coined 1924 by Ring Lardner as the title of one of his most popular short stories, the central character of which is Alibi Ike. It became an established Am. slang idiom almost at once and remains so.]

NOTE. An *alibi,* if accepted by the court and the jury, is specific and conclusive evidence of innocence (except as noted above). An *excuse* [L. *ex,* away from; *causa,* accusation] is a defense offered against a charge. An explanation [*Ex-* used as an intensive; *planare,* to make plain] is an effort to make clear. *About being in bed with your wife, sir: I do have an explanation. I do not mean to offer it as an excuse, you understand. From the way you are holding that gun, I wish, in fact, it were an alibi.*

allemande A standard square-dance call for a prescribed step to the right or left, as in *allemande right, allemande left* (or as often sounded, *let*). [Few common words have elicited so much uninformed nonsense by way of explanation. Among other offerings, I have seen it asserted as scholarship that this call derives from Fr. *allez,* imperative of *aller,* to go; with *man,* either as a Black English form meaning "go man"; or with Fr. *main,* hand, as if "go hand in hand." I have even seen the seriously offered explanation that it is from a dance called "The Alleyman." (Perhaps a form of the Trashcan Strut?)]

The term derives simply from Fr. *l'Allemande,* the German woman, the name of a lively late-XVIII French dance in three-fourths time. It was the characteristic step of this dance, imported into French Louisiana almost at once, that gave rise to this square-dance call.

Compare common *sashay,* now in general use, but still a square dance call, from the French dance *Le Chasseur,* the hunter. Also common *dosie-dotes,* corrupted from Fr. *dos-à-dos,* back to back.

awkward   The root sense, as in *Browser's I,* is backward, perverse, turned the wrong way; but browsers will welcome the following citation from Shakespeare, *1 Henry VI* III. ii, to fix this earlier sense precisely:

> Was I for this nigh wrecked upon the sea
> And twice by awkward wind from England's bank
> Drove back again?

blush   [ME *blusshen, blisshen,* < OE *blyscan,* to bloom, to redden. Via Gmnc. < IE *bl'-,* zero-grade form of *bhel-,* to swell; widely distributed in derivates signifying sexual tumescence and the reddening of a swollen sex organ (BULL).] *v.* To redden in a rush of blood as in modesty, shame, embarrassment. Said primarily of the cheeks, they being most visible, but who would misunderstand a blush that covered the whole body? *She stood there like September Morn in a body stocking of blushes. n.* Such a reddening.

   at first blush At first sight. [Demure maidens were once expected to blush modestly on meeting a strange gentleman or a lady of superior caste. And by cousinage, at least in Brit., rare in Am.:] *at a blush* At a glance.

boondoggling   1. Fussy, almost pointless, time-consuming hobby work. 2. *Ext. in politics.* Legislative enactment, esp. in the U.S. Congress, of government projects that work out to be a waste of time and money. (And corresponding verb forms.) But also, *to boondoggle Congressional, and also state legislature.* To exchange favorable votes on boondoggling projects (you vote a pork barrel to my constituents and I'll vote one to yours). [MMM cites the Chicago *Tribune,* Oct. 4, 1935: "to the cowboy it (boondoggling) meant the making of saddle trappings out of odds and ends of leather, and they boondoggled when there was nothing else to do on the ranch." And indeed they did, also whittling, braiding, and especially making choice ropes from the hair of horses' tails, though this last was serious professional work, for no real cowboy would consider a "store-boughten" lasso but wove his own lovingly and as a matter of professional pride.

But the *Tribune* reporter was reporting his Old West ana-chronistically, for the word was unknown to the cowboy. It was coined in the 1920s (largely for its expressive sound?) by R. H. Link, American Scoutmaster, to label the endless fussy plaiting of leather cords (Clanyards) to be worn around the neck with pendant whis-tles, compasses, and the like. In his original usage, in fact, a *boon-doggle* was such a plaited cord.

The term once coined was retrospectively apt to the work of the bunkhouse cowboy, but unknown to him. And as a further lan-guage note, bear in mind that the word was less than fifteen years old when the *Tribune* reporter assumed it had been around forever.]

boot 1. *In Am.* The rear baggage compartment of a stagecoach. 2. *Brit. only.* The separate rear luggage compartment of an automo-bile, called in Am. "the trunk." 3. A rear step once common on private horse-drawn carriages. On it footmen rode standing, hold-ing a bar (as firemen once did in the rear of American fire engines) and ready to jump off, open the doors, and place a portable step if the wagon was not made with an attached step. 4. In early horse-drawn carriages with open sides, boxes that projected between the wheels on either side to accommodate two additional passengers who rode facing out.

HISTORICAL. It is this fourth sense I have been slow to under-stand, and which I cannot explain except at some length. In the supplement to *Browser's II,* I cited Trench on these side-boots:

> Not the luggage but the chief persons used once to ride in the boot, or rather boots of a carriage, for there were two. Projecting from the sides of the carriage, and open to the air, they derived, no doubt, their name from their shape.

I could not understand how carriages with such projections could negotiate heavy traffic in the narrow streets of London without sideswiping. Nor could they. Trench wrote in the latter XIX. Side-boots disappeared from English carriages ca. 1700, by which time the crush of traffic made them unmanageable. Trench could have made his note clearer by dating it. He was also rather uncharac-teristically wrong about the source of the name, which is perhaps from Fr. *bout,* end, extremity, but more likely from Fr. *botte,* the name given the portable step placed below the boot by the foot-men. These steps were once carried either in the rear boot or in a forward compartment under the coachman's seat, also called a boot.

Horse-drawn carriages were first developed in France and must have been instruments of torture before the development of semiadequate springs. *Wheels: A Pictorial History,* by Edwin Tunis (1964), says, "In 1457 in Paris the mother of Louis XI rode in a wagon suspended on chains" and adds that it was called "the wobbling chariot." He also notes that "as late as 1550 there were only three carriages in Paris"—and so much for the dangers of sideswiping in heavy traffic.

There were few carriages in XVI England. The first with boots was "an exceeding marvelous princely coche" presented to Elizabeth in 1584 by the king of France. It was a six-passenger, roofed, open coach with two rear seats facing forward, two forward seats facing backward, and two seats facing out in the boots on either side. Elizabeth kept her old royal coach and assigned this one to her ladies in waiting.

Side-boots (called simply "boots") persisted into XVIII on stagecoaches, being manageable on the open highways and providing two additional seats, but the ride was so rough that passengers who rode in the boots sometimes took to their beds to recover from the pounding and jouncing. Englishmen long resisted carriages. Persons of station were horsy. They liked cutting a fine figure on an elegantly caparisoned mount. They associated wheeled wagons with the wains and drays of country louts, and scorned them accordingly. And it was certainly a torture to bounce over rough roads without springs to absorb the shock.

I am grateful to Walter Newman of Sherman Oaks, California, for pointing me to Tunis and to this explanation of Trench's accurate but scant note.

boss   Person in charge, overseer, foreman, employer, the one who gives the orders. [Am. only. < the colonial Dutch of New Amsterdam *baas,* master, patroon.]

A BROWSER'S NOTE. James Fenimore Cooper fancied himself an authority on usage and word origins. (In *Browser's I,* see *Yankee* for his authoritative mispronouncement on the word's origin.) In 1838 he wrote to Noah Webster to enlist his aid in drumming out of the language such vulgarisms as *boss, advocate,* and *deputize.* But language is pelagically indifferent to beachcombers. In 1710 Jonathan Swift inveighed against a number of neologisms, including *mob* as an ignorant corruption of L. *mobile vulgus,* the fickle multitudes. Yet in 1755 the arch-Tory Dr. Samuel Johnson included *mob* in his *Dictionary* as standard English, citing it with no disapprobation from the works of Dryden and Addison.

Boss entered deeply into the patois of immigrant workers. As *bosso* it has acquired some small currency in southern Italian, courtesy of returning immigrants. *La bossa mia* is common in It.-Am. patois for "wife"; and *far lo bosso/la bossa* serves in both It.–Am. patois and in southern Italian colloq. for "to be bossy."

Boss and its derivatives take more than a full page of the OED but never in this Am. sense. (See also in *Browser's I, boss, bossie* for "cow," which is mentioned only in OED's supplement and only as a rare dialect form.) Most OED entries have to do with embossment.

A rare usage and etymologically obscure (perhaps < Fr. *buse, buisse,* water conduit) is *boss* for tube, passage, spring, or flow of water.

Attentive browsers may welcome a partial note on a book published 1520 by Wynkyn de Worde titled "Treatyse of a Galaunt, with the Maryage of the Fayre Pusell the Bosse of Byllyngesgate unto London Stone." I have never tracked down a copy of de Worde's book and do not know its tenor nor the meaning of *London Stone. Pusell* appears as *pusle* in Bailey as "a dirty wench." And *boss* is there defined as "a water conduit, running out of a Gor-bellied [a glutton, at root, "a filthy belly"] figure." I am left to guess that this "boss of Billingsgate" is a Rabelaisian term for the phallic tube connecting the filthy-belly and the dirty wench. Whatever my confusion on these London Stones, this *boss* is not akin to Boss Tweed or to the American foreman or employer.

castles in Spain   Grand, idle daydreams. [By XI *chateaux en aire* was established in Fr. with ref. to great palaces conjured from airy nothing by the genies of Arabian tales; and also *chateaux en Asie,* prob. partly from the same association, but also because there were in Asia no castles of the European sort, though there were palaces enough. But Spain lay just next door, and in XI under the Muslims it also had no castles of the European–Christian sort, whereby the most common French idiom became *chateaux en Espagne,* castles in Spain. All of these forms signified grand, idle, nonesuch daydreams.

In late XII and XIII Spain became a place of enormous rewards for French warlords who would join the Christian Spaniards in driving out the Moors. So Henry of Burgundy invaded and established modern Portugal, raising protective castles and placing his son on the throne of the new kingdom. For a time, therefore, *castles in Spain* came to symbolize the enormous rewards conquerors could reap in Spain, but this sense has receded and the sense of the idiom has reverted to its original "cloud cuckooland of never-never daydreams."]

cheat *n.* 1. A fraud. 2. A fraudulent person. *v.* 1. To practice a fraud. 2. With *on,* To be dishonest in love: *to cheat on one's lover, wife, husband*—to have sexual affairs with others while professing love of a main partner. 2. To elude consequences as if by a secret trick: *stunt men cheat death for a living.* [The form of the word may be from (unattested) L. *excadere,* to fall out; whence OF *escheoir,* to fall out, p.p. *eschete,* an act of falling out. As a legal term, this became ME *eschete, escheat(e),* under feudalism the reversion (falling out) of land to the liege lord or sovereign when there are no legal claimants to it. So the form, but our sense of *cheat* is from the chicanery of history:]

HISTORIC. In feudal England an *escheatour* was an official of the shire who kept accounts of entailed properties and estates that had reverted to the crown because the last holder had died without legal heirs, or had been executed or banished for treason, forfeiting his estate(s). This official assessed these properties *(escheats)* and certified their value to the Exchequer. He was conceived as what we might now call a county assessor, and he was appointed as a man of honest principles.

He suffered, however, from the common infection of having been born of man and woman. His presumably accurate search and audit allowed such latitude for skimming money chests, furnishings, articles of value, and choice livestock before reporting the remainder, that *escheatour* readily altered to *cheat* in the modern sense.

Falstaff, in *Merry Wives of Windsor* I.ii, catches the word at its point of transition: "I will be cheaters to them both, and they shall be exchequers to me."

The form of the English word may have been influenced by obs. Brit. *chouse,* a swindle, a swindler, which is derived from Turkish *chiaus,* at root, an interpreter, but by long association a diplomat, a person with ambassadorial functions. Trench says that such a man "in 1609 succeeded in defrauding Turkish and Persian merchants resident in England of 4,000 pounds," then a huge sum. Ben Jonson, in *The Alchemist,* knew of this swindler in the original spelling *chiaus,* but by XVIII Bailey had it as *chowse,* a cheat, to cheat.

cheer 1. Pleasure. Gaiety. Buoyant disposition. 2. The source of such feelings. 3. *Rare or obs.* Good food and drink as a source of pleasure: *a table spread with good cheer.* 4. A shout of approval, encouragement. And as a verb, to give cheer to. Also *to cheer on,* To encourage. [A much traveled word beginning with IE *ker-,* head, also horn, hence horned head. (And horned heads once figured commonly in idols, part of the image of a god.) Etymologically *ker-,* with k/h and suffixed *-n-* in Gmnc. → skeletal *h'r-n-* → OE *horn.* Same stem into Gk. as *karē,* head, face; and prob. via L. *cara,* OF *chiere,* → ME *chere,* face, countenance. This sense has now receded from our word, but note that in the King James version, Genesis 3:19 reads, "In the sweat of they *face* shalt thou eat bread," and that the same text is rendered in Wyclif's ME, "In swoot of thi *cheer* thou shalt ete thi breed."]

HISTORIC. The connection between *cheer* and *face* is not entirely explainable, but clinging to it is the classic notion *imago animi vultus est,* the face images the soul. In Dante, for instance, the damned cannot dissemble, but project on the air about them a seemingly physical image of their distorted inner being, whereas the divine radiance of the heavenly elect images forth their blessed inner being. So *cheer* was earlier *countenance* in the now archaic "we found him in good countenance" or "in good cheer."

Chic Sale   Also commonly *Chic Sales* (but this form is a swallowed genitive, as "the Chic Sale's thing"). An outhouse.

I was wrong in dating this (vanishing?) Americanism from ca. 1920. The firm date is 1929. In that year, Charles Partlow, character actor, humorous writer, and close friend of Stephen Leacock, published a booklet titled "The Specialist" under the pseudonym Charles (Chic) Sale. It is an account purportedly by a back-country carpenter proudly dedicated to his craft, who calls himself "the champion privy builder of Sangamon County," and who gives not only specific instructions on how to build a good privy but who discourses on the wisdom of his specifications.

Before the stock market crashed in October 1929, "The Specialist" appeared in at least eleven reprinted editions, the eleventh proudly announcing "More Than a Half Million Copies Sold." Its popularity immediately established *Chic Sale* as an Am. slang-colloq. term.

In numerous stage and platform appearances, Partlow may have come on as Chic Sale and presented some of the material of "The Specialist" before 1929, but the term can only be securely dated from the publication—which occurred, oddly, at just about the time the outhouse had disappeared from all but the most backward rural areas, though it lived on in nostalgia.

Christmas stocking

> The stockings were hung by the chimney with care
> In hopes that St. Nicholas soon would be there.
> —Clement Clark Moore (1779–1863),
> "A Visit from St. Nicholas"

The origins of this now firmly established custom were touched upon in *Browser's I* under *Christmas* but merit a fuller accounting. In the piously exaggerated legends of the saints' lives, St. Nicholas is reputed to have aided a poor but honest man who had three daughters but no money for their dowries. He was about to sell them as concubines when St. Nicholas, a fourth-century bishop of Myra in Lydia in Asia Minor, supplied him with three purses of gold to secure for the girls a marriage obviously made in heaven. For such deeds of generosity Nicholas became the patron saint of gift givers, emerging via Du. *Sint (Ni)colaes* as the New Amsterdam *Sinterclaas,* Santa Claus. The "poor but honest man" of the legend must have been a decayed aristocrat whose daughters were above earning their living as washerwomen, preferring concubinage to peasant toil. In any case the details of St. Nicholas's benefaction are worth a closer look.

Santa now comes down the fireplace, but there were no fireplaces in fourth-century houses. (See *focus, Browser's I.*) Rather, they had firepits under a hole in the roof. In traditional fear of the night air, moreover, the tiny windows of ancient houses (really little more than air slits) were sealed shut at night. In later versions of the pious legendry of St. Nicholas he is said to have come to the house at night and thrown in three purses of gold to solve the family's problems.

These later versions leave the impression that St. Nicholas simply chucked three purses through the window and went his way. His donations were in fact rather more miraculous. To begin with, it was once well-established custom that a younger daughter could not marry before her elder sister(s). Saint Nicholas had to make three separate visits, one for each daughter. Since there were no window openings available, he must have chucked his purses up over the roof and through the smoke vent into (here we must assume) the stockings the girls had washed out and left to dry on the rail around the firepit. To understand the real nature of the miracle, one must realize that he threw his purse into Big Sister's stocking on the first night, into Middle Sister's on the second, and into Little Sister's on the third. Such marksmanship will do for a hat trick (halo trick?), but why pretend to be a saint if three miracle shots in a row are too much for you?

The custom of hanging one's Christmas stocking by the fireplace may have become merely homely, but it is good to know it derives from a generosity more miraculous in the giving than in the gift.

copasetic   All in order. All okay. Fine and dandy. [As noted in *Browser's II,* this term is rare as the only example I know of Am. slang from nonbiblical Hebrew. *Shekels* remains in slang usage but it is biblical. And many Yiddish terms function in modern Am. slang. But what else is there from Hebrew? This, in fact, is from modern Hebrew, *kohl ba seder,* all in order, and began as black Eng. but popularized by Bill "Bojangles" Robinson (1878–1949), popular Negro comedian and tap dancer who made the term his personal catchphrase.

I speculated in *Browser's II* that perhaps a Jewish storekeeper in the South passed it on to his Negro customers. This note is to withdraw that speculation and to locate the source in the Jewish population of late-XIX Harlem. The orthodox hired Negroes as *shabbas goyim,* sabbath foreigners, who could turn lights on and off, start fires, and cook, as Orthodox Jews were forbidden to do on the Sabbath.

In time a number of Negroes became converted to Judaism and black congregations with black rabbis developed in Harlem. Howard Brotz, *The Black Jews of Harlem* (New York, 1964), states that there were at least eight black Jewish congregations in Harlem between 1919 and 1931, and that by 1915 the first congregations had developed others in Washington and Philadelphia.

As noted, *kohl ba seder* is modern rather than biblical Hebrew, but it is a common phrase readily picked up by anyone studying for the rabbinate. Leslie Fiedler, returned from Israel about 1977, told me he heard it everywhere in the streets there, where it must long have been in use by Palestinian Jews. Scratch that speculative Southern storekeeper; short of absolute attestation, which is lacking, *copasetic* was born in Harlem.]

crapper   Thomas Crapper was a XIX sanitary engineer of London, never knighted as stated in the popular but shoddily researched *People's Almanac.* He installed the first plumbing in Westminster Abbey, and one may still find there cast-iron manhole covers with his name cast on them. He was one of several who worked on the flushed toilet in London. He did invent entirely on his own a smoke bomb to drop into a plumbing system, the escaping smoke to locate leaks. At his Marlborough Works he manufactured a line of toilet seats, the top of his line being called the Marlborough, an ornate easy chair with elaborately upholstered back and arms and a teak seat, which needed no paint and was therefore never frigid to the touch. *Crapper* for "toilet seat" or "place of defecation" was rare in Brit. use, though it did occur. It seems to have been Am. doughboys who found Crapper's name in the vitreous toilet bowls and brought it back to the U.S., where it passed into common slang.

But *to crap* is an independent form in Brit. slang use in XVIII, well before Thomas Crapper was born. The verb form is from Du. *Krappe,* labeling the mixture of straw and dung swept out of a barn. Did the surname Crapper originally mean "barn-sweeper-outer?" I know of no way to trace it, but if the substantive *crapper* is eponymously from Thomas (not Sir Thomas) Crapper, the verb form is from a Du. barnyard.

damn: not worth a damn   A seemingly natural and even inevitable idiom, as if *not worth damning to hell,* but as pointed out in *Browser's II* this form contains a discrete buried idiom. Originally, in late XIV, the form was *not worth a kerse,* not worth a weed. Then in XV *kerse* was metathesized to *kresse, cresse, cress.* (At root, OE *cerse,* weed.) Cf. *watercress.*

But elders continued to say earlier *kerse,* which must have sounded like *curse* to the young, and therefore, since a curse is a damn(ation) → the new idiom *not worth a damn.*

Then in what might be called a second evolution, as a gift of the British Empire the Eng. language acquired the word *dam,* a small coin of India worth a fraction of a farthing, and XIX Brit. slang acquired the curious expression *not care a two-penny damn,* in effect not care at all, and often rendered *not care a damn.* A curiously illogical idiom; for twopence equals eight farthings; and a damn only a fraction of a farthing, whereby a two-penny dam is a substantially inflated coin. Logic aside, the whole exchange deals in very small stuff, and *not worth a dam* (or *damn*) would have had the emotional ring language forms to. The trick is to recognize idiom when it is happening, for it often comes disguised, as in *forlorn hope* (for which see *Browser's II*).

dukes: put up your dukes   Fists: Put up your fists (and fight). [< Brit. XIX rhyming slang *Duke of Yorks,* fingers (used as forks); hence, when closed, fists.

Barrow's *Romano Lava-Lil, Word Book of the Romany,* notes

dukkipen, dukkerin, fortunetelling, palm reading, perhaps suggesting an alternate derivation from Romany via the uncertain corruptions of Brit. thieves' cant, but this possible Romany source seems best mentioned only to be dismissed, Brit. rhyming slang being more proximate and apter than palm reading to sporting or to street fisticuffs. To the best of my knowledge there has never been a Gypsy prizefighter: Gypsies are natively programmed to escape punishment, not to take it.]

dust: bite the dust   To die, esp. to fall in battle. [Most immediately from a ubiquitous cliché of latter XIX Cowboys-and-Indians pennydreadfuls: *and another Indian bit the dust* = and another Indian attacker was shot off his horse, landing (dead) on his face. American boys grew up with this formula as a central catchphrase of competitive play; but the idiom has ancient precedent in Psalm 72:9, "lick the dust," to fall in battle (not necessarily—in fact rarely—off one's horse).]

escape   *n.* Flight from present or impending dread, peril, confinement. *v.* To flee from such conditions. [The finely specific root image is of one seized by the cape who slips out of it and flees, leaving the cape in the hands of his pursuers. < L. *cappa,* cape, cloak; prefixed *ex-,* out of. The likely vulgar L. form *excappare* is unattested but may be inferred from both It. *scappare* and OF *eschaper, escaper,* to run away from, to escape.]

escapade 1. A more-or-less infamous incident from which one emerges intact. 2. *Softened ext.* A prank. An adventure. [< Sp. *escapada,* the act of escaping/of getting away with. < *escapar,* to escape.]

escape artist 1. A criminal who has repeatedly escaped from imprisonment. 2. A performer (a Houdini) who thrills audiences by escaping from seemingly secure and perilous confinement.

escape hatch 1. A hatch or emergency door, as in a submarine or airplane, through which crew members can leave a stricken craft. 2. *Ext.* Any means of relieving an oppressive situation: *The one workable matrimonial escape hatch is mutual forgiveness.*

escape mechanism More commonly *defense mechanism Psychology.* In states of anxiety, any unconsciously motivated action or illusion prompted by a felt need to disguise one's feelings. [Whether with *escape* or *defense, mechanism* is an insensitively nuts-and-bolts word.]

escape velocity The minimum speed required for an object to escape the gravitational pull of a heavenly body. (From earth's gravity, about seven miles per second or about 25,000 mph. Objects that approach but do not reach escape velocity will orbit and eventually fall back.)

explode Now primarily with ref. to detonation or to the violent bursting of bounds of unstable or flammable substances. But note the common form *to explode a myth,* which has nothing to do with detonation. [And this form is directly related to the root sense, which is < L. *plaudere,* to applaud; *explodere,* to drive an actor offstage by derisive applause, jeers, hoots, rhythmic clapping, stomping, and shouted insults. When we speak of an *explosive temper* we probably intend, by late association, an emotional detonation; but the paradigm is in this angry eruption of the Roman audience.

The Romans knew volcanic eruption, and they must have known that fermenting wine will burst a sealed container, but they did not have gunpowder, and hence had no knowledge of detonation.

Gunpowder came into European warfare in late XIV, and Shakespeare spoke of the engineer "hoist on his own petard" (mine, bomb), but no one then called that detonation an explosion. Nathan Bailey gives: "To EXPLODE, to decry, to cry down, to dislike absolutely." Johnson, 1755, gives: "1. To drive out disgracefully with some noise of contempt, etc. 2. To drive out with noise and violence." The first cited OED usage of *explode* with the sense "to detonate" is from Gouverneur Morris, "All Europe is like a mine ready to explode." The date is 1790, but clearly Morris uses the detonative sense as a familiar one. L. *explodire* was prob. metaphorically applied to a detonation at some time in XVII, perhaps before either Bailey or Johnson, either of whom might well have been aware of this emergent sense but have scorned it as an offense to their classical insistence. (See also *implode.*)]

fool [Ult. < IE *bhel-,* to blow, to swell. (BELLOW, BULL.) With regular shift of voiced stop *bh-* to *f* in Latin → skeletal root *fl'-* → L. *follis,* usu. rendered as "bellows." And this rendering underlies the common assumption that a fool is, at root, a windbag. But *follis,* plu. *folles,* also means "inflated skin, leather bag." (Both senses prob. function in Juvenal's *folles spirant mendacia,* swollen cheeks breathing out lies.) And in this sense, *follis* is the bladder flailed about by clowns since at least (and almost certainly before) low Attic comedy. *To flail the bladder* is still good English idiom for "to perform farcically." The successor to the bladder was the Renaissance slapstick, and the slapstick is still in use by burlesque comics.

Hence, one may argue that *fool* is at root a bellower (the loud laugh that bespeaks the empty mind) but the more persuasive root image may be "bladder flailer." And for centuries it was traditional for court jesters (fools) to carry an inflated bladder on a stick or thong.

In English *fool* has acquired many extended senses:] *n.* 1. *Old style.* A clown, a farcical performer, a buffoon, a court jester. 2. *By association.* A dimwitted, easily duped person: *A fool and his money are soon parted.* 3. One who acts stupidly in a given situation: *Norman Mailer was a fool to say no to Marilyn Monroe, but then, she never asked him.* 4. One who is incredibly expert: *a flying fool* [He seems to do easily what someone else would be a fool to try.]

v. 1. To mislead, to dupe: *Fool me once, shame on you: fool me twice, shame on me.* 2. To take by surprise, to prove someone else to be wrong: *We never thought she could keep her job, but she fooled us all by marrying the boss and taking over the company.* 3. To convince another of what one is only pretending: *Vince Clemente was only fooling when he told Annie he wasn't the marrying kind, but Annie wasn't fooled.*

to fool around Slang. 1. To trifle, to engage in aimless activity, to putter. 2. To be sexually promiscuous, to play the field. [When the truck driver says to the waitress, "Do you fool around?" He is saying, in effect, "Will you slip into bed with me?"] *to fool around with Slang.* 1. To associate with someone aimlessly up to no good. 2. To putter at something. 3. To get involved with: *That dude is nobody to fool around with. to fool with* To get more or less ignorantly involved in something one knows little about: *Don't fool with that nitro.*

to make a fool of oneself To bungle embarrassingly. *to play the fool* To pretend, usually with sufficient justification, that one is stupid. *fool's errand* A wild goose chase. *fool's gold* Iron pyrites (ferric sulfide), a low-grade ore often taken by the ignorant to be full of gold flecks. *fool's paradise* Any reasonably bearable pause this side of reality. (And for the rather complicated history of *fool'-scap* see *Browser's I.*)

funeral   1. The obsequies of burial or cremation, especially the more-or-less ritual procession to the graveyard or crematorium. The wake and ritual viewing of the remains are intimately connected with the funeral in common American practice, but distinct from it. [IE *dheu-*, to reach exhaustion, to die. Suffixed *-d-* in Gmnc. →

OE *dēad,* dead. DEAD. (But the root IE sense "to reach exhaustion" survived into early XVII when slang *to die* meant to achieve a sexual climax, i.e., reach exhaustion, and this sense provided a punning point in various Elizabethan and post-Elizabethan love poems.)

The voiced stop *dh-* of the IE stem regularly changed to *f* in going into Latin, as demonstrated by Grimm, whence, suffixed -*n*-, → the L. stem *fun-, funer-* → L. *funus,* burial rites → late L. *funerālis,* of burial rites, funereal, funeral → OF *funerailles,* ME *funerelles.* The ME form referred to all final observances for the dead (wake, requiem mass, burial procession, graveside rites). *Funeral* became specific to the burial procession in XVIII. Cremation was rare in England after the great common pyres (bonefires, bonfires) of the XIV Black Plague associated cremation with the horrors of the plague.]

funeral home, funeral parlor An American undertaker's unctuous label for his mortuary. [I lack a precise dating, but these terms are generally of XX. It was earlier custom, surviving well into XX, to hold the wake in the home of the deceased, a practice first abandoned in the cities whose generally small apartments and flights of stairs made it difficult to maneuver a casket.]

not one's funeral A bad situation, but not one's proper concern. Variantly *that's your (his) funeral* (implying, "and not mine"). *So you wanna hold up traffic to tell the cop his fly is open—that's your funeral, but leave me out of it.* [Am. First attested 1854 as a joke-filler in the *Oregon Weekly Times,* its familiar usage implying that it was a long-familiar term, and perhaps of West Coast origin, though it might have been imported by the regular flow of immigrants from the East. Perhaps a work camp idiom where funerals were common enough but work always remained to be done. It follows that any funeral observed by *X* does not contain *X,* who is thereby left with a day's work to get done.]

gab   *n.* Talk. *v.* To talk. *gabby* Garrulous. [To the extent that one would hardly expect to find this form in a Supreme Court decision or a formal document, it must be classified as slang, or at least colloq., yet it is of ancient solid lineage, and could be used formally in Chaucer's time with the senses "to brag, to mock, to lie." So, in The Miller's Tale, "I am not life [lief] to *gabbe*"; in The Nun's Priest's Tale, "I *gabbe* not" (here prob. with the transitional sense "I do not chatter idly"); in The Parson's Tale, "He is a japer and a gabber."

But in early Sc. and Erse *gob,* mouth, which is prob. the source of XVI Brit. slang *gob, gab,* the mouth, < Irish *gob,* beak, mouth; Gaelic *gabb,* a mouth that is never at rest, and *gabbach,* garrulous. It is prob. the generalized and long-standing English contempt for things Irish (cordially reciprocated) that has relegated the word to informal status.]

the gift of gab Ready loquacity: *Teddy gabs as fast as the next man, but he has no gift for it.*

(we were) just gabbing We were just using a lot of Teddy words with nothing really to say.

gaff [ME *gaffe,* hook, < OF **gaffe,* dial. of Provence. In limited nautical usage, a *gaff* is an extension to the top spar of a fore-and-aft sail. The word has various applications in Brit. colloq., including "place of cheap amusement, a fair, an arcade, and also what Am. calls "guff," gab. The two functioning senses in Am. are:] 1. A large hook secured to a stout pole. (When a large fish is reeled alongside, it is commonly boated with a gaff.) 2. *Cockfighting.* A sharp metal spur (heel) attached to the back of a gamecock's leg, whereby cockfighting, normally a squabble, becomes a duel, often to the death.

NOTE. So in what may be called "northern" cockfighting. Generally throughout the Caribbean, and among the Cubanos of Florida, the practice is to remove a cock's natural spur and to tape a wooden one to the back of the legs of contesting cocks. This practice makes for a less deadly, but no less intense, sport. It is a prudent conservation, since prized cocks fetch prices of around $1,000. The fight is over as soon as the vanquished hunkers down submissively. Having been so defeated, it may come back to win its next match.

to stand the gaff Usu. in a neg. construction, as *he just can't stand the gaff* To endure (not be able to endure) hardship, punishment. [From cockfighting. Prob. with ref. to "northern" cockfighting with a lethally sharpened heel. MMM's first citation is from George Ade, 1896, but cockfighting was a passion in colonial Maryland (see *blue hen* in *Browser's I*), *gaff* for spur or heel is attested in 1837, and must have been in XVIII colonial use.]

gatecrasher Originally one who gains admission to major sporting events without paying admission. By extension, one who attends a party or other restricted social event without invitation. "Crashing" parties has become a basic folkway of the aggressively ignorant young. (See *gate, Browser's II.*) [The term may precede the 1920s but did not become common until then. P. *Slang* notes its anglicization "in late 1926" as a result of newspaper coverage of two renowned early gatecrashers. Walter Newman of Sherman Oaks, California, writes me about one of them:

> The first Dempsey-Tunney fight took place in Philadelphia in 1926. A "character" named Tammany Young (later a stooge for W. C. Fields) received wide newspaper coverage for crashing this event, his first publicized crash. Thereafter it was difficult to open so much as a pay toilet in NYC without a newspaper reference to the fact that Tammany Young got in free. I was struck by the simpleminded ingenuity that fooled the ushers and doormen: he got a white jacket and a tray of peanuts and went through as a vendor.

A concurrently famous gatecrasher was One-eyed Connely. The London *Daily News,* Jan. 28, 1927, cited him as "the champion American gate crasher," and as testimony to the newness of the term defined it as "one who gains admission to big sporting events without payment."

Early gatecrashers, it should be added, made use of simpleminded ruses that simply would not work in the current era of identity cards and security guards at the employees' entrance. Today it is all but impossible to crash, let us say, the Super Bowl, and the original reference to sporting events has passed from the language for lack of practitioners. *Gatecrashing* has come to mean the new form of *party crashing,* and the common form today is simply *crashing* or *to crash.*

goose: sound on the goose   (To expand the note in *Browser's I.*) 1. *Am., now obs. but passionately common in the days of Bloody Kansas.* A formula for declaring oneself to be pro-slavery. (In the conflict between free-soilers and the pro-slavery faction, the common formula for determining friend or foe began with the question, "How do you stand on the goose?" This was a pro-slavery question. The answer, "Sound on the goose," or "All right on the goose," declared the respondent to be pro-slavery. [*Goose* was the then current way of referring to Article G (*G* for Goose, but why?) of the proposed pro-slavery state constitution. See historic note.] 2. *Brit.* [anglicized ca. 1880 with the altered sense:] Of orthodox conservative political views.

HISTORIC. The idiom remains as a footnote to bloody American history, though long fallen from common use. Before Kansas became a state in Jan. 1861, two proposed state constitutions were drawn up. The so-called Lecompton Constitution was drawn up by pro-slavery forces in convention in Lecompton, Kansas, now Lawrence. Article G of this constitution (the Goose) was an especially powerful assertion of the right to own slaves and was passed without objection by the free-soilers, who boycotted the LeCompton Convention. They met instead in Topeka, at a convention shunned by pro-slavery forces, and drew up a constitution for Kansas as a free state. It was under the Topeka Constitution that Kansas became a state. See D. M. Potter, *The Irrepressible Conflict.*

grapefruit   A ridiculous name that has misled both lexicographers and botanists. As noted in *Browser's II,* NWD goes as far as to suggest that this fruit grows in "grapelike clusters." Such is the power of words, moreover, that in 1814 the botanist John Luman, in his *Hortus Jamaicensis* (The Garden of Jamaica), persuaded himself that he had found a variety of this fruit that tasted like grapes (sour ones, perhaps).

But what is the source of this ridiculous name? Jamaican grapefruit is botanically *Citrus paradisi,* its varieties developed there from root stocks brought from Malaya or Polynesia by an otherwise obscure Captain Shaddock (and *shaddock* still does for "grapefruit" in Jamaica). That imported stock was botanically *C. grandi.*

Grapefruit, I must trepidate, though I cannot attest, must derive from *great fruit* as a lost XVIII effort to translate *C. grandi,* the great citrus (fruit). If so, the modification from *greatfruit* to *grapefruit* must have occurred almost immediately for ease of saying. For if *grapefruit* is a ridiculous name, *greatfruit* is hard to pronounce. In the choice between convenience and good sense, language has normally inclined to the convenient.

growler   [Echoic.] 1. One who growls. 2. An iceberg. [Because as it drifts into warmer waters and begins to melt, the strains of its changing weight and mass give off sounds resembling growls.] 3. A usually tin bucket of beer. And so in now obsolete Am. **to rush the growler** To run to the saloon for a bucket of beer to take home, usually for Daddy's after-work pleasure.

HISTORIC. In this age of canned and bottled beer and of refrigerators this earlier Am. ritual (common until ca. 1920) has vanished, but it was once a standard of U.S. city life to send Junior (or Mother) for a growler of beer for Daddy-home-from-work. Growlers commonly held about two quarts and economy-minded beer-guzzlers were careful to butter them to reduce the amount of head on the beer (it works: some beer companies still hand out special detergents for washing a pub's beer glasses to reduce the head).

Some sources have suggested that *growler* is an archaic liquid measure; but if so, I cannot find it. It seems, rather, to be a metal beer bucket, as in this ritual of rushing the growler; and *growler* is at root ca. 1865 Brit. slang for a four-wheeled cab (the name derived speculatively by P. *Slang,* either from the fact that it creaked and growled in motion, or from the fact that the cabby grumped and growled as he drove). Whence the slightly later Brit. slang *to work the growler,* to go from pub to pub in such a cab; the Am. idiom being a later adaptation of the Brit.

Hell's Angels   I was wrong in saying *(angel, Browser's I)* that the original group was formed in the San Francisco Bay area. By 1965 Oakland had become the "spiritual" chapter of Hell's Angels, but the organization was formed in 1950 in San Bernardino, and the San Berdoo chapter chartered all new chapters for the 15 years before Oakland's ascendancy.

Several sociological studies have shown that the first Hell's Angels were substantially drawn from the sons (and daughters) of the migrant Okies of the 1930s. These were the children of a violently uprooted culture bred to the violence of frustration and to back-breaking stoop labor—the outcasts of Steinbeck's *Grapes of Wrath.* The San Bernardino Valley had a greater concentration of these migrants than was to be found in the relatively more industrialized Bay area.

honcho   *n.* The head man. The boss. The person in charge. Often, redundantly, *head honcho. v.* To oversee. To direct work, especially the work of a crew: *Mac Cordray did a tour at Thule honcho-ing the deep-freeze operations.* [Because the word, though not Sp., suggests a Sp. origin, I long sought it in Mexican and Tex-Mex slang. It is, however, from GI slang of the Korean War, once the label for the head man of a native village, later for the officer or NCO ramrodding a work detail or a military unit. I conjectured earlier that it might be a GI corruption of a Korean word, but could not find such an origin. It is, in fact, from Japanese, and I am indebted to Richard Scorzo of USIS, Tokyo for locating its source accurately in Japanese *cho,* a leader, boss, foreman, with *han,* a small military or work unit; whence *hancho,* the man (sergeant) in command of such a unit; altered in GI usage to *honcho.*]

hypocrite   One who self-seekingly dissembles, pretending to be what he is not. [As an ancient assessment of theatrical people, the root sense is "an actor." < Gk. *hypocritos* < *hypos,* under, below (hence, "hidden"); with *krites,* a judge; hence actor, but with the root sense "one who measures things in a hidden way," hence, "person of concealed motives."]

jamoke A ham-and-egger. A street lounger doing the best he can, which is not much. A worthless guy around town. [Passé, but recently widely disseminated in the popular TV police series in which Robert Blake starred as *Baretta,* a bigmouth street cop with a heart of fool's gold. I speculated earlier that the term was via thieves' cant from Romany *mochsa,* ass, mule, corrupted from *ja(ck) moch(sa),* jackass, but that speculation must certainly yield to the common USN term (up to WWII) *jamoke* for coffee (from *ja(va)* plus *moch(a),* hence a "coffee-and-guy," a ham-and-egger, a small-time, no-account guy. (And as trivial pursuers may recall, great-heart, bigmouth Baretta had been a merchant marine before he took to tarnishing the gold badge.)]

Jay Hawker, jayhawker 1. *In Bloody Kansas,* A free-soil guerrilla. At least some bands of jayhawkers were simply bloody looters and rapists taking license from political unrest. 2. *Now.* A fondly self-asserted nickname for a Kansan. *the Jayhawk State.* 3. The mascot of the University of Kansas. A nonheraldic cartoon figure or stuffed doll of a nonexistent bird that resembles a miniature pterodactyl with a thyroid deficiency. [And so from historic carnage to cute nomenclature, Kansans making a quaint joke of their historic agony. As a nature note there is no hawk that preys specifically on jays, nor would such a hawk be likely to survive, for jays are territorial and do not flock as, say, sparrows do. They are, hence, too scattered to be any hawk's specialty. *Jayhawk* is, therefore, a nonesuch.]

HISTORIC. But why the specific term labeling a nonexistent bird for a bloody Kansan guerrilla? Hyamson offers the ponderable suggestion that Colonel Jennison of New York State, in command of the free-soil forces during the Kansas bloodshed, was known as the *Gay Yorker.* I have not been able to verify that nickname, but if so, *Jay Hawker* would follow readily.

Be it noted also that John Jay, first chief-justice of the Supreme Court, left his surname as a bitter pejorative in Am. idiom when, as our first ambassador to the Court of St. James, he made so many concessions to the British that he was accused of betraying his country. That feeling of bitterness passed, but *jay* kept a pejorative connotation in Am. idiom.

jerkwater town   1. *In late-XIX railroading.* A town along the railroad lines that had a water tank for the thirsty steam locomotive but that was too backward and unimportant to have a station. 2. *Ext.* Pejoratively, any backward small town. ["Jerking" water was the work of the fireman, who reached up to jerk the chain on the long spout of the water tank to turn it into the water intake opening in the locomotive. In *Browser's I,* I defined *jerkwater town* as one too insignificant to have even a water tower, a lack that forced train crews that stopped there when they were out of water to "jerk" buckets of water from the local well (or water trough), passing it up painfully to the man on the locomotive, an extra labor that left the men with unfavorable sentiments toward so backward a place.

I am grateful to Tom Shine of Redding, California, for leading me to see that this bucket-brigade system was not the same thing as "jerking" water. Since railroad water towers occurred frequently along the right of way, sometimes where there was no town ("in the middle of nowhere," so to speak), a town that was no more than a jerkwater stop would be little more than Nowheresville.]

joy stick   I fell into a common error when I explained this name for the early airplane control stick as deriving from the fact that it is the means to the exhilaration of aerobatics. I am indebted to Mr. Denver Elkins of Cardiff by the Sea, California, for setting me straight. Mr. Elkins cited for me the following passage from Jack R. Linke's *Jenny Was No Lady,* a history of the Jenny biplane published by W. W. Norton:

> The main control, originally called the "Joyce Stick," after its inventor, was made of laminated wood. Later this elevator-aileron control became the "Joy Stick," owing to its function in acrobatics. Now, where used, it is simply called, "The Stick."

I have not been able to identify the Joyce here referred to, but the time of his invention can be fixed quite accurately. On the first powered flight in December of 1903, the Wright brothers' controls consisted of a forward elevator, some device for a technique called "wing warping," and probably, or very soon thereafter, a rear rudder. Their "Flyer," like all the earliest planes, was designed to be unstable and to require constant working of the controls in flight.

It was, I believe, this built-in instability Joyce's "stick" was meant to remedy. In Dec. 1906 and in Jan. 1907 three patents were issued for controls that combined the Joyce stick with a foot-operated rudder bar. It follows that, whoever Joyce was, he developed his "stick" between 1903 and 1906.

junket [< L. *juncus, iuncus,* a reed, a rush. Baskets were woven of these reeds, and such baskets were called in OF *jonquettes,* whence ME *junket,* such a basket. But also *jonket,* an egg custard (because it was commonly wrapped in green rushes).] 1. A custard made with rennet. 2. A festive outing. [Because festive country folk—and gentry playing at being country folk—used to pack reed baskets with picnic goodies.] 3. A festive outing by a government official or group of officials, ostensibly on government business and always at government expense, but in fact undertaken as a free-spending holiday. [This specifically Am. sense is cited by MMM from the Detroit *Free Press,* Sept. 4, 1886: "The term 'junket' in America is generally applied to a trip taken by an American official at the expense of the government he serves so nobly and unselfishly." I do not understand "is generally applied," but it suggests that the word and the practice were already long established by the time the *Free Press* exercised its irony. The pork barrel has always been with us. Even George Washington raised some eyebrows when he submitted his expense accounts.]

kike Pejorative name for a Jew. *Mend Your Speech* by Frank H. Vizetelly (New York and London, 1920) has the following entry: *"kike, kyke.* An unpardonable vulgarism in the cant of the clothing trade. The word Kike is an adaptation from the Scottish *keek,* which designates 'One who peeps; especially in the clothing trade, a person engaged by a garment-maker to obtain the latest styles from a rival concern.'"

As managing editor of the Funk and Wagnalls *New Standard Dictionary,* and as a once-prominent authority on usage, Vizetelly cannot be ignored, but I doubt that there is much of a case for referring *kike* to a Sc. origin. John Jamieson's *Etymological Dictionary of the Scottish Language* (4 vols. London 1879–1882) does not list *kike.* It does give *keek* as 1. To peek, to pry. 2. Linen dress for the head and neck. [Would that be a peek-a-boo cowl?]

Sense 1 might readily suggest a spy (an industrial secret-peeker), but such spies were, if not peculiar to the late-XIX garment industry in New York City ("the rag game"), unknown in Scotland. It is possible that some Jewish garment worker had come to the U.S. rag game by way of Scotland, but Sc. must at least be noted as having had no visible effect on the Am.–Yiddish patois of the garment industry. By its nature, moreover, kike is not an Am.–Yiddish word, but one applied to Jews by bigots.

P. *Underworld* cites *kike* in Brit. usage from 1911, but as an acquired Americanism. Partridge follows Godfrey Irwin's *American Tramp and Underworld Slang* (New York 1930), which refers it to "the names of many Russian–Jewish [he should have mentioned Polish–Jewish] immigrants which typically ended in *-ki* or *-ky*." He adds that "these people were known as *kikis,* and that the name was shortened to the logical (sic) *kike.* I find Irwin's "logic" less than self-evident. Certainly, it does not explain the vowel shift from *kēk* to *kīk.*

As noted in *Browser's I,* Leo Rosten, *The Joys of Yiddish* (New York 1968), refers *kike* to *kikl,* the small circle (pronounced *kēk'l*) with which illiterate Jews made their mark, shunning *X* as the sign of the cross. Rosten explains *kike* as an alteration of *kikl* by late-XIX Ellis Island immigration clerks. But though Rosten's *Joys of Yiddish* is a book to admire and love, I doubt this explanation as I doubt Irwin's, if only on the grounds that the vowel alteration is unlikely.

For these reasons I return to my original guess (I cannot call it more than that) that the origin lies in Ike-Ikey (for Isaac), a once-common generic nickname for a Jew. Orthodox Jewish peddlers backpacking their wares through an American town certainly struck children as an outlandish sight. I remember young brats in Medford, Massachusetts dancing along behind such oddly dressed, bearded men, chanting *Ikey-Ikey-Ikey.* In singsong repetition it readily became *Ikey-Kikey-Kikey,* whence, as the least cause suffices (though from an earlier chain of dancing brats), *kikey* and *kike.*

knuckle A bone joint of the prehensile hand, especially the joint at which the fingers meet the palm, but also the joints at which the segments of the fingers flex. [Ult. < IE *gen-*, to compact, to make into a wad, a ball. With g/k and in zero-grade form → IE *kn'-*, and suffixed *-k-* → Gmnc. *knuk-* → OE *cnōcian* (both *c*s pronounced as *k*s), also MLG *knōkel,* knuckle (perhaps, "that with which one knocks"—and so in Ger. specific to finger joint, our modern Eng. sense, but:) ME *knokel,* any bone joint, as the knee (which has the same *kn-* stem), elbow, or even the vertebrae. The IE stem *gen-* survives in L. *genū,* knee, It. *genocchio,* Fr. *genou,* knee. GENU-FLECT. Since XV the Eng. form has been specific to a finger joint, but various idioms based on *knuckle* derive from the pre-XV ME sense.]

to knuckle under To yield to pressure, to authority. [In the ME sense, to kneel to, to bow to.] *to knuckle down (to the work)* To bend over one's work industriously. [In ME sense, "to bend the vertebrae." But:] *to knuckle down Am. XIX, in the game of marbles, migs, taws,* To put one's knuckles (first finger joints) to the ground in preparation for shooting the marble or glassie with one's thumb.

knuckleduster Also *brass knuckles* [Am. XIX. Not necessarily made of brass.] A metal bar with ring holes for at least two fingers. Slipped over the knuckles, it tends to "dust off" any opponent one then punches. Murderous varieties were variously studded and spiked.

knuckle ball Also *knuckler* A slow, spinless, often erratic pitch. [So called because the pitcher holds the ball between his thumb and the knuckles of the first two fingers—however that may be done. Catchers seemed to be fooled by the knuckle ball almost as often as the batters are.]

knucklehead A dolt. [One whose head is a bone joint. Am. XIX. In Brit. XIX slang a *knuckler* was a pickpocket. *Knuckleduster* (above) was Am. ca. 1855, anglicized, according to P. *Slang,* ca. 1865, and by 1900 was Brit. colloq. for a large, heavy, or gaudy ring.]

lief   As soon, to one's liking. *liefer* Rather, more willingly, preferably, the sooner: *I'd as lief (liefer) not attend my hanging, sheriff.* Archaic but survives regionally, esp. in upper New England. [< OE *leof,* love; *leofan,* to love. See *leman.* Cognate with Ger., *liebe,* dear. "I had as lief have the foppery of freedom as the morality of imprisonment."—Shakespeare, *Measure for Measure* I.ii.]

lobster shift   Also *lobster trick, dog watch Journalism* 1. A third work-shift on a big-city newspaper, commonly from 2:00–9:00 A.M. when little is happening and matters can be attended by a skeletal staff. (Which would be true on an evening newspaper, but on a morning paper these would be the prime working hours.) 2. The small-hours shift that edits the morning paper and the printing crew that puts it out. [Journalists, so professionally busy about everyone else's doings, have tended to be vague about the origins and the meaning of some of their own basic idioms. Many histories of journalism have explained this idiom variously. Though all seem to agree that it developed in New York City in the 1890s when relatively new morning papers were locked in a fierce competition for circulation, the professional explanations are mere guesswork.

The International Typographic Union *Review,* Sept. 15, 1983, asserts without attestation that *lobster* was a common derogatory term at this time (as *turkey* has now become, I interject). The *Review* goes on to explain that the head of an unidentified composing room, watching his dog-watch crew report for work, remarked that it "looked like a bunch of lobsters." ("Boiled" with drink?)

On about the same level of reportage other historians of U.S. journalism have said: 1. that this crew stopped to eat at fish and lobster houses on the way to work; 2. that it came to work at a waterfront newspaper plant just as the fishing boats and lobster boats were putting out (nonsense, of course, for they would put out with the tide rather than the clock); 3. that the crews scuttled to work across the floor of the night like lobsters scuttling across a dark sea bottom (call this one a touch of Pulitzer Prize poetry). Since all is guesswork, my preferred guess was made by a Nathan Goldstein, an old newspaper hand, in a letter to the editor of *Editor and Publisher,* August 25, 1979. Mr. Goldstein explains that workers on this 2:00 A.M. shift always stopped at a saloon before stumbling to work, and that William Randolph Hearst (not elsewhere attested) said, with reference to their red noses, that they looked like lobsters. Mr. Goldstein's explanation at least conforms with the tradition of devout drunkenness among newspapermen of that time.

lout   A clumsy, stupid, ill-mannered oaf. [A word of scorn derived from the pure arrogance of aristocratic assumption. Lordlings kept their peasants as ignorant as they were themselves. They also insisted that the peasants doff their hats, tug their forelocks, and shift stupidly from foot to foot while bowing in The Presence. They then belittled them for doing what was demanded of them. < *to lout,* to bow low, to be servile. < OE *lutan,* to bow. Ult. < IE *leud-,* small; via Gmnc. with d/t and suffixed *-l-* → OE *lytel,* little. LITTLE. So with the associated sense, to demean oneself ("make oneself small").]

miracle   [At root, "a smile (from God)," though the Deluge, the destruction of Sodom and Gomorrah, and the parting of the waters of the Dead Sea (from the Egyptian point of view) were rather lowering miracles. Ult. < IE *(s)mei-* to smile, *but also,* to be surprised, suffixed *-r-* → L. *mirus,* wonderful, *mirari,* to wonder at, to regard with awe. ADMIRE.] 1. A supernatural action, intervention, revelation. 2. *Weak ext.* A remarkable event: *Miracle of miracles: Benn Ciardi tidied his room.* 3. *Further ext.* An outstanding example: *He made seven miraculous passes with honest dice.*

the age of miracles is not past! A rather hyperbolic formula to express wonderment at an unusual event, as when Daddy returns sober from the country club. [Commonly used ironically, but our surviving revivalists assert seriously the working of supernatural wonders. In XVIII England and France the rational agnostics of the Age of Reason asserted the reverse, that the age of miracles was past and mankind had entered the age of reason. When the marquis de La Place, XVIII astronomer, mathematician, and philosopher, published his theories of the universe, he was asked, "What about God?" A true child of the age of reason, he replied, "Je n'eu pas besoin de cette hypothèse," I had no need of that hypothesis. (But what else will explain the fact that Benn *did* tidy his room?)]

mitten: get the mitten   To be jilted. *to give someone the mitten* To dismiss someone as a suitor. To jilt. [A once-popular, now-faded, XIX Am. idiom. As if a suitor had asked for the girl's hand in marriage and was given only her mitten, the hand slipping out of it. And many, I cannot doubt, so understood this idiom, though it derives, in fact, from an arch play on *demittance,* a sending away or a going away (from office, employment, attendance), as if the rather formal turn "She give him his demittance" had been rendered "She gave him de mitten(s)." < L. *mittere,* to send; *demittere,* to send away. Luke 2:29 reads, in the Vulgate, "nunc demittis servum tuum," Now let they servant depart.

Hyamson relates the idiom to Fr. *mitaines,* mittens, and assigns it a French–Canadian origin; but the trace from *demittance* and the constant presence of church Latin seem to make such side-conjecture (esp. when unsupported by evidence) merely random.]

oaf   1. *Now,* Dolt, half-wit, lout. *But* 2. *Up to XVII (now obs.),* Elf, goblin. [Ult. < IE *albho-,* white. (ALBINO, ALBION, ALBANIA, ALPS, ALBANY.) One early associated sense seems to have been "ghost, white apparition." Cf. surviving "pale as a ghost." Stem *albh'-* with bh/f in Gmnc. → ON *alfr* and OE *aelf,* elf, goblin → ME *elf,* elf. But the variant forms (all of which occur in Shakespeare) *ouph, aufe, aulfe* also survived, with the sense "deficient being, bumbling simpleton," emerging in early XVII as *oph, oaf,* oaf in the present sense.

The intermediate sense starting with OE *aelf* was "changeling," not exactly an elf, for that would imply supernatural powers, but a deformed and mentally deficient child left by elves in place of a stolen human baby. Such a changeling may have been understood to be a rejected elf-child or a human freak left as a substitute as a piece of elfin mischief. Logic is hardly the key to folk superstition. For language purposes the association was with "deformed, dim-witted, 'queer' one." Whatever the final explanation, the etymological branching of *elf* and *oaf* is firmly documented, as is the rather surprising XVII sense shift from "elfin-mysterious" to "queer wrong one."]

oracle   1. *In Greek and Roman religion.* (a) A spiritual medium who contacts a deity under the influence of drugs or of autohypnosis, through whom the deity speaks, often in gibberish ("speaking in tongues"), which attendant priests interpret for a fee, without which how shall God be served? (b) The message so spoken and interpreted. 2. *In a Jewish temple.* The Holy of Holies. I Kings 6:16, "even for the oracle, even for the most holy place." 3. *In nonreligious loose extension.* Any wise person whose pronouncements are received as authoritative. [At root, "a mouth" (of God, being understood). < L. *oraculum,* an oracle, < *orare,* to speak formally, to pray, < *os,* mouth, the stem visible in the genitive *oris,* of the mouth. Ult. < IE *or-,* a ritual pronouncement, to utter such a pronouncement.]

orgy   plu. *orgies* [The essential senses are "unrestrained abandonment to the appetites," including sex, and therefore, "temporary,̤" for a reveler cannot sprint forever. At ult. IE root < *werg-,* to do (WORK), whence Gk. *ergon,* work, labor (ERG). Variantly Gk. *organ,* a swelling, an afflatus. (ORGASM.) Also Gk. *orgia,* sacred rites, especially Dionysian rites, which sometimes included sexual abandon.]

HISTORIC. In Rome *orgia* gradually lost religious significance and became an elaborate feasting and drinking with slaves providing music, entertainment, and sex, A.C. or D.C. The scale of the overindulgence may be gauged by the once-common practice of the *vomitorium* to which one who had eaten and drunk to the point of crapulence could retire, have a slave tickle his throat with a feather, upchuck, and return to the feasting. There was, however, no restorative feather for the male organ, which set an obvious limit on the number of slave girls (and boys) even the lustiest Roman could use.

Orgy lost all religious and pagan association by XVII and has come to mean any unrestrained indulgence: *There has been an orgy of rumors on Wall Street. And in Atlanta, Dr. John Stone spent the evening in an orgy of diet cola, peanut butter sandwiches, and undergraduate reminiscences.*

paraphernalia   As noted in *Browser's I*, the word is based on the Gk. legal term *para phernē*, outside the dowry, with reference to clothing, small ornaments, toilet articles, and other intimate possessions a wife brought to the marriage apart from the dowry, which became the exclusive property of the husband.

I am indebted to Paul F. Stavis of Albany, New York for the information that *paraphernality* still functions in our law codes. The court findings in a recent Louisiana divorce case explain the all-but-unchanged legal sense. Appellant (the husband) claimed as community property assets that appellee (the wife) claimed to be exclusively hers. The court's findings, as summarized in *U.S. Law Week*, Oct. 22, 1985, stated:

> Unbeknownst to appellant, at the time of the marriage appellee recorded a declaration of paraphernality under the authority of Article 2386 of the Louisiana Civil Code. This declaration allowed a wife to reserve for herself the fruits from her paraphernal property (non-dotal property she brought into the marriage); it also gave her the right to manage such property and the fruits from such property.

Appellee obviously brought some reasonable doubts to the marriage, and they moved her to retain better legal counsel than the appellant was moved to find. The court, accordingly, gave the appellee her paraphernalia along with her share of the community property.

pirate   1. A corsair. (Pirates have come ashore to attack coastal settlements, and Vikings regularly raided in this way, there being at that time nothing worth attacking on the open sea; but piracy is essentially the act of attacking and raiding ships at sea, usually with riotous bloodshed.) 2. One who makes illegal use of copyright material. So *pirated edition* An edition of a popular work brought out without the knowledge and permission of the author and without payment of royalties or acknowledgment of copyright. (Illegal in the U.S., but differences in the international copyright laws allow printers in such places as Taiwan to print and distribute such editions.) [The word is only slightly altered from Gk. *peiratēs*, sea raider, < *peiraō*, I attempt, I try, I venture upon. The word *pirate* now has invidious connotations of bloody excesses. Among the Greeks, however, who extended their sympathies only within a small ethnic circle, excluding all others as barbarians and enemies, piracy was an approved and heroic venture against "them."

I do not know how this sea-raider's term acquired its specific second sense as a violation of copyright material. Why is it piracy to violate another man's literary rights for profit, or why is it more piratical than forging his signature, stealing his livestock, and debauching his wife? I have no answer, and my only clue is that the ODEE dates this usage < XVIII (toward the end of the age of piracy) and labels it, without explanation, "figurative."]

quail 1. The widely distributed wild bird that in many ways resembles a small chicken. The most common New World species is probably the bobwhite, so called because Americans have so rendered its two-tone call, a low short *bob* followed by a high long *white*. [And the old wail quail was similarly named, though the L. rendering of its cry was *coacula,* whence medieval L. *quaccula* → OF and ME *quaille.* (The New World quail need not, of course, have the same cry as the Old World one, but echoic renderings vary widely from one language to another.)] 2. A slut, a whore. [And so in XVI slang. So in *Troilus and Cressida* V.i Shakespeare has "an honest fellow enough and one that loves quails," which his audience immediately understood to mean, "a guy who chases whores." The source of this sense of quail is not easily dated but arises from the folk belief that the quail was an oversexed bird, perhaps from observation of its mating ritual. Whatever the obscure base of this sense it survives in (now limited) American slang:] **San Quentin quail** Girl(s) sexually eager but under 18. [Because to dip into such a teeny-bopper is statutory rape and can land a man in San Quentin for felonious entry.]

quarter [< L. *quattuor,* four. In all senses signifies either "four" or "a fourth." So *quart,* fourth of a gallon; *quarter,* 1. fourth of a dollar. 2. section of a city *(Latin quarter),* as if cities were restricted to only four such subdivisions; *quarto,* a book page made by folding the paper four times; and *living quarters,* implying "within four walls" (rather than out of doors).]

 no quarter In battle, signifies death to the losers. [The defeated will not be given living quarters (and rations) because they will be put to death.]

 quartered In medieval torture and execution, the death penalty imposed by roping a victim's hands and feet, fastening the ropes to horses, and whipping the horses in opposing directions to tear the wretch apart. Aside from the fact that he is a folk reincarnation of Greek Hippolytus, St. Hippolite/Hippolytus was said to have been martyred in this way.

 drawn and quartered In medieval practice surviving in England into early XIX a common practice in official hangings. Hanging by being dropped through a trapdoor results in instant death (or should so result) of a snapped neck. British hangmen regularly let victims dangle and strangle, in the style of U.S. frontier justice, "while dancing on air." London crowds seemed to enjoy this spectacle, and a substantial part of the hangman's income was from the boxes he rented to ladies and gentlemen for a properly amusing view of the spectacle.

At times the death sentence further specified that the hanged were to be drawn and quartered and the remains impaled on spikes on public view as a warning to evildoers. According to law, therefore, and for a more memorable spectacle, Jack Ketch played to his paying audience.

A hanged man tends to die with a great erection caused by the constriction of his blood, and a good hangman knew how to feature this natural phenomenon in his spectacle so that the ladies and gentlemen might exchange witty remarks on his terminal extension. Additionally, while the wretch still dangled, and before he was entirely dead, a star part of Jack Ketch's performance might be to slice his belly open and pull out ("draw") his guts. After these preliminaries and further pleasantries from the paying customers, the wretch might be cut down, beheaded, and hacked into four parts to be impaled around town on spikes, as above. At the standard rate of execution in earlier London, this quartering and impaling had to be limited for lack of enough display spikes, or London might become a fetid plague scene. The full treatment was therefore reserved for traitors and other notable felons, but a certain amount of butchery of the dead (or not-quite dead) body long remained part of the popular hangman's theatrical offering. In quartering, he offered no quarter.

quasi *adj. and adv.* As if. Almost but not quite. Purportedly but not in fact. Partially resembling (the real thing): *quasi-humanoid Nancy Walker.* (Often, but not necessarily, hyphenated.) *A quasi honest lawyer. There is nothing quasi about Mr. Reagan's economic ignorance.* [L. *quasi,* as if, so to speak. And cf. common It. *quasi-quasi,* nearly almost.]

quid A cut or wad of chewing tobacco. [Ult. < IE *gwet-, gw't-,* resin. Via Gmnc. with g/k and t/d → OE *cwidu, cudu,* and ME *quide,* cud. In XVIII *quid* and *cud* became distinct, *quid* becoming specific to tobacco chewing and *cud* to the feeding habits of cows and other ruminants. But note the IE sense for its small but certain insight into the homely habits of our early language ancestors as gum chewers back there in deep B.C. (before chicle). Their gum was the aromatic resin of the mastic tree, which derives its name, concordantly, from Gk. *mastikhē,* chewable stuff, < *mastikhān,* to chew, to grind the teeth (MASTICATE).]

quidding I have this word, previously unknown to me, on the assurance of Mr. Joseph Snyder of Myrtle Pond, Oregon, who tells me it is in common use there by farmers and veterinarians. "Old horses whose teeth have worn to sharp points," he writes, "have trouble eating grain, and tend to spill it from the corners of their mouths. . . . This is known as 'quidding.' " [I do not find this term in any of my dictionaries and must think of it as a regionalism, but it follows from firm precedent. Francis Grose, *A Classical Dictionary of the Vulgar Tongue* (London 1785), gives *quid* in XVIII use for "chew of tobacco." P. *Slang* notes that about that time wags would say to a man chewing tobacco, "Quid pro quo," (as if, "Quid? —Pro quo?" = "You're chewing tobacco? —What for?"). And tobacco chewers, of course, often dribble from the corners of the mouth, just as the old nag does when it quids.]

qui vive Fr., "who lives?" Naturalized to Eng. in *on the qui vive* Watchfully, alertly, vigilantly. [*Vive!* is the form of the common Fr. acclamation, (Long) live! as in *vive le roi!* or *vive le duc!* In *Browser's I,* I interpreted this sentries' challenge to mean *"For whom do you say vive?"* i.e., "Whom do you support?/Which side are you on?" a simple equivalent of the modern formula "Friend or foe?"

This interpretation of the original intent is not wrong and can be well defended, but I have come to prefer the simpler, more direct rendering, "Who lives?" i.e., "Who moves there?" the simple Eng. equivalent being "Who goes there?" or in the full sentries' formula, "Who goes there, friend or foe?"]

rigmarole In *Browser's I* I set out what is known about the derivation of this word from an obscure and rather elaborate party game called in OF *Ragemon le bon.* The game seems to have involved a scroll that offered intricate clues to the identity of a mysterious person called Ragemon. *Ragemon le bon* passed into early Eng. (exact date unknown) as *Ragman rolls* as a general label for legal documents and their obscurantist language.

I offer here an additional note from the Reverend H. Percy Smith, *Glossary of Terms and Phrases* (London 1883): *"Ragman Roll.* A name of uncertain origin, denoting the instrument by

which the Scottish nobility and gentry subscribed allegiance to
Edward I, in 1296." It must have been a profusely worded "instrument," a true ceremonial *rigmarole.*

ropes: know the ropes   1. *Nautical.* To know basic seamanship.
[*Ropes,* here, for rigging. And also for skill in splicing and tying
knots. Thus, the first skills one must acquire to be an able seaman.
(Cf. *tell it to the Marines*—they might believe it; because they
know nothing about seamanship, i.e., they do not know the ropes.)
Also *learn the ropes, show someone the ropes.*] 2. *In any context.*
To be competent in a particular situation: *When Jack Ketch shows
a man the ropes, he soon gets the hang of it.*

ruffian   [In discussing this word in *Browser's II* I should have been
more emphatic in discussing its sense shift, which is traceable to a
confusion of *ruff-* and *rough.*] A scoundrel. (*Scoundrel* is a word of
unknown origin.) A low person. *Also,* A thug, a strong-arm man, a
hoodlum. (But these are late-accreted senses almost certainly suggested by *rough,* as if *ruff-* implied "rough, tough, violent.") [But
at root, "a scabby, cruddy person," hence, a low person. Cf. current
Am. slang *don't be a crud,* don't be low and despicable. Ult. < IE
kreup- scab, crud. With k/h → Gmnc. stem *hreup-,* and with p/f
OE *hrufa,* scab, crud and *hreof,* scab, crud, filth (terms that easily
extend to the idea "despicable, disgusting, low, low person." The
point is that violence is nowhere implicit in these roots, but only
disgusting baseness. Thus when the Gmnc. stem entered early It.
it became *ruffiano,* pimp, and *ruffiana,* dirty whore—two sorts of
"low" (but not necessarily violent) persons.]
    But note that *to ruff,* to play a trump card, is from OF *roffle,
ronfle,* < early It. *ronfa,* a card term meaning to win a trick by
trumping, and is almost certainly < *trionfare,* to triumph (if you
are not overruffed and set because you forgot to draw trumps,
which entitles your partner to call you a ruffian).

Saturnalia   An unrestrained orgy. [L. *Saturnalis,* feast of Saturn.
Saturnalia is the L. neuter plural, but functions in English primarily as a singular, though it may have a plural and even frequentative
sense in, for example, *the saturnalia of Norman Mailer's quotidia.*]
    HISTORIC. The feast of Saturn was celebrated annually by the
Romans as a wildly abandoned revel in which masters waited upon
their slaves, who were given license to revile the masters under
religious sanctions that forbade later retaliation (but wait and see

what dirty work you get assigned to, Infradigus, if you go too far). The *Saturnalia* turned all the standards of Roman behavior upside down in a rule of disorder, and it is this sense of riotous disorder that survives as the gist of English *saturnalia.* In *Browser's I,* under the entry *sa-,* see subentry *satire* and the note on the early Fescennine Festival for a similar festival of wild abandon.

shinplaster   In *Browser's I* I gave 1863 as the first date for this term for worthless paper money, citing Shelby Foote, *The Civil War* (3 vols., New York, 1958–1974), II: XXXX "bills of smaller denomination being known as *shinplasters* because a soldier once used a fistful to cover a tibia wound." Despite a common agreement, even among lexicographers, the term was in much earlier use.

I am indebted to Richard C. Rostrum of Chicago for a citation from Ray Allen Billington's *Westward Expansion* (New York, 1949). In describing the currency crises of the 1830s Professor Billington quotes from a traveler's diary of that period:

> At Wheeling exchanged $5.00 note, Kentucky money, for notes on the Northwest Bank of Virginia; reached Fredericktown, there neither Kentucky nor Virginia money current; paid a $5.00 Wheeling note for breakfast and dinner, received in change two $1.00 notes on some Pennsylvania bank, $1.00 Baltimore and Ohio Railroad, and balance in Good Intent *shinplasters;* 100 yards from the tavern door all notes refused except the Baltimore and Ohio Railroad.

This earlier dating attested, our dictionaries will need to reassign *shinplasters* from the commonly given Civil War origin and reconsider it, probably as one of the many exuberant terms that came into Am. in the boisterous Age of Jackson.

tandem   The sense, by the language convention, is "one behind the other," as: 1. *Rare since XVIII,* A team of two horses hitched one behind the other; also, a carriage drawn by such a pair of horses. 3. A bicycle built for two; also, any paired apparatus similarly arranged. [But the conventional specification of a tandem as a pair is nowhere implicit in the roots. < L. *tandem,* so many, that many, exactly so many, exactly so long; whence, by association with counting soldiers, slaves, animals in a file, exact count, final count. < L. *tam,* so much, so many; *-dem-,* demonstrative pronoun stem (THEM). Cf. It. *tanto,* Fr. *tant,* so much, that much. English *tantamount,* amounting to that much; hence, equal to. Nothing in these roots implies that the measured file consists of any specific number, nor can I account for the way *tandem* came so specifically to imply a pair. At root the chained minutes go in tandem to eternity.]

thirty   Also *Thirty,* —*30*—, and earlier *XXX Journalism.* The traditional signoff at the end of a piece of copy; equivalent to a telegrapher's signal meaning "end transmission." And the term was in fact borrowed by journalists from early telegraphy.

There seem to have been various sign-off signals in telegrapher's use; perhaps the number 30 (in Morse code . . . — — — — — — —) or variantly XXX (— . . —, — . . —, — . . —). Either would be a distinctive and easily transmitted code signal.

Several historians of American journalism have said it was once standard telegrapher's practice to end a transmission by tapping out the number of words in each message, and all of these sources assert that the first Civil War message wired to the press services contained 30 words, whence the signoff. There seems to be no way of denying such an assertion, but since none of these "historians" seems to be able to cite the message, the case must be dismissed for lack of evidence, especially since this numerical signoff, if briefly in local use, was abandoned almost at once.

uncle   A pawnbroker. [In English use since XVIII. Commonly explained as if the pawnbroker were a kindly old uncle who lets one have money at need. But *uncle,* here, is a corruption of L. *uncus,* hook, *unculus,* little hook, because many small pawned items were hung on rows of hooks in the pawnshop. Note that early pawnbrokers in England were Lombards, their trade sign being the three golden balls from the shield of the Medici, once Europe's leading moneylenders. *Uncle* is also close to It. *onchia,* claw, fingernail. A literate British hack pawning some small body ornament would have no difficulty in punning from *unculus,* little hook, to L. *avunculus* and even perhaps to It. *onchia;* whence Uncle Hook or Uncle Claw. Insofar as I have been able to determine, Eng. is the only European language in which the word for *uncle* doubles for *pawnbroker.*]

unwashed: the great unwashed   The masses of the poor. [The label originated with Edmund Burke (1729–1797), Brit. statesman and orator. In those days before internal plumbing the attended wealthy might have hot baths hand-poured for them by servants, but the poor had no such resources in their hovels, whereby the poverty of that time remained notably rancid.]

HISTORIC. Most U.S. slum areas now have some form of indoor plumbing and in-house bath facilities, but only since WWII. Earlier slum-dwellers washed at the kitchen sink or went to the local public bathhouse, the more fastidious doing so as often as once a week. In many European cities the public bathhouse is still the principal body-dunk of the poor.

Utopia   The nonexistent perfect land. *utopian* Idyllic. From *Utopia* (1516) by Sir Thomas More, a romance about a land of perfectly righteous and moral people with an ideal government on an edenic island. [*Utopia* was Sir Thomas's coinage from Gk. *topos,* place (TOPIC, TOPICAL, TOPOGRAPHY); with modified neg. prefix *eu-* (but note that *eu-* can also have the sense "good, well," as in *euphoria,* at root, bearing up well under things and, in effect, in flowering good condition).

Utopia is almost universally glossed as meaning "no place." But that would be *Utopos,* the singular form. *Topia* is the plural, places, from which it follows that Utopia would signify "no places," an absurdity. Greek *topia* also meant "little fields," as Sir Thomas would certainly have known. I do not exactly scorn the gloss of *Utopia* as "nowhere," but I suspect Sir Thomas might well have thought on, with *eu-* taken to mean "good, well, excellent, happy," as "the little happy fields (that do not exist except in dreams).")

Valentine's Day, St. Valentine's Day   As noted in *Browser's I,* there were two saints named Valentine. Neither was especially associated with young lovers, but the feast day they share, having more or less coalesced into one piety, coincides with the date of ancient fertility rites held in Rome on Feb. 14.

Hyamson further notes "the belief that birds began to pair on that day" (so why not you and I, sweetheart?). Hyamson gives no reference in support of his assertion, and I can find no ancient reference that so designates Feb. 14, but it is the sort of natural-history invention to which the ancients and folklore are given, and certainly it should be mentioned.

Many saints, whether unique or fused, have had special powers attributed to them by association with pagan rituals long established on what became their Christian feast day. (See *Walpurgis Night, Browser's II.*) It is well to remember that Christianity took root in the cities, the rural areas (*i pagani* or, in England, the heaths, whence *heathen*) clinging to their old rites through at least the first half of the Middle Ages. When finally converted, these people of the "outback" naturally mingled pagan and Christian memories in their pious legends. My own mother was essentially an It. mountain pagan who had acquired a Catholic vocabulary in which to express her essentially unchanged pagan views and emotions.

yegg 1. *Now,* A burglar. A criminal tough. 2. *But earlier, and still properly,* A safecracker. [As noted in *Browser's I,* most dictionaries refer this term to "a famous safecracker named John Yegg." Having searched lists of criminals great and small for some years, however, I have had to conclude that this John Yegg (or any related criminal Yegg) exists only in the mythology of clerk-lexicographers.]

The pertinent annals are not endless. The original sense of *yegg* as professional safecracker sets a technological level, for before mid-XIX there were not enough safes in existence to provide safe-crackers a dependable profession. P. *Slang,* it should be noted, defines the word as "traveling burglar." (As distinct from "resident burglar"?) He glosses it as Am., anglicized by 1932, but he seems to overlook "the case of Vanderbilt and the Yeggman," mentioned by Sherlock Holmes in "The Case of the Sussex Vampire," written, I will guess, about 1900 when Sir Arthur Conan Doyle was about 41. Partridge, however, may be brilliantly intuitive in suggesting a derivation from Sc. and Brit. dial. *yark* or *yek,* to break, to smash. This suggested derivation leaves something in doubt but does seem far more to the point than John Yegg, who seems to be more famous in our dictionaries than in reality.

yo 1. A hail: *Yo there!* 2. A response to a hail or summons. [A common language form neglected by most dictionaries because they tend to copy one another and this vocalism has failed to attract the first editor's notice (*oop, oops* may be cited as similarly neglected standard language).

Yo is, among other things, a standard armed-services response to one's name during a roll call. The basic senses are "you there!" and "here!"

J. L. Dillard, author of *Black English* (New York, 1972), writing to William Safire of the *New York Times,* traces the form to black Eng.: "I have nonprofessionally assumed a derivation from *here,* based on *hya,* a rather frequent Afro-Creole form. . . . The '*r*-less' dialects of which Black English is one, have final *-schwa* in such words, and *schwa* becomes *ow* [Note: pronounced as in *know,* I believe], just as *dynomite.*"

Hya for *here* is, of course, common Dixieland, and *dynomite* as cited by Dillard is ample precedent for the variant *hyo,* whence *yo.* I take Dillard's derivation to be ponderable in context, yet nonprofessionally I must assume that *yo* is also a more general bodily-expressive syllable (like *oop! oops!* and also *yuk! ugh!*). I have no disagreement with Dillard, but I should not be surprised to find "yo" in relatively early Eng. usage, though professionally I cannot find it attested except in "yo ho ho and a bottle of rum!" the refrain of a familiar sea chantey.]

About the Author

JOHN CIARDI (1916–1985) taught English at Harvard and Rutgers, and was poetry editor at *The Saturday Review* from 1956 to 1972. His many books include poetry (*Homeward to America*; *Other Skies*), humorous verse for children (*I Met a Man*), limericks (*Too Gross*, with Isaac Asimov), essays (*Dialogue with an Audience*), and a translation of Dante's *Divine Comedy*.